LABOUR AFTER COMMUNISM

David Mandel

LABOUR AFTER COMMUNISM

Auto Workers and Their Unions
in Russia, Ukraine, and Belarus

Montréal/New York/London

Copyright © 2004 BLACK ROSE BOOKS

No part of this book may be reproduced or transmitted in any form, by any means electronic or mechanical including photocopying and recording, or by any information storage or retrieval system—without written permission from the publisher, or, in the case of photocopying or other reprographic copying, a license from the Canadian Reprography Collective, with the exception of brief passages quoted by a reviewer in a newspaper or magazine.

Black Rose Books No. HH326

National Library of Canada Cataloguing in Publication Data
Mandel, David, 1947-

Labour after Communism : auto workers and their unions in Russia, Ukraine, and Belarus / David Mandel.

Includes bibliographical references and index.
Hardcover ISBN: 1-55164-243-3 (bound) Paperback ISBN: 1-55164-242-5 (pbk.)

1. Automobile industry workers—Labor unions—Russia (Federation) 2. Automobile industry workers—Labor unions—Ukraine. 3. Automobile industry workers—Labor unions—Belarus. 4. Labor policy—Russia (Federation) 5. Labor policy—Ukraine. 6. Labor policy—Belarus. I. Title.

HD9710.R92M35 2004   331.88'1292'094709049   C2003-905802-61

Cover design: Associés libres

	BLACK ROSE BOOKS	
C.P. 1258	2250 Military Road	99 Wallis Road
Succ. Place du Parc	Tonawanda, NY	London, E9 5LN
Montréal, H2X 4A7	14150	England
Canada	USA	UK

To order books:
In Canada: (phone) 1-800-565-9523 (fax) 1-800-221-9985
email: utpbooks@utpress.utoronto.ca
In United States: (phone) 1-800-283-3572 (fax) 1-651-917-6406
In the UK & Europe: (phone) London 44 (0)20 8986-4854 (fax) 44 (0)20 8533-5821
email: order@centralbooks.com
Our Web Site address: http://www.web.net/blackrosebooks

A publication of the Institute of Policy Alternatives of Montréal (IPAM)

Printed in Canada

CONTENTS

Preface	viii
Chapter One The Legacy Of The Soviet Period	1
Chapter Two The Socio-Political Context In Russia	25
Chapter Three The Union Of Auto And Farm-Machine Workers Of Russia	59
Chapter Four Resistance In The "Traditional" Unions	105
Chapter Five Resistance In An Alternative Union	128
Chapter Six The Socio-Political Context In Ukraine	153
Chapter Seven The Union Of Auto And Farm-Machine Workers Of Ukraine	167
Chapter Eight Transformation Of A "Traditional" Trade Union	195
Chapter Nine The Socio-Political Context In Belarus	213
Chapter Ten The Union Of Auto And Farm-Machine Worker Of Belarus	223
Chapter Eleven Three Factories	249
Conclusion	265
Bibliography	275
Index	281

Abbreviations

ASM	auto and farm-machine sector
ASMB	Union of Workers of Auto and Farm-Machine Building of Belarus
ASMR	Union of Workers of Auto and Farm-Machine Building of Russia
ASMU	Union of Workers of Auto and Farm-Machine Building of Ukraine
BATE	Borisov Starter Factory
BNF	Byelorussian National Front
FNPR	Federation of Independent Trade Unions of Russia
FPB	Byelorussian Federation of Trade Unions
FPU	Federation of Trade Unions of Ukraine
GAZ	Gorkii Automobile Factory
IMF	International Monetary Fund
KPRF	Communist Party of the Russian Federation
MAZ	Minsk Truck Factory
MTZ	Minsk Tractor Factory
NPG	Independent Union of Miners
PT	Byelorussian Party of Labour
REP	Radio-Electronics Workers' Union (Belarus)
STK	work-collective council
TIE	Transnationals Information Exchange
VAZ	Volga Automobile Factory
YMZ	Yaroslavl Motor Factory

To the memories of

Grigorii Stepanovich Artemenko
(October 8, 1942–February 7, 1999)

and

Dan Benedict
(September 20, 1917–September 16, 2003)

PREFACE

This comparative study of the trade-union movements in the auto and farm-machine sectors of Belarus, Russian and Ukraine in 1991-2003 grew out of my longstanding interest and involvement in the Soviet and post-Soviet labour movements, first as an academic, and over the past decade, as a labour educator. The study seeks to understand the obstacles to the development of an effective labour movement that would be a force for social justice and democracy and what it will take to overcome those obstacles.

The book is thus written from a committed, activist point of view. At the same time, it seeks support in an honest analysis of the available facts and the determination of their interconnections. Much of the data was collected in the course of my activity within the framework of the School for Worker Democracy, which conducts rank-and-file education in the three countries. This put me in contact with hundreds of activists, some of them union officers but many with no elected position. Over the years, I have visited dozens of plants, attended numerous union meetings, participated in collective protests. Beyond the enterprises, I have spoken at length with union leaders and staff at the regional and national levels, attended union meetings, conferences and congresses. I have also had good access to union documents and publications at the various levels.

The choice of the auto and farm-machine sector was to some extent dictated by my privileged contacts with its unions, initially facilitated by the Canadian Autoworkers' Union. But another consideration was the economic importance of the auto sector for modern economies and the key role its unions have played in the labour movement around the world. The machine-building sector, the largest industrial employer in the three countries, has in general been little studied.

The book's theoretical framework is Marxist. This is not a concrete set of propositions about unions or "industrial relations," but a general approach to understanding society from the vantage point of workers' interests, the ultimate goal being their liberation from exploitation. (The term "workers" is used here in the broad sense of non-managerial wage and salary earners.) A basic premise of the book is the fundamentally antagonistic nature of the relations between labour and capital. Their conflicting interests arise out of the different positions they occupy in society. This is reflected, for example, in the fact that what is economic freedom for employers is unfreedom for workers and vice versa. Unions, therefore, are—or should be—fundamentally about power. Another basic premise is that society constitutes a dynamic "totality" of interdependent parts. "Industrial relations" cannot be understood in abstraction from the other aspects of society, including ideology, politics, the international system and the international balance of forces.

It is a cliché to write that the too many people to be named have contributed to this book, but it is unavoidable. I owe a great debt of gratitude to the worker activists who over the years shared their experiences and thoughts with me, and sometimes also their friendship. In the bleak post-Soviet reality, they insisted on their human dignity and fought back. Some eventually tired and abandoned the struggle. Others, tireless fighters like Grigorii Artemenko, Petr Siuda, Viktor Vetchinkin, died well before their time. All have inspired me in my own union and political activity and have greatly enriched my life. They were and are genuine heros. For me, they are Russia, Ukraine and Belarus, and the main reason I keep returning there.

My understanding of the labour movement and my overall intellectual development have greatly benefited from my collaboration with Galina and Boris Rakitskii, two original Marxist thinkers with whom I have had the good fortune to work together in the Russian School for Worker Democracy. Long discussions over the years with Nikolai Preobrazhenskii, another good friend, have helped me to see beyond the surface of post-Soviet reality, in which the first rule is that nothing is ever as it appears. Vladimir Zlenko, former national president of the Ukrainian Union of Auto and Farm-Machine Workers, who presently heads the Ukrainian School for Worker Democracy, proved to me that union leaders even in the bleakest of circumstances have options other than to embrace "social partnership." He was an invaluable source of information and insight into the complex inner workings of the union movement. Both he and the late Grigorii Artemenko, another good friend, proved to me that even sixty years of totalitarian rule did not completely break the continuity with the magnificent workers' movement that dared in 1917.

Among the many other people who over the years have helped me in various ways in this research, I should mention especially Serezha Agapov, Boris Maksimov, Fatima Bianchi, Aleksandr Bukhvostov, Lyudmila Bulavka, Aleksandr Buzgalin, Seymour Melman, Simon Clarke, Don Filtzer, Dave Melnychuk, Leo Panitch, and Nikolai Pokhabov, as well as my friends from the Canadian Autoworkers' Union—the late Dan Benedict, Sam Gindin, and Herman Rosenfeld, together with whom I also had the privilege of doing labour education in the countries studied. Their union and its educational programme were an inspiration to me and of great practical help.

Finally, I want to thank my wife, Sonia, for so graciously tolerating both my long absences, and also my presences, these many years.

A Note on References

Much of the material for this book comes from informal conversations with workers and union leaders and from discussions in educational seminars. These sources are often unnamed in the book. Sometimes this is because the person so requested; at other times, it is because I did not have a chance to ask their permission. Sometimes I have purposefully changed the name, position or place of employment to protect the source. In order not to encumber the text with references, I have not bothered to cite the exact date and place of interviews, even where the person is identified, unless I felt it was particularly pertinent.

Chapter One

THE LEGACY OF THE SOVIET PERIOD

No simple formula can adequately characterize the Soviet system. It was a contradictory, hybrid system that evolved out of a workers' and peasants' revolution in an economically backward country encircled by a hostile capitalist world. Though workers constituted a relatively small part of the population, the Russian labour movement emerged at the end of the nineteenth century as the most determined and effective force in the struggle against Tsarist absolutism that culminated in the February Revolution of 1917.[1] The strength of the labour movement, on the one hand, and the weakness and largely reactionary character of the Russian bourgeoisie, on the other, gave rise to dual power: a bourgeois government flanked by soviets of workers' and soldiers' deputies. The issue was finally decided eight months later when the Bolshevik-led soviets seized state power in an effort to stem the rising tide of counterrevolution and economic collapse and in the hope of inspiring revolutions in more developed countries that would come to Russia's aid.[2]

After a brief interregnum, the October Revolution was followed by a prolonged and cruel civil war fueled by foreign intervention. Coming on the heels of World War One, this terrible struggle left the economy in ruins and destroyed the working class as an independent political force. Power shifted from the soviets to the Communist Party, a substitution that the Communists at the time viewed as temporary until the economy could be restored and revolutions abroad ended their isolation. But over the course of the 1920s, power within the party shifted to its functionaries, who had themselves become an integral part of the state's administrative machinery. By the beginning of the 1930s, all independent organizations had been eliminated, and the whole economy was under the direct control of this bureaucratic élite, which was busy restoring the authoritarian and chauvinist practices of Tsarism behind the mask of socialism.

But hiding behind the socialist facade, the bureaucracy was unable to legitimate its domination. Until the very end in 1991, it remained a usurper. To remedy that would have required the restoration of capitalism and the transformation of the functionaries (the *nomenklatura*) into a class of property owners. That was ruled out both by the élite's own sense of legitimacy, which, despite everything, was still linked to the revolution, and by its fear of the popular reaction. This anomalous and ultimately untenable situation persisted as long as the regime was able to promote economic development and maintain the state's independence and territorial integrity, tasks at which the old Tsarist regime had failed.

The totalitarian nature of the Soviet state—which allowed no independent social organization or free public expression—was dictated, more than anything else, by the ruling bureaucracy's need to compensate for the fragility of its ideological and social foundations. Not only could the *nomenklatura* not establish its popular legitimacy (it was forced to hide its very existence behind a democratic and egalitarian facade, though it was quite an open secret), but it also had to use direct political means to "pump" the surplus out of the workers. As a result, economic struggle was inseparable from political struggle, something that added significantly to the *nomenklatura*'s vulnerability.[3] If the system seemed so unshakeable for so long to most observers, it was because of the elaborate and systematic prophylactic measures necessarily taken by the totalitarian state to avert any open expression of opposition or dissidence. But the regime's fragility was exposed as soon as Gorbachev loosened political controls. Almost at once, the leaders were inundated with complaints about the privileges and arbitrary power of the *nomenklatura*. Before long, a democratic movement was demanding "all power to the soviets."

Trade Unions

Trade-union independence, like soviet democracy, did not survive the civil war, during which the unions functioned as quasi-state organs of economic administration and military mobilization. Once the emergency had passed, there was considerable debate within the party over the role of unions. The position finally adopted was a deeply ambivalent one: the unions were to support the state in reconstructing the devastated economy but they were also to defend workers against possible abuses by management.[4] In practice, the unions' managerial functions had priority over representation of workers' interests, particularly in the state-sector (most of large industry). On the other hand, the Labour Code adopted in 1922 was very liberal and afforded considerable protection to workers against dismissal, no small matter in a period of high unemployment. The party encouraged unions to channel dissatisfaction into arbitration, but strikes were legal and when they occurred (not often, because of high unemployment), they frequently ended in full or partial satisfaction of workers' demands and were treated sympathetically by the press. Strikes were officially viewed as a sign that the unions were neglecting workers' needs. On the national level, within the limits set by party policy and discipline, union leaders acted as advocates for workers' interests, though without direct input from workers themselves. The trade-union leader M. Tomsky successfully opposed for several years Stalin's attempts to broaden wage differentials and weaken workers' legal protections, until he was finally ousted in 1929.[5]

That coincided with the collectivization of agriculture and the introduction of centralized economic management, a transformation that consolidated the bureaucracy's hold over Soviet society. Henceforth, unions lost their last shred of autonomy and were fully integrated in the economic and social administrations. In the enterprises, the union president was the least influential corner of the famous "triangle," after the director and the party secretary.[6] Unions played a major part in disciplining workers—and discipline under Stalin became increasingly draconian—and also in encouraging "socialist" competition among them. The liberalism of the Labour Code was gradually eroded. Strikes became illegal in practice, if not de jure, and a tabu subject for the press. Unions lost all say in wage matters, and differentials became extreme. On the other hand, they were entrusted with the administration, or co-administration, of social benefits, as well as of the technical (health and safety) and legal inspectorates.

Despite the end of terror after Stalin's death in March 1953, unions remained as undemocratic and subordinate as before. Although union officials gained more room to defend workers against violations of the law and of other centrally-established norms, the system could not tolerate independent organizations, and least of all labour organizations. Even from a purely economic point of view, the chronic labour shortage would have allowed unions to drive up wages to intolerable levels and to fatally undermine managerial authority. But the most immediate threat was political, since, as noted, economic struggles threatened quickly to become politicized, a threat that was exacerbated by the highly centralized nature of management. This was graphically demonstrated by the Novocherkassk strike of 1962, where a spontaneous protest in one factory over a centrally mandated increase of output norms and food prices quickly spread to the whole city and turned against the political authorities. It was only the quick action of the state in cutting the city off from the outside world that prevented the movement from spreading.[7] Labour upheavals in Eastern Europe were, of course, more frequent and powerful, in part because of the colonial aspect of the regimes.[8] But the same characteristics were again demonstrated in the Soviet Union at the end of Perestroika by the coalminers' general strikes of 1989 and 1991 and by the Byelorussian strike movement of April 1991.[9] These powerful labour mobilizations all occurred in the absence of independent workers' organizations and, for the most part, of any experience of collective struggle.

The state, because of its vulnerability, put tremendous effort into prevention and was careful not to overstep certain bounds in its relations with the workers. After the Novocherkassk strike, workers' wages in the Soviet Union rose steadily and basic food prices remained stable for almost three decades (there were, however, hidden increases), despite the serious economic inbalances that resulted from this policy. The next time the state increased basic food prices was in April 1991, and that provoked a vast strike movement in Byelorussia and breathed new life into a waning miners' strike already in progress.[10] When spontaneous strikes occurred in the Soviet period, the policy was to isolate and extinguish them as quickly as possible through concessions. Once tempers cooled, there would be followed by selective, but usually relatively mild, repression of the leaders. It was not uncommon for managers and party officials to be dismissed for allowing worker discontent to reach the explosion point. In the early 1980s, workers of the assembly shop of the First Moscow Watch Factory downed tools over management's reneging on a promise to raise wages. Within minutes, the plant's top managers were standing trembling in front of the district party secretary, who threatened to take away their party cards (an end to decent job prospects) unless the conflict was resolved immediately. Two hours later, the workers were back at work with their wage increase. Two managers were dismissed.[11]

Unions had three main functions under this system: administration of social benefits, assisting management in meeting production targets, and, lastly, defending their members. In the later years, especially in the 1980s, as wages continued to rise and shortages increased, unions became increasingly drawn into the distribution of scarce consumer goods, including cars, furniture, clothes, and food. But even before that, the administration, co-administration or monitoring of benefits with the aid of an army of volunteers (who usually received some material "encouragement") took up the largest part of union time. These benefits included sick leave, pregnancy and maternity leave, pensions, vacation benefits, child care, housing, catering, cultural, leisure and sports programmes. But assisting management in meeting production targets always had priority if the latter came into conflict with the other functions. In a manual for union activists of the metalworking sector published in 1972, the chapter on "production-oriented activity" preceded those on wages, health and safety and social welfare. "Production-oriented activity" included the organization of "socialist" competition, the promotion of technical innovation and quality improvements, encouraging workers to submit rationalization proposals, the organization of conferences with workers to discuss production goals and problems. (This was termed "worker participation in management.")[12] The priority given to meeting production targets was justified by the official ideology: since the Soviet state was democratic and the society harmonious, the unions' concern for production was by definition concern for the people's welfare. Economic and social progress depended above all on meeting output targets.

The basic decisions concerning wages, social benefits, and labour rights were made by central party and government bodies. The central union bodies officially participated in these decisions, and even co-signed some of the laws and decrees. But in doing so, it is by no means obvious they were defending their members' interests. In any case, the political clout of the union apparatus in the Soviet system was slight. The agreements signed in the plants (one cannot really speak of negotiations, except to some degree in the area of health and safety) were oriented essentially to ensuring that the centrally set norms and rules were respected. These agreements did not deal with wages but with health and safety improvements, housing construction and standards, catering, cultural and health and leisure facilities, and the like.

The unions' role in defending workers was thus mostly one of "controlling," that is, of monitoring the application of decisions made by higher authorities. In this area, at least on paper, unions had extensive rights. The unions in the plants had their own health and safety commissions, and the regional and national union organizations administered the health and safety and legal inspectorates. These inspectorates had an army of full-time specialists with broad powers to investigate, fine and issue binding orders to management.[13] Unions also participated in the periodic revision of output norms (a major irritant to workers), and they had the formal power to reject changes. Workers' grievances had to be reviewed by a joint union-management committee within five days of their submission, and the union could issue a binding unilateral decision if no agreement could be reached. From 1958, union consent was needed for dismissals. Enterprise unions also had the right to ask higher union bodies to remove or otherwise punish administrators for violating collective agreements or the Labour Code.[14]

Some union leaders were more committed than others to defending workers' rights. But on the whole, they exercised their formal powers only to the extent they did not seriously interfere with production targets or when they had support of higher political authorities. Most union officials were content to act as adjuncts to management and to administer social benefits. That is how they saw themselves and that also is also how workers viewed them. The political authorities periodically promoted campaigns to strengthen the representation function of unions, but they had little real impact because of the state's deeply ambivalent attitude toward the unions' role and their fear of independent organizations. In evaluating one of these campaigns, the national trade-union paper *Trud* mockingly described the unions as "semi-defenders"of the workers.[15]

The subordination of unions was systemic. Meetings of regional and national union organizations followed closely upon party meetings at the corresponding level and they adopted decisions in light of party decisions. The dates, agenda and list of participants of regional and national union gatherings had to be approved in advance by party authorities. Union leaders, except sometimes at the shop level, were appointed by the party authorities. A union appointment was typically a temporary, often unwelcome, step in the career of an engineer on his or (more rarely) her way up the administrative ladder. In 1985, when party authorities informed A. Bukhvostov, a high-ranking engineer at Gomsel'mash (a farm-machine factory) that he was to head the enterprise's union committee, they were quick to reassure him that it was not a sign of disapproval and that his tenure in the union would be brief. ("I had a negative view of unions," he recalled. "I didn't like the way they spent their time divvying up carpets and crystalware. I found that rather disgusting.") Workers were practically excluded from the position of plant president and anything higher than that in the unions.

It was also rare for union officials beyond the enterprise level to have come out of a union background. Regional and national union leaders, as a rule, were chosen from among "non-perspective" party functionaries. For this reason, unions were commonly referred to as the "grave-yard of party cadres." The last Soviet president of the Union of Auto and Farm-Machine Building Workers, A. Kashirin, had been an assistant department head in the Moscow city party apparatus for eight years, when he was appointed national president of the union. At that time, he was already forty-nine, and his party career was going nowhere. He is remembered by union officials as an exceptional leader because he promoted people with practical union experience from within the union's ranks and interfered minimally with their work.

In view of these conditions, and since, moreover, it was a serious political crime to mobilize workers or assume the leadership of their spontaneous protests, there was really no room for union independence in this system. Only the boldest individuals, people prepared to risk their career prospects—workers had none to speak of, which is one of the reasons they were excluded from leadership positions in unions—dared take very seriously their role as defender's of workers rights and interests. For example, in 1974, party authorities removed L. Kal'yanov, president of the union of the Kharkov Bicycle Factory, for refusing to consent (union consent was formally required by law) to an administrative order for the plant to work on Saturdays. I. Gorbik, the Kharkov regional president in the same Union of Auto and Farm Machine-Building Workers was dismissed two years later for taking a similar position. In the late 1970s, V. Zlenko, then president of the Chernigov regional committee of that union, refused consent to the opening of a newly-constructed technical school because the technical inspection had revealed serious safety hazards. He recalled what followed:

> I was called into the regional party committee: "Sign. We'll take it under our supervision, and all the problems will be corrected in January." They really turned up the heat, since without our signature the construction project wouldn't appear as completed in the region's annual plan for capital construction, and they would look bad. But we insisted that the problems first had to be corrected. We didn't budge. They nearly got the union's inspector fired, but he stood his ground and he's still working today. They called in the union's chief inspector from Moscow, but he also supported us…He said he wouldn't allow children into unsafe facilities. We won that battle but we didn't win them all. There were also a lot of defeats. I sometimes got into serious trouble and was summoned before the regional party committee, where they threatened me: "We'll have you fired and you won't find work anywhere else in the Soviet Union." It came to that, and many times I really believed they were going to do it. But I said to myself: "What the hell! Let them. I've worked as a repair mechanic and as a machine-repair foreman and I like the work."[16]

The Workers' Situation

Stalin's death and the dismantling of the terror apparatus did not end bureaucratic absolutism, which was subsequently enshrined by Brezhnev in article six of the 1977 Constitution with the euphemism of "the leading role of the party." But the end of terror meant that the regime had to pay more attention to workers' interests. Stalin's severe disciplinary laws were repealed, allowing workers, for example, to change jobs freely. Absenteeism, from being a crime, became a mere violation of discipline. It became difficult to dismiss workers as a disciplinary measure. Even when unions gave their consent, workers could turn to the courts with a reasonable chance of success.[17] And layoffs for purely economic reasons were extremely rare. Wage differentials were also significantly reduced, and real money wages, even by the lowest estimates, grew at an average of 2.5 per cent par annum between 1955 and 1975.[18] Other aspects of living standards also improved markedly, including housing, healthcare, education, culture, and leisure. (The progress began to slow from the second half of the 1970s.)

As a result, the workers' situation in many ways came to resemble that of their counterparts under capitalism. In both systems, labour was alienated, in the sense that workers had no control over the wealth they produced nor any real say in the organization and goals of production. But there were important differences. In the Soviet Union, the surplus product was not appropriated by a class of owners but by a party-state administration that did not hold legal title to the means of production. This title, according to the Soviet Constitution, belonged collectively to the Soviet people. While the bureaucracy was free to manage the economy in its own interest, it could appropriate only a small fraction of the wealth that was produced in the form of consumption privileges that could not be bequeathed to others and that had to be hidden from public view, since they were illegitimate.

As far as the management of labour was concerned, the situation was, as Rudolf Bahro put it, one of "no longer but not yet,"[19] that is neither capitalism nor socialism: the efficiency of the wage system, borrowed in its essential aspects from capitalism, was undermined by the chronic labour shortage and de facto job security, as well as by the size of the social wage, estimated in 1984 at two-thirds of the individual (money) wage.[20] And even the individual wage, despite the widespread practice of piece-work and bonus systems, was largely guaranteed. Soviet workers' living standards lagged behind those in the wealthy capitalist countries but they were well above third-world levels. But beyond that, full employment and the social wage (which included more-or-less free housing, healthcare, and education, and subsidized basic food products, transport, and leisure), meant that even the poorest workers were less vulnerable economically than most of their better-off counterparts in the West.[21] Today, workers recall nostalgically a time when "we didn't have to worry about tomorrow."

Of course, workers could lose their jobs, and much worse, for political dissidence. But the elimination of terror and liberalization of the Labour Code meant that the bounds of the permissible were much broader and clearer than under Stalin. Workers' physical security was guaranteed as long as they respected the political limits, and the overwhelming majority did. As for work discipline, management's powers were hemmed in by the factors already mentioned. Moreover, especially after Khrushchev's demise in 1964, a more tolerant attitude to labour discipline became quasi-official policy. It was, in a way, the counterpart to the relaxed discipline within the ranks of bureaucracy itself and a reflection of the latter's ardent desire for stability and social peace. This situation, along with the strong individual bargaining position afforded workers by the labour shortage, moved one worker to recall the early 1980s as the "golden age of the working class."

As this suggests, the repressive framework, though a crucial aspect of the situation, cannot by itself explain the workers' relative quiescence. When A. Belanovskii, former chairman of the union committee of the foundry shop at the Minsk Truck Factory (MAZ), was asked in 1992 if his predecessor had defended workers, he replied: "Conditions were totally different. You have to have experienced them from the inside…The system at that time didn't allow for much open conflict. But it wasn't just a matter of repression; it was also people's mentality. I'm trying to understand these things now."[22] While the dictatorship did foster among workers a sense of "us," the powerless and unprivileged, against "them," the bosses (*nachal'stvo*), other elements of the system muted antagonism and confused the lines of opposition. For one thing, the ruling group, which, as noted, did not hold title to the enterprises, was organized in a hierarchy of power and privilege. Administrators at each level were under the thumb of their superiors. Directors, even of large plants, trembled before ministers and higher party functionaries. This made it possible for workers to see themselves as merely the lowest rung of a continuous hierarchy of authority. Social mobility slowed down in later years, but advancement, especially inter-generational, was not blocked. Most of the later Soviet leaders, including Gorbachev and Yeltsin, did not come from privileged families. Children of high functionaries tended to shun *nomenklatura* jobs, and conscientious workers were encouraged to study for higher degrees that opened the prospect of administrative careers.

But more important was the regime's paternalism. Workers were powerless, but they had important social rights, especially a guaranteed job, job security, a social wage. Wages rose steadily, the social wage expanded, prices were stable. For workers in the large factories, the growing shortages of consumer goods were mitigated by the system of internal distribution. Official propaganda aside, this provided a basis for workers to feel that the state had a fatherly concern for them, even if it acted as an authoritarian and corrupt father. And it was also seen as defending them—not entirely without basis—from the pressures of a hostile capitalist world.

There has been debate in the academic literature as to whether there was a tacit "social contract" between the regime and the workers that would explain the latter's quiescence.[23] Sarah Ashwin, on the other hand, has argued that repression and material benefits cannot explain the social peace of the Brezhnev period, since workers have remained passive even after the repression and benefits have been eliminated.[24] But in fact, the final years of the Soviet regime, marked by political liberalization and declining living standards (mainly in the form of consumer shortages and price rises), did see a significant upsurge of labour protest, which, however, fell off rapidly once the system was dismantled under "shock therapy." In general, the influence of various social and political factors cannot not be analyzed in abstraction from the totality of the social relations of which they are a part. That totality was radically transformed by the fall of the Soviet system.

The paternalistic relations between the bureaucratic élite and the workers were even more pronounced on the enterprise level. The general director, sometimes referred to simply as "our general" (*nash general*), was the state's representative in the enterprise but at the same time a lobbyist for, and defender of, his or her "work collective" vis-à-vis the central state authorities. (This dual role, in fact, characterized every territorial level of the administrative hierarchy. It became especially pronounced under Brezhnev's rule with its de facto decentralization and tolerance for corruption.) Profits (a rather meaningless term in the Soviet economic context) were not the goal of directors, whose incentive to save on labour costs was weak. What mattered was meeting centrally-fixed output targets. Despite the "planned" nature of the economy, managers had to operate under inherently uncertain conditions, especially as regards the material supply of the enterprise. They were thus interested in maintaining a relatively large and flexible work force. Despite pressure from Moscow to save on labour, management was more interested in expanding the work force and they tried to hold onto it by offering the best wages and benefits they could. Because of the arrhythmic nature of supply and the need for periodic "storming," the administration tolerated lax discipline during slack periods. Moreover, to the degree that bonuses and social benefits depended on enterprise performance, workers did share management's interest in meeting plan targets.

And so when management, seconded by the union, called on workers to "consider the situation of the enterprise" (*vkhodit' v polozhenie*), that is, to agree periodically to forego their leisure, particularly Saturdays, or to tolerate sub-standard conditions for the sake of meeting plan targets, workers generally responded positively. Of course, fear of reprisals played a role, but there was also a widespread sense among workers that they should support "their" enterprise (sometime referred to as "native" (*rodnoe*)), a sense reinforced by the fact that much of the social wage was allocated through the enterprise in the later period. This was all part of an elaborate system, including the widespread use of piece-work, bonuses and the brigade system, calculated to make workers bear the cost of the bureaucracy's inability to organize production more rationally.

Perestroika

The choice of Mikhail Gorbachev in 1985 to head the party reflected the leadership's realization that major reforms were required to reverse the long-term economic slowdown that threatened the international status and internal stability of the regime. Gorbachev's initial approach followed traditional lines: administrative reorganization, reinforced discipline, increased investment in the machine-tool sector. But he soon decided that a bolder approach was needed and announced Perestroika (restructuring). The basic idea was to replace vertical, centralized management of the economy with horizontal, decentralized coordination through the market. The increased autonomy of enterprises, that would still be state-owned, would free up the energy of the central government for strategic planning. This would be achieved mainly indirectly through the manipulation of macro-economic levers rather than by detailed central planning and direct intervention into the activity of the enterprises.

This type of reform had already been tried with mixed results in some Eastern-European countries. What was unique to Perestroika was its political dimension: Gorbachev declared that "democratization" was the very essence of his reform. By "democratization" he had in mind the gradual, controlled liberalization of political life: relaxed censorship, limited freedom of association and workers' participation in management. But there was never any intention of letting the people decide the basic orientations of the economic reform. Even as mounting pressure from below forced open the limits of "democratization," Gorbachev continued to insist that there was no alternative to his reform, whose contours nevertheless kept changing.

Perestroika was originally presented to the Soviet people under the banner of socialist renewal and a return to Leninist norms and it initially evoked genuine enthusiasm among broad sections of workers. However, Gorbachev's goal was to rationalize the bureaucratic system, not restore the soviet democracy of 1917-18. "Democratization" was a means of exerting pressure on a reluctant bureaucracy and of winning popular adherence to reforms that would challenge long-standing social arrangements.[25] On the enterprise level, the reform provided for the election of managers and of work-collective councils (STKs) for employee participation in management. These measures were designed to strengthen workers' interest in their enterprise's performance and to allay fears of increased managerial power resulting from broadened enterprise autonomy. As Gorbachev put it: "The well-being of the worker will depend upon the abilities of managers. The workers should therefore have real means of influencing the choice of director and controlling [monitoring] his activity."[26]

However, the workers' enthusiasm for Perestroika was short-lived. They soon understood that the bureaucracy had no intention of yielding power in any meaningful way. Election of managers was subject to approval by higher authorities, and the STKs' powers were vague and circumscribed. Moreover, self-management was limited to the enterprise. There was never any question of submitting the central planning bodies and ministries to democratic control. As a result, workers could not influence the broader conditions that determined the performance of their enterprise. Had Perestroika been the result of struggle from below rather than an ambiguous gift from above, workers might have eventually been able to enlarge the scope of self-management and "democratization" and turn them to their interests. As it was, enthusiasm gave way to cynicism and to rising discontent with the growing shortage of consumer goods and profiteering by the new private ("co-operative") sector.

Nevertheless, Perestroika did give a significant impulse to labour activism, which would continue to rise until around 1991. Initially, collective protests occurred over traditional grievances, mainly wage cuts and increased output norms. An early reform of the wage system aimed at strengthening the incentive role of wages provoked many conflicts. The reform was to be introduced gradually in the enterprises, in consultation with the workers, and to be accompanied by wage increases paid out of the resulting productivity gains. But, as usual, it was marked by widespread administrative arbitrariness and formalism. Workers reacted with hostility to the abrogation of traditional practices without commensurate compensation.[27]

Another traditional grievance that provoked widespread protest was Saturday work. As they shed their fear, workers grew less willing to pay for management's inability rationally to organize production. This issue, along with management's refusal to heed the democratic will of the workers, led to one of the biggest strikes of early Perestroika in December 1987. At the Yaroslavl Motor Factory (25,000 employees at the time) delegates' conferences in each of the sixty shops all adopted resolutions to limit to eight the number of Saturdays to be worked in 1998. Nevertheless, the STK ratified management's schedule of fifteen "black Saturdays." About a quarter of the employees went out on a strike that lasted seven days. It ended when a factory-wide delegates' conference of delegates—as usual, the delegates were elected by the "work collective," that is by all employees including management—supported management's position by a narrow margin. However, the conference also decided to ban completely "black Saturdays" from 1989.[28]

Although workers were becoming more assertive, collective actions were limited to individual factories and, more often, to individual shops and sometimes even brigades. This line was finally crossed in July 1999, when the coalminers, over 400,000 strong, went on strike in four coal basins thousands of kilometers apart. Their immediate grievances were not very different from those that were provoking smaller conflicts in other sectors. But the miners were solidary, thanks to their relative social homogeneity, common bonds forged by the hard, dangerous work conditions, and their concentration in mining towns. Their strike was different also in eventually putting forward overtly political demands: an end to bureaucratic privileges, dismissal of odious local political and administrative officials, immediate elections to local soviets. The most radical region, Vorkuta, in the far north, demanded repeal of article six of the Constitution and the election by universal suffrage of the Congress of People's Deputies. These demands amounted to an end to the bureaucratic dictatorship.[29]

Almost all the mobilizations of this period were led by informal leaders and elected strike committees, bypassing the unions. The latter either took management's side or watched passively on the sidelines. For example, after a strike of welders at Ryazsel'mash (farm machinery) over increased output norms in the fall of 1998, the union suspended the membership of two of the most active participants. In the strike at the Yaroslavl Motor Factory, the union openly acted as the arm of management, urging workers to "consider the situation of the enterprise." And in the negotiations that ended the coalminers' strike, the union leaders sat beside management across the table from the strike committee leaders.

The All-Union Central Council of Trade Unions met a few weeks after the miners' strike. Its discussion of the workers' problems and of the unions' shortcomings was unprecedentedly frank. A resolution was adopted calling for a radical shift in policy in favour of defending workers' interests and away from the traditional concern with production. But the rank-and-file mobilization had not been powerful or widespread enough to radically change the conditions that kept union leaders subservient to management. During their strike, the coalminers had demanded new union elections. Subsequently, many of strike leaders were elected to leadership positions at the local level. But the union included all the employees of the coal ministry, that is, besides miners, thousands of factory and service workers who had not participated in the strike, as well as a vast number of engineering, technical, office and managerial personnel. The voice of the more militant and independent underground miners was drowned out in this largely inert mass.

The failure of elections to transform the old unions contributed to the decision by activists of the strike committees (which had not disbanded after the strike) to found a new, minority union in October 1990, the Independent Miners' Union (NPG). The NPG was distinguished by its policy of independence from management. Its statutes expressly forbade membership of administrative personnel (and, initially, of all non-miners) in the union. Some attempts to reform the unions from the inside were made in enterprises in other sectors but, with a few exceptions, they too failed. The founding of the NPG was soon followed by the establishment of "alternative" unions in other branches of the economy.

Perestroika for all practical purposes ended in 1989. The evident failure of the "socialist-market" reform, the growing popular opposition to the bureaucratic dictatorship, and the fall of the Communist regimes in Eastern Europe, persuaded a major part of the Soviet élite to opt for capitalism. From the second half of 1989, the word "socialism" disappeared from Gorbachev's lexicon. His declared goal now was now a "full-blooded market economy," and the immediate task was "de-statization."[30] This new orientation, despite the risks it entailed—and the leadership did not conceal its fear of a "social explosion"[31]—held out for the élite at least the hope of holding onto power and privilege, albeit in new forms. With the old system so widely discredited, the Gorbachev faction had little trouble keeping opposition from the conservative elements of the *nomenklatura* in check.

As for the workers' movement, it lacked a coherent programme of its own. A significant part of the activist stratum, however, embraced self-management, which Gorbachev at this point decided to jettison as incompatible with a "full-blooded market." Accordingly, the Supreme Soviet adopted a new enterprise law in 1990 that abrogated earlier self-management rights. (Election of managers had been formally abolished even earlier.) Upon learning this, the assembly-line workers at VAZ (Volga Automobile Factory, 120,000 employees who make "Ladas") adopted a resolution condemning the Supreme Soviet's action as grossly undemocratic, since the law been adopted in virtual secret (not to mention that the Supreme Soviet had not been elected by universal suffrage), without prior publication of the draft or public debate. "A gross provocation has been perpetrated. A law affecting the interests of every work collective has been adopted without any consideration for the opinion of the toilers themselves."[32]

The shift in Gorbachev's policy to the STK's was the catalyst for the emergence of a national self-management movement. This took place on the general background of mounting economic chaos[33] and conflicts over power in the enterprises, as workers accused managers of incompetence and corruption. In December 1990, a congress in Moscow founded the Union of Work-Collective Councils and Workers' Committees. Representatives from the auto sector, notably VAZ and the Moskvich factory, played a prominent role in the initiative.[34] This movement was the closest that workers came to developing an independent programme for transforming the Soviet system. But it suffered from several important weaknesses. Although it firmly opposed the bureaucratic dictatorship, it lacked an overall conception of how the economy should be organized beyond self-managed enterprises. There was also no unanimity about the desired status of the enterprises themselves. Most of the activists favoured collective employee ownership, but a minority wanted the state to retain ownership and to lease the plants to the employees. No one really thought through the practical implications of complete enterprise economic independence, the universal demand. This demand was a reaction against the workers' experience with centralized bureaucratic control of the economy. The movement, however, was silent about any planning or a regulatory role for the state or any other organism.

Although many of the activists of the STK movement viewed themselves as socialists, the programme, as it stood, made their movement easy prey for the radical liberal forces that opposed Gorbachev from the "left" (in fact, the right–the times were confusing). This weakness might not have been fatal had the movement been able to gather the force necessary to begin to apply its programme. Experience might have led to corrections and filling in the missing elements. But the movement's leaders failed to mobilize the necessary rank-and-file support for this to happen. Nor did they really try. From the start, they devoted their main efforts to lobbying government. Almost nothing was done to educate and mobilize a base for the movement, even though such a based was potentially available: opinion polls showed a majority opposed to the privatization of large enterprises.[35] At the founding congress of the movement, a heated debate took place over whether to organize a strike in support of the programmatic demands. But instead, it was decided first to try working through the republican soviets (which had recently been elected by universal suffrage). The Union of Work-Collective Councils never organized any mass actions to test the real force behind its claim to represent millions of workers. Instead, the leaders in Russia supported Boris Yeltsin in his quest for power against Gorbachev. In the Ukraine, the movement's leaders similarly gave their support to Leonid Kravchuk in his presidential bid. Both candidates boldly promised that the STKs would be the very foundation of their governments. Once firmly in power, both adopted reforms that excluded workers from any real say in management. The eventual disappearance of the STKs went almost unnoticed.

The attitude of unions, both traditional and alternative, to the STKs and to self-management tended to be hostile. The traditional unions saw in them rivals encroaching on their monopoly as representatives of employees. Moreover, the unions subservience to management meant that they would could not support anything that management opposed, and management certainly did not want any limitations on its freedom of action. To justify their position, union leaders often advanced the curious argument that "you need real owners to have real unions." The alternative unions also opposed to the STKs, which they saw as collaborationist. A. Ivanov, the first president of Edinstvo (unity), the alternative union at VAZ, recalled that the unions founders had already decided for themselves that the STKs had no future and did not provide an answer to the workers' problems. "The director was usually a member. He would present an unpopular measure, and the STK as a rule would approve it. Then he would hide behind the STK and tell the workers that it was their own decision. We felt workers should have a say in management, but through their unions."

Meanwhile, important changes were taking place in the traditional unions. Although little progress was made toward establishing their independence from management, the Ninth All-Union Central Council of Trade Unions in the fall of 1989 decided radically to decentralize power in favour of the local, enterprise unions. This was a reaction to the decentralization of economic management and to the democratic changes occurring in society as a whole: the rapid decline of party control meant that any centralism in the unions would have to be rebuilt on a voluntary basis. The national leaders of the branch unions, including the Automobile and Farm Machine-Building Workers, supported the change in the hope of acquiring some of the power and resources that had hitherto been concentrated in the national and territorial federations.[36] But they failed to take into account the legacy of the bureaucratic regime: the weak solidarity and strong aversion to any centralism. As will be seen, decentralization as such had little impact on union-management relations or on the fundamentally undemocratic character of most local unions.

A related change was the formation of national sectoral unions and union federations in the fifteen republics that made up the Soviet Union. Until then, most industrial unions had only had bureaus at the republican level. Their functions were limited mainly to relaying information to and from the central councils in Moscow. Regional union committees were affiliated directly to their central councils in Moscow. But at the end of 1990 and the beginning of 1991, republican councils were elected, and the old central councils were reduced to "international trade-union associations" (MOPs). With few resources, they mainly organize occasional international meetings in their sectors and disseminate legal and statistical information.

Apart from the coalminers, who continued to engage in collective actions after their strike in July 1989,[37] one of the most impressive labour mobilizations of this period occurred in Gomel, Byelorussia.[38] Its background was the Chernobyl nuclear disaster of 1986, which affected the Gomel region the most severely. The workers demanded government support to deal with the consequences. The strike at Gomsel'mash (farm machinery, 60,000 employees) was organized and led by its union, a rare occurrence. Responding to growing unrest and scattered wildcat strikes at the plant—forty localized strikes had occurred in 1997-99—the union committee decided to systematize the demands and put the union in a legal position to strike. Its president, A. Bukhvostov, was elected to head the strike committee. A delegates' conference voted overwhelmingly for a one-day strike on April 26, 1990, the anniversary of the Chernobyl disaster. It adopted demands addressed to the various levels of government and to management. In a somewhat curious turn of events, the workers struck an additional day to protest against the attempt of the regional party authorities to remove their director for failing to prevent the strike.

Following that, the other factories in Gomel elected strike committees, and a citywide strike committee was formed that immediately became the main political force in the town, to the point of assuming certain government functions. In July, it organized a caravan of thirteen busses that headed for Moscow, where the Communist Party of the Soviet Union was holding, as it turned out, its final congress. Prime Minister Ryzhkov received the entire delegation in the Kremlin and signed an agreement on liquidating the consequences of the disaster, an agreement that the Soviet government carried out until it disappeared at the end of 1991.[39] The relative openness of the Soviet government of the time to popular pressure stands in quite striking contrast to the attitude of the Yeltsin regime in the years that followed.[40]

The rise in worker activism culminated in the strike wave of March and April 1991, which played an important, if indirect, role in the final demise of the Soviet regime. This was the first protest that involved the machine-building sector in a major way. As before, it was not the unions that led but elected strike or workers' committees, which may or may not have included individual union officers.[41] The movement began with cascading coalminers' strikes. The demands varied but eventually all agreed on the need for Gorbachev to resign and for the transfer of power from the central government to a council of the republics. These demands paralleled those Yeltsin had made in February 1991. The NPG, and the Russian miners that supported it, had linked their fate to Yeltsin's struggle for power, a strategy that would yield bitter fruit for the miners in the years to follow. The miners' strikes evoked relatively little active response among workers in other sectors, though the recently created Union of Workers of Auto and Farm-Machine Building of Belarus (ASMB) expressed moral support and condemned Gorbachev for his refusal to negotiate while the miners were on strike.[42]

But just when Gorbachev agreed to negotiate with the miners, his Prime Minister announced a major price increase, the first in three decades, promising only partial compensation by increasing wages and social allocations. Although this move added new fuel to the miners' movement, the miners' appeal for a general strike went almost unheeded in Russia. There were some scattered strikes in other economic sectors but they were quickly settled by concessions from management. A similar appeal by Ukrainian miners evoked a somewhat stronger response, but it was much less than a general strike. In Belarus, however, Minsk, the capital city with a large concentration of auto and electronics factories, erupted in practically a general strike. A city-wide strike committee was elected that included Bukhvostov, who had recently been elected the first president of ASMB. Most, though not all, enterprise union leaders stood aside from the movement, which continued with some pauses until the end of April. On April 23-25, the strike movement briefly took on republican proportions and then was called off, as the main economic demands had been won. Despite efforts by the Byelorussian Popular Front to politicize the strike, the workers had remained focused on economic demands.[43] The miners' strike also ended about that time after Gorbachev announced a plan to radically decentralize power in the Soviet state in favour of the republics.

Eight months later, the Soviet Union was no more. The workers' movement had played an important role in its demise. Nevertheless, the end came as a revolution from above, not from below. Since the beginning of Gorbachev's liberalization, only a minority of workers had participated in collective actions and gained experience of independent organization. And that minority had no programme of its own. Petr Zolotarev, one of the founders of Edinstvo at VAZ, recalled in 1999: "Yeltsin embodied change but, as it turned out, he didn't represent what we or society wanted. Society wanted changes, but in what direction? It didn't know. We ourselves had no strategic orientation." Even among the more active workers, there was a strong tendency to look to leaders and forces outside the labour movement rather than to develop their own independent force.

On the tenth anniversary of the July 1989 coalminers' strike, a group of miners gave the following assessment of their movement. It can be applied to the entire workers' movement of the final years of the Soviet system:

> Allow us to congratulate each one of us—those who are working, who have retired, who have been laid off, or who are waiting to be laid off—on this date and to remind you that we were not always crushed by circumstances created by bosses of all levels and kinds; that there was at time when we took the situation into our own hands and showed them what was what. We forced them to consider us, the miners, whose profession is the harshest, most dangerous and difficult in the world, and the workers of other sectors, the people in general. And, friends, it was glorious! We walked an untrodden path. We did what we felt was necessary and what we felt we were capable of doing. Moved by the unquenchable desire to defend our human dignity, we by no means always knew where we should be going, but we very clearly sensed what we had to be leave behind us—a dead-end situation, hopelessness, and submission.[44]

Worker Consciousness

The way in which the Soviet system fell, in a revolution from above, meant that the large majority of workers entered the new period still strongly marked by the legacy of over half a century of totalitarian oppression. This included traits such as unquestioning submission to authority coupled with deep cynicism toward authority, lack of solidarity, weak self-confidence and a weakly developed sense of dignity. The mobilizations that occurred under Gorbachev were too limited and brief to have undermined radically these tendencies, which would be subsequently be reinforced by profound insecurity and demoralization resulting from "shock therapy."

The historian E.P. Thompson argued that class is not a thing but a process. It is a process that is structured by the antagonistic relations of production but it is shaped historically by the lived experience of men and women. "It is an active process that owes as much to agency as to conditioning."[45] In the Soviet case, however, the long period of totalitarian rule left little room for agency, if by that one means the independent, collective action and interaction of workers. In the words of one auto worker, "There was no working class; only isolated people in the same situation." He recalled a strike on the assembly line at VAZ in September 1989 that was preceded by brigade meetings. These meetings, which adopted demands that were then consolidated and presented to management, stuck in his mind as the first time the workers had ever met independently of management to discuss their problems and adopt a course of action.

It was argued above that even though the Soviet regime was able to deprive workers of that lived experience, it still had reason to fear them. This was because key features of that system facilitated collective mobilization and radicalization of this atomized mass, even in the absence of experience: the state as unique employer in this nationalized, centrally-administered economy; the workers' relatively homogeneous socio-economic situation; the official socialist ideology that cast the ruling élite in the role of usurper. But all that changed with astonishing speed when the regime collapsed. That helps to explains the paradox of Gorbachev's much greater responsiveness to popular pressure as compared with Yeltsin, even though Gorbachev had a vast repressive apparatus at his disposal and presided over an economy that was only beginning to fall into depression. Yeltsin, by contrast, was at the head of an immeasurably weaker state and he presided over a collapsed economy.

Even with those structural advantages, the nascent labour movement of Perestroika was unable to develop its own alternative to the liberals' programme. Just as workers first greeted Perestroika when Gorbachev presented it to them as a renewal of socialism, so they perceived Perestroika's failure as the failure of socialism. This perception was reinforced by a powerful propaganda campaign from 1989 onward that presented the Soviet experience as a foolish and cruel experiment and the "market economy" as the only form of "normal" economy. The success of this indoctrination was facilitated by the workers' atomization and almost complete ignorance of capitalist reality (another legacy of the totalitarian system).[46] An independent alternative to the liberal programme could have emerged only from much broader, richer and more extensive experience of struggle and from a much more confident labour movement. As it was, there was no clarity among workers about who their friends and adversaries were.[47] This was a period when magical thinking about social change abounded. The only real question, so people thought, was whether Russia wanted to be like Sweden or like America. The international situation also discouraged workers from searching for their own alternative, since the Communist regimes of Eastern Europe had all fallen in 1989, while those in South-East Asia were busy restoring capitalism themselves. Beyond those countries, there was not a significant workers' movement anywhere, except perhaps in distant Brazil and South Africa, that was marching behind a socialist banner. Labour everywhere was in retreat before the neo-liberal offensive.

While most Soviet workers remained wedded to the values of social justice, egalitarianism, and popular democracy,[48] in the absence of any alternative vision (the small socialist intelligentsia was kept out of the mass media), the liberals' individualistic concept of economic freedom appeared as a logical response to the oppressive bureaucratic regime. For example, until they had gained practical experience with the "reforms," workers found ideas like the reduction of the social wage in favour of a promised higher individual wage quite attractive, since the social wage had often served as a means of control and a source of corruption in the Soviet system. The leaders of the alternative trade unions, unable to conceive of a society without bosses and owners, also espoused the liberal alternative, at least as they vaguely understood it.[49] The leaders of the traditional unions were less enthusiastic about the brave new liberal world, but their hostility arose out of their conservatism. In any case, they lacked the independence and popular base to mount any serious opposition. As for the STK movement, which came closest to presenting a workers' alternative, it could not, as already mentioned, conceive of democratic planning and so limited its programme to enterprise autonomy and the transfer of ownership to the employees. At the time, this programme did not seem incompatible with the liberals' "de-statization."

It is interesting, in concluding this chapter, to contrast the programme of the STK activists with the goals of the movement for workers' control in Russia of 1917. The latter movement, which arose out of the workers' concern to save their livelihoods and the revolution, led them almost immediately to demand soviet (that is, workers' and peasants') power and the nationalization of the enterprises (with workers' control). There was never really any question in their minds of taking direct possession of their enterprises or of demanding "full autonomy." From their lived experience under capitalism, they understood that they could not—and that it would not be in their interest to—run the enterprises without strong support and regulation by a workers' state.[50] Unlike the STK movement, this labour movement had behind it two brief, but very rich, decades of struggle, decades during which the socialist movement was on the rise around the world (despite the temporary setback of the world war). Socialism, that is the belief that capitalism can be replaced and that it is the task of the working class to emancipate itself by doing that, was an ideology widely shared by the workers in 1917, who had their own socialist political parties and never even thought to cast ballots for representatives of the propertied classes. Indeed, the most striking characteristic of that workers' movement was its class independence, a characteristic sorely lacking sixty years later.[51]

Notes

1. On the eve of the revolution, there were 3.5 million factory and mine workers and about ten million wage-labourers in all (not counting family members) in a population of 134 million. (L.S. Gaponenko, "Rabochii klass Rossii nakanun'e velikogo Oktyabrya," *Istoricheskie zapiski*, no. 73, Moscow, 1963, p. 51.)
2. I analyzed this process as it occurred in the Russian capital in D. Mandel, *The Petrograd Workers and the Fall of the Old Regime* and *The Petrograd Workers and the Soviet Seizure of Power*, Houndsmills, Basingstoke: Macmillan, 1983 and 1984.
3. This vulnerability is also characteristic of capitalist states that play a more direct role in exploitation, a point made by E. Meiksins Woods in her *Democracy Against Capitalism*, Cambridge: Cambridge University Press, 1995, p. 46.
4. Lenin, who promoted this compromise position, described the Soviet regime after the civil war as a worker-and-peasants' state, which suffered from a bureaucratic deformation. (I. Deutscher, *Soviet Trade Unions*, London: Oxford University Press, 1950, p. 56.)
5. On unions in the early Soviet period see, Deutscher, *Soviet Trade Unions*, pp. 2-76; E. H. Carr, *Socialism in One Country*, Baltimore: Penguin, vol. 1, 1970, ch. 7; E.H.Carr and R.W Davies, *Foundations of a Planned Economy*, Harmondsworth, U.K., Penguin, 1974, ch. 20; D. Filtzer, *Soviet Workers and Stalinist Industrialization*, Cambridge: Cambridge University Press, 1986; and W. J. Chase, *Workers, Society and the Soviet State: Labor and Life in Moscow, 1918-29*, Chicago: University of Illinois Press, 1990, pp. 258-64. For a good summary the situation of unions in the whole Soviet period, see S. Ashwin and S. Clarke, *Russian Trade Unions and Industrial Relations in Transition*, Houndsmills, Basingstoke: Palgrave Macmillan, 2003, ch. 2.
6. The offices of the trade-union committee were usually located in the administration building next to those of the party and the Communist Youth League committees, and often also next to the personnel department.
7. On the Novocherkassk events, see S. H. Baron, *Bloody Saturday in the Soviet Union, Novocherkassk,1962*. Stanford: Stanford University Press, 2001; V. A. Kozlov, *Massovye besporyadki v SSSR pri Khrushcheve i Brezhneve*, Novosibirsk: Sibirskii khronograf, 1999, pp. 302-83; D. Mandel, ed., *Novocherkassk 1-3 yunya 1962 g.: zabastovka i rasstrel*, Moscow: Shkola trudovoi demokratii, 1998.
8. The main protest movements in Eastern Europe were in East Germany in 1953, Poland and Hungary in 1956, Czechoslovakia in 1968, Poland in the 1970s and early 1980s.
9. See D. Mandel, *Perestroika and the Soviet People: Rebirth of the Labour Movement*, Montreal: Black Rose Books, 1991.
10. *Ibid.*, pp. 175-90.
11. *Sovetskaya Rossiya*, Aug. 5, 1999.
12. V. M. Grigoriev et al., *Profsoyuznaya rabota na mashinostroitel'nykh predriyatiyakh*, Moscow: Profinzdat, 1972.
13. B. Ruble, "Factory Unions and Workers' Rights," in A. Kahn and B. Ruble, *Industrial Labor in the USSR*, N.Y.: Pergamon, 1979, p. 69.
14. D. Filtzer, *Soviet Workers and de-Stalinization*, Cambridge: Cambridge University Press,1992, p. 35-46.
15. Cited by V. Mozhaev, *Nezavisimaya gazeta*, Nov. 11, 1994.
16. "Interview with V. Zlenko," in D. Mandel, ed., *Looking East Leftwards*, Montreal: Black Rose Books, 1998, p. 122.

17. According to official statistics, this occurred in half the cases. See Filtzer, *Soviet Workers and De-Stalinization*, 38-39; Ruble, "Factory Unions and Union Rights," in Kahan and Ruble, *Industrial Labor in the USSR*, 59-84.
18. J. Chapman, "Recent Trends in Wage Structure," in Kahan and Ruble, *Industrial Labor in the USSR*, p. 168. For a higher estimate, see J. Pavlevski, *Le niveau de vie en USSR*, Paris: Economica, 1975, pp. 98-132.
19. "As far as the immediate producers are concerned, the dynamic of productive forces suffers from a twilight between "not yet" and no longer." R. Bahro, *The Alternative in Eastern Europe*, Manchester: NLB, 1978, p. 211.
20. V.M. Rutgaizen and Yu. E. Shevnyakov, "Raspredelenie po trudu," *EKO*, no.3, 1987, p. 5.
21. M. Mathews, *Poverty in the Soviet Union*, Cambridge: Cambridge University Press, 1986, p. 178.
22. "Interview with Nikolai Belanovskii," in *Rabotyagi: Perestroika and After Viewed from Below*, N.Y.:Monthly Review Press, 1994, p. 148.
23. For a summary of these views see S. Ashwin, *Russian Workers, the Anatomy of Patience*, Manchester: Manchester University Press, 1999, pp. 3-5. This is also a position put forward by Kozlov in *Massovye besporyadki*.
24. Ashwin, *Russian Workers*, p.24.
25. See D. Mandel, "Economic Reform and Democracy in the Soviet Union," in R. Miliband, L. Panitch, and J. Saville, *Socialist Register 1988: Problems of Socialist Renewal East and West*, London: Merlin Press, 1988, pp. 132-53. D. Kotz and F. Weir present an excellent and detailed analysis of Perestroika in their *Revolution from Above*, N.Y., Routledge, 1997. However they are not very convincing when they cast Gorbachev in the tragic role of socialist reformer undermined by the perfidious bureaucracy. For a detailed analysis of labour policy under Perestroika, see D. Filtzer, *Soviet Workers and the Collapse of Perestroika*, Cambridge: Cambridge University Press, 1994.
26. *Pravda*, Jan. 28, 1987.
27. See " 'Revolutionary Reform' in Soviet Factories: Restructuring Relations Between Workers and Mangers," in Mandel, *Perestroika*, pp. 7-42, and Filtzer, *Soviet Workers*, ch. 2, pp. 56-77.
28. Mandel, "Revolutionary Reform" in *Perestroika*, pp. 26-29.
29. "Rebirth of the Soviet Labour Movement: the Coalminers' Strike of July 1989, " in Mandel *Perestroika*, pp. 51-78.
30. It is often not appreciated that large-scale privatization began under Gorbachev. However, neither Gorbachev nor the more radical pro-capitalist elements used the word "capitalism." They claimed the term was not longer relevant: there was only more or less market, more or less state regulation. See "A Market without Thorns: the Ideological Struggle for the Soviet Working Class," in Mandel, *Perestroika*, pp. 91-116.
31. See, for example, Prime Minister Ryzhkov's speech to the Supreme Soviet in May 1990, *Trud*, May 25, 1990.
32. *Sobstvennoe mnenie* (Togliatti), no. 7, 1990.
33. In 1990, the Soviet economy experienced its first year of negative growth since the Nazi invasion. In 1991, Russia entered a full-blown depression, as GNP fell 13%. See Kotz and Weir, *Revolution from Above*, p.75.
34. On this movement, see Mandel, "'De-statization' and the Struggle for Power in the Soviet Economy," in Mandel, *Perestroika*, pp. 117-54; and Filtzer, *Soviet Workers and the Collapse*, pp. 82-93.

35. This continued to be true even years later. See *Mir mnenii i meniya o mire*, Moscow, no. 5, 1993.

36. Some later thought they saw in this a conspiracy. For example, M. Abramov, former president of the Union of Workers of Auto and Farm-Machine Building of Russia: "Now it is obvious that these destructive principles were consciously inculcated by those forces that were interested in weakening the trade unions. At the time, union sovereignty was seen as synonymous with democracy." *(Golos profsoyuza*, no 2-3, Apr.-May 1998)

37. In the year following their general strike, the coalminers, led by their workers' committees (the former strike committees), engaged in a series of regional strikes that put forth mainly political demands. These were followed on the first anniversary of the 1989 strike by a massive one-day strike demanding the Soviet government's resignation and complete democratization of the state. Mandel, *Perestroika*, pp. 159-60.

38. On this movement, see A. Bukhvostov, ed., *Chernobyl'–nezatikhshaya bol'*, Minsk, 1999.

39. This is account based on conversations with Bukhvostov and on Bukhvostov, ed., *Chernobyl'*.

40. This was true not only of the government's relations with the labour movement. See, for example, F. Daucé, "Les mouvements de mères de soldats à la recherche d'une place dans la société russe," *Revue d'études comparatives Est-Ouest*, June 1997, pp. 121-53.

41. Mandel, *Perestroika*, pp. 130-31; *Rabotyagi*, pp. 248-253.

42. *Rabotyagi*, p .158

43. Mandel, *Perestroika*, pp.175-86.

44. Letter of P. Shumkin, P. Pastukhov, and N. Glyuzidi in *Rabochaya politika*, no. 14, July 21, 1999.

45. E. P. Thompson, *The Making of the English Working Class*, London: Penguin, 1991, p. 8. For an enlightening discussion of Thompson's thinking on this subject, see Meiksins Wood, *Democracy Against Capitalism*, ch. 3.

46. As late as 1991, workers typically refused to believe that under capitalism conscientious, disciplined workers could be laid off during recessions and enterprise "downsizing" and that the unemployed were not lazy people who preferred to live on generous social allocations rather than work.

47. In 1990, a group of activists at the Arsenal aerospace factory in Leningrad succeeded in forcing democratic union elections. A new president, Nikolai Prostov, a young, skilled worker committed to union independence, was elected. A few months later, Prostov was shocked to see that the shops had elected a majority of managers to represent them at the plant's collective-agreement conference. When he asked the workers about this, they replied: "But they are educated *(gramotnye)*." At the conference, majority supported management's positions against the union. The workers' perceptions gradually changed, but not fast enough. Faced with a combative union, the director organized another one than was loyal to him and physically (and illegally) barred Prostov from the plant.

48. See "A Market Without Thorns" in Mandel, *Perestroika*, pp. 91-116.

49. One should note, in this context, the AFL-CIO's support (fully funded by the U.S.-government) for the alternative unions. Behind this backing of "free trade unionism" was the hidden political agenda of building labour support for Yeltin and "shock therapy." See P. Bracegirdle and D. Mandel, "The AFL-CIO Comes to the Community of Independent States," *Socialist Alternatives*, vol. 2, no. 2, 1993, pp. 173-98.

50. See D. Mandel, *Factory Committees and Workers' Control in Petrograd in 1917*, Amsterdam: IIRE, 1993.

51. See Mandel, *The Petrograd Workers and the Fall of the Old Regime*, ch. I.

Chapter Two

THE SOCIO-POLITICAL CONTEXT IN RUSSIA

The abrupt collapse of the Soviet Union in December 1991 opened the way for Russia's rapid integration into the world capitalist system. This was accomplished largely on terms set down by the wealthy states (the G-7), terms embodied in the so-called "Washington consensus" and the "structural adjustment" policies of the International Monetary Fund.[1] While those terms were willingly, even enthusiastically, embraced by the leaders of the new Russian state and by the bourgeoisie-in-formation, they had to be imposed on the mass of the population, which saw their collective wealth pillaged and living standards slashed.

The basic elements of this standardized economic strategy have been applied widely to peripheral and semi-peripheral economies around the world, with usually disastrous consequences for the popular classes. They include price liberalization, macro-economic stabilization (anti-inflation policy based on budget austerity and tight credit), privatization of public enterprises and services, "openness" to the world (elimination of barriers to trade, to foreign investment, and to capital flows, encouragement of export-oriented sectors), and reduction to a minimum of state intervention and regulation (ending public subsidies, lowering marginal tax rates, loosening environmental controls, weakening social and labour rights.)

These policies were the major cause of one of the deepest and most prolonged peace-time depressions in modern history. The 42.5 per cent drop in GDP in 1990-98 was greater than that suffered by Russia in World War Two. (By way of comparison, the GDP of the United States during the Great Depression never fell below seventy-two per cent, and negative growth occurred only in the first four years of the crisis.²) Industrial production in the same period dropped even farther than GDP—by almost fifty-five per cent, as compared to the twenty-four per cent drop that occurred in 1940-46. The area of cultivated land shrank steadily, as did the yield on most crops; farm livestock decreased by half.³

The level of capital investment in 1990-98 fell by eighty per cent; investment almost ceased entirely in industry outside of the resource sector.⁴ By 2000, fifty-five per cent of the capital stock in the machine-building sectors had passed retirement age, and the annual rate of replacement was only 0.7 per cent.⁵ Spending on research and development fell more than ninety per cent.⁶ But more than fixed capital that was being used up. "Human capital" too was being rapidly depleted, as some 400,000 scientists left Russia and hundreds of thousands of engineers and skilled workers left industry for jobs in petty trade, services, housing repairs and the like, where they quickly lost their skills. A large part of the work force that stayed in industry was approaching retirement age. Meanwhile, the once-extensive network of technical schools almost stopped training young people for worker professions, shifting instead to educating accountants, legal assistants, economists, and managers. When the recovery began in 1999, the shortage of skilled workers was acutely felt and was an obstacle to expanding production.⁷

The metalworking sectors declined more than the average in manufacturing. Their output in 1998 was thirty-seven per cent of its 1990 level. In the auto and farm-machine sectors (henceforth: ASM, the Russian abbreviation), only the automobile and bus sectors avoided complete collapse. Passenger car production dropped twenty-eight per cent (to 840,000 units) and bus output fell eighteen per cent (45,700 units, mostly smaller models). On the other hand, truck production declined by seventy-nine per cent (to 141,000 units), and most of that was light vans first produced in Russia in 1992. The farm-machine sector was hardest hit: tractor production was down by ninety-seven per cent (to 8,300 units), grain-harvesting combines by ninety-eight per cent (to 1,000 units), fertilizer-spreaders by 99.5 per cent (to 600 units).⁸ A union leader was only slightly exaggerating when he declared in 1999: "Our sector is not just sick—it is clinically dead."⁹ In Manufacturing as a whole, employment declined considerably less than output—by thirty-eight per cent in 1990-98. However, the ASM sectors lost 900,000 job, almost half of its 1990 workforce. Moreover, a significant number of those formally employed were on involuntary, partially-paid, or unpaid layoff, or else they were only working part-time.¹⁰

Economic growth resumed in the wake of the ruble's collapse in August 1998. Devaluation—which the IMF and U.S. Treasury Department had long opposed¹¹

—gave a strong boost to import-substitution. The period following the devaluation has also coincided with record high international prices for oil. The windfall income financed a recovery in investment spending in the oil sector, whose rapid expansion has made Russia the second largest exporter after Saudi Arabia. Average real GDP rose more than five per cent annually in 1999-2002 and was set to grow by more than six per cent in 2003. Industrial output expanded even faster–at an average annual rate of eight per cent in 1999-2002 and seven per cent for the first half of 2003.[12] But the growth has been very uneven. Recovery in the ASM sectors, in particular, has been weak. Truck production grew from a very low starting level at an annual rate of 7.6 per cent in 1999-2002, but car production rose on average only 0.7 per cent annually, bus production 0.4 per, and tractor output 4.7 per cent also from an extremely low starting point. And despite the upturn, ASM continued to bleed jobs. Between January 1999 and mid-2003, its workforce fell by 19.5 per cent to 765,000, a loss of 175,000 jobs.[13]

It is far from obvious that the present high growth rates can be sustained, as the ruble continues to appreciate in real terms, undermining import-substitution, and high oil prices at some point have to come down. The economy's most fundamental weakness, however, is low domestic demand, a consequence of the government's policy of suppressing individual and social wages (see below). But even if the growth rates of 1999-2003 are maintained, Russia will return to where it was before the transition only towards the end of the present decade. Meanwhile, the structure of the economy has been transformed. From an industrial giant, Russia has become a natural-resource exporter. This did not happen because Russia inherited technologically backward enterprises from the Soviet Union. Even the advanced sectors, like aerospace, have suffered severe, probably irreversible, decline because of a shortage of investment and the loss of "human capital." In 2002, fuel and metal accounted for over seventy per cent of exports. Oil and gas alone accounted for sixty per cent of exports in 2003, as well as for a quarter of budget revenue, and for at least half of all investment spending.[14] This leaves the economy highly vulnerable to fluctuations in volatile international commodity prices. The economic structure, along with the accompanying political and social dimensions presented below, attest to Russia's integration into the world capitalist system as a semi-peripheral, dependent member. With such a status, if development occurs at all, it is extremely unequal and partial. In essence, a section of the economy has been delimited, basically the resource sector, for integration into the world market, and all the rest is excluded because of low productivity that is not sufficiently compensated for by cheap labour.[15]

The State

The Russian government, as already noted, willingly adopted the West's economic programme. Given its fragile legitimacy and its lack of a solid social base, which it had yet to create, the political élite felt a strong need for Western support, political, ideological and financial. Besides, "shock therapy" was well-suited to the relatively small window of opportunity that it thought it saw before it. Spokespersons of both the government and the IMF in the early years frequently expressed their concern to make the transition "irreversible." But an even more important factor in its adoption was that the chosen strategy made possible the rapid accumulation of vast fortunes by those holding political power or with links to it. This explains why the same economic policy has been pursued with renewed vigour by President Putin, despite the relative stability of the regime has achieved, the radical reduction of foreign debt after 1999, the present ability to dispense with foreign aid, and, finally, the complete lack of perspective this policy offers for qualitative improvement of the state's position in the world system.

Even political figures and analysts close to the government describe the political system as a "managed democracy."[16] In practice, this is a regime headed by a president with unchecked power, whether on the part of parliament (the State Duma), the judiciary, or the people itself. Abuse of the "administrative resource" and government control of the electronic media make Russian elections grossly unfair contests. In any case, results can be falsified to change the outcome, as occurred in the constitutional referendum of December 1993, the presidential elections of 1996 and 2000, the referendum and presidential elections in Chechnya in 2003.[17] At the same time, however, the regime tolerates freedom of association and speech and of the printed press. (Putin has brought the electronic media, already quite subservient even under Yeltsin, fully under state control and has moved to shut down at least one obstreperous newspaper. But printed-press freedom still remains quite broad.) Despite all this, Yeltsin's coup against the Supreme Soviet (the former parliament) in 1993 and the government's terrorist policy in Chechnya make clear that the toleration of civil liberties is conditional on the non-threatening character of opposition.

The system of "managed democracy" was established through a bloody presidential coup against parliament in October 1993. The substantive issue in the confrontation was "shock therapy." A majority of the deputies, many of whom had voted for the reforms in 1991 and had accorded Yeltsin special powers to carry them out, became appalled at the social and economic consequences. They wanted to change course and to rein Yeltsin in, and the Constitution gave them the power to do it. Yeltsin, with a green light from the G-7, dispatched tanks against the parliament, killing in the process several hundred mostly unarmed defenders.[18] The new constitution gave the President near-absolute power and reduced parliament to an essentially symbolic role. (One of the Constitutions's highlights is that the Duma may twice vote for the government's resignation without the latter having to comply. But after a the third vote, the Duma itself is dissolved.) The Duma has become little more than a collection of lobbyists, for mostly business interests, and a source of personal enrichment for the deputies, themselves increasingly drawn from business. The rigged constitutional referendum of December 1993 and the later presidential elections all received the G-7's stamp of approval.[19]

The 1993 coup established the rules of the game for Russian politics: no effective opposition to the President would be tolerated. All the major political players, including the main opposition party, the Communist Party (KPRF), and the main trade-union federation, the Federation of Independent Trade Unions of Russia (FNPR), accepted these rules. In a speech to the FNPR Council in June 1995, its president, M. Shmakov, explained the political reality (Shmakov succeeded I. Klochkov, who had come out in defence of the Constitution during the 1993 confrontation. Klochkov was sacrificed to mollify Yeltsin.[20]):

> Today it is clear that a decisive, open confrontation with the state would throw our trade unions onto the backwaters of public life, deprive them of all constitutional means of defending workers' interests. It would be a real threat to the existence of the Federation and to FNPR-affiliated unions as a whole.

He went on to admit that by accepting the new rules his federation would be unable to defend its members against the state-led assault on their living standards and social rights:

> Of course, one cannot help but recognize that the course of social partnership with the present government institutions allows us to resolve only isolated, essentially tactical problems. We realize that it could not and cannot enable us to gain sufficient influence to change the state's policy, the overall course of the reforms, in the interests of workers, of the majority of the population.[21]

Another key aspect of the political regime is the de facto moratorium on legality. This unstated policy, which was made possible by the 1993 coup, has been an integral part of the government's economic policy. Its most striking manifestation was, of course, the privatization campaign, the most rapid and massive in history. It was also quite probably the greatest theft in history—Marx called this process "primitive accumulation"—one actively organized and promoted by the state.[22] According to a government assessment in 1995, the state received a mere 3.6 per cent of the real value of the 500 largest privatized enterprises. Independent analysts place the figure even lower.[23]

Strikingly, no one, not even right-wing liberals, like A. Chubais, architect of Russia's privatization, denies the criminal origins of the great fortunes. Chubais's party, the Union of Right Forces, is a vigorous champion of private property (which it conveniently identifies with "democracy"). He told an interviewer in 1995 that "the distribution of property in Russia, as, for that matter, in other countries, is taking place in proportion to the power of existing élites." A. Kokh, Chubais's former deputy and a fellow party member, made the following exasperated retort to critics of the privatization campaign: "They shout: 'Pillage! Pillage!' But who prevented them from taking part!?"[24] And in a letter to Russia's main business paper, *Kommersant*, Boris Berezovskii, the most notorious "oligarch" (the term will be explained presently), recalled that in those years, anyone who wasn't steeping by the stove obtained huge chunks of state property for small bribes to bureaucrats."[25] This original sin of Russian capitalism, still very fresh in the minds of the population, has prompted periodic declarations from the government to the effect that there will be no "review of the results of privatization." (Opinion surveys indicate that over eighty per cent of the population desire such a review.[26]) It was and remains undeclared state policy at the highest level to prohibit prosecution of crimes related to privatization, except in exceptional cases when the government finds it politically expedient.[27] This policy, it goes without saying, makes rather problematic Putin's declared goal of a "dictatorship of the law"(though the dictatorship part has been making headway).

The state thus led the way in teaching contempt for the law. Besides Yeltsin's tearing up the Constitution in 1993 and the criminal nature of privatization, the government's austerity policy has been marked by massive legal violations, again with the IMF's tacit approval. The government has regularly disregarded laws requiring indexation of the minimum wage and pensions and has refused to make social expenditures required by the state budget duly passed by the Duma. It has withheld payment of wages to its civil servants and pensions on a massive scale, sometimes for months on end. (This practice declined after 1998 but it has not disappeared.) And, of course, the more usual forms of corruption were and remain rampant in the public administration. One estimate puts the annual loss to the state from public corruption at thirty billion U.S.$, twice the current defence budget.[28] The same figure was cited by M. Khodorkovskii at the February 2003 meeting of the President with the "oligarchs," when he told Putin: "Your bureaucrats are bribe-takers and thieves, Mr. President."[29] Khodorkovskii, of course, was well-placed to know.

The Annual Corruption Index of Berlin-based Transparency International regularly identifies Russia as one of the most corrupt countries in the world, although there has been limited progress under Putin.[30] Property rights are still far from secure, and contract enforcement is uncertain.[31] Besides the corruption and lack of independence of the judiciary and law enforcement organs and still widespread business-related violence (much of which goes unpunished[32]), the state administration itself remains the ultimate source of business insecurity. This was graphically illustrated by the prosecution of Khodorkovskii in 2003, which followed two similar cases involving the "oligarchs" Berezovskii and Gusinskii.[33] Khodorkovskii's fortune is without doubt ill-gotten. But no one has made big money in Russia without violating the law. The selective targeting of Khodorkovskii means that anyone's property—and not only property, but freedom—is fair game.[34] The new capitalist class realizes this, of course, but it is too weak, socially isolated, and probably also too greedy to make any real effort to free itself from the state's embrace.[35]

Russian Capitalism

At the beginning of 1992, ninety-one per cent of Russia's fixed capital stock was publicly owned, and nearly all of the GDP was produced by the state sector. By 2001, only forty-two per cent of capital stock was still in state hands, and the private sector accounted for seventy per cent of GDP. Eight-one per cent of the enterprises in the machine-building sector, and virtually all in ASM, had been privatized, and ownership was becoming increasingly concentrated.[36]

When "shock therapy" was launched, the lucrative financial and resource sectors (especially oil and metals), as well as the mass media, quickly fell into the hands of what became known as the "oligarchs." This term refers to big business in a symbiotic relationship with the state administration: members of the business class depend on their connections in the corridors of power to hold onto their wealth and to continue accumulating; while members of the state administration grow rich from the tribute they extract from business. In Russia, the state appoints the millionaires and billionaires.[37] As Khodorkovskii explained in a newspaper article he penned in 1997:

> The most profitable business in Russia is politics, and it will always be so. We drew lots here among ourselves to see who would go into government. It fell to Potanin [nickel baron]. He did a lot at that post [vice

prime minister] for his company ONEKSIM. Next time, someone else will go.[38]

One of the more plausible hypotheses concerning the government's decision to prosecute Khodorkovskii—after all, he had not sinned more than others, though he was more successful at it—was that he wanted to end this system and bring business out of the shadows, to make it legitimate. The dominant faction in Putin's administration, the so-called *siloviki,* that is, people linked to the so-called "power structures" (KGB, Ministry of Internal Affairs, and military), were appalled. They insisted on their share of the wealth and the more.[39] Despite some short-lived and low-key public whining, Russia's new capitalist class was not prepared to take on the state to defend their colleague.

Outside of the resource sector, control of most industrial enterprises has passed through two overlapping stages. In the first phase of privatization, vouchers for the purchase of shares were distributed to the population at large. In addition, employees were given the option of acquiring individually up to half of the shares of their enterprises. The resulting dispersion of ownership, given the balance of forces in society and in the enterprises, left most of the latter under the virtually unlimited control of the existing management.[40]

Meanwhile, "shock therapy" had created conditions that made it very hard for most secondary-processing enterprises to make money through production: demand had collapsed; hyperinflation had devoured operating capital; the tight monetary policy contributed to the widespread use of barter; high interest rates made credit inaccessible; and the resulting overvalued ruble made imports relatively cheap and exporting difficult. In addition, enterprises were saddled with heavy tax burdens and the cost of maintaining the vast "social spheres" they had inherited from the Soviet era. Even where domestic demand had not collapsed, enterprises could not find the investment capital needed to make them competitive in the unprotected market.[41]

The ASM sectors in particular has seen very little investment even after the start of recovery in 1999, and most of what there has been is internally generated.[42] Only the passenger car sector has attracted significant foreign investment, but even that has been quite limited because of weak domestic demand for cars selling for more than a few thousand dollars (a new Lada in February 2003 sold for about 4,000 U.S.$), low protective tariffs, better conditions for export production in Eastern Europe, and general business insecurity.[43] The "oligarchs," of course, had plenty of capital, but in view of the low foreseeable return on investment in Russia and the risk of losing their fortunes if the government changed, they preferred to send their wealth abroad, which they did, according to a 2002 estimate, at an annual rate of forty billion U.S.$ a year, about equal to the what China was receiving in foreign direct investment.[44] It is worth emphasizing (as does, for example, Joseph with Stiglitz, Nobel price laureate and chief economist of the World Bank during much of this period) that most of the above-mentioned consequences of the economic policy were foreseeable and were indeed foreseen by the reformers and their IMF patrons.[45]

While it was hard to make a profit from legitimate production, legal impunity, the weakness of the labour movement, and the dispersal of ownership all combined to make rent-taking, asset-stripping, and just plain theft easy and lucrative activities for managers.[46] One of the most notorious cases was that of the giant auto-maker, VAZ (exceptional only in that the cheap cars made by this enterprise enjoyed relatively strong demand). Workers say that "organized pillage" rather than "theft" best describe the situation here. In the first post-Soviet years, VAZ was the milch cow that made the Berezovskii's original fortune. Of course, the top management received its share. With the latter's assistance, he became the sole distributor of Ladas for several years. Through commissions, delays in payment in a time of high inflation, and other machinations, his Logovaz dealerships made an estimated one-hundred-per-cent net profit on each car they sold during 1993-1994. Meanwhile, VAZ was losing money on each car it made, despite the strong demand and the cheap labour force. The enterprise accumulated huge debts and avoided bankruptcy only because of its political clout—the survival of an entire city of 600,000 depended on it.[47] (Another major car-maker, Moskvich in Moscow, that once employed 25,000 people, did go under.) Berezovskii's chain of dealerships was only the biggest of the myriad of parasitic intermediary suppliers and marketing firms that entwined VAZ. Many of these firms were headed by VAZ's managers or family members.

Rent-taking from these mediation activities was based upon monopoly situations that resulted from corruption and violence, rather than from particular business skills. When law-enforcement authorities moved against VAZ 1996 (one of several fruitless campaigns), they uncovered at least sixty-five contract murders whose victims had been managers or dealers.[48] To be fair, not all managers that became involved in illegal activities were willing participants, at least not at first. Some even tried to prevent it but found that they and their families had become targets of threats and violence.

Outright theft of VAZ's materials, parts and cars also occurred on a vast scale. In 1997, it "lost" (misplaced) a trainload of cars. ("Losses"during shipment were common in all branches of industry.) One of VAZ's directors jumped off the administration's skyscraper in connection with the case. Workers also reported unaccounted for production at the plant using its equipment, energy, and materials. The workers involved were paid by criminal organizations. Theft of parts became so well organized that workers no longer had to run the risk of carrying them out the gates themselves: representatives of criminal organizations placed orders right inside the plant, paid for them and then and picked up the parts, arranging themselves to get them out. In the spring of 2003, a member of VAZ's production council (successor to the STK with purely symbolic functions) confided that forty per cent of the profits were lost to theft and other forms of crime. However, he seemed resigned to this as a quasi-natural phenomenon, even referring to the Russian national character. The federal Assistant Prosecutor-General, V. Kolesnikov, who began yet another investigation into VAZ in 2003, estimated the plant's annual losses from the theft of parts at thirty-three million U.S.$. Reported net profits in 2002 were twenty-three million U.S.$. Theft on that scale, in his view, was not possible without management participation.[49]

With the economic upturn and the windfall profits from high oil and metal prices, and especially after Putin's election in 2000, the "oligarchs," who had their made fortunes in the resource sectors, began buying factories in other manufacturing sectors. These sold for a tiny fraction of their real value because of their poor financial situation. Moreover, ways were often found to further reduce their attractiveness prior to the sale.[50] As a result, industrial ownership became increasingly concentrated. A survey conducted in 2002 found that ninety-seven per cent of large privatized enterprises were controlled by single shareholder groups.[51] By 2003, according to some estimates, twenty large conglomerates controlled seventy per cent of Russia's GDP.[52]

All the sectors of ASM have experienced this wave of acquisitions. The Ruspromavto holding company became the biggest owner, with auto, truck, bus, motor, earth-moving equipment and other plants employing a quarter of a million people, or a third of ASM's total work force at the end of 2002.[53] VAZ employed another sixth; Severstal', owner of the Ulyanovsk Auto Factory (making Russian jeeps) and of the Zavol'zhskii Motor Factory, employed nearly a tenth. Other companies were buying up farm-machine and ball-bearing plants. One of the main owners of Ruspromavto is Oleg Deripaska, a thirty-four year old aluminum "oligarch." (The other owner is Roman Abramovich, an oil baron.) Deripaska's is a typical success story. In the Alger Hiss version, young Oleg, a physics student at Moscow State University, stood shivering in the Siberian cold in early 1993 outside the Sayansk Aluminum Factory, buying up privatization vouchers from impoverished employees. Two years later, he was running the plant. From there, his natural business abilities led to control of three quarters of the aluminum industry.[54] A more complete version, however, would include the fact that O. Soskovets, then First Vice Prime Minister in charge of the metals sector, whose daughter Deripaska was dating, gave him his entry into the aluminum business at the age of twenty-six. Eventually, Deripaska married the daughter of V. Yumashev, former Kremlin chief-of-staff and close relative by marriage to Yeltsin. The story would also include Deripaska's record of fund diversion and asset stripping, and the accusations of extortion and murder (contract killings were rampant in the aluminum industry) that barred him from entry into the U.S. It is widely rumoured that none other than Putin encouraged Deripaska's purchases in the ASM sector.[55]

The new owners quickly moved to assert their property rights, usually replacing most of the old top management. With minimal investment, they began to cut non-productive expenses with a view to squeezing whatever immediate profit they could from the plants and to make them more attractive to potential buyers as the prices of the enterprises rose with the improving economy.[56] (There are some signs that the reselling may have already begun.[57]) For example, after the purchase of GAZ, Deripaska moved quickly to cut twenty per cent of the 100,000-person work force and slashed output of the large and non-competitive Volga automobile, concentrating production on Gazelle light trucks and vans.[58] Similarly, in 2003 he announced plans to end production of large Russian-designed diesel motors at the Yaroslavl Motor Factory and to switch to assembly of smaller Italian (IVECO) motors using mostly imported parts. This would involve a more than seventy-five-per-cent reduction of the 22,000-person work force. He fired the enterprise's widely-respected general director, after the latter denounced the plan at a press conference as signifying the destruction Russia's diesel-motor industry.[59] The new owners also accelerated the tendency to shed of the enterprises' "social spheres," that is housing, summer camps, holiday resorts, rest homes, clinics, day care facilities, libraries, sports clubs, etc. These were either sold off or transferred to the municipalities. But the latter are in no financial shape to maintain most of this. As a result, many of the services were lost to workers or deteriorated. The new owners have also been very stingy negotiating benefits, trying their best to take back anything that is not required by law.[60] As for wages, ASM workers have yet to really experience the economic recovery in this area. Most of the increase in their real wages has been due to overtime and speed-up.

The Government's Social and Labour Policies and the Situation of Workers

The overall decline in the quality of life of the mass of the Russian population is starkly reflected in demographic data. Life expectancy in 1990-2002 fell from 63.8 years to 58.5 for men and from 74.3 to 72.0 for women. (By way of comparison, life expectancy in Canada in 2001 was 82.2 years for women and 77.1 for men.)[61] In the late 1990s, death rates for adult males reached levels not experienced in Russia since the late nineteenth century. Coupled with the drop in the birth rate (from 1.9 children per woman over her lifetime in 1990 to 1.2 in 2000), this has led to an accelerating natural decrease in population, which fell by 2.8 million between 1992 and 2000 (from 148.3 million) and would have fallen by 5.3 million were it not for the compensating effect of net in-migration from other former Soviet republics in the early years.[62] By 2003, the population was falling at a rate of one million a year.[63] This situation prompted an American specialist in Russian demography to remark: "If demography is said to be destiny, the destiny of Russia for the next fifty years or more is appalling."[64]

A study of the Yeltsin period concluded that 3.4 million premature deaths occurred in 1990-1998, that is deaths that would not have occurred had pre-existing demographic trends not been disrupted. By the same token, 2.7 million additional births would have taken place. The author concluded:

> During the 1990s, Russia suffered a catastrophic decline in GDP, industrial production, the quality of its health system, its social safety net and living standards, accompanied by an acute inegalitarian shift in the distribution of incomes and mass involuntary unemployment. These physical factors, social disruption and psychological stresses are more than ample to serve as the primary cause of Yeltsin's premature deaths and birth deficits.[65]

Some Russians qualify the government's policy as "economic genocide." In any case, "economic crimes against humanity" would certainly seem appropriate.

In 1989, only two per cent of the population lived in poverty by the World Bank standard of two dollars U.S. a day. In addition, as noted, poverty in the Soviet Union did not entail social exclusion to the extent it does under capitalism, since there was a high common denominator of free, or highly subsidized, decent quality education, housing, healthcare, childcare, cultural and leisure services.[66] By late 1998, 23.8 per cent of Russians were living under the two-dollar bar, and more than forty per cent earned less than four dollars a day. More than half the children were living in poor families. (According to the Deputy Prosecutor-General, there were three million street children in 2002.[67]) At the same time, inequality increased dramatically, reaching third-world levels.[68] The renewed growth of GDP has not affected the level of poverty.[69]

Average real wages before taxes fell by two-thirds during 1992-1999, according to official estimates, and climbed back to half by 2001, continuing to rise thereafter.[70] But these figures include management salaries, as well as earnings from overtime and bonuses for exceeding output norms (speedup). They do not, however, fully account for the fall in social benefits from the enterprises and the state. The average monthly wage (including management salaries) at the start of 2003, that is, four years into the recovery, was only 176 U.S.$ in the auto and truck sectors and $137 in farm machinery.[71] At the same time, the official subsistence minimum (a term to be taken quite literally) for one person was $67.5 (A quarter of the general population had income below that minimum), and the FNPR's estimate of the minimum consumer basket for one person was $168.[72] At educational seminars, when workers discuss how much they would need to earn to have a minimally decent living standard, they typically come up with the figures $500-750, and considerably more in the case of young workers with families who have to rent housing.

The government, by far the largest employer, sets the example in paying low wages. In 2000, civil servants in education, healthcare, social welfare and culture earned on average half of the wage in industry. Even as late as 2002, many state employees were earning less than the subsistence minimum. Meanwhile, the government was sitting on a foreign currency reserve of forty billion dollars.[73] The government has regularly disregarded the law requiring indexation of the minimum wage (also the basis for calculating various social allocations), with the result that it fell to ten per cent of the subsistence minimum in 1999-2000. It was last raised in October 2003 to reach twenty-seven percent of the subsistence minimum.[74] A government forecast predicted it would finally catch up to the subsistence minimum in 2028.[75]

Remonetarization of the economy after 1998 helped to alleviate the problem of wage arrears that had plagued workers from 1994 and was the source of almost all of the strike activity. Here, too, the government set the example by accumulating by far the largest debt toward its employees. Together with unfulfilled budgetary obligations, this had been a major instrument of its anti-inflationary policy, a practice that had the IMF's tacit blessing. (The latter suspended payments when the government abandoned budgetary discipline to give added support Russia's poor but turned a blind eye to the systematic robbing of state employees and pensioners.) In industry, even when wages were paid, they were often given in overpriced bartered good rather than rubles. In March 1999, workers in the auto and truck sectors workers were owed an average of 4.2 months of wages; 7.4 months in the farm-machine sector. By March 2002, average wage arrears in ASM had fallen to 1.25 months. The total owed ASM workers at the end of 2002 was equal to about 330 million U.S.$.[76]

Unemployment rose from virtually zero in 1990 to an official high of 13.6 per cent in 1999 and fell back to 7.6 in 2003.[77] But there was also massive disguised unemployment that was no less painful for workers. This includes people who were only formally employed or were involuntarily working part-time, discouraged workers who had stopped seeking employment (the economically active population fell from 84.6 to 78.6 per cent in 1992-2000[78]), as well as workers earning less than the subsistence minimum. Taking all these into account, the FNPR estimated real unemployment at closer to thirty per cent in 1999.[79] Most jobs lost to industry prior to 1999 were officially due to workers "leaving of their own accord." In fact, they were "squeezed out" (*vydavleny*) by low wages or non-payment of wages. The government did not force insolvent enterprises into bankruptcy during this period, and by tolerating, in fact promoting by its example, non-payment of wages, it held down potential political pressure to do something about unemployment.

Speaking to a group of steelworkers in 2000, Putin announced that "state paternalism" had to end. That would finally force people to stand on their own two feet. He acknowledged that "labour has been undervalued for too long" but he promised that his reforms would attract investment and so eventually lead to higher living standards. "We need reasonable policies to create stability and investor confidence," he told the workers.[80] In other words, the needs of capital had priority, but the workers' turn would inevitably follow.

The audience must have been puzzled by Putin's reference to state paternalism, since most workers had long since felt abandoned by the state. A woman worker from the UralAZ truck plant exclaimed during a discussion held in 2002: "The state is our chief oppressor! Why does it allow the people to be oppressed and degraded?" The Constitution declares Russia a "social state," but the economic policy of the government has consistently been based on the principle that workers and their families should bear the entire cost of "building capitalism." "About the only thing 'social' that remains in this state," wrote the Shmakov, President of the FNPR, "is its policy of social Darwinism."[81] The government's "Conception for Development in the ASM Sector," adopted in March 2002 without the slightest intention of actually carrying out, was silent on the issues of employment, wages, benefits and work conditions. In preparing the document, the government did not respond to union proposals on these matters.

Workers have also seen their social wage slashed. Although the Constitution guarantees free health care, primary and secondary education, chronic underfunding of these services and the miserable wages of their employees force medical institutions, schools and their staffs to demand illegal payments for services. Collections from parents for the maintenance and cleaning of schools is widespread. In hospitals and clinics bribes are required to get attention. Tests and procedures that are formally free in practice require payment. Hospitals without basic medicines and equipment and schools without heating, electricity or textbooks are common in smaller towns.[82] Even after a significant increase in the state's education budget in 2002-03, it amounted only 0.6 per cent of GDP. The state covers less than a third of the cost of universities, most of the remainder coming from student fees. Half the students are estimated to pay (and in Moscow the annual amount often comes to more than one thousand U.S.$). Bribes for admission into better faculties are commonplace.[83] The cost of housing, municipal services and utilities, virtually free under the Soviet system, has also been rising steadily under an IMF-promoted reform to make users bear their full cost. Renting an apartment that was not already occupied by the person during the Soviet period (Soviet-era apartments were de jure or de facto privatized by their occupants) is beyond the reach of workers, placing severe limits on labour mobility and making it impossible for young people who want to start families to live apart from their parents. A VAZ worker summed up the uncompensated decline of the social wage in these words: "Our wages are still socialist, but our conditions have become capitalist."

Despite the rise of mass unemployment, the fall in the social wage, and the liquidation of savings from the Soviet period by hyperinflation (deliberately unleashed in 1992[84]), the government did not put in place a social safety net. Of the seven million officially unemployed in 2000, only thirteen per cent received any state support.[85] Only a small fraction of the unemployed even bother to register because benefits are so small and paid irregularly, and the policy of the cash-strapped Employment Service is to make registration difficult. Officially, the maximum benefit is two thirds of the last wage (up to a ceiling of the average national wage) for up to three months, diminishing thereafter over the course of a year. But more than half of those registered at the end of 1998, when unemployment peaked, received only seventeen per cent of the subsistence minimum, that is, enough to survive for about six days.[86] With the introduction of the Unified Social Tax in 2001, the government abolished the separate unemployment, pension, health insurance, and social security funds, integrating these taxes into general revenues. This led to a sharp decrease in money available for unemployment allocations and other work-related benefits, including subsidies for vacations and children's summer camps. The minimum pension in mid 2003, which was received by over four million Russians, was the equivalent of twenty-two U.S.$. A senior official at the Ministry of Labour himself described it as "a joke." But even the average pension, which was worth forty-five U.S.$ in the first quarter of 2002, was below the subsistence minimum in the years 1999-2001.[87]

The Russian tax system is highly regressive. In 2001, the government introduced a flat, thirteen-per-cent, income tax that dramatically reduced the tax rate for the well-off (supposedly to persuade them to pay at least something), while raising the rate for the eighty per cent of taxpayers who had been paying twelve per cent. It also extended coverage to previously untaxed parts of the social wage, including subsidized lunches, vacations and certain social allocations. The Unified Social Tax, also introduced in 2001, sets lower rates for the well-off, and changes to be introduced in 2005 will further deepen its regressive character.[88]

Until February 1, 2002, when a new Labour Code came into force, the legal framework for union activity compared quite favourably with developed capitalist countries, thanks mainly to laws inherited from the Soviet period. Among the pro-union aspects were the unions' right to ask for (and generally obtain) the dismissal of managers for violation of the labour laws or of collective agreements and the requirement of union consent for overtime, layoffs, changes in work schedules and wage systems, and for most cases of disciplining. Upon union demand, management was required to eliminate unsafe conditions. The work collective (that is the delegates' conference, elected by all employees, including management) could elect a labour disputes committee to rule on individual grievances with the power override managerial orders. Management then had ten days to appeal in court. Union recognition was automatic when as little as three people had signed membership cards, and dues had to be automatically transferred upon written request by union members. Management also had to provide unions with the information necessary for their activities and with office space, a meeting hall, heat, lighting, means of transportation and communication, and it had to negotiate collective agreements with the unions. Without union consent, management could not transfer or discipline elected union representatives, and they could not be dismissed or laid off for two years after leaving their post.[89]

The government's motive in reforming the labour code was to make Russia more attractive for investors. The guiding orientation was reduce state regulation of worker-management relations to a minimum and to provide management with a maximally "flexible" workforce. This neo-liberal thrust was somewhat blunted as the reform went through parliament, and in a few areas, the old code was even improved. For example, the required payment for involuntary temporary layoff is now two-thirds of average, not base, pay; an extra holiday was added; and workers were given the right to refuse work if wages had not been paid for fifteen days (this repeated an earlier Supreme Court ruling). But overall, the reform significantly weakened trade-union rights. It ended the requirement of union consent for dismissals or for changes in conditions of employment, such as the work schedules and the wage system. A worker can now be dismissed for violation of safety norms, which occurs very frequently due to the age of equipment and the combination of low wages and output-based bonuses. The severity of disciplinary measures is no longer has to correspond to the seriousness of the violation. Protection against dismissal (there is no protection against lesser disciplinary measures) of elected union officers is now limited to chairpersons and vice chairpersons of plant and shop committees, and even they can be dismissed with the consent of higher union bodies. Payment in kind, previously illegal but widely practiced in the 1990s, can now constitute up to twenty per cent of the wage. Labour disputes committees are no longer elected by the work collective (this allowed strong unions to dominate them). Instead, half the members are appointed by management and half by the work collective. The procedure for legal strikes has been somewhat simplified, but the decision to strike was taken away from union members and given to the delegates' conference, which management can usually control. And the decision to strike requires a majority in a quorum of two-thirds. This makes legal strikes practically impossible, especially for the small alternative unions, the ones most apt to want to strike. (Since sanctions apply only after a court has ruled on the illegality of the strike and the ruling has been communicated to the union, in practice strikes that last at least several hours can be organized with relative impunity.)[90]

Even in relatively law-based states, management's respect for legal norms that are meant to protect workers depends to a great extent on the balance of forces in the given workplace. Russian workers lose out on both counts, since the state is far from law-based and the correlation of forces in the enterprises strongly favours management. The immediate impact of the new Labour Code was therefore not that great. In the new private sector (that is, outside of the formerly state-owned sector), it was hardly felt at all, since in practice the Labour Code was never applied there. In this sector managerial arbitrariness is unchallenged.[91] Although wages are often higher there, hours are longer, there are fewer or no social benefits (such as paid sick leave, holidays, pensions), and there is frequently the threat of violence and or arrest. This existence and dimensions of this sector weigh heavily on the legal labour market. Work in it socializes workers into a culture of illegality and promotes the idea that laws and unions are not needed.

The negative impact of the new code has been felt most by the minority alternative unions, since they had been most active in using the law to defend their members. But even before the new Labour Code came into effect, the relative success that these union had known in the early post-Soviet years in acting through the courts was declining, as the pro-management bias and venality of judges became more pronounced. Moreover, whenever a conflict concerned issues of ownership or managerial corruption, then legal recourse was always futile. Violence against trade unionist has been mostly related to this sort of issue, not to disputes over wages and conditions. Despite the changes that have been introduced into the Labour Code, it is worth emphasizing again that Russian workers have enjoyed and still enjoy a high degree of freedom of association that is quite remarkable in the context of Russia's history.

Inside the Factory

Soviet factories were large, highly integrated enterprises. Spinning-off and outsourcing have only recently begun. The typical factory in the ASM sector is situated well within city limits, sometimes close to the centre, and occupies a large territory, as land was free under the Soviet system. Dogs and cats, fed by cafeteria employees, often share the space and can sometimes even be seen wandering through the buildings. If the work force is very large, the enterprise has clinics, sports, cultural and daycare facilities, as well as vacation resorts and summer camps, now gradually being sold off or transferred to the municipality. The production buildings are visibly beyond their prime. Piles of discarded equipment and parts lie rusting under the open sky.

Inside, the shops are also untidy. Temperatures in many of them are frigid in winter and baking in the summer. Leaky roofs are common. Many of the shops, built for better times, are half-deserted. Much of the equipment is old, well behind Western technology. Little attention has been paid to ergonomics and worker comfort in organizing production. In this overall depressing setting, the administration building stands out. It has recently undergone "*evroremont*," that is, repairs and refurnishing according to "European standards." Temperatures inside are comfortable. Its toilets are clean, with seats, and there is paper.

One sees few young workers. The average age is close to fifty. The younger workers, especially the more skilled ones, were more adventurous and left early in search better wages in the new private sector. Older workers were more apt to stay on, as their chances in the "grey" labour market were not as good, and work there is very demanding physically. Having spent many years at the plant, they were less adaptable and they valued the relative security it seemed to offer as compared to the new private sector. It has proven hard to recruit and retain young workers because of the low prestige of factory work, the bad conditions and low wages (compounded by the tendency of older workers to monopolize better-paying jobs). Despite the unemployment, outside of Moscow and St. Petersburg, the turnover rate for young workers is high. Of 13,000 new hires at VAZ in 2001, 6000 left within the year.[92]

According to official statistics, at the end of 2000, 20.2 per cent of workers in the machine-building and metalworking sectors were employed in harmful or dangerous conditions, and forty-three per cent of all industrial workers received some form of compensation for harmful, dangerous or otherwise bad work conditions, that is, wage supplements, extra holidays, early pensions, free milk, etc.[93] The Minister of Labour and Social Development reported in 2002 that many more Russians die at work each year—4,372 in 2001—than in the Afghan and Chechnya wars and he decried the neglect of industrial safety.[94] Meanwhile, the state's Health and Safety Inspectorate is hopelessly underfunded. The system of compensations, inherited from the Soviet Union, discourages workers from fighting to improve conditions, to the point where workers even resist union efforts to transfer them to safer jobs. In one striking case, a woman at the Tutaev Motor Factory was tending a machine that required her repeated lifting of heavy parts. She was covered head to foot in an oily liquid that the machine spewed out. A makeshift metal awning protected the machine from water dripping from the roof but it did not cover the worker entirely. This job gave her three "harmfulnesses" (*vrednosti*), which, besides supplements to her wage (based entirely on piece-work), allowed her to take retirement seven years early. In fact, she was past retirement and was receiving her pension in addition to her wage. She said she could move to other work but this job let her earn more. Many of the most harmful jobs are occupied by single mothers.

Even when the union negotiates health and safety improvements, they are often not carried out. In a system that places so much responsibility for safety on the individual worker, the insufficient provision and poor quality of safety equipment and clothing is a major source of complaint. At the same time, workers themselves generally do not attach high priority to health and safety. The irregular nature of work over the last years, old and poorly-maintained equipment, low wages, widespread overtime, the output-based bonus system—all conspire to foster a lax attitude to safety norms. Under the present system, compensation for injuries is reduced if the worker is found to have violated technical norms.

Most of the factory cafeterias have been shut, and those still open are not frequented because subsidies have been reduced and prices are high. Most workers now bring their own food and eat it at tables in the shop next to the machines. In the 1990s, and sometimes still today, workers could be seen in the colder months huddled around metal drums in which they burned wood to keep warm. A sociologist described the scene in a tractor-assembly shop in St.-Petersburg in 1995:

The line is not moving. A few half-assembled tractors stand motionless.
The vast spaces of the shop are unusually deserted. One sees hardly any

people. But the main thing is that it is really freezing, even though it is already April outside. Along the assembly-line that stretches into the distance, bonfires are burning. Yes, honest-to-goodness bonfires. Only not right on the floor but in metal boxes. Workers stand beside them warming themselves. They also eat there…They are wearing padded cotton coats, and the women are covered in warm shawls, almost like during the blockade [in World War II]. They are eating sandwiches from home and warming up tea.[95]

The proportion of women in the industrial work force fell from forty-eight to thirty-eight per cent between 1991 and 2000.[96] In ASM, women are still forty-five per cent[97] of the work force but they work disproportionately at unskilled, low-paying and unhealthy jobs. Most workers in light and medium assembly, stamping, paint and galvanic shops, most storeroom employees, janitors and unskilled white-collar employees are women. There are very few women among tool-and-dye makers, electricians, repair persons, machine adjusters. Even in assembly, women are often concentrated in lower-paying operations, even though their work does not qualitatively differ from what the men are doing. In stamping, for example, if there are some automatic machines, men will be assigned to them, while the women feed theirs by hand. Work on the automatic machines is more skilled but also it is lighter and better paid, and there is no objective reason women cannot be trained for them. The situation is similar in engineering- technical jobs, where women occupy the lower rungs. Management is overwhelmingly male, the more so the higher up the ladder. Women have a much harder time to be accepted to training for skilled jobs. They also apply less frequently, either because they expect to be rejected or because they fear the added responsibility on top of an already "double shift" (factory and domestic work). Sexual harassment happens in the former state enterprises, but its frequency pales in comparison to what is normal practice in the new private sector. Consciousness of this issue, and to a lesser extent of discrimination on the basis of sex, is not developed among women workers, though it is easily awakened when they are exposed to education.

Despite the presence of unions in all large and medium ASM enterprises, management wields a tremendous amount of arbitrary power. The wage system is at once a primary manifestation and major source of that power. According to M. Gorenkov, economist of the Central Committee of the Union of Auto and Farm-Machine Workers of Russia (ASMR), "managers in Soviet times could generally find ways to make wages vary from one worker to the next. But the situation today is one of complete arbitrariness (*bespredel*)."

Wage differentials among workers in the same factory can be as much as four to one. Occupations are grouped according to skill and difficulty, and each occupational categories in turn has five to eight skill levels. Particularly valued workers, such as rare skilled tradespeople or brigade leaders, for example, in additional to the regular supplements, might be assigned a special bonus. The guaranteed part of the wage (*tarif*) is usually less than half of take-home pay.[98] The remainder takes the form of bonuses and compensatory supplements. The following items appeared on the pay stub for October 1999 of a skilled machinist at VAZ: basic wage—2092.50 rubles; supplement for fulfilling the output norm—648.68; supplement for night shift—20; compensation for three days not worked for family reasons—743.88; bonus for "professional mastery" (tidiness, care of tools, etc.)—502.20; unspecified bonus from the incentive fund—418.50; other unspecified bonus—1300. The total was 5,825.8 (224 U.S.$ at that time), of which thirty-six per cent constituted the guaranteed part, twenty-six per cent were supplements, and thirty-eight per cent bonuses.[99]

The compensatory supplements are more or less guaranteed, though they can still depend to some degree on the goodwill of managers. Bonuses, on the other hand, are subject to a higher degree of arbitrariness. Management's decision not to pay them is, in practice, a fine. The back of the pay stub actually lists two fines: for material damage and for defective output. At a Moscow Ball-Bearing Factory (this sector is part of ASM) management was illegally docking wages if workers took sick leave or a leave of absence at their own expense during the month.[100] "Our wage system," reported the bulletin of Edinstvo,

> leaves a lot of room for the arbitrariness of dishonest managers. Codes 3 [supplement for production delivered], 23 [for exceeding output norms] and 14 [?] are, as a rule, handed out by the foreman and brigade leader 'without noise,' so that no one else will know, since they are often given for mercenary reasons. All this undermines the psychological climate. [The bonus for] 'professional mastery,' in fact, depends on whether the boss finds the worker to his liking [*ugodnyi*] or not. If there is a conflict, you can kiss those parts of your wage goodbye. Few workers can easily find their way through this wage system.[101]

Payment for essentially the same quantity and skill of work can vary considerably from one shop to the next, and even from one worker to the next within a shop. In auto factories, for example, workers painting cheaper models are normally paid less than workers painting more expensive ones, even though the work is identical. But even the exact same work can be paid differently. According to the chairperson of a stamping shop:

> Two people are doing exactly the same work, but you are the friend of the supervisor the other is his enemy. You both stamped the same number of pieces on the same machines. But he marks you down for more. The number of pieces won't appear on your pay stub, only the sum. Well, you might bump into the other worker and find out that she earned more. You might get mad and try to find out what happened. But you might not be able to find anything out. And most often you won't even know the other is being paid more.

Asked what a worker can do if he or she feels his wage is lower than it is supposed to be, a foreman at the now defunct Moskvitch Factory replied:

> You can only try to talk to the foreman and ask him to put you on an operation that pays at a higher rate. You ask, you complain. Because every worker, besides his own operation, is doing an additional job, since none of the parts fit. To mount the part you have to bend, bang, reshape it, and you get nothing for that work unless you make noise or are in good relations with the foreman. In that case, he'll fill out a supplement form, and they'll pay you extra. Usually, it's one group that does the bending and banging, while another lives well with the foreman. So one worker can earn 1,500 and another 4,500, even though they seem to be doing the same work in the same shop. That's why relations with management are so tense—some get nothing at all, while others make pretty good money.

Bonuses and even wage indexation are often dependent on the performance of the given brigade, shop, or the enterprise as a whole. (Regular and full wage indexation of wages is rare, despite persistent inflation.[102] Even wage arrears are at best partially indexed.) This practice, like the entire organization of production, shifts responsibility for management's shortcomings onto the workers, a principle inherited from the Soviet period. This is what really lay behind Soviet workers' relative autonomy in the work process that observers sometimes interpreted in a rather too positive light.

Besides the wages system, management's other "levers" for keeping troublemakers in check include refusal of overtime or of requests for time off to be made up later (*otgul*), refusal of training for promotion to higher skill grades, involuntary job transfers. While the law limits involuntary transfers to jobs with similar conditions and pay, in practice a transfer even from one brigade to another within the same shop can result in substantial loss of wages and discomfort for workers. For example, if the former job provided a lot of overtime and the new one does not, take-home pay will fall.

The same is true if the supervisor in the former section was a fair person and skilled in finding licit and illicit ways to increase the workers' wages. In general, older workers, accustomed to their jobs and to their comrades (especially important when work is organized in brigades), often find the prospect of a transfer threatening even when wages and conditions will not suffer.

But the ultimate source of management's arbitrary power—apart from the failed policies of the unions, the subject of the next chapters—is widespread insecurity and demoralization among workers, which undermine solidarity and the will to resist. The main sources of insecurity have already been outlined: fear of unemployment, absence of savings, poverty-level wages, the weak social-safety net that is growing weaker, open and suppressed unemployment, the advanced average age of the work force, corruption of the judiciary and law-enforcement systems. A major illness in the family, the need to replace an expensive appliance or to make repairs to one's apartment constitute major crises for workers. Moreover, the average worker lives in fear of loss of his or her job. This is the case even at plants like VAZ, where management is having trouble finding workers for the assembly line. Managers' stock answer to workers' complaints is: "If you don't like it, you can leave." And it works. It might be possible—at least for younger workers—to find other work, but that work lacks even the relative stability of the factory and the protection provided by legal norms that are at least minimally respected there. Workers know the present recovery is fragile and that large plants have shut forever. In the Russian context at least, insecurity fosters conservatism among workers. After all, "things could get worse"(*kak by khuzhe ne stalo*) if one makes noise. Insecurity discourages workers from looking beyond the present moment. Its psychological and moral impact is all the greater on the background of the many decades of solid economic security of the Soviet period. The change came very suddenly and unexpectedly.

Insecurity, of course, need not undermine the will to resist, if there is a programme for change that workers they believe in. But, as noted, that is not the case. Workers, of course, can be very active in adapting individually to their circumstances. But these circumstances are accepted as objective facts that cannot be changed through collective action. The deteriorating socio-economic situation resulting from "shock therapy" undermined an already weakly developed sense of dignity and confidence among workers. This demoralization has found its most striking expressions in abuse of alcohol and theft of enterprise property, both of which have reached epidemic proportions.

Workers of both sexes agree that demoralization has hit men more strongly than women. Women workers commonly describe men as "infantile" and "gone to seed" (*degradirovany*). At the Tutaev Motor Factory, for example, the union gives small subsidies to workers to pay for their daughters' high-school graduation dresses. But it gives the money only to women workers, wives or mothers, since "the men will drink it." The differential impact of the crisis is perhaps linked the stronger identification of men with their jobs and their role as provider. Both have been seriously undermined. Workers themselves quip that "only fools, pensioners and millionaires [corrupt managers] remain in the factories." With the collapse of the Soviet Union, the old system of values was turned upside down, and once-respected working-class professions are now viewed with contempt by the younger generation and the media.

Another reason why drinking on the job and theft have mushroomed is management's tolerant attitude to these violations, which are formally grounds for dismissal. It is commonly recognized that management was much stricter on these matters under the Soviet system. Of course, it is hard to enforce discipline when work and the payment of wages are irregular. Moreover, many managers are themselves involved in illegal activities and are reluctant to go after workers who are guilty of smaller sins. The two might even be part of the same illicit operation. And it can be dangerous to try to stop theft, if it is organized. Nevertheless, there is a widespread view among worker activists that management's indulgence is policy: a worker who drinks or steals is "on a hook" (*na kriuchke*), that is, the threat of dismissal hangs permanently over the person, who will do virtually anything management asks. This is the ultimate "flexible work force." For example, at VAZ, a job on the assembly line involving repeated lifting of twenty-kilogram panels from high overhead and inserting them into the front of the cars is done, according to other workers, exclusively by "drunks," since no one else will do it.

The view that management's tolerance is policy is supported by the fact that vodka is sold almost openly inside the plant. (And, according to workers, these vendors even receive their bonus for "professional mastery.") One can even sometimes see the bottle standing openly on the workers' table next to the assembly line. At a collective-agreement conference at the Tutaev Motor plant in 2002, a worker delegate demanded to know from the director: "When are you finally going to put an end to the drinking and theft?" The director replied that this required the co-operation of honest workers, who should report the thieves. The reply provoked general indignation. The union chairperson of the metrological shop of this factory fought for months with director to remove her supervisor, an far-gone alcoholic who was frequently absent from work and who tolerated drinking by others. This struggle was going on while the plant's very existence was threatened by mounting debt, something the director never failed to cite when workers asked him to raise wages. With the arrival of new owners, there have been efforts to tighten discipline. But it remains to be seen how far these efforts will go or how much success they will meet.

On the political level, there are also grounds to believe that the pandemic of alcoholism is, if not policy, at least viewed as convenient by the government. The logic here is similar to management's: abuse of vodka undermines the potential for resistance. The state monopoly on vodka was historically a major source of revenue in Russia. Yeltsin relinquished it, and vodka became cheap and easily accessible. In Moscow in September 2002, a half-liter of medium-quality vodka cost the equivalent of one dollar U.S.. A litre of whole milk cost 75 cents. And vodka can easily be purchased almost anywhere at any time of day or night. Consumption of alcohol is fifty per cent higher today than twenty-five years ago under Brezhnev's the lax regime.[103]

In the general atmosphere of insecurity and demoralization, the thin stratum of committed labour activists comes disproportionately from among skilled tradesmen and semi-skilled women workers. This was not always the case. In the relatively favourable economic and political conditions of the late Gorbachev era and early 1990s, the core of labour militancy in the auto and tractor plants was the men on the assembly lines. The lines bring together large numbers of workers doing similar work for similar pay and who are strategically placed to paralyze the entire plant. In those early days, it often took only a few informal leaders with virtually no organization and little preparatory work to shut down the line. But from the second half of the 1990s, whenever collective conflicts broke out—almost all over non-payment of wages—women workers were disproportionately active, while men often limited themselves to a cheerleading role.

Skilled tradesmen are an exception, at least those that opted to remain in the factories, because they are relatively secure. If they are fired, they can find other work that pays at least as well. (As one skilled adjuster [seventh skill level] in a ball-bearing plant explained: "I'm not afraid. I'll always find work. I'll just write my letter of resignation, slap it down on the supervisor's desk, and tell him to fill in the date whenever he likes.") These workers are the masters of their machines, not their slaves. Their shops are clean and tidy and they run them virtually on their own. The speak with management as equals. They are proud of their skills, love their work, and find it challenging, which is one of the reasons they stayed on. They rarely drink to excess and do not steal, though they might make use of the plant's machinery and energy to work on the side (*khalturit*). This, however, is done more or less openly with management's consent, as a legitimate supplement to their scandalously low wages. At the same time, this ability to earn more money can act as a brake on their activism. An activist tool-and-dye maker at the Pekkar carburetor factory, who could have easily have defeated his corrupt president in elections, refused to run since it would have meant foregoing extra earnings. An instrument-maker at the Yaroslavl Fuel-Pump Factory (who claimed mastery of forty-five professions, including furrier), leader of the city's protest movement, explained:

> I could easily get another job. I have an entrepreneur friend who is forever courting me. But while I have the energy, I want to fight and maybe make a difference. Others have left. But if we all go, it will be complete tyranny (*bespredel*), and in the end the others will feel it too, wherever they may be. Yes, it's a plus to be educated, competent and to know own's worth—you can talk to management on equal terms. But it's also a minus. Having spent time in the protest movement, someone like me gets to thinking: wouldn't it be better if I used my capacities to make money? Many former comrades are doing that. Even I think about it.

In the summer of 2002, with labour activism at an all-time low, he left the factory to work in his friend's shop making parts for engines.

The most striking trait of workers who become active is their pronounced sense of dignity, the weakness of which they decry in the mass of workers. The often shocking lack of concern among workers for their own health and safety, both inside and outside the plants—Westerners sometimes find this "devil-may-care" attitude an attractive part of the "Russian character"—is but one measure. The dominant reaction among workers to their deteriorating situation has been passively to renounce needs that only yesterday they considered a normal part of civilized life. Active workers, on the other hand, insist on living "like people." Dignity, and the lack of it, are constant themes among activists. "They treat us like cattle (*bydlo*)," complained one. "And the tragedy is that the vast majority of workers agree that they are cattle." "We have to squeeze the slave out of us," exhorted another activist. And a woman lamented: "Seventy per cent of our male workers are drunks, and so they do what they are told, like slaves." During a discussion following the viewing of a film depicting the struggles of members of the Canadian Autoworkers' Union, one worker remarked: "You can see the confidence and dignity see in their faces. They won't let themselves be stepped on like our workers." A labour educator summed up the challenge: "Our task is not so much to make workers understand, since the basic issues are really quite straightforward. The challenge is to make them *want* to understand, since understanding would call for action, and for that they lack the confidence and self-esteem."

In the period under study, worker—management and working-class—state relations presented a paradoxical picture. For all their arbitrary, unlimited power, both enterprise management and the state administration were in important ways considerably weaker than their Western counterparts. Their vast freedom of action vis-à-vis the workers was not a reflection of their own strength, since both their legitimacy and their social bases were really very fragile. It was rather a function of the profound weakness of the working class itself.

Except on the most superficial levels, very few Russians believe the state's democratic and patriotic claims. Even the ideologues of the new bourgeoisie, as already noted, openly speak of the "managed democracy" and bemoan the absence of a "national idea."[104] But this "idea" is especially lacking among the political élite itself, which is hopelessly cynical and corrupt. The same is generally true of enterprise management. Russians are universally convinced that the economic and political administrations are stealing on a large scale. Popular awareness of the criminal origins and nature of the big fortunes is strong, and, as the case of Khodorkovsii illustrates, the state administration periodically reinforces it. To workers, the new bourgeoisie is not a class of wealth-generating "captains of industry" but a gang of rapacious pillagers.

The social bases of the state and of the enterprise administrations are also very weak. The economic strategy has produced only a narrow stratum of moderate winners, the much-touted "middle class." And their situation is precarious, as the financial collapse of 1998 forcefully demonstrated. In the factories, the economic situation and identity of non-managerial engineering and technical staff are closer to the workers' than the administration's. But even among lower and middle management, the ideological divide from workers is often absent. At least in the 1990s, many secretly sympathized with workers' struggles, and some even participated actively.

This explains what at first glance is the surprising tendency on the part of the enterprise and state administrations quickly to retreat and offer concessions when faced with even relatively small, but united and determined groups of mobilized workers. Ten years after the fall of the Soviet Union, a vote by workers could still often force the dismissal of managers. In a some cases, workers were able to impose elements of control over management in areas where Western unions do not even think to venture. As late as 1998, the government tolerated railroad and street blockades and responded with real concessions. But all the gains from these struggles proved ephemeral, because the mobilizations were so exceptional and isolated.

Notes

1. For critical analyses of Russia's economic strategy, see J. Stiglitz, Globalization and Its Discontents, N.Y.: W.W. Norton, 2002, ch.5, pp. 133-165, and J. Sapir, Le chaos russe, Paris: la Découverte, 1996, as well as his Le krach russe, Paris: la Découverte, 1998. For Russian analyses that foresaw its consequences before its application, see Voprosy ekonomiki, no. 3, 1991.
2. U.S. Census Bureau, *Statistical Abstract of the United States: 1999*, Washington, 2000, p. 881.
3. Goskomstat Rossii, *Rossiiskii statisticheskii ezhegodnik, 2001*, Moscow, 2001, pp. 337, 38, 141; Stiglitz, *Globalization…*, p. 143.
4. Stiglitz, *Globalization…*, p. 143. Investment in the machine-building sector fell ninety-two cent in 1990-97. (A.R. Belousov, "Uroki postkrizisnogo rosta," in E. Yasin, ed., *Modernisatsiya ekonomiki Rossii*, Moscow: Vysshaya shkola ekonomiki, 2002, p. 117.)
5. Goskomstat, *Rossiiskii…2001*, p. 349.
6. *Ibid.*, p. 569; A. Kiva, "Rossii nuzhen natsional'nyi konsensus dlya vyzhivaniya," *Nezavisimaya gazeta*, Apr. 5, 2002.
7. V. Soyfer, "Russian Science's Comeback," *The Wall Street Journal*, Aug. 30, 2002; *Nezavisimaya gazeta*, Apr. 16, 2002, p. 5.
8. Goskomstat Rossii, *Rossiiskii statisticheskii ezhegodnik, 1999*, Moscow, 2000, pp. 326-27.
9. *Finansovye izvestiya*, Apr. 1, 1999.
10. Goskomstat, *Rossiiskii…2001*, p. 141; *Golos profsoyuza*, no. 3, 1991; ASMR, "Report of the President to the Third Congress," Oct. 1997 (unpublished).
11. Stiglitz, *Globalization…*, pp. 135, 151.
12. Economist Intelligence Unit (EIU), *Country Profile, Russia*, London, 2003, pp. 34, 40; "Industrial Output on Rise in Russia," *RIA Novosti*, July 15, 2003.
13. Goskomstat, *Rossiya v tsifrakh 2003*, Moscow, 2003, p. 189; ASM-kholding, *Analiticheskii obzor, yanvar'-avgust 2003*, Moscow, 2003, pp. 18-20.
14. Goskomstat, *Rossiiskii…2001*, p. 609; EIU, *Country Profile, Russia*, p. 34.
15. See M. Husson, "Mondialisation, nouvel horizon du capitalisme," in *Mondialisation et impérialisme*, Paris: Les cahiers de Critique communiste, 2003, pp. 7-31.
16. See, for example, E. Yasin's "Demokraty, na vykhod!" *Moskovskie novosti*, no. 44, Nov. 11-17, 2003, pp. 5-6. Yasin was Minister of Economic Development under Yeltsin. Currently scientific director of the Higher School of Economics, he is the main ideologue of the Party of Right Forces, which reflects the interests of big capital.
17. *Nezavisimaya gazeta*, July 21, 1995; D. Remnik, "Yeltsin to the Brink and Back," *The New Yorker*, July 15, 1996; www.themoscowtimes.com/election_fraud.html; M. Bevins, "Looking Back at Election Frauds Past," *St. Petersburg Times*, Sept. 23, 2003; A. Politkovskaya, "Za chto Kadyrov nevzlyubil dedushku Balu," *Novaya gazeta*, Nov. 20-23, 2003, pp. 7-8. Referring to the 1993 constitutional referendum, a close associate of Yeltsin remarked: "The main thing is that the constitution passed, and it doesn't matter how—through the ear or through the ass." *The Financial Times*, May 6, 1994.
18. For accounts of this confrontation and its background, see See A. Buzgalin and A. Kolganov, *Krovavyi oktyabr' v Moskve*, Moscow: Ekonomicheskaya demokratiya, 1994; M. Roche, *Thérapie de choc et autoritarisme en Russie: la démocratie confisquée*, Paris, L'Harmattan, 2000; and P. Reddaway and D. Glinksi, *The Tragedy of Russia's Reforms: Market Bolshevism Against De-*

mocracy, Washington: U.S. Institute of Peace, 2001, ch. 7, pp. 369-434. The latter study is one of the best critical treatments of Russian politics in the period covered by the present study.

19. Roche, *Thérapie de choc...*, pp. 178-80; G. Simon, "Ukraina i Rossiya: dve strany –odna trasnformatsiya, *Connections,* no. 2, Apr. 2002, p. 5. During a visit to Moscow at the height of the 1996 presidential campaign, Clinton, alluding to the war in Chechnya, likened Yeltsin to Abraham Lincoln. At this time, the IMF granted Russia the second biggest loan in IMF history and turned a blind eye to the government's abandonment of budget austerity. After the elections, however, it almost immediately suspended payments because of the government's overspending. Monetarist orthodoxy was quickly restored. *The Economist*, July 13-19, 1996, p. 71.

20. In response to the FNPR's support for the Constitution, Yeltsin cut power and telephone connections to the federation's headquarters and let it be known that he had a decree on his desk ready for signing to dissolve the federation and confiscate its property. In anticipation of an immanent seizure of the federation's buildings on Leninksii Prospekt, union staff rushed to carry out the office equipment.

21. *Solidarnost'*, no. 12, 1995, p. 8.

22. The state's role is graphically presented in P. Klebnikov's *Godfather of the Kremlin: Boris Berezovsky and the Looting of Russia*, N.Y., Harcourt, 2000. Not surprisingly, Klebnikov, today senior editor at *Forbes Magazine*, whitewashes the G-7 and their international financial institutions, portraying them as duped benefactors. For Marx's analysis of the process in sixteenth and seventeenth-century England, see K. Marx, *Capital*, N.Y.: International Publishers, 1972, vol.1, pp. 713-60.

23. B. Rakitskii, *Ugol ataki*, Moscow: Institut perspektiv i problem strany, 2003, p. 9. The same government report, dated January 18, 1995, stated: "In essence, the greatest giveaway (*razbazarovanie*) of state property in the history of Russia has occurred. This in itself has become one of the sources of the crisis and has laid the ground for many future conflicts over the redivision of property." (ibid). See also B. Kagarlitsky, "'Political Capitalism' and Corruption in Russia," *Labour Focus on Eastern Europe*, no. 71, 2002, p. 81.

24. Quoted in Rakitskii, *Ugol ataki*, p. 9.

25. Cited in A. Piontkovskii, "Tovarishch Prezident i gospodin oligarkh," *Novaya gazeta*, no. 85, Nov. 12-16, 2003, p. 2.

26. EIU, *Country Report, Russia*, Aug. 2003, p. 15.

27. One of these cases is the prosecution of "oligarch" M. Khodorkovskii. In this connection, an obviously gleeful, high-ranking officer of the Federal Security Service (FSB, successor to the KGB) told a reporter under the cover of anonymity: "For many years they didn't let us enforce the law." ("Anonimnyi istochnik: A ne nado v sviterke khodit' k Prezidentu," *Novaya gazeta*, no. 85, Nov. 12-16, 2003, p. 4).

Nikolai Prostov, former union president at the Arsenal aerospace factory in St. Petersburg, summed up his experience fighting massive legal violations by management in the early phase of privatization:

> Even though abuses are everywhere, inquiries are rarely conducted, since they inevitably lead to politics. As soon as the state prosecutor begins to dig for abuses...shouts rings out: "You are blocking the privatization process, the political course of the government!"...If they try to move on it, open a criminal file, then a powerful state agency called the State Committee for Property, headed by a certain Chubais, will inevitably intervene. And Chubais usually covers for the directors. He has the support of Yeltsin. His is probably the most powerful state administration today...The Prosecutor-General can do nothing

against him. (D. Mandel, "Conversion in a Russian Defence Plant: Interview with N. Prostov," *Socialist Alternatives*, vol. 2, no. 2, 1993, pp. 139-40.)

28. "Oborotni v pidzhakakh,"*Izvestiya*, Nov. 11, 2003, p. 1.
29. Cited in Piontkovskii, "Tovarishch President…" p. 18.
30. V. Korchagina, "Russia Fares Better in Annual Corruption Index," *The Moscow Times*, Aug. 29, 2002. In 2002, Russia tied Tanzania, India, Zimbabwe, Cote d'Ivoire and Honduras for seventy-first place out of 102 in this ranking. Russia was seventy-ninth out of ninety-one countries in 2001 and eighty-second out of ninety in 1999.
31. EIU, *Country Profile, Russia*, 2003, p. 33.
32. Under Putin, contract murders of businessmen, journalists, and even prominent political figures have remained frequent and mostly unsolved. Even the contract murders of the three Duma deputies over the past five years have not been solved, and no law enforcement officials have been sanctioned for the failures. ("Country Is Still Stuck in Deadly Rut" *The Moscow Times*, Apr.21, 2003.) In 2002 the business daily *Kommersant* reported that several entrepreneurs were being murdered each month in the Russian Far-East region (A. Chernyshev, "Primorksie killery rabotayut bez vykhodnykh,"Nov. 9, 2002). Seven mayors and high functionaries of Moscow's suburban towns have been murdered since 1996. (*Kommersant*, May 5, 2003) In Togliatti, six directors of local newspapers and television stations have been murdered over the past eight years. (*Novya gazeta*, no. 84, Nov. 10-12, 2003.)
33. At the time of writing, Khodorkovskii is in jail, awaiting trial for economic crimes, including massive tax evasion.
34. The point, of course, is not that the state should not have prosecuted these people, but rather that it prosecuted *only* them. Most Russians, unfortunately, failed to appreciate the implications for their own rights of this selective, politically-motivated approach to law-enforcement and were happy to see Putin go after an "oligarch."
35. There was some protest from business circles and from the business-oriented press immediately after Khodorkovskii's arrest but it faded quickly. When Putin addressed the Union of Industrialists and Entrepreneurs shortly after the arrest, he was met with a long ovation. ("Kampaniya 'Svobodu Khodorkovskomu!' zavershena," *Izvestiya* , Nov. 29, 2003.)
36. Goskomstat, *Rossiiskii…2001*, p. 305; ASMR, "Itogi raboty mashinostroitel'nogo kompleksa i ASM za 9 mesyatsev 2001-go goda," 2001 (unpublished).
37. "Oligarch" P. Aven of the Alfa Group explained: "To become a millionaire in our country it is not at all necessary to have a good head or specialized knowledge. Often it is enough to have active support in the government, the parliament, local power structures, and law enforcement agencies. One fine day, your insignificant bank is authorized to, for instance, conduct operations with budgetary funds. Or quotas are generously allotted for export of oil, timber and gas. In other words, you are appointed a millionaire." Cited in Reddaway and Glinsi, *The Tragedy…*, p. 603.
38. Quoted in Piontkovskii, "Tovarishch Prezident…"
39. This is Piontkovskii's view in "Tovarishch Prezident," which is more or less shared by Yasin in "Demokraty na vykhod." Piontkovskii aptly described the affair as "a revolt of the dollar millionaires against the dollar billionaires." Of course, there were other ways in which Khodorkovskii set a bad example, in the opinion of the "power faction": he was financing parties not favoured by the Kremlin and even expressing presidential ambitions himself; he called for the breakup of the gas monopoly Gazprom and privatization of the pipelines; he openly opposed Russia's position on the Iraq war (wanting Russia to participate in the coali-

tion), and he even mused about the restoration of a parliamentary republic. It was obvious that Khodorkovskii had forgotten his correct place in society, that is, subordinate to the state administration. In the above-mentioned anonymous interview (see note 26), the FSB officer was especially indignant at Khodorkovskii's coming to see Putin in a mere sweater, not a suit.

40. On the unchecked power of directors in this period, see G. Kleiner, "Za granitsamy demokratii: kto i kak upravlyaut rossiiskimy predrpiaytiaymy." *Nezavisimaya gazeta*, May 8, 2001. On the dispersal of ownership, see R. Kapelyushnikov, "Krupneishie i dominiruyushchie sobstvenniki v rossiiskoi prommyshlennosti," *Voprosy ekonomiki*, no. 1, Jan. 2000, pp. 99-119.

41. The main competition for VAZ's cheap Ladas, as noted, are used imports. China, India, South Korea, Thailand and Brazil, all have either very high prohibitive tariffs on used imports or else they ban them outright. Russia imposed a twenty-five-per-cent tariff only in 2002. (AMSR, "Spravochnye materialy k soobshcheniyu 'Sovremennoe sostoyanie avtomobil'nogo i sel'skokhozyaistvennogo mashinostroeniya Rossii,'" Moscow, 2003. See also EIU, *Country Profile, Russia*, p. 29.)

42. *Kommersant*, Sept. 7, 2002; ASMR, "Itogi raboty..."

43. K. Palyshin, "Za kitaskoi stenoi," *Izvestiya*, May 16, 2003. One of the main foreign- investment projects is GM's joint-venture with VAZ to produce 35,000 Nivas, a VAZ-designed jeep, annually. GM invested ninety-nine million U.S.$, and the EBRD loaned 100 million. ("Largest Joint Venture in Auto—Chevrolet Nivas," Associated Press, Sept. 24, 2002.) In 2003 GM and VAZ announced plans to build 25,000 Opel Astras at the VAZ plant. The other major foreign investment, 450 million U.S.$, is a Ford plant in Vsevolsk near St. Petersburg, with a potential annual capacity for 25,000 Ford Focuses, though it presently produces much less. Finally, a small number of BMWs are being assembled in the Russian enclave of Kaliningrad. (*The St. Petersburg Times*, Oct. 31, 2003) Foreign direct investment in the Russian economy as a whole has been growing over the past few years. However, China received more foreign direct investment in 2002 than Russia did during the whole previous decade. (*The Financial Times*, Feb. 18, 2002.)

44. V. Golovachev, "Rossiikie den'gi vokrug sveta," *Trud*, Sept. 13, 2002. See also S. Menshikov, "Big Business Wants Reform but Starts at the Wrong End," *Moscow Tribune*, Feb. 13, 2002.

45. Stiglitz, *Globalization*, p. 156. While Stiglitz concludes that "shock therapy" failed in most of the transition countries, an IMF study published in 2000 found that "the radical reforms were, on the whole, effective. The benefits of a successful transition are now evident." (S. Fischet and R. Sahayam, "Un bilan nuancé," *Finances et développement*, Washington: IMF, vol. 37, Sept. 2000, p. 6.) It is thus difficult to avoid the conclusion that the reformers' plan was to restructure the economy through the destruction of a large part, if not most, of existing industry. (See S. Clarke et al., *New Forms of Employment and Household Survival Strategies in Russia*, ISITO/CCLS, Coventry and Moscow, 1999, p. 17, and R. Medvedev, *Kapitalizm v Rossii*, Prava Cheloveka, Moscow, 1998, pp. 15-17.) Klebnikov quotes the words of Yasin from 1993, when he was a senior minister in Yeltsin's government: "The Japanese and Germans had it easier [after World War II] because their industry was simply destroyed; there was an occupation government, and much had already been done to clear the ground and start anew. Russia, unfortunately [!] is not in that situation."(P. Klebnikov, *Godfather of the Kremlin*, p. 103. A study of the recent economic collapse of Argentina, another star pupil of the IMF, similarly concluded that the destruction was deliberate and the consequences known ahead of time. (F. Chesnais et J.-F. Dives, *Le peuple argentin se soulève*, Paris: Nautilus, 2002, ch. 4.)

46. As Stiglitz put it:

Why spend energy to create wealth when it so much easier to steal it? Privatization typically turned over large national enterprises to the old managers. These insiders knew how uncertain and difficult the road ahead was. Even if they were predisposed to, they dared not wait for the creation of a capital market and a host of other changes that would be needed for them to reap the full value of any investments and restructuring. They focussed on what they could get out of firm in next few years, and all too often, this was maximized by stripping assets. (*Globalization*, p. 158.)

47. Klebnikov, *Godfather*, pp. 88-102; Sapir, *Le krach russe*, 79.
48. Klebnikov, *The Godfather*, p. 93.
49. *Volzhskii avtostroitel'* (Togliatti), Apr. 26, 2003; "Ne vse v poryadke v nashem gosudarstve," *Tolyattinskoe obozrenie* (Togliatti), Apr. 30, 2003, p. 6.
50. As one banker put it, "Factories that are worth millions today were snapped up for as little as $60,000." ("Picking Up and Passing On the Pieces of Russia's Privatization," *The St. Petersburg Times*, Nov. 26, 2002.)
51. B. Boone and D. Rodionov, "Reformed Rent-Seekers Promoting Reform?" *The Moscow Times*, Aug. 23, 2002; S. Tavernise, "Handful of Corporate Raiders Transform Russia's Economy", *The New York Times*, Aug. 13, 2002.
52. EIU, *Country Profile, Russia*, Aug. 2003, p. 27.
53. *Golos profsoyuza*, nos. 3-4, Mar.-Apr., 2002. For a list of owners and their holding in ASM as of May 2003, see M. Rozhkova and S. Tselibeev, "GAZ razocharoval," *Vedomosti*, May 29, 2003.
54. V. Lavrentieva, "Whatever Happened To Those Vouchers?" *The Moscow Times*, Aug. 15, 2002.
55. S. Tavernise, "Lubricating the Rust Belt", *The Moscow Times*, July 25, 2002. pp. 12-13; L. Kaftan, "Ya tebya porodil, ya tebya i pristroyu," *Komsomol'skaya pravda Belarusi* (Minsk), June 6-13, 2003.
56. A. Hurst, "Russian Companies Lead Surge in Investment" Reuters, Sept. 4, 2002.
57. Y. Latyinina, "Flight Capital and Doubling Russia's GDP," *The Moscow Times*, Oct.15, 2003; Rozhkova and Tselibeev, "Gaz razocharoval."
58. *Golos profsoyuza*, nos. 8-9, Sept.-Oct. 2001.
59. Personal communication from A. Smirnov (Yaroslavl ASMR regional president).
60. ASMR, "Ob itogakh kollektivno-dogovornoi kampanii 2002-go goda," May 2002 (unpublished).
61. Goskomstat, *Rossiiskii...2001*, pp. 125 and 629; EIU, *Country Profile, Russia*, p. 16; K. O'Flynn, "The View from Moscow: The Rich Get Richer While the Poor Die Young," *The Guardian* (UK), Oct. 17, 2003; A. Dunsfield, "Life Expectancy at Historic High," *The Globe and Mail* (Canada), Sept. 25, 2003.
62. Goskomstat, *Rossiiskii...2001*, p. 81.
63. *The Guardian*, Sept. 24, 2003.
64. M. Feshbach, "A Comment on Recent Demographic Issues and a Forbidding Forecast," *Johnson's Russia List*, Aug. 11, 1999. (www.cdi.org/Russia/Johnson.) See also. M. Feshbach, "A Sick and Shrinking Nation", *The Washington Post*, October 24, 1999. p. B7. At that time, he forecast a probable population decline of forty-five percent by mid century. By comparison, the U.S. population would grow by forty-five per cent in the same period.

65. S. Rosefielde, "Premature Deaths: Russia's Radical Economic Transition in Soviet Perspective," *Europe-Asia Studies*, vol. 53, no. 8, 2001, p. 1163. See also V. Kantorovich, "The Russian Health Crisis and the Economy," *Communist and Post-Communist Studies*, no. 34, 2001, pp. 221-240.

66. Stiglitz, *Globalization*, p. 153.

67. "Number of Street Children in Russia Gets Close to 3 million," *RIA Novosti*, Feb. 19, 2002. Others put the figure closer to five million. See T. Shakhverdiev, "Vokzal'naya Rossiya," *Izvestiya*, May 5, 2002.

68. Stiglitz, *Globalization*, pp 153-54. According to Academician Dm. L'vov, the share of wages in the Russian GDP is two times lower than in developed countries: 31.5 per cent as compared to 69-72 per cent. ("Russia Produces Three Times More for One Dollar of Wages than an American Does," RIA Novosti, Dec. 16, 2002.)

69. "Russia on the Edge of Social and Economic Crisis," *Pravda.ru*, Oct. 24, 2003.

70. Goskomstat, *Rossiya v tsifrakh 2003*, p. 97, "Osnovnye ekonomicheskie pokazateli," Aug. 2002, www.gks.ru.

71. ASMR, "Spravochnye materialy k soobshcheniyu…" p. 17.

72. M. Grigorev, "Uroven' zhizni—zatyagivaem poyasa," *Profsoyuzy i ekonomika*, no. 4, June 2003, p. 4.

73. Goskomstat, *Rossiiskii…2001*, p. 196-97; "Uroven' zhizni naseleniya," www.gks.ru, July, 2002.

74. *Golos profsoyuza*, no. 6, Sept. 2003.

75. Ministry of Economic Development and Trade, "Prognosis for the Correlation of Minimum Wage and Subsistence Minimum," 2002 (unpublished). Article 133 of the new Labour Code of February 1, 2002 requires that the minimum wage be not less than the subsistence minimum. But article 421 states that a separate federal law will determine when and how equalization will occur. (*Trudovoi kodeks rossiiskoi federatsii*, Moscow: Trud i pravo, 2002, pp. 113, 186.) Putin, however, made clear that the government alone would decide when the budget could afford it. (Ashwin and Clarke, *Russian Trade Unions*, p. 113.)

76. ASMR, "Report to the Eleventh Central Committee," Apr. 15, 1999 (unpublished); "Ob itogakh…2002."

77. Goskomstat, *Rossiiskii…2001*, p. 134; EIU, *Country Report, Russia*, Aug. 2003, p. 8.

78. Goskomstat, *Rossiskii…2001*, p. 134.

79. *Solidarnost'*, no. 15, April 1999, insert p. 2. Similarly, a study by the Institute of Macroeconomic Research of the Russian Ministry of Economics found that, besides the 12.4 per cent officially unemployed in the second half of 1999, another 5.8 per cent were involuntarily working part-time, and 5.9 per cent were on involuntary unpaid layoff. (E. Shindyashkina, "Russians Prefer Moonlighting," *Ekonomika i zhizn'*, no. 50, 2000. See also S. Rosefielde, "Premature Deaths…," p. 1163.)

80. F. Weir, "The Kremlin Takes on Workers," *Christian Science Monitor*, Dec. 21, 2000.

81. M. Shmakov, *Profsoyuzy Rossii na poroge XXI-ogo veka*, Moscow,1999, p. 30.

82. *Izvestiya*, May 5, 1997 and Mar. 3, 2002; *Nezavisimaya gazeta*, Nov. 1, 2000 and Dec. 12, 2000, p. 2; EIU, *Country Profile, Russia*, 2003, p. 18.

83. EIU, *Country Profile, Russia*, 2003, p. 17.

84. Not only was hyperinflation a foreseen consequence of the way prices were freed in 1992, but it was in fact the prices that were still controlled by the state that were the major driving force of hyperinflation. As an analyst of similar reforms in Ukraine concluded that it "was a well-thought-out confiscation."(H. Van Zon, *The Political Economy of Independent Ukraine*, N.Y.: St. Martin's Press, 2000, p. 52.) Additional confiscations were to follow, including the currency collapses in 1995 and 1998 and the reform of housing and municipal services under Putin.

85. Goskomstat, *Rossiiskii...2001*, p. 133.

86. "Rossiya pogruzhaetsya v tryasinu massovoi bezrabotitsy," *Profsoyuzy*, nos. 11-12, 1998, p.15; *Solidarnost'* insert, no. 15, Apr. 1999, p.5.

87. Goskomstat, *Rossiiskii...2001*, pp. 196-97; Goskomstat, *Rossiya 2002*, Moscow, 2003, p. 11; EIU, *Country Profile, Russia*, 2003, p. 16; E. Vykholeva, "Polzkom iz teni," *Izvestiya*, June 9, 2003, p. 7.The statement was made by A. Zimin at a seminar for workers in May 1999.

88. Grigorev, "Uroven' zhizni..." p. 7.

89. K.D.Krylov, *Zakonodatel'stvo Rossii o professional'nykh profsoyuzakh*, Moscow: Profizdat, 1996, pp. 119-120, 133-7, 249, 258-60. For a detailed discussion of Soviet and Russian labour legislation, see Ashwin and Clarke, *Russian Trade Unions...*, ch. 5.

90. Articles 8, 66, 81, 82, 112, 131, 142, 157,192, 193, 374, 410. V. Pavlenko, ed., *Trudovoi kodeks Rossiiskoi federatsii*, Moscow: Trudi pravo, 2002, pp. 9, 43-46, 58, 76, 71-72, 89-90, 166, 175-81.) In April 2002, locomotive drivers in Moscow struck for about ten hours late at night and in the early morning hours before management could obtain a ruling. This was enough time to seriously disrupt suburban train movement. (*Izvestiya*, Apr. 20, 2002)

91. See, for example, *Sovetskaya Rossiya*, Feb. 1, 2000.

92. Personal communication by P. Zolotarev, president of Edinstvo, May 2002.

93. Goskomstat, *Rossiiskii...2001*, pp. 154-65.

94. "It Is Dangerous to Work in Russia," *Pravda.ru*, Feb. 20, 2002;. Goskomstat, *Rossiya v tskfrakh 2002*, Moscow, 2002, p. 92.

95. B. Maksimov, "Gegemon, gde on?" in D. Mandel and G. Rakitskaya, eds., *Govoryat rabochie Kirovskogo zavoda*, Mosocow: IPPS, 1998, p. 31.

96. Goskomstat, *Rossisskii...2001*, p.141.

97. *Golos profosyuza*, Mar.-Apr., 2002.

98. Many enterprises in the new private sector pay a straight guaranteed wage. But it has two parts: one is reported (this can be as little as a quarter of the take-home wage); the other (black cash, *chernyi nal*) is not. Taxes are paid only on the reported part, also the basis for calculating sick pay, vacation pay, and other benefits. As a result, although wages are often higher in this sector, benefits are much smaller and overtime is not compensated.

99. The stub also indicated sums withheld, including the mid-month "advance," income taxes, pension fund contributions, union dues, insurance payments, direct payment for the cafeteria and rent—a total of 1762.60 rubles.

100. S. Trokhin, "Kogda nachinaetsya ponedel'nik," *Al'ternativy*, no. 3, 1999, p. 43.

101. Edinstvo bulletin of Feb. 21, 2002.

102. *Profsoyuzy i eknomika*, no. 7, 2001, p. 9.

103. A. Uzelac, "Demographers' Conference Confirms Putin's Warnings," *The St. Petersburg Times*, July 14, 2000.

104. They have been unable to find one in Russia's pre-revolutionary past, since the regime and ruling class were so reactionary.

Chapter Three
THE UNION OF AUTO AND FARM-MACHINE WORKERS OF RUSSIA
From "Transmission Belt"[1] To "Social Partner"

One can legitimately argue about whether any union, regardless of its strategy, could have achieved much success under the very harsh and complex conditions of post-Soviet Russia. However, if one asks to what extent the major union in the ASM sector—or, for that matter, in any sector—actually tried to defend its members, the answer can be more conclusive: it did not even attempt to mobilize the better part of the resources at its disposal.

This chapter analyses the predominant response in the Union of Auto and Farm-Machine Workers of Russia (ASMR) to the situation after the collapse of the Soviet system and the launching of "shock therapy." The response was to exchange subservience to management and to the state in the name of "socialism" for subservience to management and to the state in the name of "social partnership." That was also the prevalent response, despite important differences to be examined, in Ukraine and Belarus. The following analysis, therefore, can serve also for the other two countries and need not be repeated in any detail in considering their cases. In all three countries there were, of course, deviations from the norm that took various forms. They will be the subject of subsequent chapters.

The Union of Auto and Farm-Machine Workers of Russia

ASMR was founded in December 1991 by the local (enterprise-based) unions of Russia's ASM sector and by their regional associations. Until that time, Russia had not had its own national union. All the local and regional organizations of the sector in the various Soviet republics had been directly affiliated to the All-Union (that is, Soviet) Trade-Union of Auto and Farm-Machine Workers. The latter ceased to exist in 1991.

ASMR is affiliated with the Federation of Independent Trade Union of Russia (FNPR),[2] which at its last congress in November 2001 claimed thirty-five million members and fifty-four per cent of the wage and salaried work force (down from fifty-four million and seventy per cent at the time of its founding in 1990).[3] The FNPR in 2001 had forty-eight affiliated (or contracting) sectoral unions (these previously corresponded to Soviet branch ministries) and seventy-eight regional union councils (in essence, federations of sectoral unions at the regional level).

ASMR is by far the largest union in the auto and farm-machinery sector. At the beginning of 2003, it counted 621,000 employed members, a little more than a third of its membership at founding, who belonged to 491 local organizations. Between the enterprise and national levels of the union stood twenty-six regional committees.[4] The supreme union authority within the enterprise is the delegates' conference. It elects the plant president and committee, who are the local executive. Enterprises are divided into shops (sometimes also larger departments), whose delegates' conferences (sometimes general assemblies) elect shop chairpersons and shop committees. Below these, there are sometimes union groups, which elect group leaders. There were once strict norms governing the number of full-time officials (in the shops—one for every thousand workers), but today it depends mainly on the financial situation of the organization. When it was first established, ASMR was dominated by a handful of plants employing close to, sometimes even more than, a 100,000 persons each. By 2002, only two of these colossuses were left: VAZ in Togliatti (124,000 employees in 2003) and GAZ in Nizhnyi Novgorod (69,000 employees). Together they accounted for a third of the membership. But most of the other members were still working in factories that by Western standards are large, each employing several thousand people.

At the start of 2003, ASMR claimed that its membership represented eight-four per cent of the sector's work force. Less than three per cent belonged to alternative unions, that is unions that were not inherited from the Soviet era nor affiliated with the FNPR. The remainder of the work force did not belong to a union.

With the fall of the Communist regime, the ideology and forms of "social partnership" were vigorously promoted by international organizations, such as the ILO, and they were officially embraced by the Russian government, which also proclaimed Russia a "social state." The new Labour Code even contains a section entitled "Social Partnership in the Sphere of Labour." FNPR-affiliated unions, on their part, took up "social partnership" with enthusiasm, since it corresponded to their own conservative inclinations, while allowing to mask them in phraseology appropriate to capitalism. The term "social partnership" might seem innocuous enough (rather like "globalization," in another context). No serious trade-unionist would object to a good working relationship with the employer and with the state that is formalized in negotiated agreements. However, it comes with heavy ideological baggage, in particular the assumption that the three parties—workers, employers and the state—share fundamental interests that permit the reconciliation of their differences to the common benefit of all. Not all FNPR-affiliated unions subscribe to that vision. But those that do not are very exceptional and isolated and so have little room for manoeuver

"Partnership" in the Enterprise

At the local level, the claimed common interest is to strengthen the economic health of the enterprise, as measured by profits, or to defend its very existence in the depressed economic conditions. When asked in 1996 if he saw any progressive change in the union's work over the past year, a shop chairperson at GAZ replied that the term "progressive" cannot be applied to unions:

> Some might want to see the union on one side and the administration on the other. Is that what "progressive" and "modern" are supposed to mean? Thank God, that isn't the case at our plant. We live together as a single family; we all depend on each other. Simply put, the plant is doing well, and that means that its union organization is also doing well, that it can send more people on subsidized vacations, give those in need financial support, etc…We're all in it together, a collective, and that includes the administration, the union leaders and the rank-and-file workers.[5]

Unions that hold this view do not see themselves as being about power, about increasing the power of their members and restricting that of management. For example, the authors of an American study on privatization, economists who cannot be suspected of pro-labour sympathies, were genuinely surprised to find that Russian unions made no attempt to concentrate the stock that their members received in the course of privatization—often a potentially controlling share—in order to prevent management from pillaging the factories and destroying their jobs.

> Theoretically, groups of workers and their trade unions could have meaningful independent power on these company boards. [This was written before workers had massively sold off their shares.] As large blockholders in their own right, they could nominate their own candi-

dates and use cumulative voting to elect them...Yet we have not recorded one case in which they did so. This finding reflects the fact that Russian trade unions are heavily dominated by management; they cannot be viewed as independent organizations. In what traditional free market economy could workers in most large factories belong to trade unions, own the majority of their companies' shares, yet never elect an independent representative to the board of directors?[6]

Union leaders, in fact, see their role as aides to the administration in managing the labour force. The underlying idea, to the extent there is one, is that if unions are useful to management, the latter will reciprocate by paying attention to workers' needs. Confrontation with management is studiously avoided, even over such fundamental issues as the arbitrary features of the wage system, low wages or the failure even to pay them, the failure to transfer checked-off dues to the union, extended work hours, layoffs, frigid temperatures and unsafe conditions in the shops, widespread corruption. While the unions may intervene as advocates for workers on some of these matters, they almost never think to mobilize them to apply pressure on management. And they quickly retreat in the face of a negative response from management.

But the unions rarely use even the available means available to them that do not require mobilization of their members. Few made serious use of the potentially powerful labour disputes committees to defend their members in individual grievances when these bodies were still elected by the delegates' conferences (under the old Labour Code). At VAZ, the leadership of the body-assembly department even removed the chairperson of the labour disputes committee, a member of the union committee, when management complained the committee was finding too regularly in the workers' favour. Similarly, few unions took legal action against management over unpaid wages and dues not transferred, even when the chances of success were relatively good. A. Smirnov, president of the Yaroslavl regional committee of ASMR, explained in May 2000:

> Management isn't transferring dues to the unions, and large debts have accumulated. It's a serious problem. There are some cases where the union has sued. But as a rule, that rarely happens, since experience shows that it doesn't pay to strain relations with management. I know that's not the way Canadian auto workers would see things, but that's how we are—we "show understanding" (*vkhodim v polozhenie*—literally, we enter the situation [of management]).

In a not untypical display of "understanding," the union conference at the Pavlov Bus Factory in 1998 gave a positive grade to management for its application of the collective agreement, even though it owed several months of wages to the workers and was not transferring dues to the union. "Objective circumstances" were cited.[7] At VAZ, the union even adopted a collective agreement in 1994 that permitted management to delay payment of wages, a clear violation of the labour code.

"Showing understanding" can easily shift from refusal to apply pressure to management to supporting management in applying pressure to the workers to accept concession demands. At VAZ, the union actively collaborated with the administration in twisting arms to make sure conference delegates voted for management's demand to abandon full wage indexation. The union's president himself brandished the spectre of layoffs before the members if they insisted on maintaining full indexation. (See chapter 5.) The union's role in squeezing this concession out of the workers prompted a delegate to the March 2001 delegates' conference, a worker in the body-assembly department who had apparently been coached by dissidents, to make the following tongue-in-cheek appeal to the plant's general director: "Aleksei Vasil'evich, my insistent request to you is not to support the union in lowering our living standards. Bring back monthly indexation. We place our hope in you. The proposal of the body-assembly department is one-hundred-per-cent indexation." The hall burst into laughter.[8]

But the situation at VAZ at that time was really better than in most ASM plants, where collective agreements often contained no binding language on indexation or even on raising the lowest wage level to the subsistence minimum—the phrase "if the means are available" was often tacked on at the end of the relevant paragraphs—thus giving management a virtually free hand in setting wages.[9] The section in collective agreements on wages often contains no specific language about the wage system, the level of wages and the various supplements, the form of indexation, the schedule for the payment of wages, etc. Instead, there is a vague statement to the effect that these matters are regulated by instructions decided by management with the plant committee's agreement. Yu. Novikov, ASMR's national President until May 2003, made the following comment on this practice: "It turns out that the collective agreement presented to the conference looks a lot like a pig in a poke, and people have to guess even about the level of their wages."[10]

Similarly, despite the announced economic recovery and widespread dissatisfaction among ASM workers with their wages, which are well below the average in manufacturing, ASMR unions have not mobilized to press for increases. Instead, they have tacitly or even overtly given their support to the policy of "letting the workers earn," that is to speed-up, extended shifts, overtime, and working Saturdays. Asked in June 2000 if there were any conflicts related to the level of wages, Novikov replied: "Wages are rising everywhere anyway. And in any case, what's the point of demanding higher wages if they lead to delays in payment?" Similarly, a union leader at a St. Petersburg tractor factory explained: "We meet each week with the assistant financial director and the head of the planning bureau. We ask: 'Is there any possibility of indexing wages, of raising them?' The need for pressure doesn't arise. If the possibility exists, management itself does it [raises wages]."[11]

In early 2002 at the GPZ-I ball-bearing factory in Moscow, the delegates' conference was presented for ratification a collective agreement that had been worked out by a management-union negotiating committee. (In cases were issues remain in dispute after negotiations have concluded, both positions are presented to the conference. If the conference supports the union and management still refuses to concede, the contested issues can become the object of a formal, collective labour dispute which, at least in theory, can lead to a legal strike.) However, one delegate, apparently a member of a small alternative union, complained that wages were too low, and a majority of the delegates supported him. When management still refused to raise wages, the union initiated a collective labour dispute. Asked why the union's negotiators had not demanded higher wages at the bargaining table, since they were well aware of the workers' dissatisfaction, ASMR's national Vice President, A. Fefelov, (who succeeded Novikov in May 2003) explained: "Things happened in the best way. Now the union committee can say to management: 'Look, we showed understanding, but you can see the pressure from below'." To the suggestion that the union's support among the membership would have been strengthened if the demand had originated from the leadership, he replied: "What would be gained by that? This way, the union maintains good relations with management, and the two sides negotiate a resolution to the difference."

The unions like to refer to themselves as "buffers," that is, they manage worker discontent for the administration. Remarking in 1998 on the "much calmer socio-psychological situation" at GAZ as compared to other plants in the sector, the union's vice president attributed that to his union, which acts as "a particular kind of buffer between management and the work collective."[12] In an interview to a union journal, the president of the ZIL truck factory was effusive in his praise for the "patience and understanding" of his members, who had not been paid wages for many months.[13] At another plant, a shop supervisor offered this comment about the qualities of a recently-elected shop chairperson: "I think I have acquired a sensible (*tolkovyi*) helper in him." And the chairperson, in turn, praised the members: "They understand that the shop has to work and not permit stoppages. For their understanding, I give a deep bow to the collective. Our people are outstanding, and their patience knows no end."[14] The economist in ASMR's national office explained why it would be preferable to have the main negotiations at the national and regional levels, rather than in the plant, as is current practice: "The local leaders would then be able to say to the director: 'Look, I'm under pressure from my regional and central committees'." Asked if local unions could mobilize their members to apply pressure "from below" too, he replied: "Then the director would say: 'You're not doing your job'."

The concern to avoid "straining relations" with management weighs heavily upon union leaders. In a striking case, a local leader even acquiesced to management's fixing elections and depriving him of the union post he coveted. The president of this tractor factory had resigned and he was temporarily replaced by his vice president, the leader in question. The latter decided to run for president. But the director had other ideas. For reasons of his own, he wanted to give the job to one of his assistant directors. When the acting president refused to withdraw his candidacy, the director set in motion what Russians call "the administrative resource." At the delegates' conference, the official tally was "fifty per cent plus one" for the director's candidate. Of course, no one was fooled, but since the offended party himself raised no objections, none of his supporters complained either. He later explained his silence: "Of course, I knew what was going on. They worked me over like a dog for three full days: 'Don't go for the job! We'll find you something else.' But there was a danger here of a scene (*skandal*), a division and in general of creating conflictual relations. It would have been impossible to work afterwards. I still consider that maintaining partnership relations with management is the most valuable thing. More can be achieved through them."[15]

After the collapse of the Soviet system, unions moved away from their traditional role of supporting the enterprise's production plans. But it was not long before they were again busy organizing "labour competition" (formerly "socialist competition"). Already in 1996, the union at GAZ was involved in evaluating productivity and quality in the departments and shops each month and handing out bonuses, pennants and honorary certificates to the winners. At the Volgograd Tractor Factory, the union tallies up production results daily, analyzes them, and posts the names of the best workers in a prominent place. At a bus factory outside of Moscow, a joint management-union commission visits the shops and allocates bonuses according to its findings.[16] When the director of the now defunct Moskvich auto plant fired an assembler and his section supervisor in 1999 because a loose part was found in the steering column of a racing car, he addressed an order simultaneously to the quality-control director, the supervisor of the parts-assembly department, *as well as* to the president of the union to organize meetings with workers about poor workmanship that undermines the plant's reputation.[17] As the vice-president of VAZ told a group of Byelorussian trade-unionists, "each worker has to be conscious that he is responsible for quality and so for sales."[18] In interviews, union leaders typically go on at great length about the enterprise's financial situation, its marketing and production problems, but they have relatively few words for specifically union matters. A series of articles by local ASM presidents in a recent issue of *Profsoyuzy i ekonomika*, an FNPR publication, were mostly about what the directors had done for the enterprise and the union.[19]

Union activity in support of production goals received formal approval at ASM's Second Congress in 1995, after which the national leadership itself began awarding honorary certificates for "excellent labour performance."[20] Novikov explained: "Competition today is totally different [from Soviet times]. There is no formalism."[21] The president of the union at the Pavlov Bus Factory was expressing a commonly held view when he said that "The main task of the administration and of the union committee is to mobilize the work collective to raise efficiency and obtain the needed profit." Some unions have also become involved in job training. Novikov explained that "Many plants…have stopped training machine operators…Production is recovering, but there is a shortage of skilled workers. So the union, to defend workers' interests, has to take up this very same production task and prepare worker cadres for the mass professions." At a union conference devoted to this problem in St. Petersburg in 2002, a labour sociologist asked whether unions should be trying to resolve the shortage rather than discussing how to exploit it in order to win higher wages for the workers. For this question, he was practically shown the door, and the president of a large plant which he had been studying threatened to revoke his pass.[22]

Sometimes unions go even farther in filling in for an inactive administration. For example, ASMR has been lobbying the government for several years to reduce the level of payments ASM enterprises are required to make to the government fund that compensates workers for accidents and occupational illnesses, since it considers the level unjustifiably high. "We are often asked," Novikov told the February 2002 Central Committee, 'Why are unions involved in this, when the employers themselves are inactive?' A good question."[23] The point is not that involvement in job training or in lobbying on behalf of the industry is necessarily harmful to the union. It is rather the union's failure to maintain a separate identity from management, its unquestioning identification with management's goals when it takes up these activities, and its diversion of limited resources and energy from the direct defence of workers' wages and working conditions.

Another area of union activity that harkens back to Soviet times is the administration of social benefits and the organization of leisure activities. The scope and level of these activities have been reduced because government and enterprise funds for them have shrunk and because the unions no longer administer the social security fund. Nevertheless, they still consume a lot of energy and time. More than half of local union budgets (the local unions hold onto up to eight-five per cent of the dues they collect) are typically spent on "material aid," that is handouts to workers who are in particular need, and on social, cultural and sports activities. (The other major budget item—thirty-five percent of the dues—is the salaries of union officials and employees). Unions are still involved in the allocation of vacation vouchers, in organizing summer camps for children and various celebrations and cultural events, in the provision of free legal counsel on non-union-related matters. It is this sort of activity and the unions' role in saving at least part of the "social sphere" (palaces of culture, libraries, kindergartens, clinics, etc.) from liquidation that are most frequently cited by leaders as their major accomplishments.[24]

The continued attraction of these activities for union leaders is explained by their role in maintaining membership support for the union while not requiring conflict with management that might "strain relations." Management, on its part, welcomes this work, since it helps to alleviate worker discontent with low wages and cultivates attachment to the enterprise. A good example is a recent decision of ASMR to promote the establishment mutual-aid funds at the plant level. In presenting this to the Presidium (executive) in early 2002, P. Kuznetsova, the national Vice-President, explained:

> It wasn't so long ago that every union committee had its mutual aid fund. Can we really say that the need for them no longer exists?...As we know, the wages of the majority of our sector's workers are small, and the need for a certain sum of money can arise suddenly and insistently. Where can a worker obtain it? It's not easy to get if from a bank, and the union committee can offer only very limited material support. And that's why mutual aid funds are the best answer.[25]

In other circumstances, this initiative would be innocuous, even laudable. But the establishment of these funds has not replaced the union practice of devoting a large part of dues to handouts. The initiative is even more questionable in light of the union's failure to press seriously for higher wages. In his report to the February 2002 Central Committee, Novikov explained:

> In preparing the draft sectoral agreement we made great efforts to obtain at least a gradual closing of the gap between the basic wage at the lowest skill level and the subsistence minimum. But our efforts failed. As

you know, the FNPR also failed to obtain that in the General Agreement, even though the government had previously promised it. As a result, the agreement was signed with the outstanding differences remaining.[26]

In actual fact, the "great efforts" made by the union were limited to negotiating and lobbying the government. As Novikov rather enigmatically explained elsewhere, "Our fundamental arm of struggle remains negotiations, negotiations, negotiations."[27] In this instance, no pressure, aside from moral, was exerted. And no union action followed the employers' and government's rejection of the union's position. The same thing occurs on the enterprise level, as Novikov himself lamented at the May 2003 Central Committee:

> Another problem is the active refusal of many employers to include in the collective agreements benefits and rights whose level goes beyond that set by the government. In that case, the collective agreement itself loses all significance, since it becomes a formality that has no impact on anything. And the plant committee, when it negotiates with the employer in these circumstances, is generally at a loss, since it does not feel any real support [from the higher levels of the union] and so is forced to accept compromises.[28]

In the fall of 2003, the president of the Kamaz truck factory stated that "we consider our current collective agreement as the most successful [so far], inasmuch as it fully corresponds to the Labour Code."[29]

Although leaders often decry the ineffectiveness of their unions in defending the members, the concept of "correlation of forces" is alien to their way of thinking. Conflict has no legitimate place in their view of union-management relations, which should be based upon "social partnership." When it does happen, conflict is viewed as unfortunate, abnormal, to be quickly forgotten. ASMR is obviously not the kind of union that promotes a "culture of resistance." It makes no effort to disseminate the experience of struggles within the union, even those that have led to improvements for workers. It does not honour or hold up for emulation militant leaders who have led their members to real gains. Pressure tactics based upon rank-and-file mobilization, such as strikes, work-to-rule, road and rail blockades, demonstrations, are in practice viewed with distaste and considered counterproductive, though lip service is paid to the need to keep them in reserve. Even recourse to the courts is limited by the concern not to "strain relations" with management. An issue of *Profsoyuzy i ekonomika* dedicated to the tenth anniversary of ASMR's founding and written mostly by local union leaders did not mention a single strike, even though ASMR had seen a number of long and very stubborn strikes at the enterprise level over the previous decade.[30] In the eighty pages of the issue, there is only brief mention of two conflicts, both successful lawsuits, one that forced management regularly to pay wages and the other that made it hand over union dues that it had been withholding.[31]

"We discussed the issue of collective actions at our November plenum last year," Novikov told an interviewer in 2001, and "we concluded that we are not ready for strikes today because we don't have strike funds and because that sort of action hits the workers hard in the pocketbook. And the enterprise also suffers substantially."[32] He repeated this view at the May 2003 Central Committee, noting also that only two local unions had carried out the resolution on establishing strike funds adopted the previous year.[33] (This, of course, begs the question as to why strike funds should be created locally—a rather unrealistic policy—rather than nationally.) Strikes might not make be effective when plants are threatened with closure, but VAZ's leaders take the same position as Novikov, even though they have a "solidarity fund" (routinely used for purposes other than collective actions) and the plant has generally been working close to capacity: "In contemporary conditions, strikes, as an extreme measure, are relegated to the background. Much more relevant today is not confrontation, but the seeking of compromises, points and spheres of mutual, convergent interests."[34] Where strikes have broken out spontaneously or have been organized by minority unions, ASMR leaders most often stand aside or collaborate with management to get the workers back to work.[35]

But leaving aside strikes and their problematic character in depression conditions, the fact is that unions very rarely resort to any kind of pressure. Moreover, even if the financial situation of the enterprise sets limits on demands, one can legitimately ask if anything justifies acquiescing to management's not paying wages or transferring dues. There is also no reason why financial difficulties should restrict demands that have no direct monetary impact on the enterprise but serve to strengthen the union. Such demands might be aimed at eliminating the most arbitrary aspects of the wage system, gaining access to information about enterprise finances, or the right to uncensored publication of union materials in the in-plant newspaper. Union leaders often argue that "strained relations" with management would make it hard to deal expeditiously with the myriad of problems workers bring to them relating to the "social sphere." One cited the need for emergency repairs on plumbing in a plant dormitory. He would not have been able to get quick action if he did not have good personal relations with the director. But the need to go begging to management for such things could be reduced by precise language in the collective agreement and genuine efforts to enforce it.

Even when it comes to demands that have financial consequences for the enterprise, one should distinguish between a union's legitimate concern for jobs and for the survival of the enterprise, on the one hand, and "showing understanding for management's situation," as it is usually practised, on the other. In the latter case, concessions are typically made on faith, the unions simply accepting management's definition of the situation. Nor do the unions demand guarantees that management will restore what was conceded once the crisis has passed and profitability has been restored. The most striking case of "showing understanding" was the predominant union reaction to non-payment of wages and the non-transfer of dues—in fact, no reaction at all, not even the demand to open the books. The unions acquiesced to what amounted to forced loans at negative interest rates and asked nothing in return.

The identification of the unions with management interests is underlined and reinforced by the continued presence of managerial personnel in the unions. This includes not only the lower and middle management but often also top management up to and including the general director. Managers can and do hold elected positions in the unions and they are delegates to union conferences, the highest decision-making organ on the enterprise level. From a strictly logical point of view, this does not jibe very well with "social partnership." As a VAZ worker quipped, "It turns out that management is negotiating with itself." A. Isaev, Vice-President and chief ideologue of the FNPR, was asked in 1996: "If employers and workers are in the same union, how can the union effectively take part in resolving conflicts in the enterprise?" Isaev replied that it really was an undesirable situation. However, one had to consider that Russia was a country in transition.

> In the first place, certain traditions exist. Secondly, there is no clearly defined stratum of entrepreneurs (employers) conscious of their interests. Many directors have worked for several decades in the enterprise and they remain in the union, considering themselves part of the work collective. It would be wrong to chase them out. New employers as a rule do not wish to join the union.[36]

But seven years later, with the economy thoroughly privatized and most of the old directors replaced by managers firmly under the control of new owners interested only in squeezing maximum profit out of the enterprise, there is no longer even any discussion within ASMR or the FNPR about excluding managers. In addition to Isaev's explanations, other justifications often voiced are: management would be insulted if they were excluded; it would provoke them to get rid of the "social sphere"; they are hired employees just like workers and they need union protection; they have high salaries, and the union needs their dues. But the hard fact is that the continued presence of management in the union subverts democracy and ensures management's control of the unions. As a result, the unions are anything but the self-organization of workers for the collective defence of their interests.

"Partnership" at the National Level

The economic crisis and the role of government policy in deepening and prolonging it mean that effective, durable solutions to the workers' most pressing problems cannot be found on the level of individual enterprises but must be sought in concerted action on the national and political levels. This makes the quality of the union's national leadership and its strategy of particular importance. But here, too, the union remains firmly wedded to "social partnership."

Indeed, in the opinion of ASMR's leaders, one of its biggest problems the union faces is the absence of a "strong partner," that is, an employers' association in which membership and discipline would be obligatory. The lead article of the union's paper in January 2002 appeared under the curious headline: "A Weak Social Partner Is a Strong Minus," and the following issue published the report by the national Vice-President under the heading: "I'd Like to Work With a Strong Union of Employers."[37] These titles express the union's wish for sectoral (*tarifnoe*) agreements signed by an employers' association that would enforce it in all the enterprises of the ASM sector.

ASMR's quixotic efforts, together with two other machine-building unions, to organize the employers are a good illustration of the wishful thinking that so often accompanies "social partnership": since the union was too weak itself to enforce a sectoral agreement, it decided to invest its time and energy into organizing the employers ("we fashioned ourselves a partner," explained ASMR's economist) in the hope that they would enforce the agreement on themselves.[38] In June 1997, the three machine-building unions organized a conference to which they invited union leaders and directors of the larger enterprises of their sectors. The official goal was to discuss measures for stopping and reversing the decline of machine building. But the unions also hoped to convince the directors to establish an employers' association at that conference. Speaker after speaker, from both the union and the directors' sides, subjected the government's economic policies to withering criticism. The conference adopted a list of proposals to be presented to the government for saving the sector. These, however, were specifically termed "proposals," not "demands." For one of the most striking aspects of the conference was the complete absence of discussion of means of pressure to persuade the government to change its economic course. Indeed, the word "struggle" was dropped from the original version of the resolution at the request of the employers. And the appeal issued by the conference asked workers "not to take matters to extreme methods of struggle, strikes and acts of civil disobedience, when resolving social-labour conflicts."[39]

Not surprisingly, the conference had no perceptible impact on government policy, as the sector pursued its decline unobstructed. On the other hand, the directors did meet at the end of the conference and decided to establish a Union of Employers of Machine-Building of Russia. However, the association has disappointed ASMR expectations: membership is not obligatory, and its constitution does not allow it to enforce discipline even on the directors who join. At the September 2001 Central Committee, Novikov had to conclude that "the sectoral agreement...is not a document that exerts real influence on the level of wages in the branch."[40] Nor is there any prospect that this will change in the foreseeable future, despite the increasing concentration of ownership. The reasoning behind the unions' efforts to organize the employers is the view that the latter have an interest in providing workers with decent wages and working conditions in order to make them more productive. Unfortunately, the employers have not seen the light.

Ironically, one of the problems blocking the efforts to make the sectoral agreement binding is "social partnership" itself, as practised by the enterprise unions. After all, the employers are only pursuing their interests in refusing to submit to the agreement. The real problem is that the enterprise unions are reluctant to exert any pressure on the employers to make them submit. Some even openly support the employers' refusal. The Central Committee's report on the collective agreements of 2002 states:

> To our deep regret, we still do not have a normally functioning mechanism of social partnership. The sectoral agreement negotiated jointly with other machine-building unions has no effect in a significantly large number of enterprises. The sectoral agreement officially does not apply to a quite large number of enterprises. Directors in a series of plants have officially informed the Ministry of Labour and Social Development of this [their refusal to apply the sectoral agreement]. Well, we can at least understand that directors would not want to take on extra obligations in sphere of social-labour relations. But it is totally incomprehensible that presidents of union committees should affix their signatures beside those of the directors to the letters informing the Ministry of Labour of their refusal to adhere to the sectoral agreement...We have here either a failure to understand the essence of social dialogue and collective-agreement relations or else total dependence of trade-union leaders on the will of economic managers.[41]

As the passage shows, ASMR's national leadership does sometimes exhort local unions to show some backbone, and it has done this somewhat more often in the past few years than previously. For example, it recently urged local unions to sue management for theft of union property when management fails to transfer dues and to demand that workers be paid at the rate required by the law for involuntary temporary layoffs.[42] But these are minor, dissonant notes in the prevailing vision of "partnership" at all levels of the union, that is, identification with, and promotion of, management goals, in return for which management, it is hoped, will take care of workers' needs. This is also, as will be shown below, the vision of the national leadership in its political action. Why then should things be any different on the enterprise level? The result is a rather strange situation where the national leaders call on the local organizations to press management to apply the sectoral agreement, while the local leaders demand the very same thing of their national counterparts. The president of the Elabug Auto Factory told the September 2003 Central Committee:

> I can't complain that our general director is ignoring the union committee or the social problems of the collective. But we adopted a sectoral agreement that was signed by solid people from the union, the employers and from the government. Yet all the same, my general director says: "I'm not in a position now to join the Union of Employers." How should we understand that? How can the employers ignore this matter, when the trade-union part of the collective [Note that the employer is also considered part of the collective] is fully behind the sectoral agreement. In this matter, it is no doubt the role not only of our Central Committee but also of the FNPR to transform social partnership from its present state as mere window-dressing into something real that could force the employers on the basis of the law to carry out what was adopted in the sectoral agreement.[43]

Magical thinking thus prevails at all levels, as the union carefully avoids the issue of developing effective means of pressure on employers and the government, pressure that in the end has to be based on a mobilized membership.

ASMR's political action has been strongly marked by its desire to close ranks with the employers. During the confrontation between Yeltsin and the Supreme Soviet in the fall of 1993, the union's national leadership opposed the FNPR's unconditional support for the Supreme Soviet and the Constitution. ASMR's national President, A. Surikov, helped to engineer removal of Klochkov as head of the FNPR, after which Surikov became vice-president to the FNPR's new leader, Shmakov. Since then,

ASMR has loyally followed the federation's political line.[44] For a brief period after Yeltsin's coup, the FNPR's leadership toyed with the idea of an independent, union-based labour party. But it soon abandoned it in favour of a "centrist" electoral alliance with the Union of Industrialists and Entrepreneurs, a lobby of industrial directors that supported a policy of government intervention along keynesian lines. This alliance was crushed in the Duma elections of December 1993. All the same, the FNPR renewed it for the December 1995 Duma elections under the rather curious name of Union of Labour (*Soyuz truda*). It too failed miserably, attracting only 1.6 per cent of the vote on the basis of party lists. (Other deputies are elected by geographical circumscription.) After this defeat, the directors' association left the Union of Labour.

At no point did the FNPR or ASMR undertake a serious analysis of these defeats. The wisdom of the labour-employer alliance was never called into question. For the December 1999 Duma elections, the FNPR again entered an alliance with "centrist" forces, this time the Fatherland-All Russia list headed by Moscow's Mayor Luzhkov, supposedly a friend of labour. In the run-up to the elections, the following question was put to the FNPR's Isaev: "Unions, as I understand it, are workers' organizations. Luzhkov is a representative of the recently-formed Russian bourgeoisie. What can these opposites have in common?" Isaev replied:

> If you insist on discussing this question in classic Marxist terms, let me remind you that...there are periods when the classics themselves said that workers should act in concert with representatives of the bourgeoisie...The essence of our present situation is that the labour movement and nationally-oriented capital have powerful common enemies, the financial-bureaucratic oligarchy that lives exclusively from the sale of resources and the forces in the West that want to transform Russia into a semi-colony for the extraction of raw materials. They [labour and the nationally-oriented bourgeoisie] also share a common goal: to restore the country's real economy, to raise popular living standards (without which the domestic market cannot develop), to defend the political and economic independence of Russia. These goals make possible a firm and, I believe, long-lasting union between the labour movement and the entrepreneurs engaged in the real economy of Russia.[45]

This electoral alliance, too, was soundly trounced.

ASMR, following the FNPR's lead, took a different position in the 1996 presidential elections: it refused to endorse any of the candidates, arguing that to do so would divide the membership. No one bothered to explain why the same reasoning did not apply to Duma elections. The fact is, however, that the electoral alliances for the parliamentary elections all involved loyal opposition to the President. And in any case, the Duma is only an arena for lobbying, with little power of its own. Presidential elections, on the other hand, are about real power, and in 1996 the unions did not dare come out against Yeltsin, especially after he had made it very clear that he would never give up power to a Communist, his main challenger. In the 2000 presidential elections, the union forgot its worry about not dividing the membership and endorsed mayor Luzhkov. (Yeltsin was not running, and Putin had only been acting President for a brief time and had not yet consolidated his power.) But after Luzhkov was eliminated from the running by a dirty media campaign, and it became obvious that Putin would win—one way or another. And so, ASMR followed the FNPR in endorsing Putin. So eager, in fact, was the FNPR to embrace Putin that it declared its support even before Putin had made known his programme.

Following Putin's victory, Fatherland (to which the FNPR was still affiliated through its political wing, the Union of Labour), merged with Unity (*Edinstvo*), the party recently created by Putin, to form United Russia (*Edinaya Rossiya*). The merger was greeted with exaltation by the FNPR's leadership.[46] This fusion, together with Putin's unprecedented appearance and address to the FNPR's congress in November 2001, put an end to a decade of wandering by the FNPR in the political desert.[47] It no longer had to be in the "loyal opposition." The government was welcoming it back into its strong embrace, where it clearly felt most comfortable. It is characteristic that ASMR's paper gave lengthy, front-page coverage to Putin's address, while it relegated Shmakov's report to the congress to a small inside section.[48] Asked what he thought of Putin's speech, Fefelov, at the time Vice-President of ASMR, opined: "There was one negative moment—when he referred to 'your trade unions,' as if he wanted to keep himself separate (*otdelyat'sya*) from the unions. Otherwise, it was okay."

As ever, Isaev was not at a loss to justify this latest move by the FNPR:

> The preconditions for the formation of a left-centre party in the near future are unfortunately lacking. And, therefore, we support the creation of United Russia, which is, in my view, neither left nor right, but an anti-crisis party. Its merit is to halt the disintegration of the country, to secure its modernization and development in correspondence with general world tendencies. For that, it will have to resolve both neo-liberal and socialist tasks simultaneously.[49]

The May Day demonstration of 2002 in Moscow was organized jointly by the FNPR and the United Russia party, a practice that has continued up to the present. What had never been much more than the pretense of extra-parliamentary opposition on the part of the FNPR had effectively come to an end. Over the previous decade, the federation had organized more-or-less semi-annual protests—demonstrations, marches, rallies and strikes (that is, where management agreed, the workers left work early to demonstrate)—to back demands addressed to the government. ASMR endorsed these actions but always left the decision as to whether or how to participate to the local affiliates. Some of these protests attracted very broad participation, millions of union members, according to FNPR accounts. But for the leadership, they were at most shows of force that was never meant seriously to be used. The official demands were left typically vague, on the order of "market wages for a market economy" and "for decent wages and social rights," and there was no serious follow-up after the government rejected them, as it inevitably did. The government, on its part, realized very quickly that the much-brandished specter of a "social explosion" need not be taken seriously. It tolerated the protests as a relatively harmless release of popular anger. At their high point in October 1998, when, among other things, workers were demanding Yeltsin's resignation, one could observe enterprise directors, mayors and governors, that is, people who would never openly oppose the President, marching side by side with union leaders at the head of the columns.[50] It was widely rumoured that Yeltsin himself expressed sympathy with the protesters. The FNPR forgot its demand for Yeltsin's resignation as soon as the demonstrations ended.

The federation's real attitude to these extra-parliamentary actions was expressed with surprising candor in an editorial that appeared in its paper, *Solidarnost'*, on the eve of the November 1996 protest. It was entitled "An Open Letter to Our Evil-Wishers" and began by admitting that the protests had become ritualized and resulted only in empty promises on the part of the government. But it continued:

> Let's admit that we, union activists, are very naive, that the hopes we pin on the conscience (or at least on the common sense!) of those who in power are illusory…But at least the unions are trying to fulfill *their* duty: to stop the very chaotic growth of protest, to prevent a "senseless and merciless revolt," to save the very fragile social peace in our half-ruined country.[51]

The reference to a "senseless and merciless revolt" is from a story by the Russian poet A.S. Pushkin (the phrase is often erroneously attributed to the author himself) that is set in the eighteenth-century during the peasant revolt led by Emeleyan Pugachev. To put the editorial in proper context, it should be recalled that at the time of its publication millions of impoverished Russian workers were going without wages, sometimes for many months.

Why "Social Partnership"?

ASMR leaders readily admit the failure of "social partnership." A Central Committee report noted in 2003 that:

> The results of the collective-agreement work of the unions at all levels attests to the fact that they far from always succeed in obtaining socio-economic results that could satisfy the majority of workers. The relations that exist between unions, employers and the organs of executive power can far from always be characterized as partner-like, as prescribed by the law and international norms…Often, even those elements of collective agreements that are required by law are not respected. Worse, some agreements place the bar below even what the law requires…At the same time, we see that in real life the minima that the state guarantees to workers are very low or else there are none, while laws and executive decisions are ignored right and left.[52]

On the annual tripartite agreements, the editor of the FNPR's paper wrote in 1998:

> We cannot reach any agreements with this regime…Its actions are such that every year towards December the General Agreement signed by the government, the unions, and the entrepreneurs is good for the trash can. As concerns earlier agreements on payment of arrears in wages, pensions and social allocations, they have all gone to where any worker in Russia can tell you…This government has succeeded in destroying the work of the Russian Tripartite Commission.[53]

Of course, that was in 1998, before Putin welcomed the FNPR back into the government fold. But little has changed since then in the state's approach to the unions. ASMR constantly bemoans the adoption of regressive social and labour legislation and government inaction on the union's proposals for an active industrial policy to protect and develop the sector. Indeed, the government has been negotiating Russia's entry into the World Trade Organization, a move which, in the union's opinion, will deal a death blow to the sector.[54] The president of the Mtsensk Aluminum Foundry told ASMR's Presidium in 2003:

> It is obvious that government is not carrying out the demands of the people and the unions. What does the FNPR do in that situation? It does not even suggest to pose the question of lack of confidence in the government that is in charge of the country's economy. I consider that in-

correct. It's not enough to tell us what we should do in the plants. We need to be supported.[55]

Practically the only real success that can be attributed to "partnership" is the continued existence of the union. By making itself useful to management and to the government, it has been tolerated, much in the same way that civil liberties are tolerated by the regime insofar as they do not threaten important interests. But that is small comfort to workers who have lost so much over the past years. In 1999, in a moment of unusual candor, a high ASMR official mused that it might be better if the union did not exist. At least then workers would not nurture the illusion that there is an organization trying to defend them and they might start organizing themselves.

But that moment passed quickly. And the opinion voiced by the Mtsensk foundry president is a dissonant one in the union. Although it is recognized that relations are in reality not very "partner-like," the discussion goes no further. No analysis of the underlying reasons ever follows, nor is any alternative seriously entertained. Instead, union leaders continue to affirm their faith in the failed policy. Typical in this respect is G. Nesterova, president of ASMR's Moscow committee. In an interview in 2001, she lamented the government's failure to do anything to stem the loss of jobs in her sector—more than two thirds had disappeared in Moscow, once a major ASM centre, during the previous decade and the chronic failure of average ASM wages to reach even the subsistence minimum for the capital. Yet against all apparent logic, she concluded: "We are convinced that only through the system of social partnership can you defend economic interests of workers, guarantee their employment and regularly paid wages, and provide social benefits."[56]

If Nesterova had been asked what she meant by "social partnership," she most likely would have answered that it is a system of negotiated agreements and that the alternative is anarchy and permanent class war that is destructive to all sides. She would also likely have said that unions have to cooperate with management when the very survival of enterprises is at stake. The president of Moscow's ZIL truck factory told an interviewer in 1999: "The main thing today is survival. And you can survive only by working well. If there is profit, then the social and economic problems of the collective find resolution. And for now we are forced to look people in the eye and call on them to bear it and work."[57] But this is disingenuous, and not only because ZIL had by then already practically been destroyed. Even the most radical trade-unionists recognize that under capitalism workers are inevitably dependent on employers and that an enterprise cannot function without at least minimal union co-operation with management. The choice is not between co-operation and endless, destructive conflict, but rather between independent trade-unionism that bases its action on an analysis of the workers' interests and of the correlation of forces, actual and potential, on the one hand, and the unquestioning acceptance of management's definition of the situation and identification with its interests, on the other. In some circumstances, even an independent union might have to make concessions, but only after a genuine effort to resist them had convinced the members that any alternative would be worse. Then, at least, the members might not view the union as an adjunct of management, as is currently the case for ASMR, and the union might be able to fight and win another day.

There is, however, a much more serious argument often put forth in support of "partnership": union leaders are extremely vulnerable, and this makes them avoid confrontation. Asked about relations between leaders and management in his union, Novikov replied:

> To be honest, it comes down to the economic security of union leaders, or rather to its absence, something that is felt every hour. Every enterprise president in conducting negotiations with management is thinking today about what he will eat tomorrow. We'll never get away from that problem...I won't be letting out any secrets if I say that many presidents, especially the full-timers, do not take up the challenge (*pasuyut*).[58]

Novikov was referring to the use of the "administrative resource" by management to remove uncooperative union leaders from office. And although the law requires management to find jobs for officials who have left union office and prohibits their dismissal for two years, management usually can find ways of persuading people to leave "of their own volition." A Central Committee staff member went so far as to claim that a union president who sues management for wages won't be long in that job. Union leaders propose various responses to this real problem, including: accept it as a fact of life in any country (this was Novikov's position in the above interview, the most common one); accumulate a defence fund that could give support to dismissed leaders for at least several months; replace elected leaders with "business agents" appointed from above; take the main negotiations out of the enterprise and centre them on the regional and national levels; get a law passed. All these solutions are either undesirable or unrealistic in Russian conditions.

It is striking that one never hears from ASMR leaders, at least not from anyone above the shop level, that leaders might rely on the support of the rank and file members to defend them. Of course, that is no magic formula either. Support for the union has to be "built," never an easy task, especially in Russian conditions where demoralization is a central fact of the labour scene. Indeed, mass demoralization is in reality the principle explanation for the predominance and persistence of "social partnership." But the latter is itself at the same time an important cause of the mass demoralization.

The union's subservience to management and to the state, at least in its present extreme form, would be not be possible if the rank and file were at least minimally active and possessed even a modest degree of confidence in their own force. For their part, leaders frequently complain about the members' passivity, their "consumerist" attitude to the union. Any leader who might be tempted to confront management over a serious issue would certainly have to worry about his or her future, especially if he or she were an engineer, as most union leaders are. The profession is not in great demand, and engineers who do not work in their profession lose their qualification much more rapidly than workers. But that does not explain why union leaders do not even try to overcome the workers' demoralization and passivity. On the contrary, their actions often reinforce those traits. (See below.) Yet evidence adduced later in this volume shows that workers do respond to leadership that makes a serious effort to organize and mobilize them. Moreover, when that happens, management often retreats in shock.

The economic depression and mass demoralization are the social terrain upon which "social partnership" has grown. But the interests of union leaders is the fertilizer. "Partnership" remains attractive to union leaders, despite its demonstrated inability to defend workers' interests, because it presents leaders with the least personal risk while offering them the greatest personal rewards. Union leaders are vulnerable but, as will be shown later, the "administrative resource" is far from omnipotent. Meanwhile, if reliance on support "from below" entails some risk even in the most favourable circumstances, reliance on the support of management when the membership is disorganized and passive virtually guarantees a leader's position.

But "social partnership" can and often does bring even greater rewards than job security. It is very common for local leaders to cross over into top management positions, which are very well paid today. The former president of VAZ is now assistant director for personnel. "A person needs to develop," explained M. Abramov, national President of ASMR at that time. Abramov himself soon left the union, well before his term was over, to take a job as assistant director in a Moscow factory. And the former Vice-President of the General Confederation of Trade Unions (the former All-Union Central Council of Trade Unions, now basically a liaison organization for the unions of the successor states of the USSR) became Vice-President of the Russian Union of Industrialists and Entrepreneurs. This, of course, continues a long tradition inherited from the Soviet era. But more outright corruption is also a factor behind "partnership." Russia is, after all, a society marked by widespread poverty and social insecurity.

Leaders with independent inclinations are inevitably offered, besides the prospect of a cushy administrative job, improved housing, money, shares in the enterprise, and so forth. These favours are often enjoyed by co-operative union leaders. For those leaders, at least, "partnership" does pay.

Another factor favouring "partnership" is that independent union leaders cannot count on much support "from above," from the regional and national levels of the union. These lack the resources to offer significant help. But in any case, solidarity is extremely weak. (See below.) As noted, this is not a union that promotes a "culture of resistance." The national union has provided symbolic levels of support to plants on strike, but there has never been a serious attempt on any level to mobilize practical solidarity for such struggles. Worse yet, in at least one case, a regional leader connived with directors to get rid of "trouble-making" enterprise president. This happened to N. Kuzental', president of the Pargolov hydraulic-equipment factory in St. Petersburg, who had been involved in a longstanding battle with a corrupt management that was bleeding the plant. Despite her appeals, she received no support from the regional or national ASMR or from the Leningrad Federation of Trade Unions (an FNPR affiliate). In 1994, after the president of the Leningrad regional committee of ASMR paid a visit to her director—without consulting or even notifying Kuzental'—the director had her physically (and illegally) barred from the plant. The union remained deaf to her pleas even after she had been beaten up by thugs outside the factory.[59]

Explanations of social behaviour that appeal to cultural or ideological factors always have something of a circular character. But it is worth noting that in harsh conditions, the pioneers of the labour movement have often been workers and intellectuals with socialist convictions. Their deep commitment to the working class and their long-term historical vision saw them through hard times, when most people felt that struggle was futile and wanted only to get on with their personal lives. Russia (and not only Russia) has very few socialists today. (They should be distinguished from people who are nostalgic for Soviet-type "socialism." These can be quite active but they are highly prone to wishful thinking and adventurism and they eschew everyday organizing.) Of course, the virtual absence of socialism from the Russian political spectrum is itself a reflection of the demoralization of the labour movement.

One should also add the sheer weight of habit and tradition. Any observer has to be struck by how rare it is for even militant, courageous union leaders to invest effort and resources into strengthening and consolidating their membership base. Instead, they take on management in a one-to-one contest that inevitably ends in defeat or burnout. It is as if the very concept of popular self-organization is alien to the prevailing way of thinking. Indeed, the inability of the people to organize and govern themselves is the reason most often cited by labour leaders for their rejection of socialism: a new ruling class would inevitably emerge. That is the lesson they have drawn from the Soviet experience.

"Partnership," in its various guises and under its various names, is, of course, not unique to the Russia.[60] It is a common, and sometimes predominant, tendency in trade-union movements the world over. Rarely, however (except in other "transitional" countries), is union subservience to management and to the state so pronounced and so open in the absence of political repression and of even minimal material rewards for workers. The question naturally arises as to why workers remain in these unions and agree to the monthly deduction of one per cent of their wages for union dues. Most are in the unions out of inertia: the older members—and most members are older—inherited their membership from the Soviet period. They continue to view unions as adjuncts of management and as administrators of benefits. True, the benefits have shrunk, and that is cause for some grumbling; but otherwise things seem normal to them. As for new hires, the personnel office has them join the union as a matter of course, often without even telling them. But it is perhaps significant that, while 84.8 per cent of the sector's total work force belong to ASMR, that proportion drops to 64.9 per cent among young workers.[61]

The Democratic Deficit: The View "From Above"

There is a logical and practical link between union independence, democracy and solidarity. Unions that strive for independence from management are forced to mobilize and empower their members in order to create a base for their independent power. For the same reason, they build ties of mutual support and coordinate their actions with unions in other enterprises, branches and even countries. But by the same token, "partnership" works against union democracy and solidarity. The various elements are mutually reinforcing: "partnership" favours exclusion of the members from running the union and isolation from other unions; while, on the other hand, the weakness that results from a passive membership and from the isolation of local unions encourages leaders to seek a relationship of "partnership" with management.

The end of party/state control of the unions and the decentralization of power within the trade unions greatly increased the accountability of higher union bodies to enterprise leaders but did little to increase the power of rank-and-file members. Part of the problem is the passivity of the mass of workers, who patiently tolerate frigid temperatures in their shops and often kept on working for months without being paid before there taking collective action. Some never did. Ineffective or corrupt union leaders usually have little trouble getting re-elected, not just because management supports them, but often also because no one else wants to take their place. In the fall of 1999, 452 ASM plants held union accounting and election conferences. According to the union, in only one plant did the conference give the incumbent union president an unsatisfactory evaluation.[62] That result is astounding when one considers how widespread and profound dissatisfaction was among workers at that time. At the conference of the Kirov Tractor Factory, no criticism of the union president was voiced, even though he had rubber-stamped large-scale layoffs and sabotaged attempts to organize protests. After the meeting, however, the delegates could be heard muttering: "Positive evaluation?! He should have been given a two [failing grade]." Asked why they had not spoken up, one replied "We have a load of complaints. But what's the point? It's all been decided already."[63] In fact, the outcome had by no means been a foregone conclusion. There was an informal leader who could easily have beaten the incumbent, but he did not want to run. Even so, publicly voiced criticism of the incumbent would have at least exerted pressure on him to be more demanding toward management.

Union leaders frequently complain of the workers' apathy and their "dependent" (*izhdivencheskoe*) attitude toward the union, their widespread inclination to let others put out the fire "since my house is on the edge [of the village]" (*moya khata s krayu*). The same president of the Kirov Tractor Factory lamented:

> The basic reaction I get is indifference. They're all waiting for someone else to do it for them. The standard reaction is: "You're the union; you defend us." I go around to collect suggestions for the collective agreement. I leave the draft in the shop and return a few days later: no one bothered to make any suggestions, not even in the more active sections. It's even harder to get people to go to [political] demonstrations. It's easier just to go by myself. People especially don't want to clash with the administration. I have to write the draft collective agreement on my own.[64]

The chairperson of a stamping shop at VAZ vented her frustration at the reluctance to attend conferences:

> I tell them: "You have two chances a year to deal with your problems at these conferences. For God's sake, come and vote so that the boss will be afraid of you and see that he can be challenged, if only at the shop conference. Is it such a sacrifice?" I often hold lunch-hour chats with the workers to inform them of what's going on. A lot of people attend. But

when it comes to conferences, I might get forty-five people willing to go out of 700. And yet they know they could adopt a motion of non-confidence in the supervisor. There hasn't been a case yet when this happened and the supervisor kept his job. If he's a son of a bitch that deserves to have the conference vote against him, is it too high a price to stay an extra half hour after work? They can spend the entire shift bad-mouthing him among themselves, but it's a catastrophe if they have to stay half an hour.[65]

The president of the Likino Bus Factory explained: "It's been my experience to go to the director and present the workers' demands, but when the director comes into the shops and asks about the problems, no one speaks up. So he says to me: 'Whom do you lead, whom do you represent?' " During a seminar in St. Petersburg in 1997, an enterprise president reputed for her militancy composed a poem in which she compared workers to neglected pigs who quickly abandon their thoughts of revolt the minute the farmer tosses them a bucket of slop.

The View "From Below"

That is one side of the story. The other is about what union leaders do or do not do to overcome the passivity and encourage members' participation in the union. In reality, it is very common for key decisions to be taken alone by leaders without any attempt to involve, or even to inform until after the fact, the members. For example, the leaders at VAZ failed to consult the assembly-line workers when they approved management's decision (it required union consent) to extend the second shift by an hour, a change that the workers vigorously opposed.[66] At the Pekkar Carburetor Factory in St. Petersburg, the president did not inform even his plant committee when he consented in 2000 to a reduction in sick pay and to a change in the wage system that made up to half of take-home pay dependent on meeting overall production targets for the enterprise.[67] At the Kirov Tractor Factory, it was management, not the union, that convened the workers of the assembly shop during a lunch break in December 2001 to make them a last-minute offer: a month's layoff "at their own request," that is, without pay; or a month of involuntary layoff with two-thirds of base pay (about a third of the normal wage, in this case). However, he warned, if they chose the latter, they would be required to come in every day for eight hours and do any job management assigned or possibly do nothing at all.[68] The union's president, who knew of the impending layoff and supported management's choice, the first offer, had not bothered to convene a union meeting to let the workers work out an independent position.

The members' role in the collective bargaining process is normally very limited. This is how the president of Pekkar described it:

> We met with the director about the collective agreement. He issued an order to organize a joint commission with the union. We adopted last year's agreement as the basis. We sent it around for suggestions to the shops, which were supposed to hold meetings. But there weren't many suggestions. People display passivity. Then we held a conference of the work collective, with all the managers and specialists present. It was adopted unanimously.

He apparently did not see a link between the workers' apathy and the formalism of the process or the presence of "all the managers and specialists" at the conference. In contrast, this is how a dissident shop chairperson at VAZ described her experience with the collective-agreement process:

> When I first began to work, I was very green and made a lot of proposals. But it turned out that of thirty suggestions, only one ever found its way into the collective agreement, and even that was never carried out. So people lose faith in the union's ability to change anything. Take such a basic issue as supplying boiling water for tea. I spent three years pushing it, but management said: "Oh, they want to drink tea too? That's all we need! They're not here for that. They're here to work. They have a lunch period. Let them drink tea, and they'll be sitting around for hours doing nothing." That's why people are asleep. Even when the issue is really interesting and important to them, they are convinced that nothing will be done.

As for the presence of "all the managers and specialists," this is what a mechanic at a bus factory had to say about the conferences:

> Even if management are only ten per cent of the delegates, if they see the discussion is going the wrong way, they can control things. One of them will get up and say something like "Okay, let's end the discussion and vote," and that will be the end of it. They are always maneuvering behind the scenes to keep troublemakers from speaking out. If they foresee any special problems, the director calls together his middle-level managers before the conference and tells them to make sure the right people are chosen as delegates. And in any case, people are careful not to speak out since they are afraid of losing their bonuses or other forms of punishment because management is sitting there at the conference, watching.

The following are highlights from the delegates' conference of the Yaroslavl Motor Factory (YMZ) in June 2000. It was called to vote on the draft collective agreement reached by the union-management negotiating committee.[69] In most respects, it was a typical conference, except that this factory had fared better than in the depression than many others and it had a relatively strong alternative union. 440 delegates representing some 20,000 employees gathered in the factory's "palace of culture" in the early afternoon. More than a third were dressed in suits, that is, they were managers. (A few perhaps were engineers without administrative positions.) The union president suggested the meeting be kept under two hours. The proposal was met with visible relief in the hall and was adopted unanimously. The resolutions (editing) committee consisted of two assistant directors, the chief accountant and three shop chairpersons.

The first to speak was General-Director Savil'ev. He took thirty minutes. He explained that the issue before the assembly was the extension of the 1999 agreement for an additional year and to decide "how in unison (*druzhno*) we will work and defend our interests." He painted a picture of the enterprise's economic situation: increased demand for motors that the plant could not meet, rising production costs, profits from the previous year only partially received in cash, work on developing a new motor, money owed to the government. Wage arrears had been liquidated in 1999, "though the size of the wage is something that can bother people." He reported on housing construction that had been completed, the number of children sent to summer camp and of subsidized vacations distributed. His report was packed with figures that he tossed out at dizzying speed. A Mosvkich worker once described his director's report as "casting a spell" over the hall. And, indeed, halfway into the speech, the muffled rumble of snoring could be heard distinctly from various sides. The speech clearly had one main purpose: to show that things were looking up and that management was doing the best it could under the circumstances, but that it did not yet have the means significantly to raise wages because of the debts and the need to invest in re-equipping and developing a new model. "We must keep the desired in line with the possible," he told the assembly.

Next came the union president, who took about fifteen minutes. He noted that, on the whole, the collective agreement of 1999 had been carried out to a greater degree than that of the previous year. Wages had risen and more individual protective gear had been made available, though not enough. He criticized management for failing to provide information that the union had requested in order to formulate demands for a wage increase for certain low-paid groups, particularly engineers. As he turned to other unresolved issues, his tone rose, becoming somewhat more aggressive: the failure to provide slippers in the changing room, the small number of summer-camp places for children, the failure to include union representatives in the commission that allocated the new housing. But he concluded by proposing that the new agreement be adopted, since management promised to resolve these issues in due working order.

The discussion was then thrown open to the floor. Only three people spoke. An engineer complained about the destructive consequences of the longstanding practice of paying engineers less than workers, forcing them to take on extra jobs. He too criticized the director's failure to deliver the requested information. Next, a foundry worker complained that the draft agreement was practically a secret, that ninety per cent of the workers had never seen it. He himself had seen the part on wages for the first time only that very day, and it was vague. He proposed that wages be raised two to three times and that they be indexed to inflation. This was met with some applause. A third person rather confusedly attacked the faint-hearted people who had left the plant in search of a better living. He ended by asking the director to repair the pole-vaulting equipment in the gym.

It was then the director's turn to reply. He asked if they wanted long or short answers. Shouts from all sides: "Short!" For about twenty minutes, he addressed himself to the problems of holding onto young engineers and skilled workers, of developing a motor that met Euro-3 standards, and, more generally, he defended the plant's reputation. He then turned to the foundry worker. "We know he works with Afanas'ev's free trade union. Give me the source [of funds], and I'll raise wages five times. There is no such source today." The foundry worker retorted: "We had a warning strike in the shop in November and got a thousand-ruble [about thirty U.S.$] raise. There is spare money in the factory." Savel'ev: "Yes, they did strike, and we gave in under pressure. But your time has passed. Strikes won't be repeated at YMZ. People won't follow you. You proposed a draft agreement that parallels on all points the present one. But beside each point you write: 'The union reserves the right to halt production.' That's finished. You won't be able to do that anymore." He was, however, willing to consider indexation: "Let's look at inflation." He went on to speak about slippers, the theft of non-ferrous metal, for which he blamed the foundry workers and called for draconian measures, the parking lot, a bus route, bicycle stands, the plant's vacation home, his impression of Putin, the plant's inability to raise benefits at the present time, and so forth, for about twenty minutes. After that, the union president proposed to approve the administration's performance in carrying out of the 1999 collective agreement, but taking note the failures mentioned above. He also proposed to adopt the new draft. The vote was unanimous. The meeting had lasted 110 minutes.

The most striking aspect of the conference was its complete domination by management. The union offered no leadership. The director spoke for almost half the time. His report defined the situation, what was possible. The union presented no analysis of its own, only a brief, very partial commentary that avoided the main issue of workers' wages. The delegates obviously wanted only to get it over with as quickly as possible. The reasons for that have already be noted: the outcome was considered a foregone conclusion; management was present in force; and the delegates had at least partially been vetted. As for the members of the alternative union, foundry workers are known for their independence. They often say that they have nothing to lose, since they are already in hell.

Shopfloor representation at the higher levels of the union is even more limited than in the enterprises. Most of the Central Committee members are full-time plant and regional presidents. Even the congresses have few shopfloor delegates or even shop chairpersons. Of the eighty delegates to ASMR's Third Congress in October 1997, fifty-two were plant presidents or vice-presidents and twenty-one were regional presidents. There were only sixteen women, though they made up forty percent of the membership. Seventy-one delegates had higher education, that is, they were not workers, who are by far the majority of the members.[70] And in many regions, to save money, elected committees were been replaced by councils of plant presidents, though this practice is now being reversed.

Information is the life-blood of democracy. But ordinary members typically know next to nothing about their union, the conferences, the collective agreement. These are typical remarks of rank-and-file members:

> "I don't know a thing about the union's activity, about what the plant committee is doing. All I know is that there are meetings once a year. The president doesn't talk to ordinary workers. We don't see him in the shop for years on end. Even when he shows up, he doesn't come over to us. Maybe it's below his dignity. Or maybe he's afraid." "The leaders keep to themselves. In practice, they've got their own organization, separate from ours. Our paths cross only when it comes to collecting dues." "Our union doesn't fulfill its functions. They sit in their offices, busy with their own affairs. We don't feel that they care about our working conditions, our wages. And we don't go to them. They live their own separate life, and we live ours. But when a conflict breaks out in the shop, they come running."

Many workers, in fact, are under the impression that their union is doing nothing to defend their interests. This, of course, may reflect reality and be not only a problem of communication. Asked about his union's position on permanent layoffs (at a time when the Labour Code gave unions significant rights in this area), a Moskvich worker replied: "It has no position. Our union stands for "May, Spring, Peace, Labour" [the official FNPR slogans for May Day 1999], for the rights of workers and also for those of the director. Our president is out only for himself. You should see how he has nicely filled out, all rolly-poly. We don't hear a thing from the union. It's as if it didn't exist." As these comments indicate, enterprise unions devote little attention to the flow of information between the members and leaders. Very few publish newsletters or even occasional bulletins. Many do not even possess a photocopying machine. The reason is not so much their poverty as their priorities. VAZ's union is certainly not poor. But when the chairperson of the medium-stamping shop, alarmed by the continued hemorhage of her most active members to Edinstvo, suggested that the department committee follow Edinstvo's example and put out a bulletin to report on the business discussed at its weekly meetings, the answer was: "If it's so important, do it yourself." The department committee has five full-timers.

Workers attach great importance to personal contact with leaders and frequently complain that the plant president is rarely seen in the shops. An assembly-line worker commented: "From his office to his car; from his car to his office. He never sets foot in the shops. He didn't even come before October 7 [the FNPR's national protest in 1998], although that might have helped to mobilize people."

The large size of most ASM factories means that the shop committees have an especially strategic role to play as the link between the plant committee and the membership. In any union, shop stewards are the face of the union in the workplace. But in ASMR, they are the weakest point of the union. Because of financial constraints, the number of full-time shop chairpersons has been drastically cut, and many unions have also done away with group leaders. Low wages and the resulting need to take on extra work, as well as the low-prestige and highly bureaucratic nature of the job, make workers very reluctant to run for shop president. In any case, it is often the supervisor who selects the candidate. Most shop chairpersons are office or storeroom employees, and some are foremen or assistant supervisors. On this level, women are overrepresented. The above people are not tied to machines and they therefore can find some free time during work hours to carry out minimal union duties. They can also get away to attend weekly meetings of the *aktiv* with the president. But at the same time, they tend to be distant from the concerns of blue-collar workers and their commitment to the union is weak. They also bend more easily than workers to managerial pressure.

This financial side of this problem is, again, more a reflection of union priorities than of poverty. Paid time off for elected officials and the provision of substitutes (production workers are often organized in brigades) could be negotiated. The relative sums involved are not great. Failing that, unions could cut back on what are essentially charity and social activities. As it is, shop chairpersons who are production workers cannot always attend meetings of the *aktiv*, an important source of information. When they do attend, they sit on the edge of their seats watching the clock. These meetings tend to be short, and discussion is minimal. Most often they are monologues by the president.

There are, of course, dedicated shop chairpersons who enjoy the conscious support of their members. But these are exceptional, and the plant committee's readiness to make concessions to management constantly undercuts their work. Most shop leaders spend their time in routine administrative tasks, such as allocating "material aid," subsidized vacations, day care places, organizing social activities and preparing summer camps for children. One of them explained: "There are a lot of tasks. We solve workers' problems from birth to death. We take care of the individual up to and including the funeral. One of our main problems is to find money for all that. On the whole, our work involves the resolution of 'small' problems that you can't entrust to the employer, who is busy organizing production. This everyday work takes up most of my time."[71] Little effort or time is devoted to informing the members, discussing issues with them, organizing them. Shop meetings are rare, and sometimes never occur, even though they are supposed to elect delegates to the plant conferences. When wildcats occur, the elected shop leaders tend to stand aside.

Education for shop-floor activists could be an important tool for strengthening the union's base and expanding the pool of potential leaders. But union education has been drastically cut back compared to the Soviet period. The former network of labour institutes of the FNPR and its regional federations now charge hefty fees and train young people—not union activists—mostly for the professions of lawyer, economist, accountant, manager. They have usually kept one department for union education that goes under the title of "faculty of social partnership." ASMR's national office can offer occasional training for a small number of plant and shop officers, thanks to the support of international organizations such as the International Metalworkers' Federation and the Ebert Foundation. It used to work also with Transnationals Information Exchange (TIE) and the School for Worker Democracy, but these organizations focus on educating shopfloor activists, whom ASMR has been unable or unwilling to recruit. Some education for newly elected officers is still offered by regional federations, but these are mostly "tool courses." And there is practically no education for shopfloor activists. VAZ, with its 120,000 membership, is an exception. It has built its own school and is now constructing a second. It goes without saying that the underlying orientation of the education is "partnership." According to a Edinstvo activist (who may be biased), the ASMR organization at VAZ does not even teach its group leaders how to file grievances through the labour disputes committee—they come to Edinstvo to show them.

The absence of education for shop-floor activists (which, of course, is not unique to Russia) cannot be explained solely by poverty. Paid time off could be negotiated. The alternative unions manage to send ordinary activists on their own time to education organized by TIE and the School for Worker Democracy. ASMR leaders do not, on the whole, understand the need for rank-and-file education or else they feel threatened by it. A shop chairperson at the KamAZ truck factory explained:

> Everyone needs education. And no one but the union can offer it. The bosses aren't interested in it. Unfortunately, the union doesn't bother either. I've already told our leaders: You apparently aren't interested in an enlightened membership. You want a society that consists of a crowd that understands nothing and leaders who know everything. The crowd is stupid and so should blindly follow the leaders. Their goal should be to develop the consciousness of all members of the union.

The hostility, verging sometimes on visceral hatred, of most ASMR leaders for the alternative unions is indicative of their approach to union democracy. The alternative unions represent a current within the labour movement that favours independence. Like-minded dissidents in ASMR–they are few and far between and are mostly found on the shop level—view the competition in a positive light, as a source of dynamism for the labour movement. And they co-operate with the alternatives on concrete issues. But the attitude of the majority of leaders in ASMR was neatly summed up by a national Vice-President: "They get in the way (*meshayut*). Theirs is a conscious policy of splitting." He failed to mention that the policy of most ASMR leaders is to forcibly suppress or marginalize internal dissent and to collaborate with management in harassing the alternative unions. This was also the attitude adopted by the FNPR's leaders in the reform of the Labour Code: in essence, they traded important union rights (in any case, their affiliates rarely used them, for fear of "straining relations" with management) in return for changes that give them an effective monopoly of representation and make it significantly harder for minority unions to function.[72]

This prevailing attitude also applies to other minorities, real or effective. ASMR has recently taken up the issue of gender equality. Following the FNPR's lead, its Presidium adopted guidelines for establishing women's commissions in local unions. At least some of the leaders seem genuinely to recognize that discrimination is a problem.[73] But others have adopted a purely formalistic approach and see special women's structures as divisive. The same Vice-President dismissed the commissions as "suggested by the West" (*Zapad podskazal*), that is, by international labour organizations that, among other things, provide education. He denied, for example, that women workers have specific health-and-safety problems. "Just try to shift them into a different job! They won't go for anything," he remarked, sidestepping the issues of female poverty and the system of monetary compensations and benefits for harmful work."The women's commissions will only divide the union," he opined, "when what we need is unity." The is the dominant view: unity—a genuinely urgent task—is to be achieved by suppressing differences rather than by giving minorities a legitimate place in the union to make them feel at home.

Cultivating democracy and rank-and-file activism poses formidable challenges to any union. In Russian conditions the challenges are especially daunting. This is true even for the alternative unions, whose membership is on the whole more conscious and committed. But in ASMR, there is an evident lack of interest among leaders in encouraging rank-and-file participation. An active membership would threaten the union's role as "buffer," which is the main thing it has to offer management in return for at least minimal recognition and concessions. On the second day of the above-mentioned seminar, the author of the poem comparing workers to servile pigs did not show up. One of her members explained that wildcats over unpaid wages had broken in some shops on the morning shift that day, and her president was busy trying to get them back to work. Two years later, she had left the union to become an assistant director in her plant.

Apart from the threat that democracy might present to leaders who subscribe to "partnership," there appears to be also a cultural or ideological factor at work: there seems to be a deeply embedded view, which is sometimes shared even by committed leaders and that is certainly widespread among workers themselves, that workers cannot speak for themselves but have to be represented. Related to this is the view that workers cannot be plant presidents (there are none at higher levels), although, in fact, they tend to make the best ones. As if to confirm this, the rare worker who does become enterprise president almost always signs up for night courses with a view to obtaining a university degree.

Lack of Solidarity

"Partnership" focuses the attention and energies of local unions attention on promoting the economic well-being, defined as profitability, of "their" enterprise. This necessarily occurs at the expense of their members' shared interests with workers of other enterprises. For the same reason, national leaders who espouse "partnership" have trouble uniting their local affiliates around a common programme of action, since that inevitably requires some sacrifice of short-term, local interests and the pooling of resources for the common good. In Russia, where economic and political conditions are very unfavourable for workers, this is a particularly disastrous situation, since any gains achieved in individual enterprises are necessarily temporary and partial. At the same time, "partnership" works against solidarity within the enterprise, too. In a society that promotes individualism in a myriad of overt and imperceptible ways, workers learn the value of solidarity mainly through their involvement in struggle, when solidarity is a key condition of victory. Unions that embrace "partnership" avoid struggle and rarely mobilize their members. Identification with management's goals can even lead them to support practices such as "labour competition" in the name of productivity and quality. And they are prepared to tolerate a divisive and arbitrary wage system for much the same reasons.

The radical decentralization of power in favour of the local unions was probably inevitable after more than six decades of imposed hypercentralism. And the change would indeed have been a healthy one had local unions been willing to delegate a reasonable part of their new-found power and financial resources to their national organizations. This, however, was not the case, and the problems of weak discipline and the refusal to share dues or even information with the national office are perennial topics of discussion at ASMR Central Committees, Presidia and congresses. Although the union's constitution makes decisions by higher elected organs binding on local organizations and allows the national leadership to annul local decisions that violate union statutes, these formal powers cannot really be exercised, since local unions would simply ignore sanctions or else disaffiliate. Over the years, the many resolutions and constitutional amendments adopted and aimed at strengthening unity have had little effect. For the most part, local unions just do as they please.

The financial distress of the national office is a constant refrain. The February 1997 Central Committee formally raised the national office's share of dues from 2.6 to four per cent. By way of comparison, almost sixty per cent of dues collected from members of the Canadian Autoworkers' Union go the national office or to funds and programmes administered by it. The difference, at least in this case, is a rough measure of the respective levels of solidarity. In practice, ASMR's national leadership has never received more than two per cent of the dues. (In 2002, its received 1.8 per cent, an improvement over previous years but only seventy-seven percent of a planned target that had already been lowered to accommodate the local affiliates.)[74] Novikov told the September 2001 Central Committee:

> The financial situation...is changing for the better only extremely slowly. I will remind you of the resolution of our Fourth Congress: "Unfailingly to respect financial obligations in accordance with the decisions of our collective bodies and not to permit their unilateral modification." Despite this, a series of local leaders today declare: "The conference of our enterprise organization decided to transfer such-and-such a percentage. I know it's significantly less than what the Central and regional committees are asking, but we can't give more"...But there's no sense denying it—conference resolutions [of the enterprises] are formulated as the president of the union committee wishes.[75]

Novikov was seconded by N. Skakun, president of the Yaroslavl Diesel-Apparatus Factory and a member of the audit commission:

> Financial discipline in our union is atrocious. We all hang onto our money and make decisions independently. We were given that right. That's good. But if we feel we need a Central Committee to unite us, then...As it is, we don't carry out decisions that we adopt in Moscow unanimously. You can criticize the Central Committee as much as you like, but it doesn't even have the money to travel to the regions.[76]

As Skakun noted, the national office's poverty greatly limits its capacity to provide services and to pursue coherent policies. It had to cut its staff from twenty-two when the union was founded to twelve. Only one person is in charge of the sectoral and local agreements, and no one works full-time on health and safety issues. The national office cannot offer research or educational services to local unions at any reasonable level, and there is no strike fund. The regional committees are similarly strapped for money and understaffed. The frequency of Central Committee meetings, the union's parliament between congresses, had to be cut by more than half. The national paper, a monthly that could play an important role in uniting the union and sharing information, until recently had a print run of only 5000, a tiny percentage of the membership. Recently it was reduced to 2500 (though quality has improved). A resolution of the Second Congress in 1995 to double both its frequency and circulation remained a dead letter. Local unions have not responded to appeals to take out mass subscriptions.[77]

Again, the main problem is not the economic crisis and the resultant decrease in dues. It is rather the unwillingness to share resources, a large part of which are spent on activities that should at best be peripheral to unions. VAZ and GAZ, the wealthiest organizations with a third of the total membership, gave relatively less in 2002 that most smaller unions.[78] Asked how much his union gives the national office, VAZ's vice-president replied: "It's hard to say. There isn't any specific percentage. The amount is set by agreement. But we give enough so that it won't die. We can't pull all of Russia behind us."[79] Local leaders justify their refusal to reduce the share of charitable and recreational expenses by citing worker expectations. At a 1998 Central Committee devoted to the problem of finances, the president of the Saratov Ball-Bearing Factory said:

> I am insulted by the criticism that plant committees refuse to strengthen executive and financial discipline in the union while spending their dues on material aid and the upkeep of cultural and sports facilities. Until we get legislation that guarantees state support for the social sphere of the enterprise, we have to support it. The children of our workers are using the clubs and sports facilities of our plant, and we can't throw them out onto the street. You can't speak of that as a violation of discipline.

Skakun was more candid:

> You probably could look upon the material aid we give union members as—you'll pardon my expression—a sop. But in my opinion, it is very important. There was a period when people suddenly began to leave the union in large numbers…Our explanatory work and agitation did little good. Now we are experiencing a return flow…Yes, we have to spend money on material aid to workers. For now, we can't give it up.[80]

The main reason for not abandoning, or at least cutting, spending on charity and social activities is not really the expectations of workers, since unions could, in principle, make management pay for them. After all, these expenditures amount to significantly less than one per cent of the wage bill (which is the sum total of union dues). The real reason is that they are the main attraction for workers to remain in the unions, since the latter are unable, and often unwilling, to fight for better wages and conditions. The president of the Chelyabinsk regional committee hinted at this:

> If local organizations and regional bodies had the money and sent "up" [to the national office] all that they are supposed to, they could, of course, limit themselves to purely trade-union work. But at present we frequently have to demean ourselves and beg directors for crumbs. So it's understandable that when plant presidents get any real money, they are reluctant to part with it.[81]

This was spoken in the spring of 1988 when the management practice of not paying wages and not transferring dues to the unions reached its height. Faced with this major challenge, local unions preferred to use whatever money they could "beg" from management to continue giving small handouts to a tiny proportion of their membership and to pay for social activities, rather than to concentrate on "purely trade-union work," that is, to put organized pressure on management for the payment of the wages and dues. Given the extremely serious nature of the problem and the government's role in creating and tolerating it, it would have been logical to unite around a powerful, well-financed national campaign to force—not beg—management and the state to pay the wages and to transfer the dues. Only the Yaroslavl region of ASMR rose to the occasion (see the next chapter) but it did not receive active support from elsewhere in the union.

Another argument sometimes alluded to by local leaders is their lack of confidence in how additional money would be used by the national office. The often say to it: "Tell us concretely what you want the money for, and we'll give it." It is an open secret that the national office has a "black cashbox" (*chernaya kassa*) with money earned from renting out part of its space in the FNPR building complex to private companies. This money is not accounted for. There is, therefore, a real lack of transparency in this part of the finances of the national office.[82] But that could easily be corrected if the local affiliates cared to. In fact, they seem happy with the present situation, since it provides them with a justification for not paying more.

A related problem is the limited role of the sectoral agreement, which is negotiated jointly with two other industrial unions and signed with the Union of Machine-Building Employers and the Ministry of Industry, Science and Technology. It is supposed to set minimal standards for local bargaining and should help to bind the union together. But from the start, the predominant position in the union was that it its application should not be obligatory, since conditions vary so widely from plant to plant. There is no doubt that the depression makes solidary bargaining very problematic. But the union's position on the non-binding character of the sectoral agreement flowed from a view that predated the depression, from a view that is inherent "social-partnership," namely that the level of wages and other benefits in any given enterprise should depend upon the profitability of that enterprise.

Lately, there seems to have been a move toward making the sectoral agreement binding, although it has taken the rather strange form of the union's efforts to organize employers in the hope that they will enforce the agreement on themselves. However, these efforts have not met with success. And even if the employers' association could impose discipline, the agreement's language on many issues is so vague as it render it practically meaningless. Many of the clauses in the 2002-04 accord merely restate what the law already requires. Others instruct employers and enterprise unions to conclude local agreements on such matters as free time for union health and safety activists and compensation for various types of work in difficult or dangerous conditions, but without specifying levels. (7.15, 7.10, 7.11) Another clause states that local unions and employers "can conclude" agreements on levels of compensation of injuries that go beyond what the law prescribes. (8.4). The agreement lists a series of benefits that "can be" the subject of local agreement, including improved housing, supplements for large families, rent subsidies for workers living in dormitories and for travel to and from work, the provision of workers' with garden plots. Again, there is nothing on the levels of these benefits. Moreover, the infamous phrase "taking into account the enterprise's ability [to pay]" is tacked on at the end. (8.10) On the fundamental question of wages, the agreement states that the average wage should approach the industrial average "by stages." But neither the stages nor the final date are specified. (4.3.1). On the other hand, the clause calling for the minimum basic wage (that is, the wage without bonuses and supplements) to be raised "by stages" to reach the subsistence minimum in 2003 is more specific. (4.3.2) But it violates article 133 of the Labour Code, that states that "minimum remuneration…cannot be less than the subsistence minimum." Finally, another clause calls for the basic wage to be raised by stages to no less than sixty per cent of take-home pay. This is to be achieved by 2004, and the calendar is left to local agreements. (4.3.3)[83]

Even with all this vagueness, the agreement is not binding even on employers who are members of the Union of Machine-Building Employers, since the latter's constitution does not give it the power to impose discipline. By the union's own admission, the sectoral agreement has no real influence on the level of wages.[84] On the other hand, ASMR's national office has not put much effort into pressing its own local affiliates to adopt the sectoral agreement as the basis for their own bargaining position. To be fair, its resources are limited. Yet even the limited resources it has are not fully utilized. The staff member responsible for the sectoral agreement explained: "I don't have the information [on local application of the sectoral agreement], but, anyway, it isn't necessary. What if I did have the data? If there's a problem, they can come to me." Some local unions use the sectoral agreement as an argument in bargaining. But it is obvious that most do not give it much thought. The national Vice-President complained in 2002 that "it is distressing that our union organizations did not, unfortunately, offer much active help or support in the work [of drafting the sectorial agreement]. We received a very insignificant number of suggestions and comments from local organizations. And that left its mark."[85] By the same token, ASMR's economist says that he pays not attention to the FNPR's national agreement when he works on the sectoral agreement of ASMR.

The situation is similar on the regional level. Yaroslavl, for example, has four engine and engine-parts factories, that, in a rare display of solidarity, organized a joint campaign against wage arrears in 1996-1998. (See the next chapter.) But even though the plants produce related goods and now have a single owner (Deripaska's Ruspromavto), and their unions have experience of working together, the regional president expressed shock at the suggestion that the four jointly negotiate a collective agreement that would set common minimum standards for the region, even though that would strengthen the unions' bargaining power and solidarity. "We will never have the same collective agreement in all the plants!" he replied. "Profitability is different; conditions are different. That will never be. They haven't all even applied the sectoral agreement." On the other hand, N. Volosyuk, chairperson of the strike committee of the Yaroslavl Fuel-Pump Factory from 1996 to 2001 and a union dissident, did not consider the suggestion at all outlandish. He commented: "Of course that will never be. That would make him work, and he doesn't want to." As noted, under "partnership" unions work together with management for the good of "their enterprise." It is only natural that wages in the enterprise be determined by the market performance of that enterprise. Anything else would require the unions to shift the balance of forces in their favour, that is, to struggle.

The often indifferent attitude of local unions' toward the national office is also manifested in their failure to provide it regularly with information. The national President told the Third Congress in October 1997 that "the flow of information...has become our weak point...This is not only a matter of lack of money...Some leaders fail to understand the need to keep the Central Committee informed not only of their problems, but also of the results of their work. We often lack timely information on what is happening in the regions."[86] Thus, the national office does not possess information on the level of workplace injuries.[87] It was only from the television news several days after the event that it learnt of a mass poisoning at the Dimitrovgrad parts plant in the Ulyanovsk region. In 1998, two-thirds of the local unions failed to respond to a request for information on wage arrears. Many local and regional committees do not bother sending copies of their collective agreements to Moscow, although that is required by union statutes.[88] (Over the last few years, there has been some improvement in this area.)

The financial and informational problems of the national office make it impossible to develop coherent, forward-looking policies. Its main functions have been to provide local and regional leaders with a meeting place, to supply them with information about government policies and laws, to offer suggestions on organizing their work, and to lobby the government on behalf of the sector and of individual enterprises. And that is how most local leaders want it. N. Karagin, president of VAZ, told the Third Congress in 1987: "In the opinion of the delegation from the Samara region, the Central Committee of the union should base its activity on a rather different principle: it should not so much strive to be a leading body as rather one that co-ordinates, unites, and works with the government and the Duma."[89] One might expect the smaller unions, which have more limited resources, to press for a stronger national centre. But there is little evidence of any pressure. At one time, the Yarosavl region sounded a dissident note in this respect. In June 1998, A. Smirnov, Yaroslavl regional president, said:

> What are our complaints about the Central Committee? It's work is weak. Each plant is stewing in its own juices. There's no critical analysis of the FNPR's strategy, no discussion of the future of our sector. The Central Committee has no economic programme. Could Abramov do more? True, he hasn't got any money, so that even a seminar or a Central Committee meeting is hard to organize. We pay for most of our own expenses when we go to Central Committees. Still, he could do a lot more to unify the union, at least those in the plants in the central regions around Moscow. The problem is that they are conciliators.

Smirnov saw the link between "conciliationism" (*soglashatel'stvo*—another word for "partnership") and the lack of unity. But that was at the height of his region's fight against non-payment of wages. Today, wages are being paid more or less regularly, and union life in Yaroslavl has returned to normal. Complaints about the national union are no longer heard.

In conformity with Karagin's vision for the union, decisions adopted by the Central Committee or Presidium on participation in national protests are non-binding. The February 1997 Central Committee rejected a proposal that would have made participation obligatory in a one-day general strike called by the FNPR for Match 27 to protest non-payment of wages. From the discussion it was clear that the objections were based upon the reluctance to strike by local unions whose plants were more or less functioning. The resolution called only on those unions that were already on strike for other reasons to participate in the general strike. The others could organize demonstrations, marches and picketing of government buildings.[90] (This position was not unique to ASMR, and the protest, as usual, had no impact.)

As this example shows, solidarity with workers outside of ASMR is just as weak as it is within the union. In 1995, the Union of Machine and Instrument Building proposed a merger with the Union of Heavy Machine-Building and ASMR. This would have brought significant economies and it would have strengthened the regional and national organizations, increasing the level of services they could provide. Heavy Machine-Building accepted, but ASMR opted out, though Abramov, then national President, favoured the move. The main opposition came from the regional presidents, many of whom are close to or past retirement age, and from then national Vice President, Novikov, who also stood to lose his job. Of course, had local leaders been in favour, ASMR would have accepted the merger. But they apparently feared the move would strengthen discipline (this proved to be the case in the new Union of Machine Building) and, perhaps, they just did not care.[91] ASMR's last congress in February 2002 seemed to support the latter conclusion. In the words of a high official, it was conducted in an "absolutely formalistic manner." One incident was particularly telling. The President nominated a person for one of the posts of vice president who was not a union member. This was a violation of the constitution. Although someone drew the assembly's attention to this, the person was elected anyway. Asked how that could happen, the official replied: "They don't give a damn (*naplevat*)."

Despite the complaints by the national office, the absence of solidarity seems, in fact, accepted as normal. The Central Committee of March 2002 called for the creation of solidarity funds by local and regional organizations "to give financial support to union members and to conduct collective actions."[92] But there was no central fund, even though a previous decision had called for it and it would have made much more sense from the point of view of efficacy and solidarity. These were, after all, "solidarity funds." But few union were in a rush to create their own local funds either, though the resolution was supposedly binding. A year after its adoption, only two local unions had carried out the decision.[93]

In light of all this, it is not surprising that solidarity is also very weak at the enterprise level. Already noted is the toleration of the large wage differentials, even for the same work, from one shop to the next and even within the same shop. It is not uncommon for individual shops and even groups within shops to negotiate informally with management separate raises for themselves. During the non-payment epidemic, it happened that an entire enterprise struck (though much more common were strikes by individual shops), but the first shops that were paid returned to work without even waiting for guarantees of payment to be given to the others.

ASMR's leadership is caught in a bind that is in large part of its own making: it wants and needs to justify its own existence and to strengthen its role within the union. It constantly appeals for more resources and for stronger discipline. But its support for "social partnership," which, of course, reflects the position of local leaders, reinforces and justifies the latter's refusal to respond to these appeals. It is a magic circle, and there is no obvious way out. Fefelov, who replaced Novikov as President in a sort of palace coup at the May 2003 Central Committee, has been making greater efforts than his predecessor to strengthen the national office. (For one thing, he is more active and travels outside of Moscow more often. Novikov was a career union functionary who had passed retirement age; Fefelov, former president of ZIL, is relatively young.) However, it seems doubtful that he will be able to change things significantly, since there is no real will at any level to confront employers. "Partnership" is still the unquestioned orientation.

Change in the union movement will have to come through the activation of the rank and file, whatever concrete organizational forms that may take. Ordinary workers do not benefit from "social partnership." They need effective organizations that are prepared to challenge employers and the state at all levels. And once they become active, they will not for long tolerate leaders who are unaccountable.

Notes

1. Under Stalin and later, unions were officially designated as "transmission belts" of party-state policy to the masses.
2. For a detailed discussion of the structure of the FNPR and its affiliates, see Ashwin and Clark, *Russian Trade Unions*, ch. 4.
3. *Golos profsoyuza*, no. 10, Nov. 2001; Ashwin and Clarke, *Russian Trade Unions*, p. 86.
4. ASMR, "Ob organizatsionnoi raboteTsk profsoyuza povypolneniyu reshenii IV sezdafnr," May 17, 2003.
5. *Golos profsoyuza*, nos.3-4, Mar.-Apr., 1996.
6. J. Blasi, M. Kroumova, and D. Kruse, *Kremlin Capitalism: Privatizing the Russian Economy*, Ithaca: ILR Press, 1997, p. 107.
7. *Golos profsoyuza*, no. 6, June 1998.
8. From a video of the conference made by Edinstvo.
9. *Golos profosyuza*, no. 8-9, Sept.-Oct. 2001.
10. ASMR, "Ob itogakh kollektivno-dogovornoi kampanii 2002 godo," May 2003 (unpublished).
11. B. Maskimov, "Kuda vedut lideri," 2000 (unpublished).
12. *Golos profsoyuza*, no. 5, 1998.
13. "Svezhii veter peremen," *Profsoyuzy*, no. 3, 1999, p. 12.
14. *Izhorets* (St.-Pertersburg), Feb. 3, 1997.
15. B. Maksimov, "Torzhestvo profsoyuznoi demokratii," 2001 (unpublished). The plant is un-named at the author's request.
16. *Golos profsoyuza*, nos. 3-4, Mar.-Apr. 1996 and nos. 9-10, Nov. 2003.; *Profsoyuzy i ekonomika*, no. 7, 2001, p. 7.
17. Order no. 106 by General-Director R.S. Asatryan "On Punishing Those Responsible for the Faulty Assembly of the *Duet Car*," Apr.1, 1999 (unpublished).

18. At a meeting in the BATE factory in Borisov, May 2000.
19. *Profsoyuzy i ekonomika*, no. 4, 2003.
20. ASMR, "Report of the President to the Third (Special) Congress," October 1997 (unpublished); *Golos profosyuza*, no. 11, Nov.1997.
21. *Profsoyuzy i ekonomika*, no. 7, 2001, p. 7.
22. Personal communication by B. Maskimov, June 2002.
23. *Golos profosoyuza*, no. 3-4, Mar.-Apr., 2002.
24. *Profsoyuzy i ekonomika*, no.7, 2001, passim. The issue is devoted to ASMR's tenth anniversary.
25. *Golos profosyuza*, no.1, Jan. 2002.
26. ASMR, "Report of the Presdient to the Fifth Central Committee," Feb. 27, 2002. (unpublished). An abridged version appears in *Golos profsoyuza*, no. 3-4, Mar.-Apr., 2002.
27. *Profsoyuzy i ekonomika*, no.7, 2001, p. 10.
28. ASMR, "Ob itogakh kollektivno-dogovornoi kampanii."
29. *Golos profsoyuza,* nos. 9-10, Nov. 2003.
30. Some of these were strikes at the Lipetsk, Chelyabinsk, and Promtraktor tractor factories, at the Serpukhov auto parts factory, the Tutaev motor factory, VAZ. (*Sovetskaya Rossiya*, Jan.1, 1998; Mar. 10, 1998; Sept.17, 1998; *Golos profsoyuza*, nos. 2-3,1998. See also chapters 5 and 6 here.)
31. *Prosoyuzy i ekonomika*, no. 7, 2001, pp. 29, 64
32. *Ibid.*, p. 10.
33. ASMR, "Ob organizatsionnoi rabote...".
34. "Vazovskie prioritety," *Profsoyuzy i ekonomika*, no.7, 2001, p. 49.
35. This occurred, for example, at Moskvich in 1993, at the Tutaev Motor Factory in 1996, at VAZ in 1994, at the GPZ-1 Ball-Bearing Factory in 1998.
36. www.trud.org/archive, 1996.
37. *Golos profsoyuza*, no. 1, Jan. 2002 and no. 2, Feb. 2002.
38. For a more detailed discussion of these efforts, see D. Mandel, "Why Is There No Revolt?" in L. Panitch and C. Leys, *The Socialist Register 2000*, London: Merlin Press, 2000, p. 181. Other sources are ASMR, "Report of the President to the Third (Special) Congress," Oct. 1997 (unpublished) and *Golos profsoyuza*, no. 2, Feb. 2002.
39. Resolution of the All-Russian Conference of Machine-Builders "On Joint Actions of Employers and Trade Unions," June 4, 1997 (unpublished).
40. *Golds profosoyuza*, nos. 8-9, Sept.-Oct. 2001.
41. ASMR, "Ob itogakh kollektivno-dogovornoi kamapanii."
42. *Golos profsoyuza*, nos. 7-8, Oct. 2003; ASMR, "Report of the President to the September 2002 Central Committee."
43. *Golos profsoyuza*, now. 9-10, Nov. 2003.
44. For a detailed discussion of FNPR politics, see Clarke and Ashwin, *Russian Trade Unions*, ch. 3.
45. www.trud.org/archive, 1999. On this issue, see also Gritsenko, N.N., et al., *Istoriya profsoyuzov Rossii*, Moscow: Akademiya truda i sotsial'nykh otnoshenii and FNPR, 1999, p. 327.
46. *Finansovaya Rossiya*, no. 16, Apr. 30-May 17, 2002, p. 2.

47. Putin's appearance at the congress was greeted with special jubilation and relief, since rumours had been circulating that he wanted Shmakov removed. The situation was similar in many of the FNPR's regional organizations. In St. Petersburg, the new president of the Leningrad Regional Federation, G. Lisyuk, was elected in 2001 at a conference in which the governor, the president of the regional Union of Entrepreneurs, and the directors of the region's largest enterprises were all seated on the stage. A seasoned observer remarked that "it brought back memories of the good old days." (Personal communication from B. Maskimov, June 2001.)

48. *Golos profsoyuza*, no. 10, Nov. 2001.

49. A. Isaev, "V sektakh liderstvo ne osparivayut" *Solidarnost'*, no. 21, 2002, p. 5.

50. Participation of the political authorities in these actions is noted with pride by the FNPR's official history. (Gritsenko, et al., *Istoriya profsoyuzov*, p. 497). For an account of the October 1998 protest in St. Petersburg, see *Sotsial-demokraticheskii vestnik*, no.1(5) 1999.

51. *Solidarnost'*, no. 19, 1996, p. 1.

52. ASMR, *Ob itogakh kollektivno-dogovornoi kampanii*.

53. *Solidarnost'*, no. 18, Sept. 1998, p. 2.

54. ASMR, "Report of the President to the Sixth Central Committee," Sept. 17, 2002.

55. *Golos profsoyuza*, no. 5, July 2003.

56. G. Nesterova, "Eliksir ot stareniya," *Profsoyuzy i ekonomika*, no. 7, 2001, p. 54.

57. "Svezhii veter peremen," *Profsoyuzy*, no. 3, 1999, p. 12.

58. "Interview with Yu. G. Novikov, *Profsoyuzy i ekonomika*, no. 7, 2001, p. 10.

59. See the interview with Kuzental' in Mandel, *Rabotyagi*, pp. 226-244. This is also based on personal communication from N. Kuznetal' and on my own participation in some of the events.

60. For a good analysis of the forms it has taken in the United Auto Workers' Union of the United States, see E. Leary and M. Menaker, *Jointness at GM: Company Unionism in the 21st Century*, Woonsocket, R.I.: New Directions Region 9A, n.d. For Western Europe, see A. Wahl, "European Color: The Ideological Legacy of the Social Pact," *Monthly Review*, Jan. 2004.

61. *Golos profsoyuza*, nos. 3-4, Mar.-Apr. 2002.

62. *Profsoyuzy i ekonomika*, no. 7, 2001, p. 27. Novikov felt this situation was quite normal. Noting that in the last elections, only fifteen per cent of elected officers were changed, he said: "It is characteristic that union activists and apparently even the members are sick of elections with alternative candidates."*Ekonomika i profsoyuzy*, no. 1, 2000, p.20.

63. Maksimov, "Kuda vedut lidery."

64. *Ibid.*

65. Interview with G. Pikulina, May 1998.

66. Information bulletin of Edinstvo, Aug. 7, 2002. (See chapter 5.)

67. Personal communication by N. Poplavskii, chairperson of the tool-and-dye shop, June 2000.

68. B. Maksimov, "Borot'sya ili gulyat' za svoi schet?," 2002 (unpublished)

69. It should be noted this conference in not formally a union conference but one of the work collective. In most enterprises, however, there is no practical difference.

70. *Golos profsoyuza*, no. 10, Oct. 1997. Similarly, at the FNPR's congress in November 2001, 720 of the 819 delegates had higher education. On the other hand, thrity-five per cent were women. *Golos profosoyuza*, no. 10, Nov. 2001.
71. Maksimov, "Kuda vedut lidery."
72. For details, see Ashwin and Clarke, *Russian Trade Unions*, pp. 111-14.
73. See, for example, the statement of F. Sosin, president of the Volgograd regional committee at the Central Committee of February 2002 in *Golos profsoyuza*, no. 3-4, Mar.-Apr. 2002.
74. ASMR, "Ob organizatsionnoi rabote."
75. *Golos profsoyuza*, no. 8-9, Sept.-Oct. 2001.
76. *Ibid.*
77. ASMR, "Report of the President to the Third (Special) Congress," Oct. 1997; *Golos profsoyuza*, no. 8-9, Sept.-Oct., 2001.
78. ASMR, "Ob organizatsionnoi rabote."
79. From a meeting at the Minsk Tractor Factory in June 2000.
80. *Golos profosyuza*, no. 2-3, Apr.-May 1998.
81. *Ibid.*
82. On a much vaster scale, the FNPR's accounting for income from its much larger real-estate holdings and other business assets leaves also much to be desired. See Ashwin and Clarke, *Russian Trade Unions*, pp. 90-93, and Y. Milovidov in *Izvestiya*, Aug. 25, 1999. The FNPR receives only between twenty and forty per cent of its constitutional share of the dues.(*ASTI*, no. 51-52, 2001, p.13.)
83. *Otraslevoe tarifnoe soglashenie po mashinostroitel'nomu kompleksu Rossiiskoi federatsii na 2002-2004 gody*, Moscow, 2002.
84. *Golos profsoyuza*, no. 8-9, Sept.-Oct. 2001.
85. *Golos profosyuza*, no. 2, Feb. 2002. See also ASMR, "Informatsiya ob otraslevom tarifnom soglashenii v 1998 and 1999,"Mar. 16, 1998, (unpublished).
86. ASMR, "Report of the President to the Third (Special) Congress," Oct. 1997.
87. Interview with Novikov in *Ekonomika i profsoyuzy*, no. 1, 2000, p. 22.
88. ASMR, "Informatsiya ob otraslevom tarifnom soglashenii v 1998 and 1999 gg."; *Golos profsoyuza*, no. 4, 1999.
89. *Golos profsoyuza*, no. 11, Nov.1997.
90. *Golos profoyuza*, no. 1-2, Jan.-Feb., 1997.
91. On this, see ASMR, "Report of the President to the September 17, 2002 Central Committee (unpublished); "Ob organizatsionnoi rabote," and G. Trudov, "Ob'edinenie profsoyuzov i 'udel'nye knyaz'ki'," *Solidarnost'*, no. 10, 2003, p. 2.
92. *Golos profosoyuza*, no. 3-4, Mar.-Apr. 2002.
93. ASMR, "Ob organizatsionnoi rabote."

Chapter Four
RESISTANCE IN THE "TRADITIONAL" UNIONS
The Yaroslavl Motor-Builders

Despite "social partnership," some of ASMR's affiliates have engaged in militant collective action. One of the most prominent cases involved four factories making diesel motors and parts. Three are located in Yaroslavl, a regional centre of 600,000 inhabitants on the Volga River, about 350 kilometres northeast of Moscow. The other is in Tutaev, a town of 49,000 about forty kilometres downier from Yaroslavl. The four factories employed 43,000 people in 1997, at the time of the events described here (down from 55,000 in 1990). The militant core of the movement was the Tutaev Motor Factory with a work force of 10,5000.[1]

For a provincial city, Yaroslavl saw a lot of activity during Perestroika. The strike in late 1987 at the Yaroslavl Motor Factory (YMZ) was one the earliest, large-scale labour conflicts. In 1989, a conflict at the Yaroslavl Diesel Apparatus Factory (YZDA) over managerial corruption forced the director's dismissal. Another strike in 1990 at YMZ led to the creation of a "workers' committee," which opposed the union's subservience to management.[2] Russia's first "popular front," a democratic citizen's movement, was created in Yaroslavl in July 1988 in reaction to the "election" of an unpopular party boss as a delegate to the Nineteenth Party Conference.[3] The city also hosted the first Russian national congress of popular fronts. Members of YMZ's workers' committee who were dissatisfied with the popular front's neglect of worker concerns formed a "workers' club" within the front.[4] However, as elsewhere, an independent political workers' movement failed to emerge.

The launching of "shock therapy" and the resultant fall in wages did not provoke any significant resistance in the motor factories. Nor was there any immediate response to non-payment of wages, that began in 1994. Individuals and sometimes groups of workers urged union leaders to take action, but as one of them put it, the latter "were sitting in management's pocket and defending no one's interests but their own."[5] The most significant collective response in this early period was the consolidation and growth of Solidarnost', an alternative union at YMZ that had been established in 1991 by a group of workers led by L. Afanas'ev, one of the leaders of the 1987 strike. At its high point in 1998, Solidarnost' counted about ten per cent of the work force of about 22,000. It was opposed ASMR's dependence on management and did not shy away from confrontation, including the organization of (partial) strikes. Another alternative union arose in 1994 at the Yaroslavl Fuel-Pump Factory (YZTA). It was led by two skilled workers, V. Darofeev and N. Volosyuk who had been active in the popular front. Initially, it drew about 140 members but it proved short-lived.[6] At the Tutaev factory, a group of foundry workers led by V. Popov tried in vain in 1994 to mobilize the others workers and to press the union into action.[7] Popov had successfully led a strike in the foundry in the Soviet period to support a worker who had been unjustly passed over for an apartment.[8]

The high percentage of non-union members is particular to Yaroslavl's motor factories. By the mid 1990s, about forty per cent of the employees at YMZ and Tutaev, and a third at the YZTA and the Diesel Apparatus Plant (YZDA), had left ASMR. Many quit already during Perestroika, when it was an act of some independence. Others left later in reaction to the unions' inactivity in the face of "shock therapy." (In most other Russian ASM plants, the percentage of non-union workers is small.)

The Tutaev Strikes

Mobilization on a large scale began in early 1995 at the Tutaev factory. A group of workers convinced Popov, who had left the plant to work in a grocery store, that the time was ripe: wage arrears continued to grow even though production targets were being met, and it was widely believed that management was corrupt. The group around Popov succeeded in convening a delegates' conference, which elected a strike committee. A nine-day stoppage in February 1995, marked by daily demonstrations in front of the administration building, was massively supported and it resulted in payment of the current wage and the promise quickly to liquidate arrears. But by the time May came around, they had grown to four-and-a-half-months. In July, a union conference replaced the old union leadership with the leaders of the strike committee. V. Krylov, an engineer, became president, and Popov his vice president.

In face of the mounting wage arrears, the union again began organizing demonstrations. Scattered wildcats broke out. A new strike date was set for mid-April 1996. But on March 1, one shop after the next downed tools and poured out onto the Yaroslavl-Rybinsk highway, where they blocked traffic for several hours. The strike lasted six weeks, during which several other road blockades were organized, including one in Yaroslavl on the bridge across the Volga. Even the union's new leaders were surprised at the degree of solidarity and tenacity. Management required union permission even for routine maintenance tasks. Every Monday, a general assembly in front of the gates voted on whether to continue the strike. Many workers were unhappy when it ended after six weeks without significant results.

The director, on his part, tried to sue the union for an illegal strike. But the court instead found him guilty of gross violations of the Labour Code and made him pay the workers two thirds of their base pay for the days lost during the strike. The recourse to civil disobedience during the strike reflected the workers' growing awareness that the solution to their problems was not to be found in the factory but in action against the state. All the same, they demanded the director's dismissal and obtained it in September 1997, following a campaign of demonstrations, marches and highway blockages that forced the regional government to cast its votes at an emergency stockholders' meeting for a director acceptable to the union. The new director dismissed some of the old higher administration, including the chief accountant, and opened the books to the union, revealing a huge debt. In face of this apparent goodwill, the union's leaders decided to suspend pressure tactics to give him time to turn things around.

During the strike, ASMR's national office sent Tutaev a symbolic amount of money, and the regional committee provided the union with legal counsel. But the three other plants, where wage arrears were a more recent phenomenon, remained aloof. Even as they began to feel more pain, they experienced only sporadic wildcats limited to individual shops. Several factors favoured Tutaev's relative militancy. It was a factory town built in the early 1970s by young workers who had come from all over the Soviet Union, lured by the prospect of immediately obtaining housing.[9] When the crisis hit, Tutaev workers had much less opportunity than their counterparts in Yaroslavl find alternative sources of livelihood. And the commute to Yaroslavl was too costly for most people in terms of money, time and energy. Nor could they move away in search of work, since they could not afford to rent housing and their apartments in Tutaev had almost no market value. For the vast majority, then, garden plots were the only additional source of subsistence. On the other hand, solidarity came easier in a small factory town where everyone knows almost everyone else. Tutaev's population was also left-leaning, having voted Communist in the 1996 presidential election, whereas Yaroslavl's voters overwhelmingly supported Yeltsin. The Tutaev factory even had a small group of socialist (that is, non-Stalinist) activists, a rarity.

The Political Campaign

In the wake of Tutaev's second strike, the three Yaroslavl plants, which were experiencing growing rank-and-file unrest, elected their own strike committees, which included activists of both the traditional and the alternative unions, where the latter existed. These committees, to varying degrees, acted as a spur to the union leadership. In October 1996, the four strike committees established a co-ordinating council of strike committees that met weekly in the offices of ASMR's regional committee. It organized a campaign of demonstrations, marches and picketing of the regional government aimed at forcing the state to adopt an industrial policy for their sector.[10] (At the time, the government owned a third of the shares of the enterprises.) The movement's political focus made things easier for the union leaders of the Yaroslavl factories, since they were spared from having to confront management. It also helped to save them from being booted out by the workers for their inactivity, as had occurred at Tutaev. As for the directors, though they probably felt some heat from the governor and from Moscow, on the whole they were not much bothered by movement. To the degree that they wanted to save their factories, it was doing their bidding for them. In the meanwhile, it was channelling the workers' anger away from themselves. Except perhaps at Tutaev, where the director had recently been changed, the others were all involved in intermediary companies that were parasitizing the plants. As elsewhere, management, especially the higher levels, was doing quite well for itself, despite the crisis.

The political campaign was building up to blockade of the bridge across the Volga set for December 25, 1996. (Wage arrears in October were from five to seven months.) But three days before the event, governor A. Lisitsyn, an economic liberal, summoned the directors, the union presidents and the strike committee leaders to inform them that he had negotiated a development plan with the government. They were invited to Moscow on December 25 to discuss it with the Deputy Prime Minister. The Yaroslavl strike committees called off the action, but Tutaev would not be deterred. Several busloads set out only to be stopped by the police at the entrance to Yaroslavl. The workers proceeded by public trolleys to the bridge and blocked it for two hours. In January and February 1997, the strike committees organized two massive marches down the main streets of Yaroslavl to demand the resignation of Yeltsin and his government. This represented a radicalization of their demands, which had hitherto been purely economic.

Smirnov, president of ASMR's regional committee, supported the movement, although he himself showed little initiative and was content to let the strike committees lead. He had been the union president at YZTA until 1995, where, according to Volosyuk, who chaired its strike committee, he had slept through the arrears problem. Smirnov was clearly more comfortable fighting the government than management, although, in a rare move for an ASMR leader, he did initiate a lawsuit against YMZ's director to force him to transfer dues to the union. Having embraced the political campaign, he became more aware of the unions' isolation and more critical of ASMR's national leadership. As for the FNPR, he described its national protests as "primitive, rotten and slavish." "The demands are never met, yet the FNPR has no further plans for reacting to that. If we demand the resignation of the government, we have to go all the way," he said in 1997. He even began to show interest in rank-and-file education.

The unions' political campaign resulted in the creation of Russian Motors in February 1997, a consortium of the four plants for the purpose of co-ordinating production and marketing activities. The government's anti-crisis plan also included investment credits to help bring the motors closer to Western standards. The directors, on their part, committed themselves to paying wage arrears and transferring dues to the unions.[11] On paper, at least, it was a big victory wrested from a conservative government that had hitherto shown no interest in an industrial policy.

But it turned out to be another example of the tactic of selective concessions to the parts of the labour movement that posed the greatest immediate threat. Russian Motors remained an empty shell. According to Smirnov, the directors, especially YMZ's, who enjoyed a dominant economic position (Tutaev and YZTA were smaller and mostly supplied parts to YMZ), resisted cooperation, and the governor, who had a representative on the board of Russian Motors, offered no leadership. Smirnov, on his part, did not try to mobilize union pressure to force the directors to co-operate. Meanwhile, there was a change in government in Moscow, and the Deputy Prime Minister who had signed the agreement left. The central demand of the FNPR's March 1996 national protest, which attracted quite a massive participation, had, in fact, been a change of government. With the shakeup in Moscow, FNPR president Shmakov, not waiting for a mandate from his Council, rushed to endorse the new Prime Minister, S. Kirienko, even though the latter had yet to make public his programme. Despite this, Shmakov called him a "conscientious social partner."[12] Unfortunately, the new government of "young reformers" or, as they were sometimes called, "boys in pink shorts," turned out to be even more rightwing that its predecessor. Still, from August 1997, the government began to give credits to Belarus to help its truck and tractor factories purchase Yaroslavl's motors, and that injected some cash into the enterprises. As a result, they began to pay wages on a somewhat more regular basis, though arrears continued to mount. Another relative gain was the transfer of the enterprises' "social sphere" to the municipality, which lightened their financial burdens.

These concessions, both real and only promised, seemed to take the steam out of the movement. For the next eighteen months, the only collective actions were picketing government offices and participation in the FNPR's semi-annual protests. The one in April 1998, which drew huge numbers elsewhere in Russia, attracted only 8,000 in Yaroslavl, as compared to 30,000 the previous spring. As in most other regions, the protesters demanded Yeltsin's resignation and a new economic policy.[13] The "rail wars" in May 1998 breathed new life into the Yaroslavl movement. Coalminers in Siberia, southern Russia and the far north, without any apparent co-ordination, blocked railways for several days to demand their wages.[14] These protests ended with signed pledges by the government. When they were violated, the miners sent delegations to Moscow, who on June 11 erected a tent village or "picket" next to the Humpback Bridge (*Gorbatyi most*) across the square from the "White House," seat of the executive branch of government. The bridge had seen major labour battles in the Revolution of 1905.

The picket was organized by the Independent Miners' Union (NPG), an alternative union. The FNPR and its affiliated sectoral unions largely ignored it. The picketers had three demands: Yeltsin's resignation; constitutional reform to put the executive under democratic control; an economic policy oriented to the needs of the people.[15] Asked if this was another instance of the NPG's using political demands to force economic concessions for miners and the mining sector, A. Sergeev, the NPG's president and a longtime Yeltsin supporter, insisted that this time it was different: the miners were fighting for all workers and would not abandon their political demands.[16]

The picket became a rallying point for the scattered forces of the labour movement that were fed up with the FNPR's moderation and play-acting at opposition. They yearned to break out of their isolation and saw in the miners a determined, powerful force that could unite the labour opposition and give it direction. Groups of workers came to visit the picket from across European Russian, and similar encampment were set up in other towns.

On July 2, representatives of local unions of the Yaroslavl region gathered in the conference hall of the regional council of trade unions and unanimously decided to create a Regional Coordinating Council of the Strike Movement. Besides union officials and the leaders of the strike committees of the motor and radio-electronics plants, it included representatives of the Popular-Patriotic Front (PPF), a Communist-led coalition. A Vorob'ev, a retired army officer and regional PPF leader, was chosen co-ordinator. Smirnov spoke to the meeting, calling for decisive action against the new government that was even worse than its predecessor. He cited a recently-leaked secret government memorandum to the International Monetary Fund that called for the intensification of "shock therapy."[17]

On July 3, eleven strike-committee activists from Yaroslavl's motor factories visited the miners' camp in Moscow. A week later, they returned to Moscow with a delegation of thirty-seven workers. They spent three days in discussions with the miners and activists from other towns. Back in Yaroslavl, the leaders of the strike committees and the union presidents of the four plants issued an appeal to all ASMR affiliates to join in a united movement behind the political demands of the miners. They pointed out that struggles in isolated factories could not substantially change things and they decried the absence of co-ordination in the labour movement.

The signs of growing popular discontent and of the will of at least some workers to act on it did not leave ASMR's national leaders unmoved. A brief summary of the Yaroslavl appeal was published in the union's monthly paper.[18] Its Presidium endorsed the decision of FNPR's executive to propose a general strike for October 7. But, as usual, it left participation to the discretion of its local affiliates.[19] There was a sense that popular protest was finally on the march. It was bolstered by the Communist Party's decision also to mobilize for October 7. And the expressed readiness of the FNPR to work together with "left and centre-left" forces allied to the KPRF (Communist Party) was also something new. A meeting on September 8 of the Union of Labour, the political arm of the FNPR, with representatives of the KPRF called for a "national council for coordination of solidary actions of trade unions and parties."[20] Another encouraging sign was the thirty-five-to-four vote in Yaroslavl's regional duma to demand Yeltsin's resignation. The majority of delegates had been elected as liberals (there were only eight Communists), and the year before a resolution of non-confidence in Yeltsin had garnered only sixteen votes. Yaroslavl's example was followed by the majority of regional dumas of Russia.[21]

On July 28, 5000 workers, mostly from the motor plants, marched in silence to the beat of drums to the governor's office. Even more workers would have participated, had not Afanas'ev called a separate rally at YMZ directed against management. It drew about 3000 people. Afanas'ev felt that management, not the state, was the proper target for union pressure. But the other crowd at the square in front of the regional government adopted a resolution condemning the government's economic policy and demanding resignation of Yeltsin and his government. It also called for nationalisation of the banks, natural resources and other strategic economic sectors, for a review of the legality of the privatizations, for payment of wages, and fulfillment of the government's commitments to the motor plants. Finally, the governor was to hand-deliver these demands to Yeltsin The resolution concluded with an appeal to the people of Yaroslavl and the rest of central Russia to show the government that "we are not slaves."[22]

On August 17, in what seemed like a fatal blow to "shock therapy,"the rouble collapsed, causing a major spurt of inflation that wiped out more than half the real value of workers' wages. It also decimated the new "middle class" that had formed, mainly in the financial and service sectors catering to the needs of big business and the rich. Yeltsin was forced to dismiss the "boys in pink shorts." He tried to bring back former Prime Minister V. Chernomyrdin, but the opposition was too great.[23]

The Yaroslavl "Picket"

The idea of a blockade of rail freight traffic to Moscow was discussed by the Yaroslavl delegation during the visit to the miners' picket. Tutaev had long been pressing the co-ordinating committee for such a militant action. Twice already, its workers had voted for a rail blockade, and Popov, leader of the Tutaev strike committee, was now calling for a "ring of anger" around the capital. The others accepted the idea in principle but felt it required preliminary educational work and organization. They decided first to set up a "picket" in Yaroslavl alongside the Vorkuta-Moscow railway.[24]

On August 24, 1998, about 600 people gathered on the chosen spot, mostly workers' from the motor factories, including five busloads from Tutaev. They adopted demands identical to those of the miners. About fifty people stayed the first night, despite pouring rain (Tutaev supplied the tents), and thirty or so manned the camp on a permanent basis thereafter. Although the local authorities tried at first to prevent the camp, they soon acquiesced, and before long, the governor himself spoke in favour of Yeltsin's resignation.[25] The picket became an organizing and educational centre for the movement. But more immediately, it was a permanent threat to rail traffic for the authorities. According to its activists, about 5000 people visited the picket during its first forty-five days. They took literature, read the informational boards, discussed issues with the activists. Tutaev sent at least one busload each day. The Radio Factory committed itself to send ten workers from each shift daily. Others also sent delegations.[26] The picket, in turn, sent its agitators to towns and enterprises in the region. It distributed leaflets in Yaroslavl and sent around a sound truck to mobilize for demonstrations.

The movement's focus remained exclusively political, ignoring management. The co-ordinating council, in fact, appealed to the directors to support the movement, and, in its own assessment, most of them did.²⁷ At least several of the picket's activists were released with pay from work by management (as, indeed, were the miners of the Moscow picket), and they ate lunch for a nominal price at the cafeteria of YMZ, just up the hill and across the highway from the picket. Tutaev's director also supplied the buses that brought the workers to Yaroslavl. The coordinating committee even went to persuade some YMZ workers who had gone of strike to return to work. In the words of Vorob'ev, "we told them to continue working and to send representatives to us [at the picket] on a constant basis and to work with their collective through them, to prepare for the general action, since isolated strikes yield no results. The plant has to work, to support the production cycle. After all, we will achieve its nationalization, and so it is in our interests to preserve it."²⁸

Vorob'ev's statement is a good example of the chiliastic, not to say adventuristic, bent that characterized many Communist activists and those even more to the (Stalinist) "left." Afanas'ev, though formally a member of the coordinating committee, did not take part in it. One of the reasons was his strong anti-Communist attitudes. He decried the Communist influence in the strike committees. And there was no love lost on the other side. He formally resigned from the committee after G. Khokhlov, a Communist engineer at YMZ and vice president of its strike committee, accused him over the radio of diverting workers from the main cause of their troubles by directing them against management, a secondary player. He also claimed that Afanas'ev's union existed only thanks to money from the U.S. government. (That, in fact, was not true.)²⁹

The next step of the Yaroslavl "picket" was a three-hour blockade of freight traffic headed for Moscow on September 9. The government issued orders to prevent it. At eleven a.m., between 600 and 800 people, as usual mostly motor workers, including several busloads from Tutaev, moved from the encampment in the direction of the heavily guarded tracks. A confrontation was avoided at the last moment when the railroad authorities agreed to a proposal from the coordinating ommittee that the railroad itself suspend traffic for three hours. Despite recriminations from the Tutaev workers, who wanted physically to block the line, there was a general sense of victory. The workers had shown their power.

The three-hour blockade had been intended as a warning. As a next step, the co-ordinating committee invited the enterprises and popular organizations of central Russia to send delegates to a conference in Yaroslavl to discuss further action. Some seventy people from a wide variety of protest movements and "left" (Stalinist) political organizations, whose real strength was far from clear, attended a conference on September 23 hosted and financed by the Yaroslavl regional council of trade unions. It was decided to establish a coordinating council of protest actions for all of central Russia. The new council claimed to represent seven regions. It adopted a plan to block entrances to the buildings of local and regional authorities on October 7 in order to force the latter to relay the movement's political demands to the central government in Moscow. If Yeltsin's reply was unsatisfactory, railroads and highways leading to Moscow would be cut for three hours the next day, and, if that failed, the blockade would become unlimited.[30]

Meanwhile, changes were occurring in Moscow that would undermine the apparent commitment to popular mobilization of the leaders of the FNPR and the KPRF. A majority of the deputies in the State Duma, sensing Yeltsin's weakness after the financial collapse and in face of a growing protest movement, twice rejected his candidate, Chernomyrdin, for Prime Minister. Yeltsin could have proposed him a third time and then dissolved the Duma, as the Constitution allowed, but he evidently feared that such a move would fuel the protest. Instead, he proposed Academician E. Primakov, a former foreign-policy advisor and briefly KGB chief under Gorbachev. In KPRF circles, Primakov was seen as a statesman in the traditional Russian mould, a person committed to the "national interest." Even more important, he was prepared to invite Communists into the government. Having become a government party, the leaders of the KPRF, who, despite militant gesturing, had always been exclusively oriented to parliamentary action, lost their interest in the popular movement. The leaders of the FNPR were also only too glad to declare victory. Although neither organization could afford simply to call off the October 7 protest, they both forgot it almost as soon as it was over. As for Yeltsin's camp, they knew Petrakov opposed the demand for Yeltsin's early retirement as a threat to Russia's stability. They therefore felt they could temporarily retreat to let Petrakov and the Communists deal with the crisis for which they were largely responsible.[31]

In Yaroslavl, the changes in Moscow found an echo in a joint declaration of September 28 by the governor, the vice-president of the legislative assembly and the president of the regional council of trade unions. They expressed support for the protest of October 7 as well as their confidence in the new government formed by Primakov. They also took their distance from the demands of the regional co-ordinating committee, calling merely for a "correction" of the economic course, rather than its complete "replacement" (*smena*). They also dropped the demand to amend the Constitution to put the executive (now in Primakov's hands) under democratic popular. Representatives of the co-ordinating committee had been invited to sign the declaration but they, including those who were Communists, walked out in protest.[32] Another blow to the movement came on September 30 when the NPG's leadership signed an agreement with the Primakov government that gave the miners and the coal sector economic concessions but passed over the movement's political demands in silence. On October 3, the NPG leaders called off the Moscow "picket." A week later, the remaining die-hards were unceremoniously cleared out in a pre-dawn police raid and forcibly put on trains.[33]

By all accounts, participation in the October 7 protest was massive, larger than anything Russia had seen for years. The FNPR claimed twenty-five million attended meetings, marches and demonstrations, and, of these, twelve million struck.[34] But, as noted in the previous chapter, the protest had some rather curious aspects. Most of the "strikers" were, in fact, workers let out early by management, and in many places directors and government officials marched alongside union leaders in the protest. In Moscow, Mayor Luzhkov, the president of the Union of Entrepreneurs and Industrialists, and the president of the Union of Realtors and Brokers attended the rally.[35] Yeltsin, however, was not moved. His Deputy Prime Minister O. Sysuev declared that only "a minority were on the streets. The majority stayed at their work places. And for the sake of those people, Boris Nikolaevich will continue to carry out his duties."[36]

Thus ended the largest popular protest movement the new Russia had seen. But even before October 7, the KPRF had shifted focus to its efforts to impeach Yeltsin through the Duma. It was, however, quite obvious that those efforts could not succeed without a powerful extraparliamentary movement.[37] As it was, Yeltsin had little trouble bribing enough deputies to block his impeachment. As for the FNPR, it exploited the October 7 rally in Moscow to promote mayor Luzhkov's candidacy for President. FNPR orators praised him as the man "who could unite workers and employers, left and right."[38] For the next two years, Luzhkov's election was the focus of the FNPR's political action.

But in Yaroslavl itself, the results of the protest at first appeared quite impressive, even if the main political demands had not been achieved. On October 7, the four motor factories stood idle, as 25,000 demonstrators, including ten busloads from Tutaev, marched in four giant columns to Soviet Square facing the regional government. When Vorob'ev asked the crowd if they supported a railroad blockade planned for the next day, a sea of hands shot up. A delegation led by the president of the regional trade-union federation went into the building to deliver the demands to the regional government. Its representatives were told to deliver them directly to Yeltsin. But only the Tutaev workers made good on the plan to block all the exits until confirmation from Moscow was received that the demands had been handed to Yeltsin.[39]

The co-ordinating committee agonized into the early morning hours over whether to adopt a "hard" or "soft" version of the rail blockade, that is, whether physically to block the tracks, as the Tutaev workers wanted, or again to let the authorities do it for them. That evening, the television broadcasted stern warnings from the government that anyone participating in the blockade would be criminally prosecuted. Meanwhile, the regional government also met in emergency session. An hour before the blockade was planned to begin, at 10 a.m., a top-level delegation arrived at the picket to deliver the government's resolution. It was read to the crowd by the deputy governor himself: the regional government supported the resolution adopted by the demonstrators the previous day, except for the part demanding Yeltsin's resignation and calling for a rail blockade. It offered to create a joint working group with representatives of the coordinating committee to develop and carry out an industrial and social programme for the region. The co-ordinating committee was invited to send three representatives to sit in on government meetings. It would also be given free air time on television twice a month, and the government would instruct the media to provide objective coverage of its activities. Buses would be provided to take protesters to Moscow (for a planned demonstration in support of the impeachment). Finally, this resolution would be relayed to the government in Moscow.[40]

But the government delegation implored the workers not to go onto the tracks, promising that no freight traffic would pass for three hours. The question of physically blocking the tracks was an important symbolic issue for both sides. The Tutaev workers, especially the women, insisted on going onto the tracks. Popov accused the others of "surrendering our positions and marching in place." But the majority decided to accept the offer of a "soft" version.[41] They were swayed by the government's concessions—the workers had forced the government to come to them!—and especially by the low worker turnout for the blockade after the previous day's triumph. Only about 500 people had come, and at least a third of them were from Tutaev. Meanwhile, special riot police had arrived from Moscow and they were twice as numerous as the workers. In the rest of Russia's central region, few other blockades took place. There was no "ring of anger."

Though the Yaroslavl picket remained in place for another month and the regional co-ordinating committee was never formally disbanded, October 8 marked the effective end of the movement. For a brief moment, popular mobilization had shifted the local correlation of forces, forcing important concessions from the regional government. In the following weeks, steps were taken on both sides to carry out the agreement. But as time passed, they took on an formal character and were eventually simply forgotten. Three representatives of the coordinating committee did sit in on government sessions, and the committee obtained free air time for a couple of months, until "their fear subsided," as Krylov explained. (He was one of the three who attended government meetings.) No anti-crisis plan was ever put into effect, and "Russian Motors" remained a dead letter.

To make good the government's concessions, it would have been necessary to consolidate and reinforce the popular mobilization. A combination of factors worked against that, including the temporary eclipse of Yeltsin and the neo-liberal forces, the progressive remonetarization of the economy, and the start of a recovery after the financial collapse. Wages began to be paid regularly, arrears shrank (facilitated by the devaluation that reduced their real value), enterprises began to bring idle capacity back on line in response to heightened demand for their now relatively cheaper goods. But these factors alone cannot explain the abrupt end of the protest movement. After all, Primakov's government did not break radically with the policies of the previous six years: it made no effort to raise living standards and to support domestic demand. Thus, the minimum wage and pension remained many times below the minimum subsistence level, and the government's 1999 budget was the most IMF-friendly ever.[42] Nor did the government adapt an active industrial policy, though it found money to bail out insolvent, essentially parasitical, banks. It did not renounce Russia's foreign debt obligations nor did it take measures against the illegality that had marked privatization. And finally, it did nothing to support the popular mobilization that had helped to bring it to power. In light of this, it is not surprising, when Yeltsin unceremoniously sacked Primakov seven months after his appointment and brought back the neo-liberals, it did not provoke the least popular protest.

The regular payment of wages was a real improvement in workers' lives, and that was undoubtedly a factor that undermined popular protest. But the real value of wages had fallen by at least half after the devaluation. In any case, the element of stability that the regular payment of wages introduced into the workers' lives, in other circumstances, could just as well have given birth to a movement for a living wage. One of the circumstances that worked against that were the policies of the FNPR and the KPRF, the two national organizations that might have provided coordination and strategy to the popular movement. Each, in its own way, was committed to a policy of "partnership" with various segments of the political and economic élite. The popular movement had meaning to them only to the degree that it facilitated these alliances. As Vorob'ev, himself a Communist, but one committed to the popular movement, remarked: "To a certain degree, our protest actions are being undermined by the left-patriotic opposition's particular attitude to the government of E.M. Primakov. In the State Duma, the opposition supports him. It turns out, then, that we, by developing the protest movement, are acting against those left forces. That is the complexity of the situation…Meanwhile the people continue to live miserably, and there is no ray of light."[43] The same, of course, can be said of the NPG's leadership, that cynically exploited miners' "picket" and the broad enthusiasm it evoked to make narrow, corporatist gains that themselves proved ephemeral. These three organizations also fostered the illusion among the popular activists that the movement really had a national leadership. That helped to ensure that none ever emerged. The president of the Yaroslavl regional council of trade unions later complained that "we did not see the co-ordinating role of the left-patriotic forces in Moscow. And it was sorely needed!" Vorob'ev similarly complained of "insufficient support for our actions from the centre."[44] In fact, there was none, only the imitation.

Yaroslavl thus remained isolated, despite the efforts of its activists to broaden their movement. But on October 8, it became clear that even within Yaroslavl itself only a small minority of the workers were active. The main support of the co-ordinating committee had been and remained the four motor plants, and among them, Tutaev's contribution was by far the greatest. The support of Yaroslavl's union leaders for the protest movement remained mostly on the level of words. True, they at least did not place obstacles in its path and in some ways they facilitated it. But they gave no leadership. The unions made no serious effort to inform and mobilize their members. That was left that to the picket. A. Mel'nikov, a member of the co-ordinating committee from the Diesel Apparatus Factory, complained afterwards of the "low level of information about our activities even within the work collectives of plants that had workers involved actively in the picket." Vorob'ev admitted "that we did not have enough forces. We were not even able to reach most of the work collectives of Yaroslavl. The activists most capable of working with people were busy with immediate tasks at the picket itself."[45] The latter did their best with the meagre resources at their disposal, but the camp was located away from most of the factories. That, in retrospect, was an error, even though the location beside the railway kept the authorities on their toes. Of the 5000 people who passed through the "picket" during its first forty-five days, many were not workers but pensioners and/or Communist sympathizers. The involvement of the mass of workers, apart from the demonstrations, was minimal. YMZ had 22,000 employees working just up the hill and across the highway, but few visited the picket. Most of Yaroslavl's residents, in fact, were only vaguely aware of its existence.

Even if Yaroslavl's union leaders had wanted to and knew how to mobilize their members, they probably would have been unable to do it. It was, after all, a political struggle. Yet inside the factories, the unions were as always adjuncts to management. Ordinary union members believed neither in the unions nor in their own force. The Tutaev workers were different, not because their distress was greater, but because they had experience of self-organization and they had opposed management. Even the regional co-ordinating committee, whose members were more serious about the popular movement, were not completely free of "partnership" tendencies. It appealed to the directors to support the popular movement, citing common interests "in the present circumstances."[46] Some of its members, as noted, went to persuade striking YMZ workers to return to work. And there was the rather puzzling desire to force the the regional and local governments to support their cause. Hence, for example, the demand that the regional government personally relay the demonstrators' demands to Moscow. It was as if their goal was not simply to wrest concessions from the local and regional authorities but to win them over.[47] As V. Kornilov, head of the Yaroslavl regional Communist Party, put it, "It is very important to force the governors of the regions around Moscow to work with us." The governors, of course, turned against the movement the very moment that pressure fell off. All this, of course, did not pass unnoticed in Yaroslavl. A caller to an open-line radio programme asked Vorob'ev: "Why don't you criticize the local authorities and the enterprise directors who are totally out of control (*zarvavshiesya*). There are rumours that you are friends with the governor." Vorob'ev replied that the authorities had been forced to change their attitude and to take the co-ordinating committee seriously. He also pointed out that the committee had refused to sign the declaration in support Primakov. He forgot to mention his committee's appeals to the directors.[48] In all of this, one can see the influence of the KPRF, which had its people in the co-ordinating committee and supporters among the region's union leaders.[49] This party, whose nationalism far outweighs its commitment to popular interests, has always sought salvation in the state and in the "patriotic" captains of industry and bourgeoisie, rather than in a mobilized working class. After all, the latter could get out of control.[50]

In retrospect, events largely confirmed the analysis put out by the leaders of the alternative unions at YMZ and YZTA at the start of the movement. In a joint declaration made in 1997 on the founding of the co-ordinating committee of strike committees, they pointed their finger at management, who accused the government of all sins but themselves took no action. Why were they not picketing the Kremlin or participating in hunger strikes? "Let them make public declarations of their property and income and those of their families, at least for the past year. That might really lift the suspicion of theft, machinations and self-interest from them." The authors then turned to the co-ordinating committee. Instead of demanding a change of the "bankrupt management teams" or forcing them to explain clearly when the wage arrears would be paid, it decided "to rush into street demonstrations and politics." Here the authors saw the influence of Communists and of related parties, who had no idea about workers' needs or how to organize them but wanted to saddle and ride them. And they were supported by the regional FNPR council and by the ASMR.

> The free trade unions have always considered that the FNPR-affiliated unions, before taking up the defence of workers and ordinary office employees from the oppression of the employers and the political authorities of all levels, should first exclude employers and their representatives from their ranks, since one does not keep a fox in the chicken coop. Only then will they be ready to create a regional strike committee…[The above-mentioned political forces] are consciously setting the people against the political leadership of the country, "forgetting" the main culprits, the enterprise directors…[We] consider that the strike committees should first of all, as hard as it is given our present toothless laws, get busy "squeezing" the workers' wages out of the directors, leaving in the background anti-government slogans, as justified as they may be. After all, we were hired not by Chubais and Yeltsin, but by Savel'ev, Doletskii and Pirozhkov. We have to demand of them first…Regional strike committees really are necessary, since the patience of the people is not boundless in face of the reigning lawlessness and arbitrariness of authorities of all levels…But on the other hand, there is nothing out of which to create them, since, as before, the FNPR or, as they are sometimes called, the "directors'," unions are still operating in the majority of enterprises. From them, one can create only the parody of a strike committee, and that means that they will simply not have the support or confidence of the workers. There can only be one conclusion: before creating a regional strike committee, it is first necessary to create free workers' trade unions in the enterprises, or, if it is possible, of course, to reform the old trade unions. It is necessary in the streets to demand a reckoning from the President for the economic ruin of our country, all the more as that it is easy to do, since the President will not take your wage away from you or fire you. It is much harder to demand an accounting for unpaid wages

from the one who hired you, from your own [*rodnoi*, literally "native"] director in your own [*rodnoe*] plant.[51]

The point is not whether the directors really could or could not pay wages. Even when they did not have the money, wages remained their responsibility. If enough unions had taken militant action against management, the government would have been forced to change its policy. Both the government and management were legitimate targets for the unions. The real point is that any struggle directed against the government had little chance of success as long as the unions let the directors off the hook. By focussing exclusively on the government, the unions, consciously or not, acted as tools of management, a position that was quite consistent with "social partnership."

Return to Normalcy

The decline in the frequency of rank-and-file unrest, in particular the scattered wildcat strikes, set the scene for a rapid return to "normalcy" in the unions. The Yaroslavl strike committees ran candidates in the regional elections, but, as one of their leaders put it, "money decided everything." The KPRF also saw its small caucus in the regional duma further reduced. In Tutaev, the strike committee managed to get Popov elected to the municipal council and it helped to elect a new mayor, but she proved to be "neither fish nor foul." Eventually, the strike committees just withered away, without having undertaken any serious analysis of their strategy or its results. Only Volosyuk, head of YZTA's strike committee, continued the struggle. He tried to organize workers' control of the corrupt administration of his factory but he got no support from the union committee. Increasingly isolated, he grew discouraged and in 2002 left to work in a small motor-parts shop setup by a friend, formerly an engineer at YZTA.

Collaboration between the unions of the four plants also came to an end, along with any hopes attached to "Russian Motors" and to the government's promise of an anti-crisis programme. ASMR's regional committee provided no leadership in pressing these matters. Smirnov's appreciation of the militant campaigns of the previous years, and especially of strikes, also changed: "You can see yourself that strikes yield no results. The plants have to work, and for that we need normal relations with management." He was fatalistic about local presidents ever becoming independent of management, because "they are unprotected." He also lost interest in rank-and-file education.

A return to "normalcy" was also evident at Tutaev, though it did not go as far as in the other unions, since its leadership had come out of a struggle with management. The legacy of that struggle and also of the political movement, which had consolidated a small, militant core of activists, some with socialist leanings, were to some degree able to hold the leaders in check. On the other hand, the union's failure to break out of its isolation and the critical financial situation of the factory created strong pressures for "partnership." Underlying it all was the decline of rank-and-file activism. "When the rank and file were pushing," observed S. Kvashnin, an activist engineer in the summer of 2000, "the leaders acted. But as soon as the rank and file began to calm down, the leaders seemed to fall asleep."

In the spring of 2000, the union demanded a thirty-per-cent raise, which was actually somewhat less than what had been lost to inflation the previous year. The average wage at the Tutaev factory was only half of that at YMZ. But a union survey found that not a single shop was prepared to back up the demand with collective action. The workers seemed content to be regularly receiving wages again and gradually to be paid their accumulated arrears (paid partly in kind). And so when the director unilaterally raised the base pay while at the same time cutting some bonuses, the majority of the plant committee resigned itself, even though the net result was considerably less than the thirty per cent they had been asking for and some workers ended up earning even less than before. It was pointed out that during preparation of the draft agreement, the union committee had not received any suggestions about raising wages from workers or shop chairpersons.

A visit to the union in the summer of 2000 found a situation that was not radically different from the rest of ASMR. The collective agreement that had been adopted over the objections of a minority contained vague language on indexation and the minimum wage as prescribed by the sectoral agreement. These relevant paragraphs began: "management will strive to…" The wage system remained profoundly arbitrary. Management's salaries were very high relative to workers' wages and a secret. The union was unable to publish any critical material in the plant's weekly paper, and management was stingy about giving it union access to its photocopier. There were still managerial personnel in the union, though overall membership was down to fifty-three per cent of the work force. It was very striking how much the balance of forces had shifted against the union since it had ousted the former director. Even replacing a lightbulb in a stairwell was difficult and required the intervention of the president at the highest level of management.

The mass of workers were demoralized. The dominant mood, apart from fear of losing one's job, particularly strong among white-collar personnel, was skepticism—about the honesty and commitment of the union's leaders and about the value of collective action, including the action in which they themselves had participated not long ago. Theft and drinking were epidemic. Krylov, admitted that the management knew the union had no real power behind it when it negotiated but he was at a loss about what to do. "Now that wages are being paid, I don't know how to get the workers to hate management," he complained."It was easy to mobilize before," recalled Popov: "You just had to put up a notice, and 2000-3000 came out to demonstrate."

Having relied on spontaneity in the past, they apparently do not believe the union could do anything to build support and fight demoralization. Popov resigned in disgust from the labour disputes committee because of its pro-management bias, rather than seeing that as challenge for the union. (At the time, the committee was still elected by the delegates' conference.) When workers in the stamping shop complained about the frigid temperature, Krylov got an order from the public health authorities to stop work. He hoped at least to obtain some material compensation for the workers, even if he could not improve their conditions. (The heating system is a by-product of the factory's operation, but it was working at a only fraction of capacity.) However, the workers in question were afraid to defy management and kept on working. This "betrayal" incensed Krylov, who swore he would never help those workers again. He did not see the workers' fear of management as challenge for the union to overcome.

There was little understanding among the union's leaders of the importance of involving workers in the resolution of their own conflicts with management, though that would have been a way of building their commitment and confidence. In the case of the lightbulb, the shop committee repeatedly asked the supervisor, both orally and in written form, to take action, but he failed to respond. Krylov finally took up the complaint at a meeting with the chief engineer. But the conflict could have been resolved quickly with even moderate pressure tactics in the shop, such as a lunchtime demonstration.

In early 2001, the director announced plans to send 1500 employees, mostly white-collar personnel, home on unlimited "administrative leave." His real intention was to force them to resign "of their own volition," the avoiding certain legal and political restrictions and economizing on severance pay. The union leadership informed the employees that the order was illegal and that it could successfully defend them in court. But first they had to go through the labour disputes committee. Three hundred and twenty people received notices in what was to be a first wave. The union successfully defended all those who empowered it to act for them in the courts. But few did. The others were afraid. Yet, the union leaders knew the prevailing state of mind. And the threat to jobs concerned everyone, not only those who received notice. They could have sought a collective solution that would have spared the direct targets of the layoffs the need to file individual complaints against management. A Edinstvo activist who heard this story at a seminar exclaimed: "I can't understand you. You have experience of blocking bridges and railroads! Surely your union knows that that kind of problem calls for militant, collective action?!"

The conflict over the layoffs arose only a couple of weeks before a planned seminar for shopfloor activists organized jointly by the union and the School for Worker Democracy, which was assuming most of the costs. The seminar was supposed to be a test that could lead to regular collaboration. But when the conflict broke out, the union's leaders did not see the seminar as an opportunity to discuss it with shopfloor activists and to seek solutions together. Instead, Krylov called it off, citing the deterioration of relations with management. The union's activists themselves could not understand that, though they did nothing.

In 2000, a group of women activists, again with the support of the School for Worker Democracy, established a women's commission, headed by the chairperson of the metrological shop, who also happened to be one of the plant's socialists. Despite initial skepticism, the commission slowly gained respect among the women (half the workforce) through its efforts to improve health and safety conditions and benefits and to fight wage arbitrariness and job discrimination. The commission even began to inspire fear among management, which took positive action on several of its demands, including some relating to wage discrimination. It even showed signs of taking on the problems of theft and drinking, predominantly male phenomena, that undermined the union and bled the enterprise. "There isn't a shop where the men don't drink," said one of the women activists. "We have to educate them and we do." The union leaders themselves readily admit that most of the activists are women. "In the confrontations with police," recalled Krylov, "the women were always in the forefront. The men tended to stay on the sidelines, urging the women on and offering advice." (The women usually have much unkinder words about the men.) And yet, the union's leaders have shown little interest in the women's commission and have never responded to invitations to attend its seminars. Even worse, the women learned that the union had been paying the wage of a full-time "chairperson of the women's committee," a committee no one had every heard about. No explanation was forthcoming from Krylov.

Despite their criticism of the leaders, the union's activists point out that they did challenge management over the layoffs, whereas most other unions would have rubber-stamped the order. They also note the union office is open to workers who come with problems, a far cry from the situation before the leadership was changed. And workers who come with individual problems usually get action, even if it means the leaders have to confront management. But the leaders lack any strategy. For example, they accepted the sale of the plant in 2002 to Deripaska without considering the possibility of posing conditions for the sale, something that has been done successfully elsewhere. (See chapter 8.)

The union's leaders have not bothered to establish channels of communication with the membership to get the union's point of view across: there is no bulletin nor thought of negotiating access to the in-house paper or management's photocopier. The president holds weekly meetings with the shop committee chairpersons, but the latter are for the most part holdovers from the previous leadership, insecure white-collar employees with little commitment to the union. The union has little influence over the choice of delegates' to the conferences. These are usually quick affairs that leave little time for discussion. Workers grumble that the union's leaders (there are three full-time elected officials) rarely appear in the shops. Some say that Krylov and Popov have grown close to management, and there is speculation about the size of their salaries. The committed activists do not take this gossip seriously but they speak of "bureacratization" and "detachment from the base."

Many factors help to explain the relative return to "normalcy" at Tutaev: the shaky economic situation, the union's inability to break out of its isolation, the difficulty of working with a demoralized membership. But these problems are common to most unions. One might have expected Tutaev to be more different than it is, since it went through a "revolution" and a major political campaign. Both resulted in victories, however partial and short-lived. This leads one to look at cultural and ideological factors, despite their problematic nature: the historical legacy of subordination to bureaucratic authority and the absence of traditions of self-organization. For the reliance on spontaneity is not particular to Tutaev. One can observe a similar tendency among the alternative unions, too. For several years, their leaders, many of whom had led strikes that were at the origins of their union, devoted their main energies to court actions and neglected to organize their members.

But there is a difference. Among the alternative unions that have survived—and most in the ASM sector have not done well—there is now an understanding that unions cannot succeed over the long run unless they are appropriated by their members. There is no parallel realization in ASMR, even in the affiliates, like Tutaev, that have experienced "revolutions."

Notes

1. Employment figures vary from one source to the next. These are based on Analiticheskii obzor OAO "ASM-kholding," Jan.-Dec., 1997 and Jan.-Feb. 2002, and on union sources. Some of the decline in employment reflects the partial transfer of the factories' "social sphere" to the municipality.
2. Filtzer, *Soviet Workers and the Collapse of Perestroika*, pp. 114, 116-17.
3. V. Smirnov, "Narodnyi protiv naroda," *Golos profsoyuzov* (Yaroslavl'), 13-19 Aug. 1998.
4. A. Mineev, *Moskovskie novosti*, Jan. 15, 1989, p. 8.
5. *Sovetskaya Rossiya*, Sept. 9, 1998.
6. *Rabochaya politika*, Mar. 13, 1999.
7. Interview with V. Volosyuk, Oct.1998; *Sovetskaya Rossiya*, Sept. 17, 1998.
8. A. Kudryavstev, *Yaroslavskaya zastava*, Yaroslavl', 1999, p.71.
9. "A. Malov, "Vpolne vozmozhnaya kasatrofa, " *Zolotoe kol'tso,* (Yarolsavl), May 21, 2002, p.3.
10. Letter of four union presidents to the Russian President, the Prime Minister, and the Chairpersons of the Council of the Federation and State Duma, Oct. 22, 1996 (unpublished).
11. "Soglashenie mezhdu pravitel'stvom yaroslavskoi oblasti, meriyamy g. Yaroslavlya i g. Tutaeva, OOO 'Kompaniya Russkie motory,' rukovoditelyamy predpriyatii dizelestroeniya i profsoyuzamy etikh predpriyatii," Feb. 27, 1997 (unpublished).
12. M. Shamkov, "Nastupaet vremya novykh podkhodov," *Solidarnost'*, no. 8, 1998, p. 5.
13. Kudryavtsev, *Yaroslavskaya zastava*, p. 7.
14. *RFE/RL Newsline*, May 18, 21, 25 1998; *Nezavisimaya gazeta*, May 15, 1998, p. 1; *Izvestiya*, May 20, 1998, p. 5.
15. See for example, the "Appeal to the Citizens of Russia from the Representatives of the Miners' Collectives Participating in the Picket in Front of the Government Building of the Russian Federation and from the Russian Co-ordinating Committee of Trade-Unions and Social Associations of Universities and Scientific Institutes," *Shakhterskii piket*, July 8, 2002.
16. Personal communication.
17. *Yaroslavskaya zastava*, p. 8-9; *Solidarnost'*, no. 15, Aug. 1998, p. 1.
18. *Golos profsoyuza*, no. 7, July 1998.
19. *Ibid.*
20. *Solidarnost'*, no. 17, Sept.1998, p. 3.
21. *Sovetskaya Rossiya*, July 7, 1998; *Yaroslavskaya zastava*, p. 23; *Golos profosyuzov*, July 30 -5 Aug., 1998, p. 4.
22. *Golos profosyuzov*, 30 July–5 Aug.1998, p. 5.
23. Reddaway and Glinski, *The Tragedy of Russia's Reforms*, pp. 600-1.
24. *Yaroslavskaya zastava*, p. 72.
25. *Ibid.*, p. 101.
26. *Ibid.*, p. 19.
27. *Ibid.*, pp. 87, 143.
28. *Ibid.*, p. 18.

29. Volosyuk, longtime friend of Afans'ev, reported that activists of the alternative unions, himself included, had participated in education organized by AFL-CIO representatives in Moscow. Afanas'ev also visited the U.S. on the invitation of the AFL-CIO, which paid the bill. But the only material support his union received was two computers and legal counsel. Another opponent of Afanas'ev, an engineer at YMZ, wrote:

> The treacherous Solidarnost' union was built on the despair of people reacting to the passive position of management and of ASMR…[It consists of] vain and deceived workers whose interests don't go beyond their own pocketbook. Their main slogan is "give us our wages," and to hell with what comes after, even the flood. The plants are agonizing, the equipment is falling apart, people are leaving in droves, but what do they care! "Give us our wages!" They are quite content with the [government's] destructive policy and so they are 'outside of politics'. (*Golos profsoyuzov*, Aug. 13-19, 1998, p. 6.)

30. *Sovetskaya Rossiya*, Sept. 24 and Oct. 1, 1998.
31. See Reddaway and Glinski, pp. 600-1.
32. *Golos profsoyuzov*, 7-14, Oct. 1998; *Yaroslavskaya zastava*, pp. 60, 92-4.
33. "Zayavlenie o priostanovke aktsii protesta na Gorbatom mostu," Ispolnite'lnyi komitet NPG Rossii, Oct. 3, 1998 (unpublished); *Sovetskaya Rossiya*, Oct. 13, 1998.
34. *Solidarnost'*, no. 19, Oct. 1998, p. 3.
35. *Ibid.*, no. 19, Oct. 1998, p. 3; Gritsenko et al., *Istoriya profsoyuzov Rossii*, p. 497.
36. *Mysl'*, no 20, 1998, p. 2.
37. A. Golovenko, "Impichment," *Solidarnost'*, no. 19, October 1998, pp. 10-11. Reddaway and Glinski also feel that the Communists probably never intended the impeachment to succeed. Reddaway and Glinski, *The Tragedy of Russia's Reforms*, p. 608.
38. *Ibid.*, p. 2.
39. *Golos profsoyuzov*, 7-14 Oct. 1998, *Yaroslavskaya zastava*, pp. 115-120.
40. *Yaroslavskaya zastava*, pp. 123-24.
41. *Ibid.*, p. 131.
42. Reddaway and Glinski, *The Tragedy of Russia's Reforms*, p. 602.
43. *Yaroslavskaya zastava*, p. 162. A few days after the October 7 protest, Zyuganov admitted that some party members were saying that it had all been a useless charade. *Sovetskaya Rossiya*, Oct. 13, 1998, p. 1.
44. *Yaroslavskaya zastava*, pp. 85, 161.
45. *Ibid.*, pp. 150-1, 161.
46. *Ibid.*, pp. 86-88.
47. *Ibid.*, p. 21.
48. *Ibid.*, pp. 94-5.
49. *Golos profsoyuzov*, the weekly paper of the regional council of trade unions, appeared once a month with a paid insert by the regional organization of KPRF.
50. *Sovetskaya Rossiya*, a daily newspaper close to the KPRF, gave the impression that Russia in the summer of 1998 was on the eve of a new October Revolution.
51. *Rabovchaya sila*, no. 4(28) 1999, p. 3.

Chapter Five
RESISTANCE IN AN ALTERATIVE UNION
Edinstvo

Edinstvo (Unity), the alternative union at VAZ is the most successful of the minority alternative unions in the ASM sector. It has maintained its numbers and influence, while virtually all the others have gone into decline over the last several years under the impact of the same factors that account for the hegemony of "social partnership" in the labour movement.

Edinstvo's relative success is in part due to favourable objective circumstances. VAZ, located in the city of Togliatti 850 kilometres southeast of Moscow on the Volga, is the largest auto factory in the world. With over 100,000 employees at the main site—Togliatti's total population is 750,000—it assembled seventy per cent of all passenger cars made in Russia in 2002, over 700,000 units.[1] Despite a recent move toward outsourcing, a high proportion of the parts are still made in-plant. Like the other alternative unions in the machine-building sector, Edinstvo's membership has never gone beyond four percent of non-managerial personnel. But its 3350 members in May 2003 was a high enough number to provide it with a substantial financial and activist base. (The ASMR affiliate at VAZ claims ninety per cent of total work force, including lower and middle management. Top management has suspended membership, though, according to one of its vice-presidents, the union would not mind having them.[2]) Edinstvo's other major advantage is the factory's relative stability. It has gone through shortened workdays and brief shutdowns but these have been more than matched, especially in the past few years, by extensive overtime, extended shifts, and a six-day "sliding" work schedule. (Under that "temporary" regime, Sundays are the only common day off, and Saturdays are paid at the regular rate.) Overall employment and output levels have been relatively stable thanks to sustained demand for the low-end cars, of which VAZ is a monopoly producer. Its only competition is from used foreign imports, which are partially discouraged by customs barriers.[3]

The other factors in Edinstvo's relative success are "subjective" and constitute the focus of this chapter.

Origins

The decision to form a new union was adopted in September 1990 at a meeting of 200 workers. A decade later, membership had grown to 3500, only to fall back to 3000 after an unsuccessful strike in 2000. It began to grow again in 2002, climbing back to 3350 by the summer of 2003. Edinstvo was formed by workers who wanted a union that would be independent from management and would focus its efforts on defending members' interests, not on distributing benefits or organizing social activities. Its constitution excludes managerial personnel. There is some debate in the union about whether to admit foremen and brigadiers (elected lead-hands who participate in the distribution of bonuses). That decision is left to the members of the given shop. However, there is no debate about the fundamentally contradictory interests that divide management and workers. (Unless otherwise specified, the term "worker" will designate all non-managerial personnel, including office employees and engineers).

The creation of Edinstvo was also a rejection of the STK movement, which was prominent at VAZ. The union's first president, A. Ivanov, recalled that the most active, capable workers were, in fact, attracted to the STK rather than to Edinstvo. But Edinstvo's founders felt the STK would become—indeed, to a significant degree, had already become—a screen for management to shield itself from the workers. According to one Edinstvo member, "We saw that management needed self-management 'democracy.' But that gave no power to workers and, in practice, it was under management's control." As elsewhere, VAZ's STK soon withered away, though management replaced it with "production councils," mostly advisory bodies somewhat reminiscent of "jointness" committees in UAW plants in the U.S. Their members are well-paid and typically rubber-stamp management decisions.

Edinstvo's rejection of the STK's goal of participation in management, or even complete takeover of management, was in part a reaction against experience under the Soviet system that made workers bear material responsibility for faulty management without giving them any real say in it. But it also reflected a pessimistic view of the workers' capacity at that time to manage production. The union's founders wanted workers to be able to influence management, but "from the outside." Somewhat paradoxically, the same thinking lay behind their support for Yeltsin and his liberal economic strategy, a position that was shared by the other alternative unions.[4]

Edinstvo's membership thus differs from that of the ASMR in that the act of joining, to one degree or another, is a statement of independence vis-à-vis of management. Given management's hostility to Edinstvo, it is, in fact, an act of defiance that requires a certain amount of commitment and courage. The level of administrative intimidation and harassment varies from shop to shop and takes different forms, including the refusal of training and promotion opportunities to Edinstvo members, refusal to hire their children, refusal of overtime, of emergency material support, of time off at one's own expense, and in general of requests that depend on managerial discretion. More rarely, Edinstvo members lose bonuses and benefits, they are transferred, or threatened with dismissal. And even though a shortage of workers has forced management to seek new recruits in surrounding rural districts, there is still considerable fear among VAZ workers of layoffs and dismissals. Management, for its part, constantly reminds workers of the masses at the gate waiting to be hired. In one incident, when an entire brigade in the parts-assembly department decided to switch to Edinstvo, its members were called into the ASMR office and, under the gaze of management, they were lectured about Edinstvo's hidden agenda, which was allegedly to sell the factory off to Americans who want only to destroy Russian jobs.

Of course, not all, or even most, of Edinstvo's members are committed activists. Workers join for a variety of reasons, some narrow and individualistic. But there is nevertheless an element of self-selection: to one degree or another, its members are convinced of a basic conflict of interests separates them, as workers, from management and they believe that they can defend themselves through independent organization. This sets them apart from the mass of ASMR members, who belong to their union out of a combination of inertia, lingering faith in the paternalistic benevolence of management, and, most of all, lack of confidence in their own collective capacity to change things for the better.

The Major Confrontations

Edinstvo is one of the very few Russian unions, local or national, that has a strike fund—twenty per cent of the dues. Its statutes forbid use of the money for any other purpose, and it can be disbursed only by the decision of the union conference, the union's highest body. There is a small budget for "material aid" (the most important item in ASMR's budget after salaries), but it is never fully spent. This support is limited to 200 roubles (6.6 U.S.$) per request, a symbolic sum. If it is a major emergency, the union will make a formal request to management for the worker.

The first strike ever at VAZ occurred in September 1989, a few months after the general coalminers' strike. It was led by informal leaders, some of whom went on to found Edinstvo. This period marked the apogee of rank-and-file activism, when a handful of informal leaders could sometimes mobilize large numbers of workers with minimal preparation and organization. Squeezed between this unprecedented pressure from below and contradictory and shifting policies from above, management was thrown on the defensive.

As elsewhere, activism centred on the assembly lines, and VAZ has four. Three of them are two kilometres long. The strike was preceded by brigade meetings, whose minutes were handed to management. A two-hour warning strike was announced. The workers demanded higher wages, indexation, and a thirty-per-cent supplement for assembly-line work, with additional compensation for especially onerous operations. General-director Kadannikov pleaded that he too was "hired labour, just like you"(he is a major stockholder in VAZ today), but to no avail. Some of the participants remember that management showed pornographic movies (a complete novelty for Soviet workers) on screens mounted above the assembly line in an effort to distract the workers from protesting. But following the lunch break, 20,000 workers—a figure never since even been approached—poured onto the square below management's blue skyscraper. Threatening to prolong the strike, the workers forced management to set up a loudspeaker system for them. Faced with the prospect of the second shift joining the stoppage, Kadannikov yielded on all the demands except indexation.

The strike was supported by the STK, largely thanks to the efforts of its vice-president, A. Andrianov, who enjoyed great authority among the workers. But the union remained invisible throughout. After the strike, the assembly-line workers elected a new shop chairperson, who subsequently negotiated some improvement for the workers. But, as one recalled, "before long he began to appear in the shop with his head bowed"—he had been coopted by the higher levels of the union.. "We saw," recalled Ivanov, Edinstvo's first president, "that FNPR-type unions can function well for short time when they are taken over by active people but that they soon inevitably become bureaucratized." "There are officials in ASMR who are very critical [of management and of the union leadership]," added P. Zolotarev, Edinstvo's current president, "but they will only express their criticism in a narrow circle of people and they won't organize workers for action."

In early 1991, a one-hour strike occurred over the issue representation at the delegates' conferences. The majority of the STK (itself elected by the conference) had decided that the enterprise should become the property of the work collective, that is, of the employees. Management, however, wanted the employees to receive only twenty per cent. The state would keep another twenty per cent, and the rest would go to suppliers and foreign investors. At a delegates' conference called to decide the question, the majority supported management's position. But the worker delegates claimed that managerial personnel, who made up a third of the delegates, were over-represented. In addition, management could generally count on the support of engineering-technical delegates, who are more vulnerable to managerial pressure than workers. (Their vulnerability is partly due to their career aspirations, largely absent among workers and which depend wholly on the goodwill of management. In addition, their work is often difficult to evaluate by objective criteria, and this leaves more room from managerial arbitrariness in assigning bonuses.) Workers, though the overwhelming majority of the work force, constituted less than half the delegates.[5]

Following this vote, the worker delegates, led by Andrianov, formed a "workers committee" and demanded the annulment of the decision pending new elections on a proportional basis. But the conference rejected the demand. A week later, the workers' committee together with recently-formed Edinstvo called a one-hour protest strike. It was strongly supported on the assembly-lines and to a lesser extent by the other shops. Management, backed by ASMR and the STK, condemned the strike. Andrianov was ousted from the STK and soon after left the factory altogether. But the administration could not ignore the strike. It organized a referendum that yielded a majority in favour of proportional representation of the three main groups—workers, engineering-technical personnel, and management. That rule was enforced for a few years but, as the correlation of forces in the factory shifted, it was set aside without every formally being rescinded. At the time, the strike reflected a certain aspiration to independence—the workers no longer wanted to let themselves be represented by management.

The first major collective action led by Edinstvo alone was a response to the hyperinflation unleashed by "shock therapy." In April 1992, following brigade meetings, delegates' conferences of the final-assembly and motor-assembly shops demanded full indexation and a forty-two-per-cent wage increase. When management rejected the demands, Edinstvo initiated conferences in three additional shops, which also adopted the demands. The arbitration procedure, required by law and which at various times involved municipal officials and even the Minister of Labour, did not lead to an agreement. Meanwhile, Edinstvo was posting notices calling on workers to donate to its strike fund. Only a few days before the strike deadline, management gave in. One-hundred-per-cent monthly indexation was applied in the entire factory.

The fate of indexation at VAZ is instructive. In 1997, the ASMR-management negotiating committee—Edinstvo was excluded from negotiations despite its repeated requests—decided to replace full monthly indexation with an annual bonus that would depend upon "the financial and economic activity" of the enterprise. This concession was justified by the enterprise's precarious financial situation, especially its large tax arrears. Edinstvo campaigned vigorously against it, arguing that the workers should not be made responsible for VAZ's finances, since they had no say in running the plant. It pointed to managerial incompetence, widespread theft, corruption, the extensive use of intermediaries that milked the factory. This agitation yielded results, since the delegates' conference of March 1, 1997 rejected the concession. But this was followed by several weeks of major arm-twisting, and on March 29 a reconvened conference agreed to reduce mandatory indexation to 72.5 per cent of inflation. It was only in 1999, that the conference finally agreed completely to forego guaranteed indexation.[6] But the concession did not come easily either. In some shops, it took as many as three conferences (the shop conferences elect delegates to the plant conference) before the workers got it "right." At the plant conference, both management and ASMR brandished the threat of layoffs if wages had to be indexed regardless of the plant's situation. Edinstvo's president, who was a delegate to the conference, was not given the floor. The 2003 collective agreement restored 72.5-per-cent indexation but kept it conditional on the "results of economic activity,"[7] a vague phrase that left the decision entirely in management's hands.

Despite the loss of indexation, Edinstvo can take some of the credit for the fact that wages at VAZ have kept well ahead of most other plants in the auto and truck sectors. At GAZ, the other giant vehicle maker, whose economic situation is roughly comparable to VAZ's (it is the monopolistic producer of cheap minivans that enjoy relatively strong demand), wages were half of those at VAZ for most of the last decade, a period when GAZ was famous for its paternalistic relations and its union's deep attachment to "partnership."[8]

It is also largely thanks to the workers' pressure organized by Edinstvo that the non-payment of wages, a problem that plagued the Russian economy particularly from 1994 to 1998, was kept in check.[9] The major protest against wage arrears was a six-day strike in the final-assembly shop (no. 45/3) in the fall of 1994. It occurred at a time when non-payment was only beginning.[10] Management had not paid wages in February of that year, and, despite a series of lunchtime demonstrations in the following months, it refused to say when the debt would be paid. (It should be noted that the arrears at VAZ were indexed and accumulated interest at (very low) savings-bank rates.) On September 27, Edinstvo organized a meeting of the second shift of the final-assembly shop, which voted unanimously to stop work at once in support of the demands for payment of February's wage as well as guarantees of regular payment of wages in the future and payment of the wages lost during the strike. On September 29, a formal shop conference unanimously confirmed the demands, rejecting management's offer to negotiate while production continued. During the negotiations, the administration argued that the collective agreement, negotiated with ASMR, allowed it to delay wages. Edinstvo countered that that violated the law. Management offered to pay the arrears in monthly installments of 100,000 roubles (the average wage was 520,000) from November. The delegates' conference found the offer acceptable but nevertheless voted unanimously to continue the strike until management agreed to pay for the days lost and gave guarantees against reprisals.

On October 3, the administration shut down all operations directly connected with main assembly (the paint, body-welding, suspension, motor-assembly, and some other shops) until October 10 and dismissed thirty-three assembly-line workers, in addition to nine members of the strike committee already fired on September 30. Kadannikov also threatened to shut the whole plant if work on the assembly line did not resume by October 10. The assembly workers returned to work on October 10 to find several hundred riot police stationed along the line. (The police left after a few hours.) They were not paid for the strike days or the subsequent shutdown (a disguised lockout, in the view of Edinstvo), and they were issued reprimands.

Edinstvo supported the fired workers out of its strike fund while it contested the legality of the dismissals in court. It won the case several weeks later, forcing reinstatement of all the workers with back pay. The court ruled that management had acted illegally, since it punished the workers without requesting a court ruling on the legality of the strike. ASMR (along with the production council) had supported management throughout and publicly condemned the strike. Nevertheless, it later took credit for reversing the disciplinary measures, basing this on the presence of its lawyer at the court proceedings. (He apparently did not speak.) In an interview to the company paper, the union lawyer stated that, regardless of the court's ruling, "many of the workers really deserved severe punishment for the harm they caused the enterprise."[11]

The problem of wage arrears resurfaced in 1995, 1996 and 1999, but the sums owed were kept small and paid back relatively quickly. Edinstvo, on its part, kept up the pressure with demonstrations, lawsuits, and complaints to the Labour Inspectorate and the Public Prosecutor. However, it was unable to organize more strikes. The time of relatively easy mass mobilizations had passed. Membership continued to grow at a slow rate, but the union lost its positions on the strategic final-assembly lines. This was due to a number of factors, including management's muscled response to the 1994 strike, which left a strong impression on the workers, even though the disciplinary measures were ultimately reversed. After the strike, persecution (including involuntary transfers) and harassment of activists were stepped up. But the main factor was the prolonged depression. Even if VAZ was less affected by it than other plants, its workers experienced periods of reduced workdays and temporary stoppages. At one point there was talk of bankruptcy because of the taxes owed. All this heightened the sense of insecurity. For their part, management and ASMR never tired of drawing the workers' attention to what was happening elsewhere in Russia and reminding them how good they had it.

Edinstvo, however, won a significant political victory in 1999, when it organized the successful electoral campaign to the Duma of its president A. Ivanov (who gave up his union post). He won thirty per cent of the vote in a large field of candidates in a mainly factory riding. His closest rival, a businessman, received only twelve per cent, even though he outspent Ivanov many times over.[12] (Ivanov was re-elected in 2003.) This was a sign of the authority the union had won among VAZ's workers that went well beyond its own membership. But the victory had more practical significance for the union. Although the Duma's role is largely symbolic, its deputies enjoy a measure of prestige and privilege that permits them to intervene with the authorities of various levels on behalf of constituents who would otherwise be completely helpless against the rich and powerful. Ivanov, besides usually taking progressive positions on labour and social issues, has helped to restrain VAZ's management and the local Togliatti authorities from more blatant forms of repression against Edinstvo.

The currency devaluation of August 1998 cut real wages dramatically but also increased demand for domestic goods, making 2000 was a record year for profits at VAZ. As elsewhere, management responded to the upsurge in demand by adding shifts, overtime and by speed-up. It even took credit for "letting the workers earn" but otherwise refused to increase real wages in any significant way. A typical article in the company paper ran under the title "To Live Better, We Have to Work More." It was a report on the recent extension of the second shift on the assembly line to nine hours. In the same article, VAZ's deputy director was quoted in it as saying that there were "no objective possibilities to raise wages this year."[13] The extended shift required and received the formal consent of ASMR, even though the workers had expressed their opposition to it.

As the problem of wage arrears faded in the wake of the devaluation, strike activity in Russia virtually ceased. But the economic upturn and worker discontent over low wages, longer hours and speed-up helped lift Edinstvo's membership from 2300 in the summer of 1998 to 3500 in 2000. It was in this context that Edinstvo decided to organize a one-hour warning strike in the fall of 2000. The immediate initiative came from activists in seat-assembly shop. Apart from their low wages and forced overtime, this overwhelmingly female group was upset at the outsourcing of door-assembly, which had traditionally belonged to their shop. They wanted an end to subcontracting and demanded that VAZ's collective agreement be applied to any operations already outsourced. In addition, they wanted a doubling of wages and the "thirteenth-month" bonus, which management had not paid out 1999 despite record profits. Edinstvo's leaders had been considering strike action but they hesitated, fearing the repression that would follow if the strike failed. Instead, they proposed that the workers in seat-assembly organize a collective refusal of overtime. This was accepted, and majority of the workers took part in the action, despite strong managerial intimidation.

But after a week, the shop's activists were pressing Edinstvo to broaden the movement. After much debate, the union notified management of its intention to organize a one-hour warning strike on October 10. (The legal cover for the strike was an official labour dispute already in progress over representation of Sotsprof, Edinstvo's federation, in the national Tripartite Committee. This meant, however, that Edinstvo could not officially declare its own demands, something that lent an element of confusion to the strike.) ASMR's president appealed repeatedly over the plant's radio to the workers against supporting the strike. Edinstvo planned the action for four shops, besides seat-assembly: medium-stamping, final-testing, metallurgy, and final-assembly. It was counting especially on the latter to shut down production in the whole plant. The first three shops supported the strike partially. But assembly line kept on working. The optimistic reports from the shop's chairperson had turned out to be without basis. In seat-assembly itself, strong intimidation by management made the workers hesitate. Edinstvo send three activists to give them a push, but they were immediately arrested by the police and led away. (They were released that evening after Ivanov intervened.) Then Zolotarev arrived, accompanied by Anna Perova, the very authoritative chairperson of the medium-stamping shop. She shouted: "sit!"(*sidet'*), and work ceased at once. The police tried to take Zolotarev away, too, but the workers, hammers in hand, formed a circle around him. "This one we're not giving up!" declared one of them.

The strike failed. Edinstvo tried to organize a demonstration a few weeks later to support the wage demands, but only a few hundred workers showed up. Management intensified its harassment of Edinstvo members. Some were threatened with dismissal unless they left the union. The administration also tried to paralyze the union by blocking the free movement of its officials through the plant, having its leaflets banned, prohibiting lunchtime demonstrations, and pressuring the municipal government to refuse permits for its demonstrations on public property. Most of these measures were eventually beaten back in court by Edinstvo, but the intensified pressure and the loss of confidence among workers in Edinstvo's capacity to influence management contributed to the outflow of almost a thousand members in the year following the strike.

Despite this setback, Edinstvo kept up the pressure against *kolym* (literally "bride-money," that is, earnings from overtime and exceeding production norms) and for an increase in regular wages. In 1999, management had extended the work day to nine hours on the second shift in the paint shop, as a "temporary measure." (From bitter experience, Russians say that there is nothing more permanent than the "temporary.") The shop employs 2500 people, almost all women, in very unhealthy conditions which entitle them to an early pension. The extended shift required, and duly obtained, the consent of ASMR, but it was very unpopular among the workers. Edinsvto conducted a survey among the workers in 2000 that confirmed that the vast majority opposed to the new regime. It then organized brigade meetings and obtained the eighty per cent required to call a special shop conference, which had the power to override ASMR's consent. But management also got busy and threatened the delegates with dismissal if they attended the conference. One particularly zealous foreman went around ripping up the deputies' credentials. When the bravest of the delegates nevertheless showed up at the hall that had been reserved in one of the plant's dormitories, they found it "closed for repairs" and the power shut off. The caretaker was at a loss to explain. In 2002, Edinstvo also organized collective refusals of overtime in the medium-stamping shop and in metallurgy to back demands to double wages, restore indexation, and reduce the share of bonuses and supplements in take-home pay.

In 2002, management decided to extend the second shift on the third assembly line that makes the new model "Kalina." In the weeks preceding the change, Edinstvo organized almost one hundred brigade meetings that voted overwhelmingly against the change. ASMR, nevertheless, gave its consent. On September 2, 2002, the first day of the nine-hour shift, Edinstvo's the entire plant committee observed to ensure that the supposedly voluntary character of the extra hour was respected. About a third of the workers stopped work after eight hours. Management marked the cars that went by as "defective," entailing loss of bonuses for the workers. One brigade that kept on working wrote collectively to a local newspaper: "Our bosses quietly hint that we can refuse to work but that if we do they will find a reason to punish us."[14] Workers could ask to be transferred to other lines but most find it painful to leave familiar brigades and conditions. There was also no guarantee they would really be assigned to equivalent work.

A few days later, the workers came to work wearing stickers on their chests and backs that read "I don't want to work nine hours." This was probably the first time such a tactic had been used in Russia, and it threw management into a rage. All the workers were photographed. But they were not intimidated. The entire shift walked off after eight hours. Resistance was maintained for three days but with decreasing participation. One the second day, management began to transfer workers, and that undermined resolve. Had the workers remained solidary, as Edinstvo urged, management would not have been able to replace the entire shift. A scheduled delegates' conference of the enterprise took place a few days later, but neither the nine-hour shift nor the problem of low wages was discussed.

But discontent continued to grow. The widespread perception of managerial arbitrariness and incompetence was reinforced when only six weeks after the introduction of the nine-hour shift, the workers were sent home for two weeks because of low demand for the cars.[15] Meanwhile, real wages were falling. In the body-assembly department, they fell twenty-five per cent in the second half of 2002 and another twenty per cent in the first two months of 2003.[16] Then in February 2003, the draft of the new collective agreement was published announcing important benefit concessions: reduction or termination of subsidies for meals, transportation, stays in the plant's sanatoria, and an end to interest-free housing loans for young workers. Lost also were the guarantees protecting various categories of workers against permanent layoff: invalids, women with small children and dependent invalids, workers near to their pensions, and others. The draft contained no guarantee of an increase in wages, and the language on bonuses and supplements was weakened, giving greater latitude to managerial arbitrariness. As mentioned earlier, a paragraph on quarterly indexation at 72.4 per cent was reintroduced, but its application was still dependent upon the very vague "economic performance" of the enterprise. To add insult to injury, ASMR's president Karagin broke with established practice and signed the agreement on his own, without waiting for the delegates' conference, which was scheduled for only a few days later. (The new Labour Code allowed him to do that.)

The new agreement was negotiated exclusively by ASMR, which continued, with management's support, to keep representatives of Edinstvo away. Edinstvo complained about that many times to the Public Prosecutor, who confirmed the illegality, but nothing changed. Meanwhile in a leaflet directed against Edinstvo, ASMR claimed that the alternative union refused its repeated invitations to participate in negotiations out of fear of responsibility for tough decisions. This period saw large-scale departures from ASMR, sometimes entire brigades at a time. Edinstvo estimated that between ten and fifteen thousand left in the first half of 2003. In his report on the first-quarter of 2003, a dissident ASMR shop chairman wrote:

> The observed tendency to leave the union is explained, in our view, by fact that union members, on the one hand, do not understand their personal role, considering that union is something that should do everything [for them]; and, on the other hand, by the fact that in reality they do not always find protection and support for their legitimate demands in the higher levels of the union at the plant. The decline in living standards, the absence of wage indexation, the three-shift regime and forced overtime—all that leads them to feel the union does not defend them. They take for granted the existence of the benefits in the collective agreement and do not realize that they owe them to ASMR. We have to pursue explanatory work on those questions.[17]

However, only a fraction of those leaving ASMR have so far joined Edinstvo. Although dissatisfied with ASMR, most lack confidence in the ability of Edinstvo—in essence, in their own ability—to change things for the better.

On March 12, 2003, Edinstvo organized a rally in front of the administration building to protest the concessions that ASMR had negotiated and to support demands to double wages and restore one-hundred-100-per-cent monthly indexation. The demonstration drew 2200 people. To ASMR's claim that the enterprise was in a difficult economic situation, Edinstvo replied that VAZ was working at capacity and sales were good. Meanwhile, management was unable or unwilling to stop huge losses from theft, corruption, and its use of intermediary companies. Low wages, bad working conditions, and management's contempt for workers all undermined productivity and quality. The rally also demanded an increase of the guaranteed part of wages to ninety-five per cent (bonuses and supplements account for about forty-five per cent at VAZ), to base payment of the annual "thirteenth-month" bonus on indicators that depend exclusively on workers' performance (as had been the case before 1996) and not on the enterprise's profits, and to reduce the gap between wages and managerial salaries to a ratio of one to five.

As expected, Edinstvo received no formal reply to its demands. Soon after the rally, however, management announced that first-quarter results allowed it to raise wages 6.6 percent and that it was looking into the question of vacation subsidies (which it had cut in the negotiations). It also decided now that it could pay the full "thirteenth-month" bonus, instead of only fifty per cent, as it had previously announced. Edinstvo called a second rally for April 23. Already at the March demonstration, the police had tried to prevent the sound truck from reaching the square, but the workers, supported by Ivanov, forced open a passage for it. This time, the city simply refused permission for the rally. It backed down only when Ivanov presented himself as the organizer. But the police warned all of Togliatti's sound-truck owners not to rent equipment to Edinstvo, and so the rally's speakers had to do without amplification. As usual, the police filmed the event. All the speakers were later charged with administrative infractions and summoned to appear in court. Edinstvo had the charges overturned on appeal a month later.

The 2,100 workers who attended the April rally unanimously supported a resolution to prepare a one-hour warning strike to back the demands. To that end, a campaign was launched to collect signatures from at least fifty per cent plus one of the employees. (The new Labour Code requires a vote of fifty per-cent plus one at the delegates' conference for a legal strike, but Edinstvo had no way of calling a conference.) By the end of May, 10,000 signatures had been collected. There was some doubt within the union's leadership as to the realism of a strike in the current context, but all agreed that the signature campaign was an important mobilizing tool and that management would have a hard time ignoring the expressed will of tens of thousands of workers.

Day-to-Day Struggles

In its polemics with Edinstvo, ASMR accuses it of pursuing cheap publicity through strikes, leaving to it the heavy responsibility of day-to-day defence of worker interests, which is at the core of trade-unionism. In fact, the difficulty of organizing collective protests in past years has forced Edinstvo to devote most of its energy to pursuing individual and group grievances and violations of union rights through the labour disputes committees and the courts. To this end, it employs a full-time lawyer and inundates public prosecutor with complaints.[18] Edinstvo's responsiveness to workers' complaints against management when ASMR has refused to act, especially if that requires confronting management to get results, are frequently cited by workers as the reason they decided to switch unions.

In one instance, a paint-shop worker who was living with her family of four in a single room of a plant dormitory (the kitchen and bathroom are shared with other tenants) had been seeking without success authorization to occupy an adjacent room that had become vacant. When she turned to her ASMR shop committee for help, the response she received was: "Who told you to make children?" She begun to organize a petition among fellow workers who had similar problems, when on the bus to work one day someone handed her a Edinstvo leaflet. The whole group eventually switched unions.

Early one morning, fifteen foundry workers appeared from their night shift at Edinstvo's office (a small room inconveniently distant from the factory—Edinstvo wrested it from management after a long legal battle). They complained about health and safety violations and the three-shift regime that had been introduced with ASMR's consent against their opposition. The brigadier who acted as the groups spokesperson explained that he decided he had to act when his son came to work in the foundry: he wanted to leave him a decent future. Zolotarev told them that he would not solve their problems for them but that they could count on the union's support if they decided to fight together. Thirty-eight foundry workers joined. The foundry became one of the union's most militant shops.

Other grievances that Edinstvo has frequently dealt with are health and safety violations, the arbitrary calculation of wages and the failure to pay for additional work, wrongful disciplinary measures, including punishment for refusing overtime, improper calculation of vacation time. This is not to say that ASMR is inactive on the shopfloor. The situation varies considerably from shop to shop. But ASMR's officials, especially its army of relatively privileged fulltimers, tend to be distant from ordinary workers, who often say they feel like they are talking to bosses when they go to the union. But more importantly, it is a rare ASMR leader who will pursue a grievance when that entails a serious confrontation with management. And the few that are prepared to do that do not find support in the higher levels of the union.

On the other hand, Edinstvo's ability to pursue grievances is limited by its weak presence on the shopfloor. Even in the shops where it has significant numbers, Edinstvo, unlike ASMR, has no full-timers, and management refuses to give Edinstvo's officers free time, as it does for ASMR, which also pays its activists modest sums as "material encouragement." That means that Edinstvo's activists, apart from its two full-timers, have to do union work before or after their shift, during their lunch break, or on days off. Even in Edinstvo, it is not easy to find people with that kind of commitment.

Another problem is the growing bias of the courts and the law-enforcement agencies against workers, a somewhat belated reflection of the shift of the political balance of forces in society. From that point of view, the new Labour Code really only brings workers' rights into closer conformity with the situation in society and with what had already become normal practice.

Edinstvo's Strategic Choice: An Organized Workers' Movement

Despite these difficulties, Edinstvo might well have followed most other alternative unions in the ASM sector and become a sort of legal-defence agency to the virtual exclusion of organizing.[19] Although this was a losing strategy, the temptation was great, since mobilizing had become a frustrating, even seemingly hopeless, task. If Edinstvo succumbed less than others to it, that was partly thanks to its ability to recruit a new generation of activists, who brought fresh energy into the union in the second half of the 1990s. But even at the nadir of worker activism, Edinstvo's leaders never forgot that the union's success, indeed its very survival, depended in the final analysis on its ability to mobilize. Zolotarev explained:

> Solidarity [the alternative union at the Shar ball-bearing plant in nearby Samara] is in serious trouble, and I blame its leader for that. He got carried away with the courts and lost the activeness of his members. Courts are not a union's basic activity, and I tell our members not to expect miracles from them, since they don't reflect the interests of workers. We have won small victories through the courts, like the restoration of supplements and bonuses to workers, but the main thing is solidary action, strikes, and other forms of organized collective pressure.

After much soul-searching debate in the late 1990s, the union decided that its strategic goal was "to develop a mass, organized workers' movement."

In his report to the Coordinating Council (a quarterly assembly of the union's elected officers) in March 2003, Zolotarev explained that the new Labour Code need not undermine the union's real power "because we have the potential to protest in an organized manner. For example, shop 38 struck over vacation schedules. That's organized pressure. It's more powerful than formal rights, and that's what we have to develop." "What is Edinstvo?" asked the chairperson of the paint shop. "It's workers ourselves. We have to tell our people to stop asking 'What is Edinstvo doing?' They have to raise issues and apply pressure themselves, take part in collective actions, come to demonstrations. That's what has an impact." Similarly, the leader of the medium-stamping shop said:

> Our task is to mobilize workers around problems and to demand, demand, demand. It's not enough to give information. We have to mobilize people to act with us. I explained to the workers that they were really getting only three additional rubles for their overtime. So they spat at it and walked away, even with the shop superintendent yelling after them:

"You bastards! I'll fire you!" That's protest. But how much work did it take to bring them to that point, all the leaflets, the agitation! Consciousness is rising, and people are coming to the [shop] conferences, since they understand their importance.

Edinstvo's efforts to cultivate in the workers a strong sense of dignity, a worthy goal in itself, should be seen as part of its strategy to fight demoralization and activate people. A central leitmotif running through all of Edinstvo's literature is the need for workers to demand respect, to stop allowing themselves be "humiliated," treated like "human cattle" and "rabble." A typical union leaflet begins: "The ordinary worker is used to being in the humiliating position of total dependence on the will of the employers. And the will of the employers is to survive in the marketplace by trampling on the workers' interests. Workers! It's time to respect yourselves and speak up for your rights."[20]

When an activist from the stamping shop refused to submit to a physical search at the gates, Edinstvo took up her cause. "Why go to the trouble of installing modern technological equipment to control the exits?" asked one of its leaflets. "Why take prophylactic measures to prevent crime and analyze the causes of theft? Why consider the rights and dignity of the worker rabble, when it's so much easier to humiliate a thousand honest workers in order to catch a single thief. After all, don't they say that when you chop wood, the chips must fly?"[21] The union eventually won a partial victory on this issue when the regional Prosecutor instructed management that physical searches are permissible only after external examination or metal detection provides sufficient grounds. In that case, they have to be done away from the public's gaze by police officers of the same sex as the suspect and in the presence of witnesses of the same sex, and whole procedure has to be written up formally and signed by the suspect and witnesses.

Another leaflet reported about a manager who used "choice foul language" (*otbornyi mat*) in his dealings with workers and tried to block a Edinstvo health and safety commission from doing its work. Besides being simply insulting, this kind of "impoliteness and rudeness" (*grubost' i khamstvo*) towards workers, a consequence of management's impunity, harms productivity, "since a worker whose boss tramples underfoot his human dignity will not want to do good work." The union filed charges against the manager that resulted in a police fine for "petty hooliganism."[22]

Slowly, the accent on dignity—completely absent from ASMR's discourse—has begun to have an impact. An activist on the assembly line reported how she organized fellow workers against an odious foreman,

> ...a petty tyrant (*samodur*), who made generous use of the foulest language. We collected compromising material (*kompromat*)—his insults, his

incorrect calculation of wages, his creating an unhealthy work atmosphere—and we wrote it all up. Management had no choice but to transfer him out. This gave people confidence in their strength. They saw that it's not hard to get rid of foremen, since foremen have to break rules much more often than workers do. Now, if someone calls them "*barany*" (stupid, literally "sheep"), they don't wait for me. They write it up themselves.

Related to this is the struggle to the limit management's arbitrary power, which is exercised according to the traditional Russian principle of "I'm the boss, and so you're a fool" (*ya nachal'nik—ty durak*). This is the major source of fear that keeps workers from defending their interests against management (and, at the same time, a consequence of that fear). "We are worried at the dangerous tendency of management consciously to inspire in workers a sense of fear, insecurity, unfreedom, in order to undermine their capacity for resistance," reads a union leaflet.[23] Edinstvo's activists try to teach by example. When a shop supervisor on the assembly-line tried to add new operations to an activist's job, she demanded extra pay. When he refused, so she declined to do the additional operations. To the surprise of her fellow workers, he did not punish her but merely transferred her to another job and found a more compliant replacement. "Eventually, following my example, the others began to stand up for themselves. Now they have lost their fear, and at shop conferences they stand up and tell him to his face that he's a thief."

Limiting arbitrary managerial power is the goal behind the union's demand to reduce the share of bonuses and supplements to five per cent of the wage. In its analysis of the draft collective agreement of 2002, Edinstvo noted:

> The wage system, that is so highly praised by the ASMR committee, gives dishonest managers a basis for allocating the wage fund according to their own interests. Thus, codes three and twenty-three [supplements for completed work and for exceeding output norms] are allocated, as a rule, by foreman and brigadiers "on the quiet" (*vtikhuyu*), so that no one knows, since very often they are guided by their self-interested motives. This fosters social tension and has a negative impact on the moral and psychological climate in the collective.
>
> There is really only one criterion for payments from the "professional mastery" and the foremen's funds: does the worker try to please (*ugoden*) the boss or not. If there is a conflict with the administrator, you can forget about the above parts of your wage. And in general, are there

many workers in the factory who can easily orient themselves in this wage system?[24]

Despite widespread abuse of the bonus system by management, the idea of doing away with it is so novel to Russian workers that most have trouble at first accepting it legitimacy. They say that it would be unjust for lazy workers to earn as much as a hard workers and they ask how management would get effort out of workers if they did not wield material incentives. This reaction reflects a deeply-ingrained attitude, promoted under the Soviet system and which continues to be cultivated by management and by ASMR, that workers "share" responsibility with management for the economic performance of "their" enterprise. Even if the enterprise no longer belongs "to the people," it is still "our native (*rodnoi*) factory." It is only right, therefore, that workers should "take into account" (*vkhodili v polozhenie*) its circumstances, which are almost always portrayed as "difficult," even when profits are high. The underlying premise, of course, is that workers and management share fundamental interests. VAZ's administration, explained ASMR president Karagin, "grew up at VAZ, just as we did, and it is concerned with the health of our native factory, loves the factory, wants it to remain the flagship of national automobile construction. Therefore, our task is a shared one: to protect the enterprise, to keep the collective together. Our differences usually concern only details, small things."[25]

Edinstvo decisively rejects that premise, arguing that workers have no power over the basic factors that determine profits. Management will not even give the union access to information about the true financial state of the plant. The workers cannot therefore be made responsible for its economic performance, even if they have to consider it when formulating their demands. When management, seconded by ASMR, cites the precarious financial situation of the enterprise to justify the low wages and to demand concessions of the workers, Edinstvo points to the high salaries of administrators (a "commercial secret") and the huge losses from theft and mismanagement. Edinstvo has condemned the language of Section One of the collective agreement entitled "Shared Obligations of the Parties," since it makes workers responsible for output and investment plans and for the integrity of the enterprises's property.[26]

The union's rejection of responsibility for what it considers managerial responsibility lies behind its opposition to the clauses of the collective agreement that make indexation and the "thirteenth month" depend on the enterprises's "economic performance." In addition to being unfair—workers do not make the decisions that determine profitability—these clauses are calculated to discourage activism by binding workers to management's interests. At the same time, there is some debate within the union about how far this position should be taken. For example, a member of the plant committee wrote a leaflet in which he mentioned that the temperature in one of the shops (where his wife works) often dropped very low because the workers whose job it is to mind the gates frequently left their post. Zolotarev argued that the leaflet could not be published in that form, since the temperature is management's responsibility and the union should not be seen as calling to discipline workers. For the same reason, Edinstvo will not get involved in campaign against alcohol consumption and theft on the job, even though some members feel it should. The leaflet's author maintained his position, and it was not published.

Democracy

Edinstvo's efforts to promote an informed, educated membership that can control and run its own organization are an integral part of its strategic goal of "a mass, organized workers' movement."

Edinstvo really stands out among Russian unions for its informational activity, which is usually a forgotten area. Given the vastness of VAZ and the limited number and time of Edinstvo's activists, the union relies heavily on the printed word. Unlike ASMR, that has access to the company paper (published three times a week in 16,000 copies), Edinstvo publishes its own leaflets. These appear on a more-or-less weekly basis in 3000 copies and they are written mostly by the leadership, less often by shopfloor activists. They perform several functions: they inform members of the decisions and actions of the leadership; educate them about their rights; report on problems and grievances in the different shops; and they mobilize for collective action. Their success was indirectly confirmed in 1999 when management (in the person ASMR's former president!) sought a court order to prohibit them as unlicenced periodicals.[27] He obtained it, but Edinstvo has it overturned on appeal.

The union also makes a point of functioning transparently. Plant committee meetings are open to all members and their proceedings are reported in the union's leaflets. Special care is taken to avoid anything that might arouse suspicions of favouritism and corruption. When Edinstvo is invited to send members to conferences or education in other cities or abroad, the shops are consulted and they have to approve the candidate. Upon his or her return, the person makes a written report that the union publishes. By contrast, ASMR people never make public reports of their trips, since they were typically chosen by the leaders without any consultation, as a reward for services rendered.

Edinstvo has worked closely for many years with TIE-Moscow and the School for Worker Democracy to organize education for shopfloor activists. It has also created its own education committee with a mandate to organize four seminars each year for shopfloor activists. As noted, ASMR affiliates show little interest in shopfloor education. ASMR at VAZ is exceptional in having built its own union school with money from its "solidarity fund." It is currently building a second. But, the content of its education aside, it is conducted on company time, whereas Edinstvo has to organize its seminars on the workers' own time. A few dissident ASMR shop leaders sometimes attend those seminars but they admit that they cannot recruit any of their members to accompany them, a comment on the respective levels of commitment in the two unions.

Edinstvo's leadership has rejected the use of material incentives to encourage activism. There has been a longstanding debate about offering at least token compensation to workers who attend education, especially since Saturday is a workday for many of them and they have to forego wages. So far, this has been rejected. The president (himself a full-timer), in particular, insists that money will not help if commitment is weak but it does corrupt. Moreover, when activists are paid, there is always uncertainty about how they will act when the going gets tough. In conformity with this policy, the union has kept the number of its paid elected officers to two. (There was only one before 1998. There are, in addition, a full-time lawyer, a secretary and one and a half accountants.) This is part of an effort to prevent leaders from becoming detached from the membership. It is also aimed at countering the profound skepticism among Russian workers about all authority figures, not least union leaders. Zolotarev is himself is a skilled worker with no higher education—something completely unheard of in ASMR. His earns his salary of a skilled worker and claims, with apparent sincerity, that he would gladly return to his old job if he was no longer wanted him as president. According to the union's constitution, ten per cent of the relevant unit can force a conference to recall its elected officers. (This has never occurred.)

Democracy, according to Zolotarev, is when "the members make decisions themselves and carry them out themselves." He readily admits that Edinstvo is far from that ideal. In particular, too much responsibility is concentrated in the hands of the plant leadership. The recent creation of a "coordinating council" was aimed at rectifying this. This quarterly assembly of all of the union's elected officers, from group leaders up, hears a report from the president on the preceding period and adopts a plan of action for the next. (In light of the new Labour Code, ASMR's leadership has floated the idea of convening delegates' conferences only "as needed," instead of twice yearly, as has been the traditional practice.) The creation of education and women's commissions (in addition to existing health-and-safety and social-affairs commissions) was also aimed at delegating responsibility away from the centre. The women's committee was the independent initiative of a few activists in the framework of a project developed by the School for Worker Democracy. Despite a certain initial skepticism among the (mostly male) leadership, they gave it their material and moral support from the start.

All the above policies are geared to strengthening commitment and activism. Edinstvo compares favourably with other alternative unions, which very often revolve around a single authoritative leader and not much else. Nevertheless, Edinstvo's leaders consider that the union's weakness on the shopfloor—and in particular on the assembly line—is its most serious internal problem. In their view, formal education helps but there is no substitute for collective struggle to draw out and train new activists. As shown above, the union has been trying to rekindle the dynamism of earlier years. The solution is not obvious, and there is some skepticism about the prospects of the present campaign over wages. But there are also signs that the mood at VAZ may be shifting, as evidenced in the large-scale defections from ASMR.

Beyond the Factory

Awareness of the need to find allies in the broader labour movement and society comes easily to Edinstvo, which confronts an administration that can count on the support of political authorities and law-enforcement agencies, as well as the mass media. The problem is that most of Russia's unions are themselves allied to management and to the state and so hostile to unions like Edinstvo. Various groups of workers in Togliatti, notably teachers and public transport workers, have turned to Edinstvo for advice and support during their strikes. But these conflicts did not lead to permanent organizations with which Edinstvo could form enduring alliances. On the other hand, Edinstvo has begun to forge links with Togliatti's civic organizations in connection with Ivanov's electoral campaigns. The very fact of Ivanov's election is evidence of the union's authority beyond its own membership. It also enjoys the sympathy of one of Togliatti's daily newspapers, the crusading daily, Tolyattinskoe obozrenie, whose director was murdered in 2002 in a contract killing (one of several of journalists assassinated over the past years[28]). But that does not amount to very much in a city that is so dominated economically and politically by the giant auto factory.

On the national level, Edinstvo is affiliated to two (of the four) labour federations that unite alternative trade unions, Sotsprof and VKT (General Confederation of Workers, affiliated with the International Confederation of Free Trade Unions).[29] Edinstvo gives them ten per cent of its dues. These organizations engage mainly in lobbying but, in view of the small size and minority status of their affiliates, they do not have much clout. They also helped coordinate the campaign against the new Labour Code, in which Edinstvo was very active. The campaign, though defeated, was a rare instance of coordinated action among alternative unions.

Edinstvo has participated in the general shift to the left of recent years by the alternative unions. Like Edinstvo, most supported the Yeltsin regime even as late as his second election campaign in 1996. It might seem paradoxical that unions that call for independence from employers would support a neo-liberal regime. But this was to a large extent a reaction against the subordination of unions under Soviet "socialism."(The anti-liberal KPRF, on the other hand, favours "partnership" with "patriotic" employers.) A turning point for Edinstvo was the summer of 1998, when it sent a delegation to the miners' "picket" in Moscow. The fight against reform of the Labour Code helped to consolidated the leftward shift. The political views of the union's leaders today can be described as left social-democratic: they see the state is inevitably on the side of the employers. On the other hand, socialism is not a strategic goal for them, only a very distant dream that has no real impact on their action.

Edinstvo played an active part in founding of the Russian Labour Party (RPT) in January 2002 and it remains a strong supporter today. The formation of this party, based on the alternative Sotsprof and Zashchita union federations, was a top-down affair, a reaction to the defeat of the campaign against the government's proposed Labour Code. The party's primary raison d'être was to elect deputies to the Duma who would defend the interests of the alternative unions. Otherwise, its platform was vague, though it took progressive positions on such social issues as reform of communal services and pensions. Until the Duma elections of the fall of 2003, the RPT had two leaders: S. Khramov, the head of Sotsprof, who has traditionally espoused liberal positions (though not, obviously, on the labour code), and O. Shein, deputy to the Duma from Astrakhan and leader of Zashchita, an alternative union federation that describes itself as socialist and which has links to Stalinist parties to the "left" of the KPRF. There was some talk in 2003 of an electoral alliance with the avowedly Stalinist Russian Communist Workers' Party, but the latter decided to join the coalition headed by the KPRF. In the lead-up to the election, Khramov and Shein had a falling out, and the future of the party is now unclear. Shein himself was re-elected to the Duma from the town of Astrakhan.

Ivanov, whom Edinstvo helped to elect twice, is also not without his political ambiguities. He ran as an independent candidate and is probably one of the few deputies that has not been corrupted. He has maintained close links with Edinstvo and has generally taken progressive positions on social issues, including the labour code reform. But on other matters he supports Putin and even served as his "confidential agent" for the Samara region in the 2000 presidential elections. He argues that the working class is too weak to defend itself and so it needs the support of a strong state. In addition, his support for Putin allows him to obtain more resources for his constituency. Despite the confused nature of both forms of Edinstvo's political action, they at least are evidence of its evolution toward more independent politics. ASMR, in the footsteps of the FNPR, has undergone the opposite evolution.

Although Edinstvo's membership is again growing, it remains a small minority at VAZ. This poses the question as to whether a strategy aimed at reforming ASMR from within might have made more sense. The answer was not obvious at the moment of Edinstvo's founding, a period of significant working-class activism. Today, however, Edinstvo's founders seem vindicated. Asked if he thought it was good for workers for two unions to exist at VAZ, Ivanov replied: "No, it's a bad idea. But there is really only one union at VAZ. An organization that claims to defend both workers and management is not a union."Certainly, the fate of independent shopfloor leaders who remain in ASMR has been to be marginalized. They complain that Edinstvo draws away the active workers who might otherwise support reform of ASMR. But the example of Tutaev, where a spontaneous mobilization replaced the old leadership, is not encouraging for ASMR's capacity to reform itself from within. None of ASMR's local affiliates (certainly not its national or regional organizations) has been any more successful than Tutaev in breaking out of the traditional mold.

As noted, a worker's decision to join Edinstvo implies a degree of conscious adherence to union independence and of commitment. In particular, it indicates a belief that independent collective action can make a difference. Edinstvo's members are different from the inert, frightened, and demoralized mass that is the base of ASMR, though the difference should not be exaggerated either. The relative ideological and psychological homogeneity of Edinstvo's membership and the absence of management from its ranks have allowed it to play a sort of vanguard role at VAZ that would not have been possible from within ASMR. Edinstvo's influence extends well beyond its membership and it has never stopped exerting real pressure on management. Its existence has undoubtedly been positive for all VAZ's workers. Certainly, management views it as a threat and a limit on its freedom of action and would like to be rid of it.

The fundamental factor limiting the expansion of Edinstvo's membership and influence is the passivity and demoralization of the mass of workers. As seen earlier, that is the consequence of many factors, most of which are well beyond Edinstvo's influence at present. Nevertheless, Edinstvo has not given up. It has tried to the best of its capacity to influence the moral climate. In the end, what distinguishes it most from ASMR is its capacity to learn from experience, in particular from its mistakes, and so to change. No change is evident in ASMR. Edinstvo has a deeply committed leadership that lives and breathes union and that has refused to let the daily grind of union work stop it from thinking strategically. That too is absent in ASMR.

Notes

1. Argumenty i fakty, no. 11, 2003, p. 2.
2. From a presentation at the Minsk Tractor Factory in June 2000.
3. "Khronika ob'yavlennoi katastrofy," *Izvestiya*, May 16, 2003; M. Fisher, "Little Love Lost for Russia's Forlorn Lada," *National Post* (Canada), Feb. 1, 2003.
4. Edinstvo's position was actually closer to "Menshevism," in that its leaders felt that Russian workers had to pass through the school of capitalism before pursuing the goal of socialism. The two presidents of Edinstvo both came to oppose the Soviet system after reading through Lenin's works, which made them aware of the vast gap separating reality from the revolutionary project.
5. O. A. Bol'shakova, et al., *Samoupravlenie na promyshlennykh predpriyatiyakh v usloviyakh perekhoda k rynku: iz opyta Vol'zhskogo avtomobil'nogo zavoda, 1991-1995 gg.*, Togliatti: Tol'yattinskii politekhnicheskii institut, 1995, p. 37.
6. For the language on full monthly guaranteed indexation, see *Kollektivnyi dogovor aktsionernogo obshchestva "AVTOVAZ,"* Togliatti, 1994, pp. 17-18. For the 72.5-per-cent indexation, see *Kollektivnyi dogovor aktsionernogo obshchestva "AVTOVAZ,"* Togliatti, Mar. 1, 1997, p. 16.
7. *Kollektivnyi dogovor aktsionernogo obshchestva "AVTOVAZ" na 2003 god*, 2003, p. 8.
8. Sibal (Deripaska) purchased GAZ in 2000 and carried out mass permanent layoffs and a reduction of benefits. Wages, on the other hand, were raised, so that at the start of 2003 they were at two thirds of those at VAZ. *Analiticheskii obzor OAO "ASM-kholding," yanvar' 2003*, Moscow, 2003, p. 23.
9. *Izvestiya*, Aug. 4, 1998.
10. This account is based on interviews and on the collection of documents *Zabastovka v tsekhke 45-3 Volzhskogo avtomobil'nogo zavoda, 27 sentyabrya—3 oktyabrya 1994 goda: dokumenty i materialy*, Moscow: Institut perspektiv i problem strany, 1998.
11. "Uvolennye vosstanovleny na rabote, no profsoyuz 'Edinstvo' zdes' ni pri chem," *Vol'zhskii avtostroitel'* (Togliatti), Dec. 28, 1994, p. 6.
12. *Rabochaya politika*, Dec. 24, 1999.
13. *Volzhskii avtostroitel'*, Sept. 12, 2002.
14. V. Grabov, "Razvitie kapitalizma, chast' vtoraya," *Panorama Tol'yatti* (Togliatti), Sept.10, 2002, p. 6.
15. Demand dropped when the government announced its intention to raise import duties on older model used cars beginning from the new year. People rushed to buy the imports ahead of the deadline, cutting sharply into the demand for the Ladas.
16. From unpublished figures of the production council of the body-assembly department. The ratio between the average before-tax wage and the consumer basket for a single adult dropped twenty-five per cent in the last half of the 2002, and another twenty per cent in January-February 2003. It averaged 1:13 over 2002.
17. In fact, the benefits mentioned were largely inherited from the Soviet period, and many have been eroded without resistance from ASMR. In private conversation, this leader complained

bitterly that ASMR's leaders undermine his work in the shop, that the best people he recruits to the shop committee end up leaving for Edinstvo, that ASMR is unreformable. His relations with Edinstvo, which has a strong leader in the shop, are on the whole friendly. His reasons for remaining in ASMR are complex, and, undoubtedly partly material, since he is a full-timer.

18. Zolotarev: "The public prosecutor says we're swamping him with our never-ending complaints, but I tell him that we wouldn't have to complain at all if just once he took action against an administrator who violated the law."

19. At a seminar in St. Petersburg in June 2001, the national president of the Union of Locomotive Brigades stated that the "focus on court action was a reflection of the weakness of our numbers. We became defensive, and our leaders wanted to make themselves reputations as lawyers and keep the masses at a distance and in the dark." Not long before, his union had made a major policy shift, dropping its craft orientation in favour of organizing the entire rail sector. Not unrelated, was the union's shift to the left, to opposition to the government that it had long supported.

20. "Byt' ili ne byt'," Edinstvo leaflet, Nov. 13, 2002.

21. "Vashe mnenie nam ponyatno…" Edinstvo leaflet, July 6, 1998.

22. "V edinstve—sila," Edinstvo leaflet, Feb. 25, 2003.

23. Edinstvo leaflet of Feb. 26, 2002.

24. "Analiz proekta kollektivnogo dogovora mezhdu litsamy ot profkoma ASM i rabotodatelem AO 'AVTOVAZ' na 2002 g.," Edinstvo leaflet, Mar. 21, 2002.

25. D. Pankin, "AO 'Avtovaz': peremeny k lutshemu," *Golos profsoyuza*, no. 1, (Jan.) 1998, p. 2..

26. *Kollektivnyi dogovor OAO "AVTOVAZ na 2003 god*, pp.4-5.

27. Management obtained the order, but it was overturned on appeal.

28. M. Paxson, "Dying for the Truth in Russia, *The Washington Post*, Oct. 19, 2003.

29. The differences between these federations are less ideological or political than a function of personal conflicts between leaders.

Chapter Six

THE SOCIO-POLITICAL CONTEXT IN UKRAINE

Ukraine is approximately the size of France and the second most populous of the former Soviet republics. At the time of the breakup, it had a population of fifty-two million, a little over a third of Russia's.[1] Famous for its rich black earth, Ukraine also had a large industrial base in coal-mining, metallurgy, chemicals, and machine-building. On the eve of secession, there was a widespread belief, aided by the propaganda of the nationalists and their newly-found allies in the Ukrainian *nomenklatura*, that an independent Ukraine, free of Moscow's domination, would quickly accede to Western living standards. But this did not to take into account the highly integrated nature of the Soviet economy and the cost of disrupting longstanding relations between enterprises. Even more important, however, was Ukraine's heavy dependence on Russia for much of its raw materials and most of its fuel.[2] As it turned out, Russia had been heavily subsidizing the Ukrainian economy.[3] But most of all, the ninety per cent who voted for independence in December 1991 could not foresee that independent Ukraine would be dominated by an elite so utterly corrupt and rapacious that the old Communist regime would soon start looking good in comparison.

Ukraine's post-Soviet trajectory closely resembles that of Russia. If the authoritarian drift of its political system has been rather slower, its socio-economic regression has been considerably more pronounced. Like Russia, Ukraine increasingly displays traits of a society relegated to the periphery of the world capitalist system. But unlike Russia, Ukraine is not very resource rich. The corollary of this evolution is a weak "civil society," including a labour movement that, like Russia's, is firmly wedded to "social partnership." The "alternative" union movement in Ukraine even weaker than Russia's.[4]

However, the Union of Workers of Auto and Farm-Machine Workers of Ukraine (ASMU), created in 1991 on the basis of existing Soviet trade unions, was during its first decade without any analogue in Russia. Its national leadership was determined to promote union independence and it found real, though limited, support for this in some of its regional and local affiliates.

The Economic Situation

Ukraine's depression has been deeper and more prolonged than those of either Russia or Belarus. In 2000, GDP officially stood at 47.4 per cent of its 1991 level, whereas the average for the countries of the Community of Independent States (USSR minus the Baltic state) was sixty-eight per cent.[5] Even after three years of growth, GDP per capita (at purchasing power parity) was still less than half that of Russia and Belarus and about a quarter of neighbouring Poland's.[6]

In 1999, the volume of capital investment was a quarter of the 1991 level.[7] Industrial output stood at 42.7 per cent of 1990 levels.[8] Even agriculture, in this former breadbasket of the Soviet Union, declined by more than sixty per cent, and in 1999 Ukraine had to import a large amount of wheat for the first time.[9] In ASM, farm-machinery production fell by eight-six per cent and motor-vehicle production by eight-two between 1990 and 1999.[10] ASMU's president was not exaggerating by much when he reported in 1997 that his sector "has practically been destroyed."[11]

Following nine consecutive years of decline, growth resumed in 2000. GDP rose by 5.9 per cent that year, and by 9.1 and 4.6 per cent in the next two. In the first half of 2003, the annual growth rate was 7.5 per cent.[12] Industry grew on at an annual rate of 7.3 per cent in 1998-2002.[13] However, this recovery has relied heavily on growth in the metals and chemical sectors, which have benefitted from strong demand in Russia and Asia since late 1999. Like Russia, Ukraine's industrial structure continues to shift away from high value added sectors, like machine-building, toward low-process materials, like steel and chemicals. The share of metalworking and machine-building in industrial production fell from twenty six per cent in 1991 to thirteen in 2000, while metallurgy's share rose from eleven to thirty per cent.[14] Most of the metal is exported, and in 2002 it accounted for thirty-nine per cent of total exports.[15] This makes Ukraine highly vulnerable to fluctuations in the international environment that is dominated by the wealthy, developed countries. The latter also confront Ukraine with protectionist measures in precisely those areas where it can compete—metals and agriculture. The basic problems facing the economy show no sign of resolution: weak domestic demand and lack of the investment. Real disposable money income in 2001 was only thirty-two per cent of the 1991 level,[16] while investment in 2001 was at only a third, with only four per cent of it coming from abroad. Ukraine has one of the lowest levels of foreign direct investment of the region.[17] An IMF study published in 2003 concluded that the recovery is not self-sustaining, largely because of the poor investment outlook. It predicted annual rates of growth in the range of one and 4.5 per cent up to 2010. That means that in the best scenario Ukraine will still far behind where it was in 1990.[18]

As in Russia, the ASM sector, like most other high value-added sectors, has benefitted relatively little from the recovery. Truck and tractor output continued to decline into 2002, when it stood at nine and three per cent of the respective 1991 levels. Passenger car production (mainly the Zaporizh'e Auto Factory (ZAZ) which has a joint venture with Daewoo) grew to twenty-eight per cent of its 1991 level, but in absolute terms that was only 43,500 units produced in 2002.[19]

Frustrated liberals explain the depth of Ukraine's depression by its late and hesitant "reforms," that is "shock therapy." Some even deny it ever attempted "shock therapy." But as Stiglitz has pointed out, that argument is disingenuous, since the IMF's programme contains everything, and certain elements will inevitably be left out. But the IMF itself pushed monetary targets, budget deficits and the pace of privatization. On these, Ukraine has performed "well." All the rest was secondary.[20] In the end, the main reason why Ukraine has done more poorly than Russia is that it lacks Russia's abundant oil and gas and, with a smaller economy, it was hit harder by the disruption of ties following independence. Moreover, the Ukrainian government aggravated the damage with policies consciously aimed at breaking the links with Russia.[21]

The Political System

It is true, however, that "shock therapy" got off to a later and a less determined start than in Russia. Prices were not freed to the same extent in 1992, and privatization began a few years later and proceeded somewhat more slowly. The more hesitant start was largely a consequence of the new regime's weakness. The first President, Leonid Kravchuk, had been a loyal member of the Soviet nomenklatura until a few months before secession. In fact, he had served as the Ukrainian Communist Party's Central Committee secretary in charge of ideology, which, among other things, was hostile to Ukrainian nationalism. But with the ship evidently going down, he embraced the cause of independence, together with much of the Ukrainian nomenklatura, in order to hold onto power. In this, he found a ready ally in the Western-oriented nationalist movement, which had already seen its strength peak at about a quarter of the electorate and had no hope of taking Ukraine the country to independence by its own forces.[22]

Kravchuk ran for president in December 1991 unopposed from the Left. He was all things to all people: defender of Ukrainian statehood to the nationalists of the western regions and Kyiv, and guarantor of continuity and stability to Ukrainians in the east, centre and south who wanted to maintain close ties to Russia and to preserve the welfare and egalitarian aspects of the Soviet system.[23] As in Russia, the mass of the population turned against the Western-promoted "market reform" once they began to experience its consequences.[24] But unlike Yeltsin, Kravchuk did not have a large "reserve of public confidence" as a former fighter against the bureaucratic dictatorship and privilege. His "window of opportunity" for carrying out "unpopular reforms" was a small one.

Active parliamentary opposition to the government's economic policies arose early in Ukraine, and unlike Russia, it coincided with powerful labour protest. In May 1993, the Supreme Rada (parliament) refused to renew Prime Minister Leonid Kuchma's special powers. A month later, two million miners and factory workers, mainly in the heavily industrial and russophone Donbass region, struck to protest against declining living standards. (When Yeltsin confronted the Russian Supreme Soviet in October 1993, he had the support of the still influential Independent Miners' Union; and despite FNPR president Klochkov's support for the Constitution, the rest of the labour movement remained passive.) As a consequence of this opposition, the "reformers" were forced out of the government. However, lacking their own vision for Ukraine's development, the workers settled for a referendum that posed the question of confidence in both the President and the parliament. In the meantime, the enterprise directors and local Donbass authorities were able to exploit the mobilization to obtain increased subsidies.[25]

Parliamentary elections in the spring of 1994 dealt another blow to the liberal/nationalist forces, which took only a quarter of the seats. The "anti-reform" parties (mainly the Communists, Socialists and the Peasants' Party) took a third. Almost half went to the politically amorphous "centre," which leaned to the right but not in any consistent fashion. The presidential elections of July 1994 dislodged Kravchuk, a fate that might well have overtaken Yeltsin had his coup failed in October 1993. Kravchuk's opponent, former Prime Minister Kuchma, won fifty-two per cent of the vote, most of it in the east and south. He had run on a social-democratic, even socialist, platform, promising closer relations with Russia. He even received the endorsement of the Communist Party.

But once in power, he quickly adopted right-wing policies. This put him in direct conflict with parliament, where the Left was able to block some elements of the neo-liberal programme that Kuchma unveiled in late 1994 with the endorsement of the IMF and World Bank. Immediately after his election, Kuchma launched a campaign to amend the constitution along Yeltsinian lines. He won a series of concessions by brandishing the threat of a referendum and the dissolution of parliament.[26] But parliamentary elections in March 1998 further strengthened the "anti-shock" forces. Although far from a majority, they were able to cut back Kuchma's powers, defend a minimal level of social expenditure, and block certain liberal measures, especially the privatization of 6,300 enterprises listed as strategic.[27] On a visit to Kyiv in 1999 to discuss a two billion U.S.$ loan, Stanley Fischer, then First Deputy Director of the IMF, complained that "finally Ukraine has agreed to a very sensible programme with us, but they're having great trouble getting it through the parliament."[28]

Kuchma was re-elected President in October 1999, despite his dismal record. Like Yeltsin in his election campaign of 1996, Kuchma made massive use of the "administrative resource." He also had the support of the mass media, that was either controlled by the state or by "oligarchs" who supported him. And there was also old-fashioned vote rigging. But the major factor in Kuchma's victory was the insistence of Communist Party leader P. Simonenko on running. That ensured that the much more widely respected leader of the Socialist Party, O. Moroz, would not be Kuchma's opponent in the runoff. Had the left forces united around Moroz, he might well have won, regardless of the unfair competition and massive corruption that characterized Kuchma's campaign. The three main left candidates together received forty-five per cent of the vote in the first round as against Kuchma's 36.4. It is also worth noting that Russia has no analogue to Ukraine's Socialist Party, a non-Stalinist left party. It has shifted rightwards in past years but remains social-democratic with a genuine, if limited, base. Many Ukrainians who strongly disliked Kuchma and would have supported Moroz could not bring themselves to vote for a Communist candidate.[29]

Fresh from his victory, Kuchma resumed his creeping coup against parliament. Progress was slowed down, however, when evidence surfaced that he had personally ordered the assassination of muckraking journalist, A Gongadze, in September 2000.[30] It says something of the quality Ukraine's political life that no one has been brought to justice so far and that "Kuchmagate" has all but been forgotten inside the country. A Russian journalist put it this way:

> There are three types of regimes. There are dictatorships, where people are killed on a regular basis, but the prosecutors do not look into the crimes committed by the president because it is considered the government's supreme right to slaughter its citizens in these countries. There are democracies, where any suspicion that a president may be guilty of murder will cost him his job. And then there is a country called Ukraine, where the president is a suspect in a murder case, but no one seems to

care…There is only one thing that the opposition did not take into account—in countries where the investigative authorities are no different from the bandits, *kompromat* [compromising evidence] is devalued completely.[31]

If Ukraine's Supreme Rada is somewhat less impotent than Russia's State Duma, the difference is one of mainly of quantity, not quality. The Ukrainian constitution leaves parliament some vestiges of power, but the President can generally overcome parliamentary opposition through bribery and blackmail. If those fail, he can unleash the "law enforcement" and tax-inspection agencies against recalcitrant deputies. It is thanks to those methods, the Kuchma finally assembled his more-or-less stable parliamentary majority.[32]

As in Russia, an undeclared moratorium on legality protects the rich and powerful. The government has shown the way with its unending scandals involving top state officials. Kuchma has ignored the Constitution repeatedly by refusing to sign laws after his veto had been overridden by parliament. He has also illegally "sequestered" social spending required by the budget, decreed wage freezes, and refused to raise the minimum wage in line with the minimum subsistence level. As in Russia, he made non-payment of public sector wages, of budgetary obligations, and of state orders fulfilled by enterprises, a central element of his monetarist policies in 1995-1999. This massive theft on the part of the state—in the first quarter of 1999, pension and public-sector wage arrears were equal to eight per cent of annual consolidated budget revenue[33]—enjoyed the tacit support of the IMF .

In the end, though Ukraine's road has been rather more sinuous, its political and economic systems differ little from Russia's.[34] Both are "managed democracies" with—so far at least—relatively low levels of repression (aside from Chechnya, in Russia's case). Both are very far from the rule of law, with corruption even more blatant in Ukraine,[35] a country from which two Prime Ministers have fled under accusation of massive theft and where the present one was appointed already having two criminal convictions. Both governments are wedded to monetarist policy; their economies are largely privatized (the private sector accounts for seventy-five per cent of GDP in Russia and sixty-five in Ukraine[36]), wide open to world,[37] and increasingly dependent on the export of natural resources and low-valued-added primary and semi-finished goods.

The Capitalist Class

The Ukrainian bourgeoisie is referred to as the "clans" (they began as geographically-based groupings) rather than the "oligarchs," but otherwise this class shares many basic traits with its Russian counterpart: it is a deeply cynical, essentially rent-seeking class, intimately linked both to the corrupt state administration and to the criminal underworld. But while Putin has moved to assert the state's supremacy over the oligarchs, even while serving their interests, Ukraine's "clans" have placed their people in key ministerial posts, as well as in parliament. The current Prime Minister, V. Yanukevich, is himself closely linked to Donestsk-based "clan" interests.[38]

The parasitic nature of Ukraine's new bourgeoisie is well illustrated by the country's gas distribution network, a major source of private accumulation. Almost all fuel and energy producers in Ukraine are loss-making, but that does not stop the distribution of fuel and energy from being highly lucrative. Ukraine itself produces little gas, but the system of distribution, organized under the auspices of former Prime Minister Lazarenko (now awaiting trial in California) and heavily dependent upon government protection, allowed a handful of firms to siphon off vast wealth from cash-strapped enterprises that had no access to credit.[39] The enterprises overpaid for gas with bartered manufactured goods that the energy distributors sold abroad at large profits upon which they paid no taxes.[40]

But the epitome of the short-sighted greed that characterizes this new ruling class was the theft in 1998 and 1999 of Russian gas transiting through Ukraine to the West. (Ninety per cent of Russia's gas exports pass through Ukraine.) This caused Russia to look for alternative routes, threatening one of Ukraine's major assets. If that were not enough, in 2000, Kuchma appointed Yulya Timoshenko, a woman who had made her fortune trading gas under the above-described system, to the post of Deputy Prime Minister. Incredibly, she was put in charge of cleaning up the energy sector.[41] Timoshenko soon fell out with Kuchma and formed her own party, and accusations of corruption began to fly between the two. This is typical of a political system where political parties are created on order to serve the interests of oligarchic "clans" and where competition among the "clans" is what passes for political struggle. In this system, Kuchma represents the dominant "clan," and he is constantly maneuvering to maintain its dominance.[42]

After his re-election in 1999, Kuchma was able to speed up privatization. This led to the takeover of industrial enterprises, including many in the ASM sector, by Ukrainian and Russian "oligarchs," and spelling the end of the reign of freebooting directors. Management style has become more hard-nosed and less paternalistic, but investment has remained minimal. The predominant economic orientation of the new owners is still predation, though its forms are somewhat more refined.

The other important actor in Ukrainian politics is the West, especially the U.S., well represented by the IMF and other international financial institutions. As in Russia, the IMF, with its ability to block or unlock credits and to signal potential foreign investors, has had major influence on economic policy. But the U.S. government has also intervened directly. In 1997, *The Financial Times* reported that the Ukrainian president and government were "summoned" to Washington to receive a "dressing down" for their insufficient market zeal.[43] Another report took note of the "not very correct diplomatic behaviour of U.S. officials in Kiev, who not only do not resist giving direct instructions to the political leaders of the country but also actively influence events in the Supreme Rada…A well-known Ukrainian politician…said that during one of the U.S. Secretary of State Madeleine Albright's visits to Kiev…in very inappropriate, almost ultimatum form, she instructed them how to run the country."[44] The United States' policy of "tough love," as *The Financial Times* called it, (until recently, Ukraine was the third largest recipient of U.S. bilateral aid) is largely based upon its geopolitical interest in keeping Ukraine away from Russia. But there have also been some economic gains, despite Ukraine's economic disaster. It's integration into the world economy has opened it up to penetration by Western imports, sometimes enjoying the direct financial support of the Ukrainian government and at the expense of domestic producers. And the illegal outflow of capital from Ukraine to the West—estimated at fifteen billion U.S.$ between 1995 and 1999 alone—is far greater than the total sum of Western foreign investment, aid and credits.[45]

Ukraine enjoys some room to manoeuver, thanks to its ability to play the West and Russia off against each other. The "special" relationship with the U.S. soured somewhat when the U.S. backed protests against "Kuchmagate" and sought to replace Kuchma with his former Prime-Minister V. Yushchneko.[46] Kuchma turned to Russia, and Putin gave him his support. Meanwhile, to the alarm of Ukrainian nationalists, privatized Ukrainian enterprises have been falling increasingly under the control of Russian conglomerates, whose experience at home prepared them well to venture where Western capital fears to tread. After September 11, 2001, Kuchma shifted westward again, announcing Ukraine's intention to join NATO (and abandoning the state's previous non-aligned orientation), but the reconciliation was marred by evidence that Kuchma had personally authorized the sale of radar equipment to Iraq.[47] And so it goes.

The Workers' Situation

A new Law on Trade Unions, signed by Kuchma in September 1999 after parliament overrode his veto, confirmed most of the traditional union rights, including the right to automatic dues checkoff, to obtain information, to demand the dismissal of managers for violations of the Labour Code or collective agreements, the requirement of union consent for disciplining and layoffs, and the protection of union officers from persecution. It also added a new element, inspired directly by ASMU's constitution, that declares union independence from employers and prohibits employers or their representatives from occupying elected positions in unions or from negotiating on the part of workers.[48] But in the fall of 2003, the government made public the draft of a new Labour Code that goes well beyond the new Russian code in its neo-liberal orientation. It has been denounced by the Federation of Trade Unions of Ukraine (FPU) and, as in the Russian case, it will probably be somewhat moderated in the process of its adoption.[49] Even so, the rights that workers and their unions now formally enjoy are not of much practical use when unions are so weak. And as in Russia, judicial independence in Ukraine leaves much to be desired. As far a worker-employer relations in the new private sector are concerned, it is the law of the jungle.

Outright state repression of unions has been limited, though the arrest of the leader of the miners' strike committee in Zaporizh'e in 1996 left its mark. On the other hand, police surveillance and harassment of more militant labour leaders is more widespread than in Russia. Militant leaders find their phones tapped, their mail opened, and they receive frequent visits from state security agents. In the period before the 1999 presidential elections, the late president of the Kharkov regional organization of ASMU, Viktor Vetchinkin, who actively campaigned for Moroz, was called in almost daily to the police. The local chief confided to him that he had been unable to find any compromising evidence but that he was under orders to keep after him. He suggested to Vetchinkin that, if he had high-placed friends, he should ask them to intervene to take the pressure off the police.

Of the three countries under study, Ukrainian workers have been hit the hardest economically. In 1990, Ukraine ranked forty-second on the UN Human Development Index, as compared to Belarus in thirty-sixth place and Russia in twenty-ninth. A decade later, Ukraine ranked eightieth, as compared to Russia at sixtieth and Belarus at fifty-sixth.[50] As imperfect as these rankings are, they provide a rough idea of the relative regression. A U.N. study estimated that living standards declined by eighty per cent in the first three years of independence.[51] In the spring of 2003, after three and a half years of growth, eight-five per cent of respondents to a national survey conducted by Ukraine's Institute of Sociology perceived the economic situation as "very bad."[52] During its first decade of independence, Ukraine's population officially declined by eight per cent.[53] Life expectancy fell from sixty-six to sixty-two years for men and from seventy-five to seventy-four for women between 1991 and 2000. Infant mortality is five times higher in Ukraine than in Germany and two times higher than in Poland, which began the transition on a par with Ukraine, its neighbour.[54] Ukraine's birth rate, which was the same as Russia's in 1991, fell from 12.1 per thousand to 7.7 in 2001, as compared to 9.1 in Russia. This reflects the relatively deeper poverty and insecurity of Ukraine.[55] As one worker put it, "only the bold dare have more than one child or even any children."

Real wages began to rise again in the wake of the financial collapse of 1998, and, according to official figures, they reached one third of 1991 levels in 2000 and one half by 2002. But the FPU put real wages at a only quarter of 1991 levels in 2002.[56] The average Ukrainian wage is half the Russian,[57] equivalent to about eighty U.S.$ in the first half of 2003. In the ASM sector the average wage at that time was sixty-seven U.S.$, just under the official subsistence minimum for a single person which covers only food, shelter and clothing.[58] The World Bank puts the poverty line at $4 a day for cold countries like Ukraine, and at seminars, workers say they would need at least $150 for a minimally decent living. In 2002, almost two thirds of household income was spent on food. Even so, nutritional deficiencies are widespread, as cheaper potatoes and bread have replaced vitamin and protein-rich foods. According to research by the U.N., the energy value of the average diet fell from 3,597 calories in 1990 to 2,752 in 1996. Meat consumption has fallen fifty per cent since 1990, fruit by twenty per cent, eggs by forty, and fish—by seventy-five per cent.[59]

But the official figures for wages do not take into account their non-payment, a massive phenomenon that peaked in 1999, when the workers in the auto sector were owed on average 6.4 months wages and in the farm-machine sector—4.5 months.[60] In the town of Kupensk in 1998, desperate foundry workers were reduced to demanding a loaf of bread a day per worker as partial payment of wages owed, but the director would give only half a loaf. By the end of 2002, the wage debt had been practically liquidated in the auto sector, though in farm machinery it still amounted to thirty-seven million hryvnas or about seven million U.S.$.[61] The total wage debt in the economy in mid 2003 was still equal to half of the total monthly wage bill.[62]

Industrial employment fell fifty per cent between 1991 and 2001, from 7.7 to 3.9 million, while the total employed work force declined by sixteen per cent from twenty-five to 20.9 million.[63] In ASM, employment dropped fifty-two per cent in 1991-2000, from 460,000 to 220,000. But all these employment figures include workers who were in fact laid off (on "administrative leave") or were involuntarily working part time.[64] Official unemployment was only four per cent in 2002. Those were the people registered and receiving benefits. The Economic Intelligence Unit put real unemployment in 2003 at closer to twenty per cent.[65] Another estimate that includes all those who were unemployed, laid off or working only one or two days a week in 2000, put it one third of the active population.[66] Despite the return to growth in 2000, employment in ASM has continued to fall.[67]

What there exists of a social safety net provides workers with very little security. If official unemployment is low, it is because the miserly benefits offer little incentive to report: in 1999, the benefit did not exceed nine U.S.$ a month.[68] The average and minimum pensions in 2001 were twenty-two and thirteen U.S.$ respectively.[69] Meanwhile, the government, prodded by the IMF, continues to cut subsidies to housing, utilities and public services that still provide some cushion to workers. As in Russia, services that are formally free, especially healthcare and education, are underfunded and so increasingly demand de facto user fees. State funding of healthcare is only fifty U.S.$ per capita, half the level in Russia and a fifth of Central Europe's. "The nation is dying from this free healthcare," remarked a worker at a seminar in Vinnitsa. Higher education is less and less accessible to workers' children.[70] In some towns, buildings in entire districts suffer through the winter with cold radiators. Others are without hot water for half the year, and the streets are dimly lit, if at all.

The obvious questions are: how do people survive, and where have all the industrial workers gone? As in Russia, the basic mode of adaptation has been simply to abandon needs that until very recently were considered an indispensable part of civilized life. There has also been a certain return to agriculture. Ukraine has the dubious distinction of having seen a relative, even small absolute, rise in the agricultural work force.[71] Some city-dwellers get help from family in the country and many have garden plots. Non-payment for housing and utilities is a mass phenomenon. Another important survival mechanism is migration: there are an estimated one million Ukrainians working, for the most part undocumented, in Russia alone. Many others have gone westward. Others who left industry eke out an existence in petty trade and services.

At a seminar for shopfloor activists in November 1999, Vladimir Zlenko, then national president of ASMU, gave his view of the workers' situation:

> It is important for trade unions to realize that the working class as such in the Ukraine has been destroyed. Workers are surviving however they can. They seek solutions to the problems of their lives beyond the confines of the plant, that is, they have practically lost their link to the plant. Some, while formally employed at enterprises, have become petty traders, entrepreneurs, craftspeople, and a significant part are being "lumpenized." Marx in his time observed that lumpens are incapable of organization and struggle...A trade union can function only in a plant that is working. We can beat our chests and shout that we are strong as much as we like, but if there is no enterprise, or if it only formally exists, then there are no workers and there can be no union. And I have to ask myself: is this not done by design by our government?[72]

This, of course, was the low point of the "transition." Since then, the situation has improved, though not by much.

Notes

1. Statkomitet SNG, SNG v 2001 g.: statisticheskii spravochnik, Moscow, 2002, p. 105.
2. Ukraine's fuel reserves meet only ten per cent of its needs. *Europa World Yearbook, 1998,* London: Europa Publications, 1998, p. 3429.
3. H. van Zon, *The Political Economy of Independent Ukraine*, pp. 18, 111.
4. For an overview of the union movement in Ukraine, "Profspilkovyi rukh v Ukraini," *National'na bezpeka i oborona*, no. 8, 2001.
5. Statkomitet SNG, *SNG v 2002 godu: statisticheskii spravochnik.*, Moscow, 2003, p. 26. Stiglitz puts GDP in 2000 at only one third of its 1990 level. (Stiglitz, *Globalization*, p. 153.)
6. Economist.com Country Briefings, June 20, 2003 (www.economist.com/countries/Ukraine). Per capita GDP in Ukraine was $US 2,606. Some studies claim Ukraine's shadow economy is relatively higher than in most other "transition" countries. See IMF, *Ukraine: Selected Issues*, IMF Country Report, no. 3/173, June 2003, pp. 21.
7. *SNG v 2001 g.*, pp. 7, 28.
8. UEPLAC, *Ukrainian Economic Trends, Monthly Update*, Kyiv, Apr. 2002, p. 8.
9. Van Zon, *The Political Economy*, p. 86.
10. Derzhavnii komitet statistiki Ukraini, *Statistichnii shchorychnik Ukraini za 1999 ryk*, Kyiv: Tekhnika, 2000, p. 126
11. V. Zlenko, Report to the conference "Towards a New Transnational Worker's Response to the Curtailment of Production and Neoliberalism," Frankfurt, Mar. 6-9, 1997 (unpublished).
12. Economist.com Country Briefings, Ukraine June 20, 2003.
13. EIU, *Country Profile: Ukraine*, 2003, p. 35.
14. *SNG v 2001 g.: statisticheskii spravochnik*, p. 23.
15. IMF, *Ukraine: Selected Issues*, p. 50.
16. Statkomitet SNG, *SNG v 2001g., Statisticheskii ezhegodnik*, Moscow, 2002, p. 127.
17. *SNG v 2002 g : statisticheskii spravochnik.*, p. 48; *SNG v 2001 g.: statisticheskii spravochnik*, p. 32. Ukraine has attracted less than three per cent of the foreign direct investment in Central and Eastern Europe in the post-Communist period. (EIU, *Country Profile: Ukraine*, London, 2003, pp. 31, 44.)
18. IMF, *Ukraine: Selected Issues*, pp. 13, 17.
19. *SNG: Statisticheskii ezhegodnik, 2001*, pp. 170-71.
20. Stiglitz, *Globalization*, p. 155.
21. H. van Zon, et al., *Social and Economic Change in Eastern Ukraine*, Aldershot: Ashgate,1998, pp. 49, 112.
22. T. Kuzio and A. Wilson, *Ukraine: Perestroika to Independence*, CIUS: Toronto, 1994, p. 62. See also, A. Wilson, *The Ukrainians*, New Haven: Yale University Press, 2000 (second ed.) pp. 174-178. The nationalist movement was centred in the west of Ukraine, which until 1939 had for several centuries been cut off from the rest of the country. The centre and east of Ukraine had been part of the Russian empire during that time and later part of the USSR.

23. Kuzio and Wilson, *Ukraine,* pp. 187-9, 204, 206.
24. Van Zon, *The Political Economy*, p. 49.
25. V. Borisov, "The Strike as a Form of Worker Activism in a Period of Economic Reform," in S. Clarke, ed., *Labour Relations in Transition*, Cheltenham: Edward Elgar, 1995, pp. 177-200; A. Swain, "The First and Last Ukrainian Plan? Dismantling the Coal Mining Industry, *Labour Focus on Eastern Eruope*, no. 60, 1998, p. 73.
26. K. Wolczuk, "Constituting Statehood: the New Ukrainian Constitution," *The Ukrainian Review*, fall 1998, no. 45, pp. 17- 37.
27. *Izvestiya*, April 3, 1998. V. Zviaglyanich, "State and Nation: Economic Strategies for Ukraine, in S. Wolchik and V. Zviglyanich, *Ukraine: the Search for a National Identity*, N.Y.: Roan and Littlefield, 2000, p. 253.
28. "IMF Mission in Kyiv to Decide on $2 Billion Loan, *RFE/RL Newsline*, July 25, 1998 (www.rferl.org/newsline)
29. L. Finberg, "Leçons de l'élection présidentielle ukrainienne," *Courrier des pays de l'Est,*, Feb. 2000 no. 102, pp. 4-13. The Ukrainian Communist Party, like its Russian counterpart, has remained faithful to key elements of its stalinist legacy.
30. L. Sevunts, "Headless Body May Be trouble for Ukraine Leader," *Montreal Gazette*, Dec. 21, 2000, p. B-1. For a summary of the case and its status as of August 2003, see the press communique of *Reporters Without Borders* from Aug. 19, 2003 at www.rsf.fr/article.php3?id_article=7789
31. Yu. Latynina, "Ukraine: The Soap Opera," *The Moscow Times*, Aug. 2003.
32. I. Zhdanov and Yu. Yakimenko, "Poslednii bastion demokratii," *Zerkalo nedeli* (Kyiv), no.13 (438), Apr. 8, 2003, p. 5.
33. EIU, *Country Profile: Ukraine*, p. 27.
34. This is the conclusion reached by German historian Gerhard Simon in "Ukraina i Rossiya: dve strany—odna trasnformatsiya," *Connections*, Apr. 2002, pp. 1-8.
35. EIU, *Country Profile:Ukraine,,* p. 25.
36. K. Gaiduk, et al. *Belarusskaya eknomika na pereput'e,* Berlin and Minsk, 2003, p. 94.
37. The average real import duty in Ukraine in 2002 was two per cent. (IMF, *Ukraine: Selected Issues*, p. 55.)
38. EIU, *Country Profile: Ukraine*, p. 8.
39. Interest rates in March 2003 were seventeen per cent, despite marginal inflation. Even so banks are reluctant to lend to industry, and never do so on a long-term basis. (EIU, *Country Profile: Ukraine*, p. 38.)
40. Van Zon, *The Political Economy*, p. 86; C. Clover, "Le Donbass: une économie de prédation, *Courrier des pays de l'Est*, Feb. 2000, pp. 25-27.
41. *The Financial Times*, Nov. 20, 2000; S. Vlasov, "Velikomuchennitsa ot biznesa," *Sovetskaya Rossiya*, Jan. 13, 2001.
42. See *Nezvisimaya gazeta*, 6 and 10 Dec. 2000.
43. *The Financial Times*, May 30, 1997.
44. *Nezavisimaya gazeta,* Dec. 23. 2000, p. 5.
45. van Zon, *The Political Economy Ibid.*, pp, 68, 91.
46. *Fakty i kommentarii*, (Kyiv) March 22, 2002.

47. EIU, *Country Profile: Ukraine*, p. 15.
48. *Zakon Ukraini "O professional'ykh soyuzakh, ikh pravakh i granatiyakh,"* Donteskii oblsatnoi sovet profsoyuzov: Bibliotechka profosyuznogo lidera, 2002.
49. "Zverennya Prezidii Federatsii profspilok Ukraini z privodu podanogo Kabinetom Ministriv Ukrainy do Verkhovnoi Radi Ukraini proektu Trudovogo kodeksu Ukrainy," *Profspilkovi visti*, Oct. 21, 2003.
50. UN Human Development Report, hdr.undp.org/reports/global/2002.
51. O.S. Vlasiuk and S.I. Pyrozhkov, *Indeks liudksogo rozvytku: Dosvid Ukrainy*, Kyiv: National Institute of Strategic Studies and United Nations Development Programme, 1995, cited in T. Kuzio, *Ukraine Under Kuchma*, N.Y.: St. Martin's Press, 1997, p. 137.
52. N. Drobnokhod, "Gosudarstvennyi labirint dlya ukrainskogo naroda" *Zerkalo nedeli*, Apr. 6, 2003, p. 20.
53. *SNG v 2001 g.: statisicheskii ezhegodnik*, p.105. The decline would have been greater were it not for the large in-migration of Ukrainians and Crimean Tatars from other parts of the former Soviet Union in 1991-93.
54. EIU, *Country Profile: Ukraine*, p. 19.
55. *SNG v 2001 g.: statisicheskii ezhegodnik*, pp. 115, 116 and 112. See also, V. Krasin, "Pochemu nas stanovistsya men'she," *Den'* (Kyiv), no. 33, 2002.
56. *SNG v 2002 godu: statiticheskii spravochnik*, p. 135; S. Kondryuk, "Sotsial'noe partnerstvo na Ukraine," *Solidarnost'*, no. 14, 2003.
57. IMF, *Ukraine: Selected Issues*, p. 9.
58. *Uraydovyi kur'er* (Kyiv), no. 135, 2003; *Edinst'* Kyiv), no. 3, 2003; S. Kondryuk, "Sotsial'noe partnerstvo…"
59. EIU, *Country Profile: Ukraine*, p. 19.
60. ASMU, "Materialy do zvitu Tsentral'noi Radi profspilki," 2000, pp. 20. (data of the Ministry of Industry)
61. ASMU, "Report of the President of ASMU to the Central Committee of April 10, 2003" (unpublished).
62. *Uryadonyi kur'er*, July 24, 2003.
63. *SNG v 2001 g: Statisticheskii ezhegodnik*, p. 691.
64. ASMR, *Materialy do zvitu…*, p. 1.
65. EIU, *Country Profile: Ukraine*, p. 32.
66. O. Korniyevskii, "Unemployment in Ukraine: Estimates and Forecasts," *National Security and Defence*, no. 2, 2000, p. 27. (www.uceps.com.us/eng/all/jounral2000).
67. ASMR, "Report of the president of ASMU to the Central Committee of Apr. 10, 2003."
68. O. Kornievski, "Unemployment in Ukraine," p. 28.
69. *SNG v 2002 g.: statisicheskii spravochnik*, p. 377.
70. EIU, *Country Profile: Ukraine*, pp. 18-19.
71. *SNG v 2002 g.: statisicheskii spravochnik*, p. 374.
72. ASMU, *Profosyuzy i rynochnaya ekominka*, Kyiv, 1999, pp. 34 and 48.

Chapter Seven
THE UNION OF AUTO AND FARM-MACHINE WORKERS OF UKRAINE
Promoting Independence

The Union of Auto and Farm-Machine Workers of Ukraine (ASMR) was founded in January 1991. At that time, its employed membership was 460,000, about a quarter if the Russian union's. By 2000, it had fallen to 216,000 and was down to only 129,000 at the start of 2003.[1] The decline was almost entirely a consequence of the economic crisis, since ninety-seven per cent of the work force in ASM belonged to the union in 2003. The few alternative unions in the sector are very weak.

ASMU is one of the forty sectoral unions affiliated with the Federation of Trade Union of Ukraine (FPU), which is by far the largest union federation in Ukraine, with a claimed membership of 14.4 million in 2001 or 89.4 per cent of all union members. Most of the others belong to still "traditional" unions but which are not affiliated with the FPU, such as the railroad workers. The principal alternative unions are in coalmining and transport.[2] In absolute terms, union membership fell by a third between 1991 and 2001, but in the enterprises and institutions inherited from the Soviet period, union density remains high. On the other hand, unions are practically inexistent in newly-formed private enterprises.

It was above all the determination of its first president, Vladimir Zlenko, to break with past practice that distinguished ASMU from its Russian counterpart, and, indeed, from all other FPU-affiliated unions. His ten-year tenure from the beginning of 1991 to the end of 1999 is the focus of the first part of this chapter. Since his retirement, the union has gradually shifted back to mainstream "social partnership" positions.

The Kharkov regional organization of ASMU, to which the initiative in creating an independent Ukrainian union in 1991 belonged, had an important influence on the character of national leadership. This region alone (one of twenty-five in Ukraine) accounted for a quarter of ASMU's membership. Under the forceful command of its president, Viktor Vetchinkin, the Kharkov regional council was the first labour organization in Ukraine to proclaim its independence from the state and from management in May 1990.[3] Zlenko's main base of support, it is the subject of the second part of the chapter.

Fighting "Partnership"

Zlenko's election as president of the new union perhaps reflected the more optimistic mood of the time, a period of relative social activism. Normally, the choice would have gone to someone who already had an apartment in Kyiv (Zlenko was from Chernigov), since the time had passed when the state was allocating apartments, and the union could not afford to buy or rent one for its new president. But ASM had only two plants in the capital, and neither of their leaders was considered suitable by the delegates at the founding congress. Zlenko had luck, however, in securing the help of the well-connected President of the All-Union (i.e., Soviet) Union of ASM Workers, which had not yet been disbanded. Even so, he spent his first year in Kyiv in a factory dormitory.

Zlenko's biography set him apart from most union officials. He had worked for several years as chief technologist in a parts plant in Chernigov before becoming plant president. From there, he was appointed president of the regional committee in 1978. But he insisted on keeping his office in the factory and did not move into the offices located in the building of the regional council of trade unions. "I didn't want to belong to a party organization of bureaucrats. I wanted to attend party meetings with workers. It took a lot of effort to remain in the plant's party organization [rather than that of the regional council]. I wanted to stay close to the life of the factory. I felt that if I knew what was happening on the ground in one plant, it would be easier to understand the others."[4] Zlenko was the only regional president of a sectoral union in Chernigov who had not previously been a party functionary. He was in frequent conflict with the enterprise directors, party authorities and the head of the regional council of trade unions. At ASMU's founding congress, he agreed to run for national president only at the last minute, but he won an absolute majority in a field of six candidates.

The promotion of union independence lay at the heart of his programme. It was the constant theme of his reports to the Central Council and of the union's paper, *Ednist'* (Unity). A typical cartoon in the paper showed a kneeling union president with pillows tied to his knees knocking timidly on the boss's door. The caption read: "I want to ask: is this how it is at your plant?"[5] Zlenko was always at pains to emphasize the conflicting interests that oppose workers and management. At a seminar in Lutsk for shopfloor activists, he explained:

> If workers feel that their interests coincide with those of management and that the director is the head of the family, of the work collective—in any family, of course, there can be minor conflicts—then why hold formal negotiations, why have unions at all, why the right to strike? The enterprise's father will set everything right and make a happy life for each worker. I'm not saying that they are bad people, though some are. They simply find themselves in a position where they have to carry out the employers' policy: economize on wages, on health and safety expenses, on social benefits. And in Ukraine, it is the managers who are getting rich…Government policy is to create a class of rich people, owners, at the cost of impoverishing the broad mass of the population, and managers often get rich by not paying wages. What worker has not experienced the insult and humiliation of not receiving wages? With the support of the government, employers trample underfoot the Constitution and laws and display contempt for workers' interests.[6]

Part of his strategy to promote independence was to get management out of the union. He asked his Central Council: "Can workers express themselves freely when the director is sitting right in front of their noses on the stage at the conference? And can a trade union adopt the workers' viewpoint when in its highest body, the union conference, you might find up to eighty per cent of delegates who are from management, from foreman and right up to director?"[7] But this goal, which Zlenko proclaimed from the moment of his election, came up against the strong resistance of local leaders. Even Kharkov's Vetchinkin objected at first, citing the loss of dues that it would entail. Local leaders agreed that separation was inevitable at some undefined point but not yet, and they brought out all the usual arguments. Only the most candid admitted that they were worried principally about their own welfare. Zlenko explained to a group of workers:

> Certain plant presidents have said to me: "If something happens and I don't get re-elected, I'll have to go to the director for work." This was when we were discussing the question of management's presence in our union. At that time, 2400 South-Korean trade-unionists, including their president, were sitting in jail and asking for our support. Worker leaders went to jail and didn't worry about what their employers would think. They held the interests of the working class above their own. But our

leaders can't seem to separate themselves from management. With the support of many union leaders, management does not want to leave our union because as members they can keep an eye on it...There are even instances where the director is a member of the plant committee. And he is almost always sitting in the stage at the conferences where he can observe the hall.[8]

Zlenko was forced to move slowly. His first attempt to change the statutes to exclude managers completely from membership was defeated at the May 1997 Central Council. However, in 1998, Vetchinkin finally agreed to a weaker formulation. What finally decided him was an incident during the parliamentary election campaign that year, in which he had run as candidate of the Social Democratic Party of the Ukraine: the director of the Kharkov Tractor Factory refused to let him onto its territory to campaign among the workers. Backed by Kharkov, Zlenko was able to persuaded the Central Council of May 1998 to prohibit "employers (administration)" from being elected to trade-union committees or from negotiating on behalf of the union. Regional and local organizations were given until the next round of union elections at the end of 1999 to put the decision into effect.[9] ASMU successfully lobbied to have this rule incorporated into the new Law on Trade Unions. But the definition of "employer" proved contentious. At the October 1998 Central Council, Zlenko proposed that it include anyone with the power to issue orders or discipline. But the majority wanted it limited to directors and assistant directors, department and shop supervisors and their assistants. (The parliament's definition was even narrower: the owner and the general director.) The Council also decided that no new members from the above categories be accepted into the union. This was a significant, if limited and mainly symbolic, step towards union independence.

Parallel to the efforts to separate the union organizationally from management, Zlenko sought to demarcate its policy, challenging the traditional disposition to "take into account the interests of the enterprise." The clearest expression was his uncompromising position on the non-payment of wages. Whereas most local leaders were indeed inclined to "show understanding," citing objective circumstances and blaming government policy, Zlenko consistently argued that since wages were the workers' source of subsistence, nothing could justify the union's tolerating their not being paid. Even if management had no money, that was management's problem, not the union's. He explained:

> Today workers everywhere are not being paid. That means it's a state problem and that we have to make demands on the government. And we are doing what we can to change that government. But the main culprits in this situation are the enterprise directors and their administra-

tions. After all, it is by their hand that wages are not being paid, that the economy is going to ruin. There are directors who could pay but don't, using the money for other purposes, because that's what everyone else is doing, that's the way things are. Every day we have to demand that management pay our wages on time. That's what they are getting paid for. If taxes are a problem, let them put pressure on the government to reduce them. And if they can't keep the factory working, then who needs that kind of director and chairman of the board? The same goes for ministers and prime ministers.[10]

You might find the odd honest director. But at least the overwhelming majority are getting rich by every available means: they create small enterprises, commercial firms; they sell and resell the plants's output five times over through these firms and skim off huge profits. Their interests and those of the workers were always opposed, but before, under the old system, that conflict was somewhat muted. In those days, directors were privileged and could take certain liberties, but if they stole and were caught, they were put away. There were limits. There are none today.[11]

Zlenko showed the way himself by refusing concessions in bargaining the sectoral agreement with the government. In 1998, alone among the leaders of the eleven industrial unions that were negotiating jointly, he rejected the government's demand to set the minimum wage for the eleven sectors below the poverty line, where it had been in previous contracts. In principle, his refusal opened the way for a formal labour dispute, but in practice there was not much Zlenko could do alone. All the same, it was a signal to the local unions not to make concessions in their own bargaining. In the 1999 negotiations, he was the only national president not to agree to the government's demand to free employers from the negotiated minimum wage, if the enterprise owed more than five months wages. He proposed that the presidents go back and consult their membership, but they refused. However, Zlenko was supported by his own Central Council.

ASMU's Central Council took enforcement of the sectoral agreement very seriously, in contrast to its Russian counterpart, which considered its status as recommendatory. In fact, the sectoral agreement was largely ignored in ASMR's enterprises. Application of the sectoral agreement was the activity that took the most of the time and energy of ASMU's national office. It encouraged local unions to mobilize rank-and-file pressure during their own contract negotiations, as well as to obtain payment of wage arrears and union dues. The Central Council issued concrete instructions and distributed forms to local unions for the organization of lawsuit campaigns, and it cited the miners' strikes as examples of effective action on non-payment.[12] When a union sued, results were usually forthcoming. In one case, the national office financed a lawsuit (the local union had no money) against the director of the Zhitomir Parts Factory for 18,000 hryvnyas (about 4,000 U.S.$) owed to the union. The day after the judge's decision for the union, a bailiff sealed the cars and computers of top management with a view to their sale. The director immediately paid the union its dues.

The President's reports to the Central Council and the union's paper gave prominence to local conflicts and singled out for praise organizations that took militant action. Local unions were instructed to view contract negotiations as a labour disputes that had to be accompanied by organized pressure to be successful.[13] In his report to the May 1997 Central Council, Zlenko stated:

> Enough patience! We are constantly adopting resolutions on the need to organize mass pressure, but [spontaneous] workers' actions do not always receive the support of union leaders. Even when local protest actions don't win all the demands, they have a tremendously positive impact on the development of the labour movement. Workers who stand shoulder to shoulder in demonstrations and strikes are proud, freedom-loving people. They are people who don't want to crawl into the twenty-first century on their knees but to walk in on their feet, with heads held high. Today we are recommending to all plant and regional organizations of the union to assume the leadership of all local worker actions.[14]

The national leadership, to the extent of its resources, lent its support to workers who resisted, even when that meant crossing local and regional union leaders. At the Kyiv Motorcycle Factory, for example, wages not been paid for three months. The workers were also upset at the repeated layoffs, some for a month at a time. The authoritarian director was sixty-five and well past retirement age, and it was widely believed among the workers that he was neglecting the enterprise while he prepared himself a comfortable nest-egg at their expense. In October 1995, he announced yet another month-long layoff, which the union president, as usual, countersigned without consulting even his plant committee, let alone the workers. To make things worse, the workers were to receive only thirty per cent of their base pay, not the two thirds mandated by law. This finally provoked a wildcat strike. I. Onoprienko, a machine-operator who had briefly participated in a small alternative union at the plant, assumed the leadership. At a mass meeting, after a lengthy discussion, it was decided to prepare a general assembly for the return to work at the end of the month. Its object would be to consider a vote of non-confidence in the director. Meanwhile, an organizing committee was elected, headed by Onoprienko to prepare the assembly and to lobby the government to remove the director. (The enterprise plant was still state-owned.)

When the month had elapsed, the general assembly, in a hall filled to overflowing, voted to remove the director. It also voted to replace the union's president. Zlenko urged him to address the assembly, but he refused, citing its unconstitutional character. The assembly elected Onoprienko to head the union. Although the election had no constitutional standing, Zlenko advised Onoprienko to assume the post. He wrote him a document confirming his election pending an official delegates' conference and he affixed the Central Council's stamp to it. After holding out for ten days, the deposed president gave up the keys to his office. The general director made him a deputy director. But the general director himself was soon removed by the government, though it refused to consult the union on his replacement. Zlenko explained his position in the conflict:

> While the old union committee stood by passively and let wage arrears accumulate, Onoprienko was busy organizing a lawsuit campaign. When the director got wind of this, he got so scared that he immediately found the money to pay workers the two thirds required by the law. And he didn't just pay for the latest shutdown but for all the others over the past year. So how could we not support such a man?

Backed by a mobilized membership, Onoprienko led the union in tough and largely successful negotiations with the new director. But, in a scenario that was repeated elsewhere, he gradually shifted his focus from applying pressure on management to lobbying the government for orders, credits, tax abatements, and the like. This left little time for organizing. Despite Zlenko's admonitions, Onoprienko rarely visited the shops. Rumours began to circulate that he was close to management and was receiving favours. They were false, but they were fed by the union's assumption, albeit with good intentions, of what should have been management's responsibility. Meanwhile, it did nothing to develop its base among the rank and file. Before long, Onoprienko even began to sound like management. When workers complained about mounting wage arrears and repeated layoffs, he would cite the factory's difficult financial situation.

Reflecting on events a few years after, Onoprienko's vice-president, L. Cherkovskii, said: "Never again will I fight to change directors. The real question is: after we were elected, should we have worked together with management or should we rather have pushed to get management working." Zlenko took the latter position, and he refused Onoprienko's requests to accompany him to one or another ministry to ask for a tax abatement or credit. He told him to make the director go. Zlenko took the same position in opposing unions' participation in the administration of social benefits, the distribution of services and goods to workers, campaigns against drinking and theft, not to mention "labour competition": these were all management's responsibility. He was far from always successful, however, in convincing local leaders, as, for example, when the union at ZAZ gave management a blank cheque to dock bonuses of up to twenty-five per cent of take-home pay for lateness of only five minutes. Normally, each instance would have required union consent.

Zlenko was equally uncompromising on the difficult issue of layoffs. The sectoral agreement permitted permanent layoffs of up to seven per cent annually in any given enterprise. But the law requires union consent to the laying off of any particular individual, and that potentially gives the power to block, or at least to delay, the layoffs. The advice of the national office to local unions was first to survey the members's opinion and then put the question to a conference. If overstaffing was really a problem, the members still had alternatives they could defend, such as a shortened work-week or reduced wages. In a report to the Central Council, Zlenko explained: "Only when the majority of workers are convinced that they have fought behind their union and can't win, should the union committee agree to mass layoffs. But then it must demand compensation beyond what the law prescribes, as the committee of the Lutsk Ball-Bearing Factory did. [It obtained twelve months severance pay.] Even if it can't save all the jobs...workers will still support such a union committee."[15]

The national leadership of ASMU pursued a similar policy in its political action. This put it in irreconcilable opposition to the leadership of the FPU, which is even more shamelessly opportunistic than its Russian counterpart. A. Stoyan had been a senior consultant to President Kravchuk before being elected president of the FPU in 1992. He later was elected to parliament, even while keeping his union position, a violation of the FPU's constitution that Zlenko unsuccessfully fought. Stoyan has frequently shifted fractions, but they were all right-wing and, except for one occasion, very close to the President.[16] The FPU has always been firmly wedded to "social partnership," even though the government has violated every General Agreement it has signed on its major points.[17] Stoyan himself has repeatedly undermined national labour protests, for example, by announcing last-minute "breakthroughs" in negotiations with the government that never materialized.[18] He also opposed the FPU's participation in the campaign to demand Kuchma's impeachment over the Gongadze affair, stating quite candidly that his first concern was to protect the FPU's considerable real-estate holdings (which he controls without serious oversight by the affiliates).[19] On his fifty-fifth birthday, the government awarded him the medal "For Services Rendered" third class.

Zlenko characterized the FPU as "a pro-government organization that looks to the state, not the workers, for support. Its leadership [is]...afraid to confront the state to defend workers' interests. They hold their interests in real estate and in the social security funds, sources of subsistence for the union bureaucracy, above the interests of ordinary workers."[20] ASMU's repeated proposals to organize a general strike were always defeated in the FPU. So were Zlenko's attempt to organize opposition to Stoyan among the other industrial unions, even proposing that they secede from the federation. Whenever word came to deed, ASMU found itself isolated. This happened in 1998, when the presidents of the other metalworking unions and of several regional councils abandoned at the last minute a coalition that had been formed to oust Stoyan.[21]

Zlenko is a committed socialist without nostalgia or illusions about the old system, a very rare political position in the union movement that was also shared by Vetchinkin. Soon after its founding, ASMU allied itself with the Social Democratic Party of the Ukraine (SDPU), which had elected several young leftwing intellectuals to the first post-independence parliament. Unlike the much larger Communist and Socialist parties, the SDPU actively tried to work with the union movement on the basis of equality. Its programme emphasized self-management and decisively rejected "shock therapy." But in the 1998 elections, it failed to elect any candidates, as left-leaning voters preferred the larger and more easily identifiable Communist and Socialist Parties. (Ukraine has several parties calling themselves "social-democratic," all of which, except the SPDU, are right-wing.) In the 1999 presidential elections, ASMU, alone among the major industrial unions, supported the candidacy of Moroz, leader of the Socialist Party. SPDU and Socialist Party leaders were frequently invited to ASMU Central Councils under Zlenko. But even though the union supported these left-leaning parties, Zlenko warned against illusions:

> Ukraine still does not have a party whose practice would justify it being called a "workers' party." All the parties in Ukraine were created to provide a base for one or another leader. None emerged from a social movement, and that includes the labour movement. That party has yet to be created. Even if we support the SDPU and the SPU, it is still too early for us to call them our parties. At present, like the others, they are seeking sponsors among the rich, and that means that their politics can become dependent on those people. But the SDPU is actively trying to build links with the unions, and that is positive.[22]

The contrast with ASMR's politics, which are based on an alliance with the "patriotic bourgeoisie" and "partnership" with the government, is striking. Where ASMR's leadership saw the government's policy as marked by "errors" and called for "corrections," ASMU saw the government as pursuing the interests of the ruling class and called for militant action to oppose it. At the May 1997 Central Council, Zlenko argued for "more determined efforts to mobilize workers to make use of forceful methods of struggle against the government and the employers...It is an illusion to expect a basic change of policy from this government." In an interview he explained: "This government is guided...by...[the interests] of a small group of greedy people who are enriching themselves, hiding behind the slogan of creating efficient owners...An inhuman bourgeoisie is being created that devours everything, plunders everything, uproots everything. It doesn't give a damn about the people, the country, patriotism."[23]

Despite his efforts to promote union independence, Zlenko's support at the lower levels remained limited. Even when his Central Council adopted his proposals, they were far from always carried out locally. On the other hand, ASMU did have relatively more independent local organizations and rank-and-file revolts against subservient union leaders than ASMR. The difference was in part due to the support they had in the national office, which really tried to cultivate a "culture of resistance." This created an atmosphere at the Central Councils in which even those leaders who had no intention of "walking the walk" felt pressure to "talk the talk." This gave truly independent leaders some ideological space—as well as real support from the national office—in which to operate. But they were far from the critical mass necessary to change the union as a whole.

"Social partnership" remained the norm in practice, even if it was rejected as the official ideology. When the president of the union at the Odessa Plough Factory resigned, the regional president consulted the director about his replacement, explaining that her policy was to "seek contact with strong directors." As in Russia, it was not unusual for plant presidents to be, in effect, appointed by the director, while the workers stood by passively. Showing a group of union educators around the Lvyv Bus Factory, the president proudly introduced various shop superintendents as "ours," that is, they were former shop presidents. Her union participates with management in assigning bonuses in a programme of "labour competition." Following the Central Council's recommendation, many more local unions in ASMU sued for dues than in the Russian union, but more than half did not, for fear of "straining relations."

The situation was similar when it came to political action. ASMU's Central Council took independent positions, while other unions made opportunistic alliances supporting Presidential party or those of one or another "clan." But the ASMU's position, with some exceptions, were not translated into action locally. The Central Council regularly adopted formally binding resolutions to mobilize for national protests and election campaigns, but only a minority of enterprise and regional unions showed much activity. During a discussion of the low turnout to a recent national protest, Chernigov's regional president argued that "the workers have not matured enough for protest" and that explained the low turnout. But a local president retorted: "Stop telling tales. You know as well as I do that when leaders are decisive, workers come out."

Democracy and Solidarity

Zlenko never stopped pushing, but he had few illusions about the capacity or willingness of most regional and local leaders to change. For real change, any pressure he could exert "from above" had to be matched and more by pressure "from below." His main concern was to provide ideological and organizational space in the union for forces that really wanted to resist management and the state. His efforts to promote democracy and to increase the influence and resources of the national office were dictated mainly by that concern.

As in Russia, the end of party-state control left real power in the hand of enterprise presidents, not the membership. Major decisions were often taken without consulting or even informing the enterprise committees, let alone the members. Zlenko, on his part, hammered away at the need to organize and mobilize, to include the rank and file in decision-making and in carrying out decisions:

> We have to intensify our work with the members, draw them into the resolution of union tasks…In practice, the rank and file are often pushed aside. Some plants have even stopped holding real union meetings. Their leaders are afraid to face the members, explaining that they are embittered. But don't these people, practically driven to desperation, constitute our union? They are the people who have to defend their interests within the framework provided by our organization…We have seen some paradoxical cases where the plant president has turned to the higher organs of the union to ask them to invoke article forty-five [removal of managers for violation of the Labour code or collective agreements] without first bothering to ask the membership for support. So is it really surprising that when the director turned around and asked the workers to support him against the union's leader, they did? It has even happened that they voted the union president out of office.[24]

Besides his urging to revive and strengthen the role of plant conferences and regional councils and conferences, Zlenko tried to increase the presence of rank-and-file activists in these representatives bodies. In March 1999, the Central Council adopted a resolution calling for proportional representation of workers (who make up eight-five per cent of the membership) and engineering-technical staff (including management) at enterprise conferences and for workers to constitute at least half of the delegates to regional councils and to the Central Council.[25] As one might guess, the resolution was not respected, but at least more workers began to appear where there had been very few before. Some regional councils, notably Kharkov and Vinnitsa, actually attained the fifty-per-cent goal. In the Central Council itself, ten of the seventy-two delegates were workers in 2000. This did not bring major changes to the union, but the worker delegates, once they found their bearings, did have influence the tenor of the meetings, ensuring that greater consideration was given to rank-and-file concerns.

Zlenko tried but failed to obtain the resources he needed to establish an educational fund for shop-floor education. ASMU did, however, collaborate closely with TIE and the School for Worker Democracy, which shared his outlook, something ASMR has been unable or unwilling to do. Asked what the basic message of education should be, he replied: "Fight yourself and don't wait for someone else to do it for you. That's what democratization means: the rank-and-file acting. Even when a leader can act alone, he shouldn't. He has to act together with the members, even if it's only a few of them. A leader has to inspire workers to collectively solve problems themselves. This is something very few people in Ukraine, workers or leaders, understand."

The main reason the national office could not do more to promote rank-and-file activism was its lack of resources, which local unions refused to give it. Zlenko told his Central Council: "Not all union leaders today are thrilled by the idea of responsibility, accountability and discipline. Some have grown accustomed to answering to no one. They have become independent little princes, guided by personal ambition rather than the interests of the organization and the cause they claim to serve. Some display smugness, not to say self-adulation."[26] ASMU was subject to the same powerful centrifugal forces as its Russian counterpart. However, its leadership was more determined to do promote unity and solidarity within the union. The Third Congress in 1995 adopted an amendment to the constitution that eliminated references to the plant committees as "member organizations." Instead they became "structural units." The higher elected bodies were given "leadership," no longer merely "co-ordinating" functions.[27] This, at least in principle, marked the rejection of a federative structure and of the absolute primacy of the enterprise committees. Henceforth, decisions of higher representative bodies (the regional and central councils) were binding on enterprise organizations, which could be sanctioned up to expulsion. These bodies could annul decisions that violated the constitution and even remove leaders who made them. But though discipline did improve in some respects, violations remained so widespread, especially when it was a question of dues, mobilizing membership for protests and campaigns, or confronting management, that to invoke the sanctions would have threatened the existence of the union. Moreover, expulsion would have mainly punished the rank and file, who usually had no say in the violation.

Zlenko, in fact, had few illusions about the impact of these amendments. What he really wanted was additional resources that would allow him to reach the rank and file over the heads of local leaders. The latter, for the most part, could not be relied upon to transmit the national office's point of view. Its constitutional share of the dues in was 4.5 per cent in 1995, but most regions were not paying it. The national office survived in part because it could pay some staff salaries out of the Social Security Fund, which was still under union administration. Zlenko asked the Third Congress for an additional eight per cent in order to create central funds for information, education, and strikes. The information fund was earmarked mainly for the monthly paper *Ednist'*, which would become the national office's principal means of communication with shopfloor activists. The educational fund was intended for the same group: Zlenko's unspoken goal was to train at least several workers in each of the larger plants upon whom he could depend to distribute the national office's literature and to explain and defend its positions. Some, he hoped, would eventually emerge as alternatives to the present leaders. Another five per cent of the dues would go into a strike fund to permit the union to give practical support to workers who were prepared to confront management. But the Congress decided only to give a 1.5 per cent increase for the newspaper. Still, it was a moral victory of sorts in that it gave formal recognition to the need to strengthen solidarity within the union.

Financial discipline slowly improved. By 1999 the central office was receiving a little more than four per cent of the dues, almost twice as much as in 1996 and significantly more than ASMR was receiving from its affiliates. ASMU's Fourth Congress in 2000 raised the national office's share of dues to eight per cent and in 2002 it actually received 5.5 per cent. The main problem, as in Russia, was the unwillingness of local leaders to give more. As late as 1997, there were still a total of 699 cultural and sports workers on the payroll of local unions.[28]

One of the major differences between ASMU and ASMR was the seriousness with which the former approached the sectoral agreement. In the Ukrainian union, the minimal norms set by the sectoral agreement were treated by the Central Council as obligatory. The agreement was on the agenda of practically every Central Council and Presidium. Although the depression conditions meant that exceptions would be inevitable, the union had considerable success in enforcing it. Each fall, the Central Council set priorities, after which agreement had to be reached with the eight, later ten, other industrial unions, that negotiated jointly with ASMU. The central point of the negotiations was the minimum wage in the sectors. The wages of the other skill levels were adjusted accordingly. It was generally set at the poverty line, so that, in 1999, the minimum wage of the first skills grade was 115 per cent of the poverty line. The minimum was set low to be realistic, but at least there was a concrete figure and specific language. This set the Ukrainian agreement apart from the Russian, which called on the employer merely to "try to pay." The Ukrainian agreement also set the guaranteed part of the wage (that is, without bonuses and supplements) at a minimum of sixty-five to seventy per cent of the total.[29]

As noted, ASMU took enforcement seriously. In 1999, more than three quarters of the local agreements incorporated or bettered the norms of the sectoral agreement.[30] Since ASMR did not even try to analyze its local agreements, a comparison is not possible, itself an indication of the relative importance of the two sectoral agreements. Reporting discipline was also better in ASMU. In 1999, practically all the larger plants (seventy per cent of all the affiliates) sent in their collective agreements. The Presidium (executive) met twice annually to review application of the sectoral norms, inviting presidents and directors of problematic plants. Since privatization had been slower in Ukraine than Russia, the union could still apply some pressure on management through the government, where it owned shares. However, the government was very reluctant to assume any responsibility. Eventually, an employers' association became the third signatory, but its real influence among directors was negligible. Zlenko scoffed at ASMR's efforts to create an employers' organization to enforce the agreement, explaining to his Central Council that could happen only if employers faced a powerful labour movement against which they were unable to defend themselves individually, a far cry from the situation in Ukraine.[31]

In the end, enforcement was up to the union alone, and that depended on the determination of the leadership. The means at its disposal were mostly, but not only, moral. Traditions of deference in Ukraine meant that public criticism by the national union leaders was not without impact on directors. Where the director was still a member of the union, the latter could expel him and publish a resolution of censure in the paper. In some cases, Zlenko threatened to appeal directly to go directly to the workers for a vote non-confidence in the director. Both acts usually meant that article forty-five would be invoked, after which dismissal generally followed. In 1988, it was invoked thirteen times by ASMU. Despite its limitations, the role of the sectoral agreement played an important role in holding the union together, and plant presidents in ASMU readily confirmed that it was of major assistance to them in negotiations.

Looking back over his nine years as President, Zlenko said:

> In 1991, when we founded it, we declared that we had a union, but that wasn't really true. Every regional and plant committee considered itself independent, and God forbid that anyone should intervene in their life or that they adopt a common policy. I can't say we've completely overcome that today, that all the problems have been resolved. Not by a long shot. But we have created the basis for a national union. You won't find a similar degree of unity in Russia or a sectoral agreement that plays the same role.

The drive to build solidarity did not stop at ASMU. Zlenko repeatedly proposed a merger to his sectoral negotiating partners to create a single metalworking union and he was prepared to forego any leadership position in the new union himself. But the other leaders were not ready to give up their fiefs. Instead, a loose Association of Unions of Industrial Workers was formed in December 1998. In sharp contrast to ASMR's leaders, Zlenko recognized the legitimacy, indeed the necessity, of the alternative unions. His Central Council did not hesitate to call on the members to participate in protests initiated by alternative union federations, this in spite of the FPU.[32] ASMU also contributed to the coalminers' strike fund during their big strikes and their march on Kyiv in the first half of the 1990s and it offered to organize joint actions with it. But as in Russia, the coalminers' leaders took a corporatist attitude and refused to adopt demands that could rally the entire labour movement. The head of the "traditional" miners' union even stopped accepting the ASMU's offers of material support.

After Zlenko

Zlenko resigned at sixty, the official retirement age, though he easily could have been re-elected to a third term. (Leaving a paid union position at retirement age is rare, given the small size of pensions. ASMR's last president was removed very much against his when he was well past retirement age.) The November 1999 Central Council replaced Zlenko with his vice-president, Vasil Dudnik. This was, in part, a practical choice, since any president had to already have an apartment in Kyiv. But most people, including Zlenko himself, believed that Dudnik shared the positions the national union had been defending for the past decade.[33]

But it became evident very quickly that they were wrong. Five days after that Council that upheld Zlenko's refusal to sign the sectoral agreement because of the clause freeing enterprises from raising wages to the new level if they owed more than five-months of wages, Dudnik nevertheless affixed his signature to it. He also decided not to enforce the law requiring payment of two-thirds of base pay for layoffs "when the enterprise cannot pay." Zlenko had always refused to make concessions on this matter. Even if the enterprise really could not pay, at least the money would be counted as debt owing to the workers.

It was not a complete about-face (for one thing, Dudnkik had inherited the national office's staff from Zlenko), but the change was obvious. The Central Council continued to review application of the sectoral agreement and to support local unions that invoked article forty-five, but the proportion of plants that enforced the wage levels of the sectoral agreement declined from two thirds in 2000 to a half in 2001, despite the overall improvement in the situation of industry.[34] The national office and Central Council generally adopted a less active position than before on local conflicts.

Dudnik, who had been a party official before working in the Soviet trade-union bureaucracy, did not share Zlenko's view that the path to renewal of the labour movement lay in organizing and mobilizing the rank and file. He looked instead to the support of regional union leaders and the remnants of the (always semi-mythical) "red directors."At a conference organized by TIE, he shocked shop-floor activists from VAZ's Edinstvo by his open disdain for them. His attitude to the alternative unions is also hostile. And he did nothing to enforce the statute, adopted under Zlenko, that calls for increased representation of workers in elected union bodies. Instead he called to elect "professionals" as delegates. Nor did he enforce the ban on electing managerial personnel to union positions. (The director of a Chernigov parts plant was a delegate to the Central Council held in that town in February 2000.) Accordingly, he had the wording of the union's constitution changed from "defence of hired workers" to "defence of its members." Commenting on ASMU's Fifth Congress in March 2000, Tatyana Byrdina, a strong supporter of Zlenko's positions, said: "The basic question today is whether the unions are prepared to change for the better the extremely critical situation of our country and genuinely to defend people of labour. I did not hear an answer to that question at the congress, that, on the whole, took place in a serene atmosphere. The only question that aroused any real debate was the proportion of dues that should be given to the Central Council."[35]

Although ASMU remains an exception in its official support for the Socialist Party and SPDU in elections, Dudnik dropped Zlenko's confrontational approach to the FPU and the government. Whereas Zlenko had invited representatives of those parties to the Central Councils, Dudnik invites government officials. In September 2003, for example, ASMU's paper published on its front page a biography of the newly appointed head of the Department for Farm Machinery in the Ministry of Industry. The paper also gives prominence to agreements between the government and FPU, describing them, without irony, as "social partners." Yet other articles report on the government's violation of these agreements.[36] Dudnik also rejected the idea of a merger of the unions in the metalworking sector, even though some of ASMU's regional leaders strongly favour it and the presidents of the other national unions were finally coming around. He openly argued that ASMU should worry about the corporatist interests of its own members.

The relative ease with which Dudnik shifted the orientation of the Central Council is an indication of weakness of the real support for Zlenko's positions among regional and local presidents. Nor did it not help that Vetchinkin fell seriously ill just as Zlenko retired. Vetchinkin died in 2002. In reality, Zlenko had had few illusions about his support (though he did have illusions about his vice-president.) Indeed, that was a major factor in his decision to retire: he concluded that his efforts to change the union from above were futile and he lacked the resources significantly to support potential forces of change on the shop floor. Upon retirement Zlenko, however, did not abandon his commitment to an independent labour movement or his rank-and-file orientation. He is still pursuing the same long-term goals that he did when President of ASMU but in his new capacity as director of the School for Worker Democracy of Ukraine, which he co-founded in 2000, and which works with shop-floor activists.

The Kharkov Region

The more progressive character of ASMU in this region was not due to any favourable economic conditions: the region was as depressed as any. The ASM sector, centred around farm machinery, lost two thirds of its work force between 1992 and 2000, leaving the union with only 43,000 members.[37] Vetchinkin summed up the state of the sector's sixty-five enterprises in the fall of 2000: "Five are more or less stable; six are managing to keep afloat but with difficulty; the rest are barely breathing."[38]

The main factor that set the region apart was Vetchinkin's leadership. He began his working life as a machine-operator at the Bicycle Factory. Studying in the evenings, he earned a an engineering degree, and was eventually promoted to a managerial position. A conscientious person and well-known sportsman, he was "elected" to the factory's party committee and later to its union committee. He became union president at the factory in 1974. His predecessor, an "honest and fair man," had been removed by the party authorities for refusing to authorize Saturday work. The same fate befell the regional council president, who insisted too much on respect of the Labour Code. Vetchinkin himself barely missed the same fate (he was threatened with loss of his party card) also for "failing to understand demands of the present situation."[39] Nevertheless, in 1978 he was appointed president of the regional council, where he became a major force in promoting the newly formed, union-run Labour Inspectorate, whose job it was to monitor application of labour legislation. And he continued to forbid work on Saturdays.

Kharkov is an industrial city, a major centre of machine-building, one of the few industrial towns in Ukraine that predates Stalin's industrialization drive of the 1930s. It was the first town in Ukraine in which Soviet power was proclaimed in 1917. Despite this, Vetchinkin denied that it had any special militant traditions, noting that the two presidents who followed him at the factory "were not fighters and they bought cars with management's help." He had few allies among the other unions in the region, and he considered the regional federation "conciliationist" (*soglashatel'skaya*).

Like Zlenko, Vetchinkin was a vehement opponent of "social partnership" and publicly denounced it at every opportunity:

> The lengthy procedure required for legal strikes that practically rules them out, the systematic violation by government and management of their signed agreements, the failure to pay wages, widespread contempt for the law, mass unemployment, the liquidation of social benefits—it all shows that government and the owners dreamed up "social partnership" as a gimmick to help them to hang onto their property (honest people have none) and to make big profits on the backs of workers. Can the interests of the "partners" coincide in these circumstances, as the ideologues of the ruling class would have us believe? Workers and unions must categorically reject such "partnership"…Workers' consciousness, as in the old days, is still dominated by the belief that the directors are their "providers." They believe that employers are interested in protecting and developing industry, failing to notice all the stores and small businesses they own. The goal of this ideology is to dissuade workers from independent protest…Force respects force. We have to become a force based on the understanding that…only by applying real pressure…can we succeed in changing anything in this society.[40]

Among ASMU's regions, Kharkov put the most effort into assuring that common minimal norms were respected in all its enterprises. Vetchinkin concluded a five-year agreement with the directors recognizing ASMU as the sole bargaining agent and guaranteeing union rights. Each fall, a regional union conference adopted negotiating demands. These were considered binding on the local unions. The regional council sent out negotiating guidelines to all local unions, and its representatives participated in the local negotiating committees. Another conference in the spring reviewed contract enforcement. In 2000, the regional council had two directors dismissed under article forty-five.[41] It was also the only organization in ASMU with a strike fund, based on four per cent of dues.[42]

The union members were encouraged to participate in formulating demands, but mobilization was not a regular part of the negotiating process. There were some strikes over contract enforcement, particularly the failure to pay wages, but in the end, it was Vetchinkin himself, a dynamic and imposing personality, who was the main enforcer. In the words of the president of Lozovoya Stamping Factory, which were echoed by many others: "No other regional leader is so determined, insistent or bold. He has a tremendous capacity for work and spends more time among the work collectives than in his office. He never turns down a request for help or takes no for an answer."[43] Apart from his personal qualities, he could count on the authority his position commanded among directors that lingered on from the Soviet period.

Except in extreme circumstances, Vetchinkin forbade plant presidents from making concessions from the regional norms, and, with the exception of the Tractor and Ball-Bearing Factories, local presidents did not dare to disobey him. If local negotiations were blocked, he would go to speak to the director himself. And when gentle persuasion failed, he threatened to appeal to the delegates' conference, where the union usually won. Though not always. In 1999, the conference at the Tractor Factory, which was packed with managerial personnel, rejected Vetchinin's impassioned appeal to support the twenty-eight vacation days of the regional agreement, rather than the director's proposal of twenty-four, the legal minimum. But the conference supported the director.

Vetchinkin also mobilized the prosecutor's office, the tax authorities, and the Labour Inspectorate to go after recalcitrant directors.[44] True, these rarely took action (the government was, in fact, using the public prosecutor and tax inspectorate to intimidate Vetchinkin), but since management always had sins to hide, any special interest from the authorities was very unwelcome to them. The main thing was to send the directors a message that the union was not about to let matters stand. Directors asked Vetchinkin why his union had to be different, when all the others readily "showed understanding." His only reply was that other regional leaders did not want to complicate their lives by confronting management. Kharkov was the first region in ASMU to organize systematic lawsuit campaigns to force the payment of wages.[45]

The support Vetchinkin gave Zlenko in his efforts to unify the union followed from his rejection of "partnership." If, as he argued, "force respects force," then there was not much an isolated region could achieve. Kharkov was the most disciplined of ASMU's regions, always sending the full constitutional share of dues to the national office. It was also meticulous in reporting—Vetchinkin sent copies of all the local contracts to Kyiv by special messenger. In exceptional cases, he requested formal authorization from the Central Council to allow one or another of his plants to delay application of the new wages required by sectoral agreement. Surprisingly, however, he did not support Zlenko's efforts to introduce proportional representation in the Central Council in place of the norm of two delegates per region. Kharkov would have ended up sending the largest delegation, and that meant a lot more expenses.

Vetchinkin was a strong advocate of political action. Only political struggle could really change the situation, he argued. His organization took active part in the electoral campaigns of the SPDU and SP, though the results were disappointing. Kharkov's ASMU also regularly mobilized the greatest numbers for national protests. Vetchinkin repeatedly pushed for a national general strike, but there were few takers. Like Zlenko, he had only profound scorn for the FPU's leadership. He termed its national agreement with the government "a bunch of empty slogans that don't resolve a single question in the workers' interest."[46]

Zlenko was sometimes critical of Vetchinkin for his tendency to concentrate power and to try to resolve conflicts on a personal basis, without membership involvement. He took issue with Vetchinkin at a regional conference, when the latter criticized the president of the Kupensk Foundry for leading an illegal strike. (Vetchinkin did, however, shield him from legal prosecution.) According to Zlenko's view, in Ukraine's circumstances, any activism had to be encouraged. Nevertheless, Vetchinkin's readiness to confront management and political authorities made him more sensitive than most leaders to the need for democracy and rank-and-file activism. He told his members:

> Only a militant union can defend the labour and socio-economic interests of workers. A militant union is independent of the government and management and uses all means of struggle, including strikes…A militant union tries to organize rank-and-file members…It is not enough that a leader wants the union to be militant. The rank-and-file members themselves need to be organized and show solidarity. They have to force those whom they have elected to defend the oppressed at work and in society.[47]

The Kharkov council was unique in that, of its eight-odd members, only about a fifth were full-time union officers, and about a third were rank-and-file members. The council organized each year one-day educational sessions for 1500 newly elected officers at all levels, including group leaders. In 1999, following the Central Council's example, it adopted a resolution aimed at ensuring a more balanced representation of the main categories of members: workers, engineering-technical staff, men and women, mature workers and youth.[48] It also began to publish a mass monthly bulletin in 1999, the only region to do so. When the School for Worker Democracy was established in Ukraine in 2000, it chose the Kharkov region of ASMU as its natural base.

The industrial collapse severely limited what the union could achieve for workers. Almost all its concrete gains were very relative, in the sense that things would been worse without the union's efforts. It had the best enforcement record of the sectoral agreement of any region, and management there showed more respect for the law. Among the specific achievements Vetchinkin himself pointed to, were payment of the two-thirds of base wage during temporary layoffs, four extra days of vacation, the absence of involuntary permanent layoffs, the retention by the plants of their "social sphere."

The Bicycle Factory

In Vetchinkin's estimation, only about eleven of the sixty-five plants (many were small service centres where it was very hard to mount a challenge to management) had more-or-less independent unions, a proportion that went well beyond other regions. The most outstanding of these was the Bicycle Factory. It was unique in that its union's made the shift to independence without any change of leadership.

Tatyana Byrdina came to the plant in the early 1970s as a young engineer. Workers still recall being impressed by her dignity and independent spirit, which stood out against the grey conformity of the Brezhnev era. One woman worker said she was particularly struck that Tatyana dared to wear jeans to work. Tatyana became vice-president of the union in 1985 and was elected president in 1987 in an open election among three candidates. In a society where cynicism prevails, Tatyana enjoys her members' confidence. "Our Tatyana is constantly in struggle," said a member of her union committee. "Our people won't let management devour her. If she asks them for help, they'll always come through." When she walks through the shops, workers take time out from their work to come over and chat. They know that she turned down offers from the director to become his assistant, and that the director before him had offered her money, shares, and a new apartment to drop the union's fight against him. She even faced down the local mafia when it came to buy the sports centre, a prime piece of real estate.

Asked about this, she replied: "Why should I be afraid of conflict? After all, I don't depend on the management. I've never taken anything from them, though they have tried. I've kept my dignity at work and in my personal life. I'll never let anyone humiliate me. That's how I was brought up." But she was quick to add: "I can count on the workers. If know that if I ask for their support at the conference, they'll give it to me. And I also have the support of our regional council. I don't mean the federation, of course. It's useless. I don't see any other real unions in our region. But Vetchinkin will always come through for me. That's absolutely clear."

Her union's main achievement is undoubtedly the plant's continued survival, although its work force fell from 4500 to 1800 over the 1990s. That victory was won in a bitter struggle against the factory's former director, who had support in the government. It was that struggle that consolidated rank-and-file support for the union. Otherwise, neither the situation of the enterprise nor the work force were exceptional: by the late 1990s, almost two thirds of the employees were of pension age or close to it, and the plant was heavily in debt, working irregularly at a fraction of its capacity.

In 1991, at the end of the Gorbachev period, the work collective elected a new director, a former mayor of Kharkov who had been removed for corruption. But he made a good speech, and the workers felt his administrative experience and political connections would help the factory. Well before the Ukrainian government launched its privatization drive, the new director decided to privatize the plant. He proposed that the employees take it over as a closed joint-stock company (shares could not be sold outside of the work collective) and promised them a great future. Tatyana warned against taking this leap into the unknown. After all, laws governing privatization had not yet even been adopted. But as elsewhere in the former Soviet Union, workers believed at that time that getting out from under state control was a good thing.

Three months after privatization was completed in 1994, the director announced a month-long layoff. Tatyana had to enlist a reluctant public prosecutor to force the director to pay the workers two thirds of their basic wage. Several months passed, and production stopped again, this time for three months. And so it went. Tatyana finally called a delegates' conference to invoke article forty-five. But the director persuaded the delegates to give him another chance. Meanwhile, the plant was sinking deeper into debt, as the director took out loans allegedly for reconstruction. The union also learned that he had sold stocks to unknown outsiders and was using enterprise money to purchase additional shares for himself. As the plant agonized, he was building houses and buying apartments for himself and his family. The union, supported by the ASMU's regional council, turned to every conceivable political authority, including the President, but everywhere it was told to stop interfering with a director who was doing his job.

The conflict came to a head when the plant failed to reopen in mid May 1995, as promised after a five-month layoff. The summer months had always been the busiest for bicycle production, which was seasonal. The director refused to give the union an explanation nor would he allow it to hold a meeting in the plant's auditorium. He was counting on the union not being able to mobilize the workers, who had been away from the plant for five months and lived dispersed around the city. But mainly through leaflets pasted on telephone poles and bulletin boards, the union assembled 2000 workers at an open-air meeting on the street in front of the factory. The strong presence of police armed with batons, which the workers call "democratizers," and the filming did not deter the workers. They blocked all traffic on this main thoroughfare for four hours, until they finally got the attention of the city fathers. The factory reopened the next day and worked steadily for about a year.

The union kept up the pressure, despite intimidation by management and the political authorities, who filed criminal charges against Tatyana and called in the workers for questioning. In private conversation, the director admitted to Tatyana that he was stealing but that it was small stuff compared to what other directors were doing. A series of newspaper exposés by a friendly journalist and a law-suit campaign to force payment of wages finally convinced a district judge to open criminal proceedings against the director. This was a first for Kharkov and perhaps for all of Ukraine. A month later, at the end of 1998, the director died.

A new director was elected, on the union's recommendation, by the stockholders' meeting, which was attended by 1500 former and present employees of the plant. Since it was in such terrible economic shape, the union went easy on the new director during his first year. He respected the schedule for paying wage arrears and reported regularly to the union on the enterprise's condition, which began slowly to improve. But the union resisted the strong temptation to identify with management. It allowed not a single involuntary layoff, instead pressing management to seek ways to expand production. When Tatyana refused to authorize the dismissal of a workers for theft, the director accused her of sabotaging his efforts to save the factory. She replied that management had been watching the woman because she had dared to criticize it. For Tatyana, the main thing was to strengthen the workers' confidence in the union, to convince them the union would defend them. They would in turn support the union.

The authority the union enjoyed among its members allowed it to dominate the labour disputes committee. Between November 1998 and August 1999, all 105 complaints examined were decided in the workers' favour.[49] The union's unswerving defence of its members was a virtuous circle: the confidence members had that the union would defend then made them less afraid to stand up with, and for, the union against management.

Saddled with a huge debt and without access to credit, the director decided in 2000 to attract capital by leasing out the more profitable shops and concentrating the debt on the remaining ones. To make the offer more attractive, he wanted only individual labour contracts in the leased shops, that the collective agreement not apply in them, and that the employees could be let go without reason or any union protection at the end of their contracts. The union tried but failed to block this in the courts. It therefore demanded that the collective agreement be applied to all the shops, regardless of who was managing, and that there be no layoffs. To support these demands, it organized meetings in all the shops. They voted massively to physically block management's access to the plant, if it refused to accept the union's demands. The director gave in.

By 2000, Tatyana decided that the grace period was over. She wanted to invoke article forty-five, demanding the director's dismissal for non-payment of wages. But she failed to rally a majority in her union committee, who felt that arrears of only one and half months were not sufficient grounds to call a conference. Tatyana argued that a union could not make concessions on wages: "You can tolerate a lot of shortcomings in a union's work, but payment of wages is our most fundamental issue…We need to be serious about demanding it from directors."[50] The union encouraged members to mandate the union to sue for their wages. At first, only a few took up the offer, fearing management's wrath. But soon several hundred had filed suit. Even though it usually takes half a year to see any money through the courts, it keeps up the pressure on management, which is one of the reasons arrears are relatively small.

"It's the great failure of our unions," Tatyana said in a interview, "that we did not react at once to non-payment. We should have shut down all the plants the very first month. But we let ourselves be humiliated, and so they continue not to pay. Of course, if we had a normal state, it would press criminal charges for withholding wages. All it takes is to toss a couple of directors into jail, and the rest would pay up. On the whole, I don't believe them when they say they can't pay." In her view—not shared by Vetchinkin—workers should not worry about pushing the plant into bankruptcy, since the government is clearly not interested in outright liquidation of the factories. As for the directors, if it were not in their interest, they would not hang onto their jobs. "And besides, what's the use of a job in a factory that doesn't pay you wages?" She is just as firm on union dues: "I tell the director: 'Do whatever it takes. Sell your car, if you have to. That's your headache.' Not paying dues is plain insolence. They're getting insolent because they see no one resists. They say to themselves: 'It's not causing me any trouble, so why not keep on doing it?'"

Other union leaders in the region, including Vetchinkin, were of the opinion that the bicycle workers are more active than most workers and better informed about their rights. They certainly are less resigned, despite the enterprise's very problematic economic situation. Plant conferences, which workers elsewhere typically avoid like the plague, are attended by 400 delegates, an unusually large proportion. In addition, there can be as many as 600 observers. "A lot of people are surprised that we have so many delegates," Tatyana said. "But we have a big hall; so why not get more people involved?

Even though it's after work hours, you have people complaining that they have to stand in the foyer just because they weren't elected." Delegates are elected anew to every conference in order to broaden participation.

The main point of the plant's bi-annual conferences is the collective agreement, its adoption and application. This is not a pro-forma exercise, as in many enterprises, where the meeting will note shortcomings and then vote to approve management's application of the agreement, "considering the complex situation of the enterprise." At the bicycle factory the agreement is closely monitored and violations are written up with specific instructions to management to act on them. If the problem is serious and no action is forthcoming, article forty-five is brandished at the responsible administrator.[51] Tatyana herself "drags" about twenty top managers to these conferences to answer workers' questions and to directly experience their pressure. She claims that workers are not intimidated by their presence. Those who don't want to speak, can send up written question. This shows that management's presence at union meetings need not undermine independence. But that is true only if the union is already independent and enjoys its members' support. The issue of excluding management from the union is, in a sense a symbolic one, but one that has very practical ramifications in post-Soviet conditions.

The conference of April 2000 that reviewed application of the contract adopted a fourteen-point resolution. Besides the issues of wage arrears, the shortage of protective gear and clothing, and compensation for work-related injuries, several other items touched on the quantity and quality of production, the low level of executive and work discipline, the moral and psychological climate in the plant. These points were not without ambiguity. But the union was not about to assume responsibility for these matters. It was demanding that management do its job.

Besides the plant conferences and the president's own frequent visits to the shops, the union keeps workers informed through a monthly newsletter, which it began publishing in 1998 after the administration stopped publishing the plant paper. It is possibly the only local bulletin in ASMU, maybe in all Ukraine. The union also organizes lunch-time meetings in the shops every month, which Tatyana attends, "dragging" with her the reluctant director: "Why should I have to explain why there are no wages? The shop supervisor is also in no position to answer that kind of question."

As for the shop chairpersons, normally the weakest link, Tatyana admitted that "not many want the job. I think there used to be more takers. But in general, the workers elect people on whom I can count and who know how to work. Nowadays, these are mostly women; before there were more men. You met Tanya [a shop chairperson] at the seminar. You could see how militant and bright she is. She really likes union work. And there are many militant, demanding girls, like her, who speak out and will support me when I need it. Of course, some are better than others, and some really don't do anything." The shop chairpersons meet with Tatyana once a week. These are real discussions that include reports from the shops. "Even though the plant is small," explained Tatyana, "I need to hear how people live. Of course, the basic problem today is wages. But there are also smaller ones: protective clothing, drinking water, no broom to sweep up the dirt, and a shop supervisor who does nothing. We seek solutions together." Observing these meetings, one has the sense of a close-knit, committed group, united around a respected and admired leader.

Tatyana and a number of her union's activists have been active in parliamentary and presidential election campaigns of the SPDU and SP. Like Zlenko and Vetchinkin, Tatayna is a socialist with a realistic assessment of the past. Addressing her members on May Day 2001, she said:

> In times past, on this day we used to report our labour victories and assemble in colourful columns, while brass bands played. Everyone knew that if society does not perish even in the most difficult times, if power stations function, if trains run, if grain grows—we owe it all to the working person. We knew that a decent attitude toward the working person is not a concession but ordinary civilized behaviour. Today, strange as it may seem, the working person is in the most miserable situation, and that reflects, as in a mirror, the level of development of our society.
>
> Unemployment, non-payment of wages for lengthy periods, unsatisfactory work conditions, declining living standards, workers as objects of manipulation on the labour market—that's today's reality. But we also have to remember that the difficulties about which we now speak openly were decades in the making. But they were kept hidden, covered over in embarrassed silence. Workers have not been able to resist because there are no worker politics and they are not active in defending their interests. And the unions, which had no experience of struggle, were also not prepared to fight.[52]

Since there nothing in the factory's "objective" situation to distinguish it from the rest, one has to conclude that leadership is the major factor here. But not only Tatyana's. For she could count on Vetchinkin, and he in turn on Zlenko. Since both left the scene, and Kharkov's regional president, Vetchinkin's former assistant, is not much different from the others, Tatyana finds herself very isolated. There is no doubt that the bicycle union will remain independent as long as she is president. But independence will be very hard to sustain in such isolation when she leaves.

Notes

1. ASMR, "Materialy do zvitu." At its founding, the union had also 40,000 pensioners and 20,000 technical-school students. In January 2003, there were 32,382 and 15,844 respectively.
2. "Profspilkovyi rukh v Ukraini,"pp. 5-6.
3. V.G. Antonova, ed., *Ocherki istorii profosyuzov Kharokovshchiniy*, Kharkov: Tornado, 1999. p. 318
4. "Interview with V.I. Zlenko," in Mandel, *Looking East Leftwards*, p.121.
5. *Ednist'*, no. 11, 1998.
6. *Profsoyuzy i rynochnaya ekonomika*, p.59.
7. Report to the Ninth Central Council of Mar. 31, 1999 (unpublished).
8. *Profsoyuzy i rynochnaya ekonomika*, pp. 57-9.
9. *Ednist'*, no. 7, 1998.
10. *Profsoyuzy i rynochanya ekonomika*, p. 50.
11. "Interview with V.I. Zlenko," Mandel, *Looking East Leftwards* p. 125.
12. See *Ednist'*, no. 4, 1996.
13. See, for example, V. Tsekihmeistruk's report "On the Work of Trade-Union Bodies in Concluding Collective Agreements" at the April 31, 1999 Central Council (unpublished).
14. ASMU, Report to the May 21, 1997 Central Council (unpublished).
15. ASMU, Report to the Ninth Central Council, March 31, 1999 (unpublished).
16. In the 2002 elections, he was second on the moderately oppositional list Nasha Ukraina, a coalition of neo-liberals and equally rightwing nationalists headed by V. Yushchenko, a former prime minister that Kuchma had fired and the darling of the U.S. embassy. Stoyan explained his high position on the Yushchenko's list as a mark of "confidence in the work being done by the unions." (A. Likhovod, "Profbossy za pravykh," *Rabochii klass*, no. 5 , Feb. 2002.) Right after the elections, he shifted to the pro-presidential Edinaya Ukraina fraction.
17. "Profspilkovyi rukh v Ukrainy," p. 28.
18. *Ednist'*, no. 3, 1999; V. Zlenko, "Profsoyuznoe dvizhenie v Ukrainie: proshloe i nastoyashchee," Chernigov: STDU, 2001, pp. 6-7.
19. L. Shangina, "Profsoyuzy Ukrainy: davaite druzhit', no ne trogaite nashe imushchestvo," *Narodnaya volya* (Minsk), no. 15, 2001, p. 8.
20. *Profsoyuzy i rynochnaya ekonomika*, p. 57.
21. Such sudden about-faces are typical of Ukrainian union life. In 2002, O. Khmara, well-known Communist parliamentary deputy and president of the Donetsk regional council of trade unions, Ukraine's largest, suddenly shifted into the pro-Kuchma "Edinaya Ukrania" fraction, to the consternation of his supporters in the Donetsk union movement. It was another case of principle yielding to the carrot and stick.
22. *Profsoyuzy i rynochnaya ekonomika*, p. 54.
23. "Interview with V.I. Zlenko," *Looking East*, p. 129.
24. ASMU, Report to the May 21, 1997 Central Council.

25. *Ednist'*, no. 4, 1999. By contrast, in the build-up to the FTU's congress in 2002, Stoyan had his council recommend that at least half of the delegations be full-time officials. There was no mention of workers. (*Profspil'kovi vesti*, no. 16, 2002)
26. ASMU, Report to the May 21, 1997 Central Council.
27. *Ibid.*
28. *Ibid.*
29. *Ednist'*, no 1-2, 1999; *Otraslevoe tarifnoe soglashenie mashinostroitelei na 1999 god*, Moscow, 1999.
30. *Materialy do zvitu Tsentral'noi rady profspil'ki, Ednist'*, Sept. 1998 and Apr. 1999; personal communication from V. Tsekhmeistruk.
31. Report to the May 29, 1998 Central Council (unpublished).
32. See, for example, *Ednist'*, no 8, 1998.
33. See for example Dudnik's article in *Ednist'*, no. 7, 1998, where he criticized the FPU's policy of "social partnership" which showed more concern for management's problems than those of workers.
34. *Ednist'*, May 2003.
35. *Ibid.*, nos. 49-50, 2000.
36. For example *Ednist'* no .5 2003 showcased meetings and joint resolutions of government and union representatives on its front page, while on page three the president of the union at the Kharkov Tractor Factory was highly critical of the government for "not carrying out numerous agreement, resolutions and orders" regarding support for the agricultural-machine sector that it itself adopted.
37. *Informatsionnyi listok khar'kovskogo oblastnogo soveta rabotnikov ASM*, June, 2000.
38. *Ednist'*, no. 9, 2000.
39. *Ibid.*, Sept. 1998.
40. *Ibid.*, no. 7, 1998.
41. *Informatsionnyi listok khar'kovskogo oblastnogo soveta rabotnikov ASM*, May 2000.
42. *Ednist'*, no. 7, 1995.
43. *Ibid.*, no. 9, 1998.
44. *Informatsionnyi listok khar'kovskogo oblastnogo soveta rabotnikov ASM*, Apr. 1999.
45. *Ibid.*, Sept. 1998.
46. *Ednist'*, no. 7, 1995.
47. *Informatsionnyi listok khar'kovskogo oblastnogo soveta rabotnikov ASM*, July 2000.
48. *Ibid.*, no. 4, 1999 and no. 7, 2000.
49. Icharlcov Bicycle Factory, *Profsoyuznyi listok*, July 1999.
50. *Ednist'*, nos. 3-4, 2000.
51. See, for example, *Profsoyuznyi listok*, Apr. 1999. The issue was the provision of drinking water.
52. *Ibid.*, Apr. 2001.

Chapter Eight
TRANSFORMATION OF A "TRADITIONAL" TRADE UNION
The Vinnitsa Ball-Bearing Factory

Like Tutaev's Motor Factory, the Vinnitsa Ball-Bearing Factory experienced a "revolution," a spontaneous, rank-and-file mobilization that replaced both the director and the union leadership. The difference was that the new union president in Vinnitsa sought to consolidate his base and draw the rank and file into the life of the union. This experience shows that even in the most daunting "objective" circumstances, an independent, union-building strategy is possible and can yield gains for members. It also illustrates the role that progressive leadership at the national and regional levels can play in supporting forces for change in the enterprise.

Vinnitsa is a regional capital in central Ukraine with a population of 380,000. At its high point before the collapse of the Soviet Union, the ASM sector employed 20,000 people here, of whom 9000 were at the ball-bearing plant. Many of the workers were the first generation from the village and still had family ties there. In 1998, when the "revolution" occurred, employment in the sector had already fallen to 8500, with about 3300 left at the ball-bearing factory. But half of these were on temporary layoff or childcare leave. Shutdowns lasting several weeks were common. The plant had undergone incorporation, but the state still held most of the shares. However, it had long since abandoned any responsibility for its management.

During Perestroika and in the first years after independence, the workers remained inactive. Management and the union were unchanged. Except for the social benefits it helped administer, the union was irrelevant to the workers. If they had a problem, they went to management. Conflicts rarely took on a collective dimension, and when they did, they were confined to the given shop or even section. Copies of ASMU's paper that arrived at the factory remained undistributed on the tables of the shop chairpersons.

There was one partial exception to this general picture. In 1992, the polishing-and-assembly shop elected a brigadier as shop-committee chairperson, Pavel Tyutyunov. One of the few union-led protests before 1997, possibly the only one, happened here over a health and safety problem. A liquid coolant was giving off noxious fumes, and repeated complaints to the supervisor brought no action. At a shop meeting, the workers adopted Tyutyunov's proposal to down tools and hold a demonstration in front of the administration building. But it came time to act, he had to resort to shaming and cursing the workers, who were cowering behind their machines. In the past, workers in this or that shop had spontaneously refused to work. But Tyutyunov was proposing an organized, union-led protest. That was perceived as a direct challenge to management. It had never happened before, and the workers were afraid.

The "Revolution"

The first really serious, though still spontaneous, protests were sparked by non-payment of wages, which became chronic in 1996. The most militant was the turning shop. (It makes the inner rings from pipe for the bearings.) The relatively small number of workers, about 300, and their social homogeneity—mostly skilled, male machinists and adjusters (often the same person combined the two jobs)—facilitated collective action. A few weeks or months later, workers in other shops might in turn refuse to work, but the shops never linked up with each other. These wildcats usually erupted after several months during which wages had not been paid. Workers would arrive at work one day and, as usual, ask the supervisor when they would be paid. Failing to get an answer, they would hold an informal discussion and decide, without a vote, not to begin working. A few minutes later, the general director or one of his aides would come running, usually with the union president at his side. He would hear the workers out and then launch into an explanation of the plant's objective difficulties, with special attention to government policy. He would lay out his efforts to resolve the problems and promise results soon. Sometimes he would order immediate payment of small sums to the workers. Having let off steam, the workers would start working. A few months later, the scene repeated itself.

Toward the end of 1996, as the wildcats became more frequent, a member of the plant committee suggested that the union formulate a common set of demands for all the shops and present them to management. A participant at that meeting recalled that this "revolutionary" suggestion provoked profound consternation and fear among the assembled. "Who will present them to the director?" asked one. Since no one was prepared to volunteer, the idea was put aside. The union had always acted as a servile aide to management, and the barriers to shifting to a confrontational mode were too great.

This went on for a couple of years. Then in 1998, after a two-month shutdown, the workers returned only to be learn that the administration had no idea when wages would be paid. Again, the turning shop refused to work. But this time, its workers went through the rest of the factory, calling the others to join. Before long, the entire plant had gathered at the main gates. Tyutyunov suggested they move to the factory's club to hold a meeting. Soon the general director arrived with the president and vice-president of the regional ASMU council in tow. But this time, his explanations did not calm the workers.

The plant had been without a union president for three months, as the former president, N. Nikolov, had left to become vice-president of the regional council. But the regional president and management were having trouble finding a replacement for him, since "acceptable" candidates were reluctant to place their heads in the lion's jaws: on the one hand, the level of worker mobilization would not allow the union play its traditional role as "buffer"; but, on the other hand, no one was willing to lead the workers in a confrontation with management. At the meeting, some workers from Tyutyunov's shop passed up a note proposing him for the job. He was a thirty-five-year-old, clean-cut, abstinent adjuster. He had graduated from the factory's technical (high) school with a "red-diploma" at the age of seventeen and, with a pause during his military service, had worked there since. A highly skilled electronics technician (he sometimes filled in as electrician and machinist), the prospect of getting fired held little fear for him. Before becoming shop chairperson in 1992, he had been, in his own words, "a typical worker, distant from everything." But there was a difference: he had a developed sense of dignity and a commitment to justice. If he stayed at the plant when other skilled workers left in search of a better, more secure income, it was in part because of these qualities.

As noted earlier, it was almost unheard of for a worker to be plant president. And Tyutyunov did not want the job. For one thing, he would probably earn less money at it. But he was also frightened by the responsibility, worried that his grasp of economic issues was too weak to allow him to deal with management on an equal footing. All the same, his colleagues proposed him. The proposal pleased neither the regional president nor the general-director. The former read it out to the meeting but explained that several other candidates were also being considered and that the plant committee would soon make a decision. This shocked the assembled workers, who began to whistle and stamp their feet. One shouted: "The entire collective is here in the hall, and you're proposing that the committee decide!?" The director also spoke out categorically against an election by the meeting, characterizing that as a usurpation of the plant committee's authority—and, of course, he controlled the plant committee. At this, all hell broke loose: "They just don't want him! Then we're damn well going to elect him!"

Tyutyunov took the floor and restored some order. The director proposed that the plant committee meet that same day to choose the new president. Tyutyunov supported the proposal, and the meeting adopted it. The director promised partial payment the next day of the current month's wages, and at that the workers went back to work. The plant committee met that afternoon, but to its dismay, the room was packed wall-to-wall with workers. Although the vote was secret and most committee members did not want Tyutyunov, they were left with no option.

A month later, the turning shop was out again on a wildcat over the failure to pay wages. Tyutyunov went to the shop to ask the workers why they had not come to the union. As he entered, one worker remarked: "Oh, here comes another boss!" But Tyutyunov explained he had not come to get them back to work but to consult and organize. He pointed out the futility of spontaneous, isolated actions. A shop meeting was called and, after some debate, it adopted Tyutyunov's proposal to initiate the legal procedure for a labour dispute, but to do it in the name of the entire factory. Tyutyunov later explained that he wanted to use the procedure to build rank-and-file support for the union. "I wanted to show them that if they didn't get their wages, it wasn't for the union's lack of trying. The economic situation really was bad, and I wanted to get them to stop opposing themselves to the union, which they saw as part of management." At the same time, he admitted that he was afraid the government would come after the union for an illegal strike, as it had done a few years before to the coalminers, whose leader had been arrested without any reaction forthcoming from the membership. "In sum, our members did not have much confidence in the leadership, and the leadership did not have much faith in the support of the members."[1]

Meetings were organized in all the shops, and a common set of demands was formulated and presented to the director. The director consulted his lawyer and was genuinely shocked to learn that he was legally bound to negotiate with the union. "Until then, management had always decided on its own when to speak, with whom, and what tone to assume. They hoped to pacify the workers with the support of the local authorities and the higher trade-union organ. They were convinced they were blameless and expected the ministry or someone else to solve the plant's problems."[2] The union demanded payment of the current month's wage and gradual liquidation of arrears in the form of bartered food and payment of the workers' rent and utility charges. It maintained the pressure throughout the negotiations with mass meetings and demonstrations and a lawsuit campaign to obtain the wages arrears. Enraged, management posted the names of the workers who filed lawsuits on the "black" board, describing them as "greedy" people who were the reason why the "quiet" workers were not receiving their wages. These lists were quickly torn down. The talks between management and the union ended without tangible results, except for the distribution of some bartered food in lieu of wages. Even so, the workers were made to queue long hours in the summer heat to receive it. The plant then shut down for two months.

Upon returning to work, the workers again gathered at the gate and called out the director. But this time, he did not come. Some wanted to block the highway; others even called to "go for pitchforks." On the second day of the strike, an enlarged session of the plant committee, attended by over a hundred people, decided to invoke article forty-five. A special delegates' conference endorsed the decision, and decided to call for arbitration, a move that would bring the government, the main owner of the factory, into the picture.

The union also asked for Zlenko to be included on the union's side. They knew they could count on him not to back down and also hoped he would keep the regional president, who was far from enthusiastic about confrontation, in check. Zlenko's position in the conflict was unambiguous: the union had to hold management responsible, regardless of any "objective" circumstances: "The workers were hired to make ball-bearings and they do that with skill. The job of the plant's board of directors and management is to ensure that it is well-supplied and sells its products. Though they are incapable of doing that, management still claims big salaries for itself, more and more shares, personal cars, and other benefits…They blame everything on the workers and the government, on everyone, in fact, but themselves."[3] Before the arbitration started, Zlenko made a point of visiting each shop to speak with the workers. He wrote up the conflict in ASMU's paper, presenting it as an example to be emulated by others who were not being paid.[4] The president of the regional union was uncomfortable but had little choice but to go along. Nevertheless, he tried to educate Tyutyunov, advising him to to be less "emotional" and to attend management's production meetings, since "after all, a union leader has to understand the economic situation of his enterprise."

The plant conference had decided that any proposal that came out of the arbitration had to be submitted to the membership for ratification. And in the course of the arbitration, the union's people went back four times to consult with the members. Zlenko also invited workers to sit in on the arbitration, and its proceedings were transmitted to the factory club. Tyutyunov wanted it to be clear that "if the union had to step back from some of its demands, it would not be the decision of the committee but of the entire union." Although the enterprise really had no money, Zlenko was able to uncover unproductive expenses equal almost to the total amount of the wage arrears. The arbitrator's recommendation was favourable to the workers. As owner, the government's side tried to delay any decision (the arbitration was not binding), but the strong presence of workers at the proceedings left it no choice but to accept the recommendation.

As a result, the director was dismissed, and the plant started paying for the workers' rent and communal services in lieu of the arrears. Current wages also began to be paid more regularly, though only sixty per cent in cash. According to Tyutyunov, the new director arrived with the clear understanding that "the union at the Vinnitsa Ball-Bearing Factory is not a Soviet-type trade union, not a 'transmission belt' that turns in whatever direction management points. He knows that it is an independent organization of workers; and so management's attitude to the workers and the union has totally changed."[5] But not quite, since the director had plans to replace Tyutyunov with a hand-picked candidate at the next union elections in 1999. Having got wind of this, Tyutyunov went to the regional president for support. But the reply was: "What happens will happen." "If a local union is doing its job," remarked Tyutyuov, "the regional leaders are forced to confront management. That's why they constantly advise me to "consider the situation" in which management finds itself. But if the union shows understanding for management's situation, who is left to show understanding for the workers?" The workers in the turning shop told him not to worry. They went through the factory, agitating on his behalf. Even the plant committee, which consisted in its majority engineering-technical employees held over from the previous elections, supported him. In a resolution read out to the delegates' conference, the committee condemned management's interference in union affairs.

Building the Union

There was still a long way to go for the union really to become an organization of workers themselves rather than a few people acting on behalf of a mass of mistrustful, passive workers. Tyutyunov was one of the very few leaders of a "traditional" union to make promotion of rank-and-file activism and commitment a top union priority, though he soon found that there was no easy way to achieve these goals. He began by fighting the workers' tendency to bypass the union in resolving their problems with management. This had a lot to do with the inactivity of the shop committees. The usual weekly meetings with the shop chairpersons failed to give him a clear picture of the workers' concerns and of the mood in the shops. Nor did the information he gave at these meetings always get back to the workers. He explained:

> The shop committees aren't functioning. It's as if they weren't there. I've suggested to the chairpersons to meet among themselves to discuss common problems, but it doesn't happen. I've asked them why they don't hold shop meetings after work or during lunch-breaks. The workers could tell them what issues they wanted raised with me. I offered to come myself to these meetings, at any time. But I can't get them to change. And the workers still prefer to down tools spontaneously and to discuss problems informally among themselves, rather than to meet with the shop committee and work through the union.

Tyutyunov was at least able to force the shop chairpersons to hold real accounting and election conferences, which in the past had often been mere formalities. And he made his presence at those meetings obligatory. In addition, he organized meetings in the plant's club for workers of the various shops. "It turns out," he complained, "that I'm doing the work of the shop chairpersons. But these meetings are important, since people often hesitate to speak out or ask questions at the big conferences. Here they are more open. Their questions can be very blunt and catch you off guard. But I come already knowing that the issues are complex and that the discussion will be tough." At these meetings, Tyutyunov fought the workers' traditional view of the union as a service agency to which they paid dues but for which they bore no responsibility.

> I tell them: "You elected me plant president but do you really think I can solve your wage problems for you on my own? What do you want me to do—grab the director by the throat and knock his head against the wall a couple of times? Will that make him pay up?" That throws them into confusion. It gets them thinking: "Really, how can one person do anything?" I tell them that as an elected leader I have a certain role, but they are many and they don't want to do anything. When I see that they've digested those ideas, I move on to suggest that they might at least together write a note to the union, laying out their concerns. Why write? Because when the director sees me coming after him aggressively, he gets the idea that I'm the sole cause of his troubles. Get rid of me, as he tried to do,

and things will quiet down. At most, there might be spontaneous strikes, which he can easily deal with—make a speech, toss out some promises, and walk away. Sure, that's not much fun for him either but it's better than organized resistance. If I have something in writing from the workers, I can slap it down on his desk.

A group of workers from Tyutyunov's own shop took up his suggestion. Because of the plant's precarious financial situation, the union had agreed to a gradual increase of wages in three stages to the level required by the new sectoral agreement. The authors of the letter, after describing the decline in their living standards over the past years, criticized this "conciliationism" and demanded full regular payments of wages in cash at the level required by the sectoral agreement, as well as liquidation of accumulated arrears. Twenty-eight workers signed the letter. Despite the criticism which it contained, and which Tyutyunov took personally, he brought the letter to the director. The latter was stunned by it, more by the signatures than by the contents themselves. By his own admission, he was unable to sleep for two nights. "That was the effect of a single signed letter from workers," commented Tyutyunov. "A strike wouldn't have made that impression."

A related goal pursued by Tyutyunov was the strengthening of plant-wide solidarity. The isolation of the different shops dated back to Soviet times. The formal labour-dispute procedure, in which the turning shop acted for the entire factory, was a first step. But after that, the chairperson of that shop continued to act independently, without considering the rest of the union. In fact, she was pursuing a personal agenda, but her members were unaware of it. Two days after a plant committee meeting at which she did not speak, she called a strike in the shop to demand payment of wages that were late. But now, the other shops found that conduct unacceptable. The vice-chairperson of the power shop explained:

> Everybody's wages were late. But they got theirs on the first of the month, while we had to wait for the thirty-first. We went to the plant committee, but they said they couldn't do anything about her, since she had authority in the shop. So we went to her ourselves. She told us there wasn't enough money for everyone. We replied: "Don't think you're so smart. We may be an auxiliary shop, but we can cut your power." We also spoke to the workers in the shop. Now they take the others more into consideration, and we are better organized.

Two years after his election, Tyutyunov could say: "It's very clear that the workers today are not the same as a few years ago. They are still afraid and passive, but not the same. They have come to understand certain things and they know that they cannot defend themselves in the old unorganized way."

Aside from shop meetings, Tyutyunov sought other means to keep the members informed. A newsletter was beyond the union's reach, but he did negotiate a small photocopier and an old computer as partial payment of dues that were owed. And he began dealing with management as much as possible through written documents, copies of which were posted in the shops. He also made a point of recruiting younger, rank-and-file workers for education organized with the School for Worker Democracy. Two of the "graduates" were eventually elected shop chairpersons, against management's wishes. "I wasn't on the list that management had drawn up," said Viktor, a thirty-two-year-old electrician. "The supervisor said I was a troublemaker, that I didn't let others work. But when I came from the seminars, I always showed the others the literature I had brought back and talked about what had been discussed. So at the meeting, an older worker said: 'Viktor's been to courses. He went to Kharkov for a seminar. There are so many old people at the plant. He's young and shows promise. Why not give him a chance?" The vote was twenty-eight against twenty six for Viktor.

But the main instrument for activating the rank and file was the union's readiness to confront management to promote the members' concerns. They could see for themselves that by actively supporting the union they could make real gains. "It is active struggle that unites and teaches us best," explained Tyutyunov.[6] After a period of grace for the new director—wages, after all, were being paid more regularly—there was not a single round of negotiations that resulted in union-management consensus. In the past, few workers had not even been aware of negotiations. Now a copy of the sectoral agreement was posted in each shop along with the plant committee's proposals for the local negotiations. Meetings were organized in the shops to solicit suggestions, and the shops were kept fully informed of the disputed positions, which were presented to the delegates' conference. There, the union's support was solid. If management still refused to sign, the union would initiate a formal labour dispute, which carried the threat of a strike. And it was not an empty threat. Although the procedure set down by law took at least fifty days, the union organized several "spontaneous" stoppages. In one case, all the workers "individually" decided at eleven a.m. to go the toilet. On another, they all went to management to ask for emergency financial aid. Another key tool for resolving individual grievances was the labour disputes committee, which the union controlled and which always decided for workers.

The union was gradually winning the confidence and active support of the members. It made the director see that he could not run the plant without the its cooperation. This was the antithesis of "social partnership."

Struggle for Cash Wages and the Liquidation of Arrears

The main goal in 2000 negotiations was one-hundred-per-cent cash payment of wages. It was also the central demand in the above-mentioned letter of twenty-eight workers, dated March 31, 2000. All the shops endorsed it. The minutes of their meetings were deposited on the director's desk, and he was given until the new year to meet the demands, after which the union threatened a return to strike action and to force his dismissal. Because the factory had no access to credit, any cash it received was obtained from VIRT, an intermediary firm that supplied it with metal, power, and cash to pay taxes and wages, in return for which it took the finished ball-bearings and—so the workers suspected—a hefty profit. The director showed the minutes of the meetings to VIRT's management. In January 2001, the workers celebrated a big victory: they received their wages fully in cash.

Then in February, the director informed the union that he did not have the money to pay in cash. The union stood firm: no return to payment in kind. It demanded a meeting with VIRT and repeated the demand several times, until one day a brash young member of Ukraine's new business class appeared, announcing that he had fifteen minutes to give the union and that the meeting had to be behind closed doors. In fact, the meeting went on for two hours in the presence of over fifty union members, including the entire plant committee, the shop chairpersons and about twenty rank-and-file activists. "He came as a tough businessman, but we put him on the hot seat (*ego zakalyali*)," proudly recalled one of the workers. "We let him know that without our cooperation, there would be no big profits, or any profits at all. We had information on the shady aspects of VIRT's relations with the plant." VIRT's representative offered a schedule of cash payments to be made to the plant. But the union insisted and obtained a schedule of wage payments to the shops: it wanted to make sure the money reached the workers.

From that time, wages were paid fully in cash. The union also forced management to pay two-thirds of base pay for temporary layoffs, something it had never done before. But it was not long before the factory began to accumulate debts for power and water again and was threatened with having them cut off. Asked if he felt that he had good information about the plant's financial situation, Tyutyunov replied:

> I get all the information I ask for: output, sales, average wages, costs, productivity. The figures show things are bad. I can't shout about wages and completely ignore the plant's situation. On other hand, if a worker works, he has to be paid. I can't make concessions on that, even if there's no money left for electricity. And how do I know? There could be some kind of secret deal with the supplier [VIRT]. After all, if the firm is dealing with our plant, there must be profit in it. We know they're making money.

The next major struggle was over payment of the three-million hryvnyas (about 555,000 U.S.$) of wage arrears. In 2001, as part of its accelerated privatization programme, the government put up for sale a controlling twenty-nine-per-cent share in the enterprise. (It owned fifty-two per cent.) The union resisted the temptation to get dragged into a fight over ownership, which experience elsewhere showed could not be won. (Even so, Tyutyunov and his family received threats of violence during this conflict.) It also rejected suggestions from government officials to get rid of the director because of the wage arrears. It realized that it was not a matter of the director's personal qualities. Instead, the union decided to pose its own conditions for the sale, even though it had no legal status in the transaction. The conditions included regular payment of wages in cash, liquidation of the arrears, maintenance of the plant's profile for at least five years, no job cuts, and ten million hryvnyas in investments. After talking with the holder of the main bid, the union agreed to stretch out payment of the debt over 120 days, so as not to block the sale. The prospective buyer, on its part, agreed to raise the investment commitment to nineteen million hryvnyas over three years.

A new element in this confrontation was the strong support the union received from ASMU's regional president, Nikolov. He had worked as an electrician at the ball-bearing plant before becoming a full-time union official. He moved on from there to became regional vice-president in 1997 and in 1998 replaced the president, who left for anothe job. Nikolov gradually adopted more militant positions under the impact of the mobilizations at the plant and Zlenko's influence. (Even after leaving ASMU, Zlenko kept in contact through his educational work.) "I was brought up when unions were supposed to be 'schools of communism'," admitted Nikolov. "It took time to realize that documents do not solve problems." But the union's main leverage was the high level of rank-and-file mobilization. "It was a very conflictual period," recalled Tyutyunov. "We were fighting management over the collective agreement that had not been signed. The unrest was palpable. They knew that the workers were prepared to fight. They knew that anyone who bought the factory would have a lot of trouble running it. And so they listened to us." In the end, the State Property Authority accepted the union's conditions.

The sale went through in August 2001. The buyer was a trading company called Interprodukt, linked to the Donetsk "clan." But sixty days after the sale, no payments had been made towards liquidation of the wage arrears. Tension was rising. Tyutyunov and Nikolov informed the director that the union was initiating a labour dispute. The director told them to take up the matter with Donetsk. Tyutyunov went to Donetsk, armed with the minutes of the shops meetings. There, he promised a strike that would back the demand to annul the sale, unless the arrears were liquidated within 120 days of the sale. A few days before the deadline, Interprodukt phoned Tyutyunov to inform him that the order for payment had already been signed. Interprodukt was calling him even before the director to make sure that the money was used for its intended purpose. The workers received their arrears on the 120th day after the sale. It was the equivalent of a half-year's wages, and they were jubilant, even though part of the payment was in overpriced bartered goods and in the form of communal services.

The Fight for Survival

Unfortunately, the celebration did not last long. Almost immediately, one of the plant's creditors—which happened to be a subsidiary of Interprodukt—filed a bankruptcy suit against the enterprise for a debt worth the equivalent of 7,000 U.S.$. It became evident that the plant had been bought with the intention of stripping its assets and liquidating it. Although it was loss-making, the loss had been stable for several years. The much less modern ball-bearing plant in Kharkov was not facing bankruptcy. Then in the spring of 2002, with tension already running high over stalled contract negotiations—management was refusing the wages set by the sectoral agreement, and the union was threatening to block the shipment of goods—it got wind of plans to sell some of the plant's equipment to the Kharkov factory. As usual, the union organized meetings in all the shops and handed the minutes to the director: the union made clear that the workers were determined to prevent any attempt to move out equipment, even if it took an occupation. One evening around this time, Tyutyunov got a phone call at home from Donetsk: "Is it a personal matter? Why don't you like us?" The caller offered Tyutyunov money and an apartment. (Tyutyunov was living with his wife, two children, and his mother-in-law in two rooms of a plant dormitory.) Nikolov also got a call, asking how much it would cost to reduce the union's activism.

In June 2002, the director sent the workers home on indefinite leave. Two months later, the plant stopped paying two-thirds of the base pay. In July, a leaflet appeared in the mailboxes of the buildings where many of the plant's workers lived summoning them to a meeting. It was signed "the initiative group." On July 19, 2000 workers gathered in front of the plant's locked gates. The shops elected representatives to an "initiative committee," which was given the mandate to organize a campaign to save the factory. The committee consisted of nine workers, including Tyutyunov, and an engineer. Only five of them were members of the union committee. The workers decided not to entrust the campaign to the plant committee, which had thirty members, because the work would be semi-clandestine, possibly dangerous, and not all of its members were considered trustworthy.

The union wrote to all levels and agencies of government demanding annulment of the sale on the grounds that the conditions had not been respected. It let the government know that the workers of this factory would not sit by passively, as so many others had done, while the equipment was sold off for scrap. "The owners said several times that they never dreamed they were acquiring such hard nuts (*krepkie orekhi*) when they bought the factory," proudly said Lidiya Semenovna, a leading member of the initiative committee, an engineer who had not been active in the union until two years before. As a result of this pressure, the mayor agreed to take over the plant's social sphere, a move that significantly eased its financial burden. This opened the way for an agreement with the owners, who promised to resume production on October 2. But they reneged, still intent on liquidating the enterprise. As for the State Property Committee, it informed the union that all the conditions of the sale were being fulfilled and that it could do nothing. In fact, the State Property Committee had modified the contract after the fact so that the payment of wage arrears was considered fulfillment of the investment obligation. So pleased was that State Property Committee with the new owners that it sold the state's remaining twenty five per cent in the enterprise to one of its subsidiaries in January 2003. This time there were no investment obligations. The sale was made even though the court was at the time deciding whether to declare the enterprise bankrupt. In all, the state had sold off a fifty-four-per-cent share in the factory for a little over one million U.S.$, a fraction even of the scrap value of its machinery and of the real estate.

Towards the end of September 2002, new leaflets signed by the initiative group called the workers to a protest march to the governor's offices. On October 2, fifteen hundred workers assembled at the gates. Some had come in from far-off villages where they had gone to stay with family. The initiative committee made sure the press was out in force. The government sent his deputy to dissuade the workers for marching, but to no avail. The mood was very militant. Some were calling to block the railway. The nine-kilometer march evoked widespread sympathy from all strata of the population, even the bazaar traders and the police. The Union of (retired) Officers promised to protect the workers, if they decided to occupy the plant. The Communist parliamentary deputies from Vinnitsa and activists of the Communist Party were also present. Despite some initial hesitation about politicizing the struggle, the union decided that it needed political allies to win. The support of the deputies, who raise the issue in parliament, made an important contribution to the outcome.[7]

Vinnitsa had never seen such a protest. The authorities, unaccustomed even to mild popular resistance, were shaken. They were worried that the people might finally wake up to put an end to their impunity. Besides, parliamentary elections were approaching. Vinnitsa had voted strongly for Moroz and was seen as a "red" region. The governor came out to address the crowd assembled under his windows. He announced that an interdepartmental governmental commission would be set up to look into the situation at the plant, and that everything possible would be done.[8] After the meeting, he called in Nikolov. Banging his fist on the table, he shouted: "All of Ukraine is quiet. Only you have to make such a noise!" He was feeling heat from Kyiv and he threatened to convene ASMU's regional council to remove Nikolov. Nikolov, however, had little to worry about, since the majority of the delegates would be from the ball-bearing plant, which was now far beyond the control of the governor. Meanwhile, Tyutyunov found that his telephones at work and at home were cut. The same thing happened to the other members of the initiative committee, who were called in by the police along with other workers and made to sign forms to the effect that they had been forewarned against participation in further "disorders."[9]

The initiative committee's goal was to stall the court proceedings long enough for political pressure to bring results, since the judge, if left to himself, would inevitably declare the plant bankrupt and liquidate it to pay the creditors. Among other things, the committee promised the authorities a huge demonstration, together with the opposition parties, to greet Kuchma's planned visit to Vinnitsa. Meanwhile, the union kept the members informed and let them participate in the decisions through enlarged meetings of the plant committee. Finally, the creditors' committee, which was in reality the owners and their subsidiaries (the court refused the union's request for representation on the committee, though it was a creditor) retracted its suit.[10] The court now had to adopt a restructuring plan. It met in four sessions, and each time several hundred workers demonstrated on the street below. "The judge is bought and sold," said Tyutyunov, "and he did everything to keep us from participating in the proceedings. When I asked to speak—we had no legal standing—he asked me: 'By what authority do you speak?' I pointed to the window: 'There, on the street, that's my authority.' It made me feel good."

In March 2003, the court adopted a restructuring plan that called for keeping "at least" 850 employees, about a third of the workforce at the time of the closing eight months before. The union tried but failed to obtain six months severance pay for those who would be permanently laid off, instead of the legally-required three months. Some equipment would be sold off to pay the creditors. There was no investment obligation. It was bitter, but still a victory. There was now a chance at least the plant would live and employment would increase in the future. How many times had the authorities told the union to make peace with the fact that the plant was already dead? Some of the workers had already found other jobs and would not have returned in any case. The union itself figured that plant could not operate without a minimum staff of 1300. But the union's major consideration was that it would become more and more difficult as time passed to mobilize enough workers to exert real pressure. The workers were losing faith that the plant would ever reopen.

"The key thing," explained Tyutyunov

> was to get the plant working as quickly as possible. Otherwise, there would be no way to mobilize, and no struggle. The union is going to make sure all the permanent layoffs are made in strict conformity with the law. But we have said: No one who was really active in the struggle will be laid off. Otherwise, it would be like reprisals. And after eight months of serious struggle, we have a large core of tested and tempered activists. Some are new people who were awakened by this fight. So when we hold new elections in the shops, we'll know whom to choose.

When the remaining workers were recalled at the beginning of August to prepare the plant for production, a delegates' conference elected the entire initiative committee to replace the old plant committee. "It has all changed with the election of the initiative group," explained Lidiya Semenovna.

> Before, half of the committee was inactive. Now the people in the shop committees are all committed (*ideniye*) people. Whenever there's a big question, we call an enlarged committee and invite workers. This is mandatory and regular. We are always going to the shops to work with the people, personally to convince them to participate, to give them information, to renew contact. We tell them: "We can't solve the problems without you." When the director sees the enlarged committee, the workers' burning eyes, he knows he has to act. We had to convince the new director that this was not some social club but a workers' organization, that if he didn't want to do what we asked, we would force him.

Relations with management remain basically conflictual. "Management is always trying to get around the union, to act arbitrarily. It even offers the workers incentives to ignore the union. The owners' representatives actually went through the shops, telling the workers how bad the union is and calling them to leave it. But we weren't worried." They also tried to get the workers to sign individual contracts to place of the collective agreement. But these efforts were abandoned when it became clear the workers would not sign. Only the supervisors are on individual contacts. But the union has also won the grudging respect of management. "They used to ignore us," said Tyutyunov. "Now they make an effort to inform us and to consult. They called us in to explain the restructuring plan, so that we in turn could explain it to the workers."

Breaking Out of Isolation

The union's struggles made it acutely aware of the need to build solidarity with forces outside the plant. It was obvious that none of the workers' more serious problems could be resolved within the framework of the enterprise. The support of the regional ASMU was an important factor in even the partial victories. And the struggles in the plant, in turn, helped to transform Nikolov from a "social partner" into a fighter, prepared to take on management and the authorities.

The felt need for broader support awakened dissatisfaction among workers with the national leadership of ASMU and with the FPU. This moved the local union to put pressure on them. After receiving the letter of the twenty-eight workers, Tyutyunov went to the shop to talk with them. There he learnt, somewhat to his relief, that he was not the target of their anger. The letter had really been intended for the higher levels of the union movement for failing to organize resistance to the government. The letter focused on wages, but the authors made clear that "this question is not only economic but especially political. In the nine years since independence, we have been living worse and worse. One of the reasons for this decline is the weak, we would even say, timid work of the unions." After the meeting, Tyutyunov wrote up a "declaration" addressed to the regional and national levels of ASMU and to the FPU. It was adopted unanimously by the delegates' conference. It read:

> The trade-union committees in the plants are doing what they can to stop the deterioration of the workers' situation. (Demands made to management, strikes and other protest actions, non-confidence votes in directors, arbitration, and other actions.)...But can they by their own forces resolve the very complex problems that arise? Where the plant's financial situation is bad, it is almost impossible to get wage increases, regular payment of wages, payment of the wage arrears. And even where workers get one hundred per cent of their wages on time, is that enough to allow them to pay for rent and communal services, to feed and dress their families?
>
> Even more [than the government's anti-popular policies], we are amazed at the position of the unions, that were created to defend workers' rights. In the enterprises, unions are changing their way of working in order to defend workers' interests. But change is very slow in the higher organs and federations. If a union in a factory is inactive, that affects the situation only of its own workers. But if the higher levels are passive, that affects the workers of the city, region and country. Thus,

the delay in raising the minimum wage last year damaged the material situation of all workers, and that was at a time when prices for rent, communal services, local transport, food and especially for bread, so strategic for the people, were being raised... All these actions of the government and parliament were made possible only because the unions were not sufficiently active. They limited themselves to making declarations and voicing demands, to which no one paid attention... The most effective means available to unions strikes, demonstrations, marches. These are enshrined in the Constitution and in the law. But we use these rights ineffectively, or not at all.

The letter ended by calling on the higher bodies of the union movement to adopt a programme of action "such that everyone, from the President down to the worker, will feel that in this country the trade unions are the most active defenders of the people."[11] It was read out at the regional council. One of the worker delegates (who was there as a result of the Central Council resolution of 1999) moved to officially endorse it and send it to the Central Council and to the FPU. The council refused the endorsement but it did send the letter to the ASMU's national office, asking for it to be published in its paper. "Our goal was to let the other local unions read it and so put pressure on the higher levels," Tyutyunov said. "We wanted to tell the Central Council that it should act as a catalyst to get the Federation to stop hugging the President." Dudnik at first refused to publish the declaration, which he termed "philosophical musings." He relented after Zlenko threatened to take it elsewhere. The FPU's *Prokspilkovy visti* agreed to publish it only as a paid advertisement for 2,000 hryvnyas.

Members of the initiative committee were disappointed with the weak support they received from ASMU's national office. "If we ask," said Tyutyunov, "they help. Dudnik came to the plant once during the conflict and spoke to the workers. They also published an article by Nikolov. But they take no initiative themselves, and that leaves us with a bad feeling. The Central Council should take the lead. It knew our situation. We asked Dudnik to send the editor of the paper to talk to the workers first hand, but he didn't." Tyutyunov wrote Dudnik asking why ASMU members hear about his plant's struggles only at the seminars of the School for Worker Democracy, but they are never discussed at the Central Council. Dudnik called him a "populist" but otherwise did not reply. While other ASM plants in Vinnitsa offered moral support and some of their workers even participated in the march, the other unions did nothing. One of the court sessions took place during a meeting of the regional federation's council right across the street from the court. Nikolov proposed that the delegates join the demonstrators during their lunch break, but no one went. "We are weak here down below in the union and we lack the means for linking up," explained Tyutyunov, who placed some hope in the internet. His union gained access to it thanks to support from the Canadian Auto Workers. Finally, as noted, the political support from the Communist deputies was important. The union, in turn, mobilized workers to participate in the opposition's protests against the government.

The victory in the fight to save the factory, though partial, would have been impossible were it nor for the union's struggles and painstaking organizing work of its leader during the preceding five years. They transformed the union from a tool of management into a genuine labour movement. They made committed union activists out of members who previously had not given the union a second thought. They transformed the members themselves, whose self-confidence and dignity, their active orientation and quick grasp of issues put them head-and-shoulders above others participants at educational seminars. During a discussion at one of these in November 2003, a woman worker from the plant said: "We can't say what the future will be. It looks like the owners would still like to liquidate the enterprise. But even if in the end we can't save it, we will still have won. We will have shown them all that we are people."

Notes

1. T. Tyutyunov, "Dlya pobedy nuzhen predannyi lider i aktivnye, smelye rabochie," *Profsoyuzy i rynochnaya ekonomika*, p. 43. Most of this chapter is based upon interviews, reports at seminars, personal communications, and personal observation.
2. *Ibid*, p. 44.
3. *Ednist'*, no. 6, 1998.
4. *Ibid*.
5. Tyutyunov, "Dlya pobedy…" p. 47.
6. Tyutyunov, "Dlya pobedy…" p. 47.
7. *Ednist'*, no. 10, 2002.
8. *Ibid*., *Golos Ukrainy*, Nov. 11, 2002.
9. *Golos Ukrainy*, Nov. 23, 2003.
10. *Panorama tizhnya* (Vinnitsa), Apr. 23, 2002.
11. An abridged version appeared in *Ednist'*, no. 5, 2000.

Chapter Nine

THE SOCIO-POLITICAL CONTEXT IN BELARUS

Belarus borders with Russia on the east, Ukraine on the south, and Poland, Lithuania and Latvia on its north and west. It is the smallest of the three predominantly Slav republics of the former USSR, with a population of about ten million, a fifth of Ukraine's and a fifteenth of Russia's. In area, it is a little over a quarter the size of Ukraine. Almost one in five Byelorussians lives in the capital, Minsk, and most are Russian-speaking.[1]

Belarus has few natural resources, mainly potash and wood. Russia is by far its largest trading partner, from which it imports fuel, metal and chemicals and to which it exports mainly machines, textiles and foodstuffs. Largely agrarian until World War II, Belarus saw the rapid growth of engineering and electronics industries in the decades after the war. Byelorussians often referred to their country as the "assembly-shop of the Soviet Union." Its ASM sector manufactures heavy trucks, tractors, agricultural machines, bicycles, and parts for them.

Economic Policy

Belarus has the distinction of being the only post-Communist state to have rejected the "Washington consensus." As late as the end of 1998, only twenty-eight per cent of the country's basic funds (that is, buildings, machinery and tools, livestock, etc.) were privately owned, almost the same proportion as in 1992 (and half of the level in Russia). In ASM, only twenty per cent of the factories had been privatized.[2] Thanks to corporatization of the enterprises (their transformation into joint-stock companies), the government could report in 1999 that the non-state sector produced 42.7 per cent of the manufactured goods. But, in fact, the government still owned a controlling share in the majority of corporatized enterprises (the private shareholders were mainly employees),[3] so that even in 2001 ninety-five per cent of industrial production came from large state-owned or state-controlled enterprises.[4] The number of newly-created enterprises in the private sector (mostly in retail commerce and catering) is small compared Russia and Ukraine.

Although it is no longer a Soviet-type economy, the state's role in the management of enterprises remains significant. This takes the form, among other things, of selective tax privileges, exemptions from currency controls, provision of low-interest credits. In 2001, the state still controlled about thirty per cent of prices, mainly of consumer goods.[5] It also indirectly regulates wages, linking their growth to increases in output. And it can, directly or indirectly, remove and appoint enterprise directors.

While the government has made efforts in recent years to bring down inflation—it stood at 42.8 per cent in 2002[6]—it has rejected monetarism. Its main economic priorities are to sustain and increase production and employment, and despite Belarus's heavy dependence on the depressed Russian economy, the regulatory and relatively easy monetary and credit policies have had a measure of success. GDP in constant prices in 2002 stood at 98.4 per cent of its 1991 level, as compared to 76.2 for Russia and 53.8 for Ukraine,[7] and the rate of growth in the first half of 2003 in Belarus was on a par with Russia's and Ukraine's.[8] Between 1997 and 2002, the average annual rate of fixed capital investment was forty-eight per cent of its 1991 level, which compares well with Russia at 29.5 per cent and Ukraine at 27.1.[9] Industrial output in 2002 was 113 per cent of 1991 levels, as compared to sixty-seven and seventy-four in Russian and Ukraine respectively; and agricultural output stood at seventy-eight per cent, compared to seventy-two in Russia and sixty nine in Ukraine.[10] Even allowing for the smaller size of the unaccounted-for contribution of Belarus's "grey economy" and the problematic nature of official statistics, the relative differences are significant (especially considering the absence of earnings from export of natural resources and semi-finished goods) and they are accepted as real even by unsympathetic observers.[11]

Belarus's ASM sector has also fared relatively better. In 2002, it produced almost three times as many tractors as Russia and twelve times more than Ukraine; whereas in 1991 it made only half as many as Russia and roughly the same number as Ukraine.[12] Between 1991 and 2002, truck production in Belarus fell by fifty-seven per cent, as compared to seventy-two per cent in Russia and ninety-one Ukraine. (The drop in Russia would be much greater of one compares only heavier trucks, since most of Russian truck production is mini-vans today.)[13] Motovelo, the Minsk Bicycle and

Motorcycle Factory, is producing at capacity and cannot keep up with demand; while the Kharkov Bicycle Factory, once the flagship of Soviet bicycle-making, is struggling to survive.

The Byelorussian economy is also significantly less criminalized than the other two. In 2002, Transparency International ranked Belarus thirty-sixth least corrupt among the 102 countries on its "corruption perception index." Russia placed seventy-first.[14] Belarus's enterprises have not suffered the asset-stripping and pillage that occurred in Ukraine and Russia, and capital flight has also been limited because of currency controls. Another positive consequence of limited privatization is much more efficient tax collection.[15] The paradox is that, although Belarus has the clearly the most openly dictatorial and repressive regime of the three, in matters that do not directly affect the President's power, it is a significantly more law-based state. The levels of managerial corruption and the "mafia" are comparatively modest. As a leader of the Union of Auto and Farm-Machine Workers of Belarus (ASMB) explained: "They steal, but only as much as Lukashenko let's them."[16] The class of "new Byelorussians," who live in newly-built luxury homes and drive expensive cars, is small change compared to Russia's "oligarchs" and Ukraine's "clans."

Despite this, liberal analysts do not hesitate to qualify Belarus's economic performance as "dismal." They deplore the fact that the government views the large industrial enterprises as vehicles for providing employment and incomes, "rather than simply as economic entities."[17] It is apparently of little concern to them that the economic policies of Russia and Ukraine are highly unpopular, while, by their own admission, those of Belarus "enjoy the support of major social groups," including workers, who "grumble about low wages but generally support the system, which provides them with secure jobs and access to social services financed by large industrial enterprises."[18] They argue that despite the much steeper decline of their economies in the 1990s, Russia and Ukraine, unlike Belarus, are now poised for takeoff, since they have carried out "reform." But that is far from obvious. As one might expect, the IMF is highly critical of the slow progress of "reform" in Belarus and calls for rapid privatization and deregulation.[19] It canceled all lending to the country in 1995. Ironically, economic growth resumed soon after, four years before it did in Russia and Ukraine.

Belarus under Lukashenko has thus refused to be integrated into the world economy on terms dictated by the West, which has only minimal leverage in Belarus.[20] On the other hand, in contrast to Ukraine, the Byelorussian government has put much effort into preserving and strengthening the economic ties with Russia. Integration with Russia is a popular policy that has undoubtedly benefitted the Byelorussian economy, though it will inevitably force it to move closer to Russia's liberal model. Of course, Belarus's success is only relative: in the first decade since the end of the Soviet Union, the net result was at best was stagnation. In 2002, only fifty-five per cent of industrial capacity was being used, though unemployment was relatively low. Seventy to eighty per cent of the equipment in industry had passed its replacement date.[21] And while investment has been relatively higher, it is far from what is needed. Moreover, much of it has gone just to keeping enterprises afloat, rather than restructuring.

Despite the positive aspects of the economic policy for workers, ASMB's leadership has been sharply critical of the government for low living standards, hidden unemployment, high inflation, the absence of a coherent industrial restructuring policy, the heavy tax burden carried by the enterprises that are left with insufficient working capital, let alone investment funds, and an overall economic climate that discourages private, especially foreign, investment. The union has been especially critical of the subordination of economic policy to the political ends of the President: the arbitrary allocation of tax abatements and cheap credits to punish or reward enterprise directors, depending on their political loyalty, or to buy the quiescence of potentially threatening groups of workers; the President's large discretionary budget; revenues wasted on maintaining a vast state apparatus and on pet projects, such as the construction of hockey palaces in Belarus's cities. (Lukashenko, in mid-life, decided to take up the sport.)[22]

The Political Regime

Western observers generally put the political regime of Belarus in a class apart from those of Russia and Ukraine. If the latter are "managed," "imperfect" or "fledgling" democracies, Belarus is "Europe's last dictatorship." Certainly, the Lukashenko is less concerned with appearances, and his regime is somewhat more repressive, if one chooses to leave aside Russia's war in Chechnya. But in fact, the three regimes have more in common that what separates them: all three presidents were elected in grossly unfair contests and wield nearly absolute power. The state controls the main electronic media, which is the population's main source of information about public affairs. In all three, the level of repression is, in fact, relatively mild as far as dictatorships go (again, Chechnya aside), but that is mainly a function of the opposition's weakness.

As noted, Belarus's regime is the least self-conscious about democratic appearances. All three parliaments have been reduced to a largely ornamental, consultative status, only in Belarus does the President vet the candidates. At the same time, the situation is in many ways paradoxical, and not least because, as already noted, economic policy is much more attuned to popular desires in Belarus and public and private corruption are kept much more in check. What most sets Belarus apart is the level of repression against the trade-union movement. Yet at the same time, the government has been more responsive to its demands.

Like Russia and Ukraine, Belarus experienced a wave of popular enthusiasm for liberalism in the early 1990s. Deputies close to the pro-Western Byelorussian Popular Front (BNF), though a minority, exerted strong influence in parliament and enjoyed the support of its chairman, S. Shushkevich, a well-known physicist. But Prime Minister V. Kebich, a career industrial manager, had a more sober appreciation of the "Washington consensus," and the rapid collapse of the economy in neighbouring Russian quickly put an end to the popular infatuation with liberalism. The BNF's influence plummeted.

In 1994, the Supreme Soviet amended the constitution to create a strong presidency. The expectation was that Kebich would be elected to the new post. Instead, Aleksandr Lukashenko, a parliamentary deputy and former collective-farm chairman, received eighty per cent of the vote, mainly on the basis of his anti-corruption campaign. Lukashenko had previously flirted with the BNF but was too much of a populist and too hungry for power not to see that it was a losing number. With the Russian collapse before his eyes and memories of the powerful strike movement of April 1991 still vivid, he continued Kebich's cautious policies. Then in 1996, taking a leaf from Yeltsin's book, he carried out a coup against parliament, which he legitimated through a referendum. However, unlike Yeltsin, whose coup was in large part designed to allow him to pursue "shock therapy," Lukashenko continued to reject that strategy. It is that rejection, much more than his authoritarianism, that explains why he stands condemned by Western governments as "the lone remaining outlaw in Europe."[23] At home, Lukashenko was genuinely popular, though less so as time passed. His coup, unlike Yeltsin's, was bloodless and he did not have to falsify referendum results.

Belarus is also the only post-Soviet country in which the labour movement, especially the two main industrial unions, ASMB and the Union of Radio-Electronics Workers (REP), constituted the principal political opposition. (Western analysts often wrongly attribute that role to the BNF, which, in fact, has been marginalized, despite—and partly thanks to—Western financing). That is also partly the reason why the Byelorussian state has subjected the unions to much more systematic repression. Both the unions' influence and the repression against them are, in turn, closely linked to the government's economic course. The working class has not been subjected to the same level of economic insecurity or social decomposition as in Ukraine and Russia. Those social consequences of "shock therapy," one can argue, are the functional equivalents of political repression, in the sense that they have so undermined labour's capacity to resist in Russia and Ukraine as to make systematic repression of the labour movement unnecessary there. In addition, the state's economic strategy in Belarus makes it more vulnerable to labour's pressure because it assumes more direct responsibility for the fate of the enterprises and the well-being of their workers.

As in the Russia and Ukraine, the procedure for legal strikes is so onerous and long—six-to-twelve weeks—as to practically rule them out. The government's repression of a public transport strike in Minsk and Gomel in 1995—the unions were disbanded, the leaders arrested, and many of the strikers fired and blacklisted—had a definite cooling effect.[24] As in Russia and Ukraine, oppositional labour leaders are subject to surveillance and periodic "visits" by the police, but only in Belarus has the government instituted the position of Assistant Director for Information in all the large industrial enterprises. Their function is ostensibly to keep workers informed of government and management policies. But, in fact, they are propagandists and spies for the government. Political protests are allowed, but the demonstrations are relegated to outlying areas of the city and they usually attract a strong police presence. In 1999, Lukashenko issued a decree requiring re-registration of all social organizations and political parties, imposing new, more restrictive conditions. Among other things, it forced unions to sign up all their members anew and to obtain written consent for dues check-off from each. The move dealt a serious blow to the alternative unions but it also deprived the Association of Industrial Unions, whose main members were ASMB and REP, of its official status.

Directors are under strong pressure to keep workers from union-organized protests and to makes sure that "proper" delegates are chosen to union conferences and congresses, that is, delegates who will vote to replace oppositional leaders, where they exist. Concerted efforts were made in 2000 and again in 2002 to dislodge, among others, the president of the union of Minsk Ball-Bearing Plant, the national presidents of ASMB, REP, and of the Union of Agro-Industrial Workers, as well as the president of the Byelorussian Federation of Trade Unions (BFP). These were accompanied by public slander that tarred these leaders as drunks and thieves. At the time, the efforts failed, except in the case of V. Goncharik, president of the BFP, who was forced to resign. Goncharik had been the candidate of the unified democratic opposition in the 2000 presidential elections. He was replaced by L. Kozik, a government functionary with some past union experience. Three months after the presidential elections, the government issued a decree prohibiting automatic dues check-off. It also stepped up the pressure on directors to force the unions in their enterprises to disaffiliate from ASMB and REP. In 2002, three unions disaffiliated from ASMB, followed by three more in 2003, some of them very large plants. In May 2003, about a dozen enterprise unions that had disaffiliated from their national organizations formed a Union of Industry that is loyal to the President. In December 2003, a special congress finally deposed A. Bukhvostov, President of ASMB and a prominent figure of the political opposition.

The Socio-Economic Situation of Workers

The refusal of "shock therapy" has not spared Byelorussian workers from a dramatic fall in their living standards, which stand somewhere between those of Russia and Ukraine, though rather closer to Russia. On the other hand, inequality is much smaller in Belarus. By some measures, Byelorussian workers were even somewhat better off than the Russians. Belarus ranked fifty-sixth on the UN Human Development Index in 2001, with Russia, sixtieth, and Ukraine, eightieth. (In 1990, Belarus ranked thirty-sixth behind Russia, which was twenty-ninth.)[25] But the principal economic advantage enjoyed by Byelorussian workers over the past eleven years is the greater measure of economic security, as concerns employment and the payment of wages.

Belarus's demographic indicators, as overall measures of social health, are better than in the other two countries. In the 1992-2002, its population fell by 2.4 per cent, compared to 2.9 in Russia and 7.8 in Ukraine. (In-migration to Belarus was negligible.[26]) Life expectancy in 2000 was sixty-nine in Belarus, compared to sixty-eight in Ukraine and sixty-five in Russia.[27] As the table below shows, average wages in Russian roubles 2001 stood between Russia and Ukraine, but the prices of basic goods were lower, though on the rise.

Comparison of Wages and Selected Prices in Russian Roubles in 2001

country	average wage	meat	potatoes	communal services
Ukraine	1 800	65,21	4,88	49,95
Belarus	2 700	37,29	4,18	18
Russia	3 500	78,85	7,71	54.5

Source: *Profsoyuzy*, no. 2, 2002, p. 25.

In 2001, thirty per cent of the population of Belarus was living below the poverty line. 54.5 per cent of average household income went spent on food and 16.0 per cent on services. In Russia the figures were 43.4 and 19.3 and in Ukraine 63.4 and 18.0. The average Byelorussian diet was also significantly richer in vegetables, milk and meat and their products.[28] Real wages in Belarus, despite the high level of inflation, have risen every year between 1996 and 2002. In the ASM sector, they increased from 121 per cent of the minimum consumer basket in 1995 to 193 per cent in 2001. In the first half of 2003, they were down to 175 per cent. The average wage in Belarus in January 2003 was the equivalent of 118 U.S.$, and in ASM—142 U.S.$, behind only the banking sector and the government apparatus.[29]

As in the other two countries, the social safety is weak, though benefits has been eroding more slowly. The minimum pension in 2001 was a third of the average wage and well below the poverty line. The average pension was equal to three quarters of the minimum consumer basket. The average unemployment benefit was less than a tenth of the average wage, and less than half of the unemployed qualified for it.[30] As in the other two countries, basic health care is free but patients increasingly have to pay for tests, medicine and other supplies. Higher education is still free only for the exceptional students. Utilities and basic services continue to be subsidized—the big plants have held onto to more of their "social spheres"—but fees and prices are rising The government in Belarus supports the construction of affordable housing, something it stopped doing long ago in Russia and Ukraine.

In general, the refusal of "shock therapy" has meant that the Byelorussian working class has not undergone the same degree of social decomposition as in the other two countries. Belarus is exceptional among post-Communist states in having kept a stable level of employment for most of the post-Soviet period. (The big drop in employment—twelve per cent—occurred between 1991 and 1995.)[31] Employment in industry declined by 22.5 per cent over the last decade, as compared to fifty per cent in Ukraine and 44.5 in Russia.[32] The share of industrial employment in the total employed work force dropped relatively little, from 31.1 to 27.5 per cent.[33] In ASM, which is the largest industrial sector, employment fell by a third as compared to more than a half in Russia and Ukraine.[34] (On the other hand, radio-electronics, the other major industrial sector, which was heavily defence-oriented, lost more than two thirds of its employees.) In December 2000, Ministry of Labour surveys indicated a real level of unemployment between five and eight per cent.[35] However, judging by output, industrial enterprises are heavily overstaffed, by as much as twenty-five per cent, according to ASMB. Despite the relatively low unemployment and management's complaints about high labour turnover, at least in Minsk, the fear of losing one's job weighs heavily upon Byelorussian workers, though less so on skilled workers. Technical schools and colleges preparing young people for ASM never stopped teaching worker professions, and one sees many more young faces in the factories than one does in Russia or Ukraine.

Theft and drinking at work, which are, among other things, indicators of demoralization, are also less widespread in Belarus, where the "production culture," according to experienced workers, was always better. Byelorussian workers were not been exposed to the demoralizing influences of lengthy layoffs and non-payment of wages in the 1990s. Management is also less corrupt and arbitrary than in Russia and Ukraine, a situation that apparently dates from the Soviet period.[36] On the other hand, the ten per cent increase in the number of serious or lethal work-related accidents in the late 1990s in ASM (37 deaths in 2000), despite the smaller employed work force, is an indication of the general deterioration of working conditions. That is linked, among other things, to the advancing age of the equipment and the low wages, which workers try to compensate by exceeding norms.[37]

Notes

1. Minstat Belarusi, Goskomstat Rossii, *Belarus' i Rossiya*, 1999, Moscow, 1999, p. 11; Goskomstat SSSR, *Narodnoe khozyaistvo SSSR za 70 let*, Moscow, 1987, p. 392.
2. Goskomostat, *Belarus' i Rossiya*, p. 26.
3. The state held at least half the shares in forty-nine per cent of corporatized enterprises and at least a quarter in eight-five per cent of them. V. Novak, "O reformirovanii sobstvennosti v respublike Belarus'," www.president.gov.by/gosim/publish/paper-min.htm
4. EIU, *Country Report: Belarus*, June 2003, p. 17.
5. EIU, *Country Report: Belarus*, Mar. 2001, p. 15.
6. EIU, *Country Report: Belarus*, June 2003, p. 5.
7. *SNG v 2002 g: statisticheskii spravochnik.*, 2003, p. 26.
8. EIU, *Country Report: Belarus*, June 2003, p.3
9. *SNG v 2001 g.: statisticheskii spravochnik*, p. 28; *SNG v 2002 g.: statisticheskii spravochnik*, p. 48.
10. *SNG v 2002 g.: statisticheskii spravochnik*, pp. 37, 45.
11. One of these is the Economist Intelligence Unit. See also the joint German-Byelorussian study by K Gaiduk et al. *Byelorusskaya ekonomika na pereput'e*, Berlin and Minsk, 2003.
12. *SNG v 2002 g.: statisticheskii spravochnik*, p. 171.
13. Ibid., pp. 170-1.
14. V. Korchagina, "Russia Fares Better in Annual Corruption Index," *The Moscow Times*, Aug. 29, 2002. The ranking was conducted by nine corporate and non-corporate organizations, including the World Bank, Columbia University, the Economist Intelligence Unit and Price Waterhouse Coopers, on the basis of surveys of businesspeople, analysts and locals in each country.
15. EIU, *Country Report: Belarus*, June 2003, p. 20.
16. *Byulleten'*, Moscow: Shkola trudovoi demokratii, no. 12, 1999, p. 34.
17. EIU, *Country Report: Belarus*, June 2003, p. 17.
18. *Ibid.*
19. *Ibid*, p. 20.

20. EIU, *Country Report: Belarus*, Feb. 2001, p. 15.
21. *Belorusskii rynok*, no. 6, 2003, cited in K. Gaiduk et al., *Belorusskaya ekonomika*, p. 17.
22. See A. Bukhvostov's speech to the Third Congress of ASMB in ASMB, *Materialy III-go s'ezda belorusskogo profsoyuza ASM*, Minsk, 2000, pp. 19-32.
23. *RFE/RL Newsline*, Aug. 29, 2001. The phrase belongs to the U.S. Secretary of State.
24. A. Bukhvostov, "Metropolitenskaya zabastovka: nekotorye vyvody i uroki," *Narodnaya volya* (Minsk), July 15, 1997.
25. UN Human Development Reports, hdr.undp.org/reports/global/2002.
26. *SNG v 2001 g.: statisticheskii spravochik*, individually p. 736: *SNG v 2002 g.: : statisticheskii spravochik*, p.385.
27. *SNG v 2001 g. : statisticheskii spravochik*, p. 115.
28. *SNG v 2002 g.: statisticheskii spravochik*, pp. 129-30; *SNG v 2001 g.: statisticheskii spravochik*, pp. 140-41.
29. ASMB, *Informatsionnyi material uchastniku IV vneocherednogo plenuma sovet profsoyuza*, Feb. 2002, p. 15; unpublished data from ASMB; EIU, *Country Report: Belarus*, June 2003, p. 23.
30. *SNG v 2002g : : statisticheskii spravochik.*, pp. 232-33; BFTU, *Novosti Federatsii profsoyuzov*, no. 6, June 2001, p. 32; EIU, *Country Report: Belarus*, June 2003, p. 24.
31. K. Gaiduk, et al., *Byelorusskaya ekonomika*, p. 88; *SNG v 2002 g. : statisticheskii spravochik*, p. 230.
32. *SNG v 2001 g.: statisticheskii spravochik*, pp. 260. 691, 507.
33. Ibid., p. 260.
34. *Rabochaya solidarnost'* (Minsk), Feb. 23-Mar. 1, 2001; *Materialy do zvitu ...* p. 1; ASMR, "Itogi raboty mashinostroitel'nogo kompleksa and ASM za 9 months 2001 goda," 2001 (unpublished); "Report of the President to the Fifth Plenum of the ASM Central Committee," Feb. 27, 2002 (unpublished).
35. EIU, *Country Report: Belarus*, Feb. 2001, p. 16.
36. During most of the Brezhnev period, Belarus was headed by P. Masherov, whose administration was distinguished by its relative honesty and competence, against the general Soviet background of deepening corruption and mediocrity. Masherov's memory is still revered by Byelorussians old enough to remember him. (He died in a plane crash in the early 1980s, giving rise to the popular belief that his death was ordered by Brezhnev.) Apart from Masherov's personal qualities, Byelorussians point to the impact of World War Two on the republic, which had a powerful partisan movement and lost one citizen out of four under the Nazi occupation. Well into the 1970s, a large part of Belarus's top officialdom had been former partisans, including Masherov, himself a former partisan commander. Byelorussia's leaders, so the argument goes, were formed in the crucible of guerilla struggle and so remained closer to the people. During the Brezhnev period, socio-economic development in Belarus significantly outpaced that of Ukraine and Russia.

    A respected Russian economist described Byelorussians as "partisans by nature." During a visit to Minsk in the early 1980s as part of research on living standards, he asked the republican Statistics Committee for data, knowing full well that information on incomes and their distribution were tightly kept state secrets, at least in Russia. To his amazement, the Byelorussian officials gave him free access, telling him to take whatever he needed.
37. ASMB, *Informatsionnyi material uchastniku II plenuma soveta profsoyuza ASM*, May 29, 2001, Minsk, p. 47.

Chapter Ten

THE UNION OF AUTO AND FARM-MACHINE WORKERS OF BELARUS

Opportunities Lost, And Perhaps Found

The Union of Auto and Farm-Machine Workers of Belarus (ASMB) is the largest industrial union in the country. At its founding in 1990, it had 240,000 members, down to 190,000 by 1998. Of the 190,000, 145,332 were employed in 103 enterprises, the others being pensioners and students. Another 5,880 factory employees or 3.8 per cent of the sector's work force belonged to alternative unions or were not union members.[1] The Byelorussian Federation of Trade Unions (BFP), to which ASMB is affiliated, claimed a total membership of four million in 2002, or about ninety per cent of the employed work force. The federation had thirty-two sectoral and nine territorial (regional or city) affiliates.[2]

Byelorussian Specificity

Besides the government's refusal of "shock therapy" and its repression of oppositional unions, two other elements of the "objective" situation deserve special mention: the high level of concentration of ASMB's membership and the experience of struggle the members brought into the post-Soviet period.

At the beginning of 2000, ninety-three per cent of the factory employees in ASMB were concentrated in three of the country's six regions, with Minsk and the Minsk region themselves accounting for sixty-nine per cent and for over a half of the plants.[3] Nearly half of all the factory employees in the union were employed in only six large plants all located one district of the capital. This gave ASMB an imposing physical presence at the geographical centre of state power, something the government could not ignore, especially after the strike wave of April 1991 that had so shaken the republic. The concentrated membership facilitated coordination of action and the flow of information within the union, both vertically and horizontally. Along with Belarus's relatively small size, it allowed the union to do away with regional committees, which played a mostly conservative role in Russia and Ukraine. Instead, the Republican Council appointed its representatives to the three main regions of concentration outside of Minsk. The absence of regional committees also freed additional resources for the national office, which received fifteen per cent per cent of the dues (2.5 of which went to the FPB), as compared to the de facto 4.5 per cent received in Ukraine and even less in Russia.[4]

Unlike their Russian and Ukrainian counterparts, the majority of ASMB members brought into the post-Soviet period experience of independent collective action: the 1989-90 movement in Gomel region to obtain support for the victims of Chernobyl and the April 1991 strikes set off by the price increases decreed in Moscow. ASMB members were key actors in both mobilizations, which were largely successful. This experience provided a foundation upon which a culture of resistance could be built.

ASMB also entered the post-Soviet period with a national leadership and a significant minority of enterprise and shop leaders committed to independent trade-unionism. After the strikes of April 1991, some of the leaders who had stood by passively or opposed the strikes were voted out of office and replaced by the strike leaders. Those who supported the strikes—and, surprisingly, there was a small minority that did—found new support among the membership for taking independent positions vis-à-vis management. But even where the mobilization did not lead to the ouster of subservient leaders—this was the case in the majority of enterprises—the latter came under new pressure from the members to show more firmness in their dealings with management.[5] The power of a mobilized, united labour movement left a strong impression on even the most conservative union leaders, as well as on managers and government officials. The April 1991 events had a similar impact on the Radio-Electronics Union (REP), the other large industrial union, which at the time had 260,000 members, but was reduced to 70,000 by 2000. (The sector had been heavily involved in defence production.) This gave ASMB's leadership an important ally at the national level, something that was sorely missing for Zlenko in Ukraine.

The election of Bukhvostov as President of ASMB in November 1990 was a reflection of the oppositional mood and the activism in society at the time. Bukhvostov was well-known for his role in the Chernobyl movement. He chose for his vice president a young foundry worker who had been a shop committee chairperson at the Minsk Truck Factory (MAZ) but had been removed in 1989 for fighting corruption in the plant's union and administration.[6] On the eve of the April 1991 strikes, the leaders of ASMB and REP, having failed to push the BFP into action to obtain a wage increase from the government, successfully negotiated one on their own in most of their plants. But they still did not hesitate to support the strike once it broke out spontaneously. Despite widespread of mistrust of union leaders among workers, Bukhvostov was elected to the Minsk strike committee.

Promoting Independence

Of the three unions under study, ASMB had the best initial conditions for a decisive break with the Soviet legacy of subordination to management and the state. Its national leadership was committed to independent trade-unionism and it enjoyed the support of a significant minority of union leaders in the plants. Even more important, the union had a mobilized base and informal shop-floor leaders, the strike committee activists of April 1991, who were pushing "from below." It took Zlenko almost eight years to get his union to amend ASMU's constitution to exclude management from elected positions. But ASMB's constitution, adopted at the founding congress in 1991, stated that "Membership in the union is suspended when a member moves into…a management position…or becomes an owner employing hired labour."[7] True, the wording was ambiguous, a concession made to conservative local leaders, who balked at expelling management, since it left open the possibility that managers who were already union members might remain members. The decision left with the local unions.[8] All the same, the constitution made clear from the start that the union viewed the interests of workers and managers as incompatible and that the latter should not be members of the union.

In the union's first years, the national leaders actively promoted independence at the plant level. Nikolai Belanovskii, ASMB's first Vice President, explained in 1992:

> The biggest problem at first involved breaking the old mentality of the enterprise committees. They were used to waiting for instructions from above. We put moral pressure on them; and we can do that because our authority is rising among the workers, who can see the sort of things we are doing. The rank and file are beginning to ask a lot of questions of their [plant] committees. Many of the people who haven't been able to change their ways are leaving. Others are trying to change…The experience of April 1991 pushed consciousness forward and allowed the emergence of new potential leaders…At the Ball-bearing plant, the

members of the strike committee were elected to the new plant committee. We're working closely with them, teaching them the ropes. It's a pleasure to work with these new people, since our views coincide. You see, after we created our new Republican Council, there was a gap between the republican organization and the plant committees. We wanted to pose things in a radical way and to speed up change but we had to deal with existing plant committees, who often don't understand our approach and want to smooth over problems with the administration...It's a complex issue. For example, at the Tractor Factory, the [conservative] plant committee got mad that certain shop committees were inviting us directly and not going through them...But on the other hand, there's an urgent need for change...I can't work openly with a strike committee to overthrow an existing union committee. But we do invite their representatives to plenums of our Council, and that gets the plant committees angry.[9]

In 1992, ASMB and REP formed the Byelorussian Independent Association of Industrial Unions (BNAPP), even while remaining in the FPB. There they constituted a militant pole that eventually helped to push the federation to adopt more independent positions vis-à-vis the government. But in the early years, BNAPP often organized protest actions independently of the federation.

Unlike their Russian colleagues, ASMB's leaders did not attribute magical significance to the term "social partnership." When they used it, it meant only that management and the state, on the one hand, and unions, on the other, agreed to be bound by negotiated collective agreements. That did not change the fact that the "partners'" interests are fundamentally contradictory and that the collective agreement merely reflects the balance of forces at the time of its signing. Bukhvostov told ASMB's Third Congress in September 2000:

> It would be very naive to think that you can get results and make progress in wages and living standards merely by negotiating. Without forceful collective action by the unions, negotiations usually end in concessions on the unions' part...We obtained the best results in the negotiations that were backed by the threat of mass protests in February and December 1999, and after the mass demonstrations of July 1998 and September 1999. But that's not enough. We have to mobilize much more if we are to win our goals.[10]

Bukhvostov often stressed the central importance of the strike weapon.[11] Negotiations of the first sectoral agreement with the government, which was signed in October 1991, were accompanied by a very real strike threat. In those early heady days, a union leaflet went even further, declaring that "the strike is not the ultimate weapon. The ultimate weapon is when workers pick up cobblestones."[12] ASMB's Second Congress in 1995 established a national strike fund based on contributions of 2.5 per cent of the dues. But, again, participation was left to the decision of the local unions.[13] Eventually, however, changes to the law and the threat of repression (especially after the metro workers' strike), as well as demoralization, made national strikes impossible. The strikes that occurred, and there was a considerable number, were mostly local, brief wildcats, spontaneous or secretly union-organized. The strike fund was used mainly to support persecuted activists and for solidarity with strikes in other sectors and countries and with the victims of natural disasters.[14] To encourage independence, the union guaranteed up to a half-year's wages from the fund to union officials who lost elections and could not find appropriate work.[15] ASMB also made good use of the provision of the Labour Code allowing union to demand the removal of recalcitrant directors in plants that had especially serious health and safety problems or where wages were not paid.

Although it was unable to organize national strikes, ASMB's relations with the government were marked by an almost continuous chain of mass marches, demonstrations, petition drives, picketing, and law suits. The president of the union of the Minsk Gear Factory gave the following account of sectoral negotiations with the government in the late 1990s:

> We have our demands, and the Ministry has its own. We don't make concessions but immediately organize picketing to exert pressure. But since that has no effect; we convoke an assembly of delegates elected from our plants and we invite the Minister and the directors. Again, no effect. Then we announce that we are organizing a mass demonstration to back our demands. The last negotiations, we didn't even have to hold the demonstration, since the President declared it was a threat to national security. He told his Minister: "Either you resolve the conflict or you're fired." And so we negotiated. Since our starting demands were higher than what we realistically hoped for, we finally agreed on a "rather decent" contract. Except for bank employees and state functionaries, we have the highest wages in the republic.[16]

These mobilizations, undertaken with or without other unions, were not the exercises in venting steam that Russia's FNPR conducted. They were organized around concrete, winnable demands, most often wages increases, and they almost always led to at least partial concessions on the part of government. The demands were not simply filed away after the protests. The government's response was closely monitored, analyzed and discussed. If it was judged unsatisfactory, the campaign continued.[17] The workers' attitudes and their state of readiness for collective action were constant themes of discussion at the ninety-seven-member Republican Council and the Presidium, the seventeen-member executive council. The national leaders frequently gauged rank-and-file attitudes and opinions through surveys.

Local strikes were quite common in ASM. Together with the pressure on the government by the national union and its allies, they were a key reason why non-payment of wages did not become a major problem in the sector. (At the same time, as argued earlier, the government's economic strategy and its own corresponding legitimating arguments made it particularly vulnerable to work protest.) These local strikes were openly encouraged and supported by the ASMB's national office. For example, in December 1997, over the head of the enterprise committee, it called on the workers of Gomsel'mash to conduct a general warning strike to protest a two-month delay in wages. (The unon had successfully pressured the government into granting the ailing plant [which makes combines] a large loan, but that did not solve the wage-payment problem.)[18] Where local union leaders were close to management, workers struck on their own. In September 2001, the workers of the Tractor Factory, whose union leaders were loyal to management, downed tools and poured into the street to protest a month's delay in paying their wages. ASMB's national paper wrote:

> The indignant workers of MTZ blocked traffic on Dolgobrodskii St. [a major thoroughfare]. Their decisive act again proved that workers can get respect for their rights not by idle talk in the changing rooms and or by giving the finger in their pockets, but by protest, open and bold. The bosses immediately come running, and the police hide behind the fence...This time the enterprise's unions were not the organizers, and that is a serious wake-up call for worker activists. It is easy for a union to lose a sense of the workers' mood, but with that it can also lose their trust. The union committee was not the organizer but it joined the ranks of the protesters, trying to understand and support the injured workers. At the first signal, Aleksandr Bukhvostov arrived on the street that was bristling with anger. The protest bore fruit. On the same day, branches of the Savings Bank began to pay out the wages for August...We recall that Director Leonov once said that his subordinates would never march with banners onto the square...It turns out they did and they didn't bother to ask his permission.[19]

Most of these local strikes were over unpaid wages, but some were to back demands for increased wages,[20] strike demands that had not been heard in Russia or Ukraine for many years.

ASMB's national leadership devoted a lot of effort to educating the rank and file and keeping them informed. In 1997, the union launched a campaign, asking the members to sign membership cards anew. This was accompanied by oral and printed information on the union's history and the gains it had made for the members over the years. The goal was to make membership in the union more a conscious choice. And despite fears that it might backfire and lose many members to the union, ninety-eight per cent (virtually all the non-managerial members) signed the cards. In 1998, ASMB replaced its weekly bulletin, published jointly with REP, by an eight-page weekly paper with a print run of 7,000-10,000. Since the mass media in Belarus were mostly state-controlled or loyal to the President, the paper was read with interest by members, at least when the local unions distributed it, which was not always. Bukhvostov explained the goal: "Information about the union, about the struggles we are conducting has to reach the members, attract them, call them to participate in all the union's actions. If workers know more about what we are doing, they will trust us more, and that means they will participate with us in our collective actions."[21] The Republican Council also adopted a programme of rank-and-file education and for training union educators, which carried out with the support of TIE, Western trade unions, and the School for Worker Democracy.[22] For its Third Congress in 2000, it produced a video with scenes from the unions' struggle of the preceding five years.

At that Congress, Bukhvostov gave the following evaluation of the progress that had been made in promoting union independence and membership activism:

> We succeeded in creating an authoritative trade-union association, ASMB. We drew fire from those who were accustomed to life as time-servers in the union and for whom the interests of the working person are only important up to a point, as well as from those in government who would like to turn the unions into corporatist bodies that help the state and employers to exploit workers.
>
> We are far from having achieved all that we wanted…In our opinion, one of the main reasons we have not been able better to defend the living standards of our workers and pensioners is that ASMB has not yet become a school of struggle for workers and has not taught them to fight for their rights. One thing is clear: only forceful mass action in defense of workers' rights will yield positive results in today's situation. The alternative to struggle is a miserable existence and the rule of arbitrariness.[23]

The promotion of union independence met with a lot of resistance from local leaders. Bukhvostov had to note at the congress that "some union committees dose out the information they receive from the Council; they don't distribute the paper to workers, and so forth."[24] The national office's enthusiasm for rank-and-file education was also far from universally shared. The majority local leaders rejected a proposal to create a national education fund. Only a few of them set up their own educational programmes, as the national office recommended, and the latter had trouble recruiting new workers for its courses because plant leaders were not always helpful in obtaining time off for their members.[25] Already at the Second Congress in 1995, pressure from plant committees forced an amendment in the constitution concerning membership of managerial personnel in the union. The article was further watered down to allow even members who moved into managerial positions to stay in the union. Whereas the constitution had called for their membership to be suspended, now the paragraph read: "Membership in the union can be suspended on decision of the enterprise union organization when a member moves into an employer position."[26] A decade after the union's founding, there was still at least one plant (Avtoagregat in the town of Borisov), whose president was a shop supervisor. In 2001, Aleksandr Evdokimchik, national Vice President, estimated that only between twenty to thirty per cent of the large local unions were in any real sense independent from management, and that might have been an overestimate. This was more than in Ukraine and certainly more than in Russia, but it was far from the leadership's vision in 1990.

Political Strategy and Mixed Messages

Part of the reason why that vision had not been realized lay, as was the case in Russia and Ukraine, in the demoralizing effects of the economic crisis. Although the immediately economic causes of insecurity were weaker in Belarus, the level of political intimidation was significantly greater. As worker activism and the influence of the alternative unions declined, local leaders felt less pressure "from below." But that is only part of the explanation. The other part lies in the political strategy of the national office.

In 1990, Bukhvostov was opposed to the "politicization of trade unions. Parties…mean struggle for power, the pursuit of often dubious political ambitions. That distracts workers from defending their economic and social interests…the only goal and task of trade unions."[27] This was a widely held view at the time among independent trade-unionists, a reaction against party-state control of the unions under the Soviet system. However, it did not take Bukhvostov long to change his mind. In December 1992, the national leaders of ASMB and REP created an organizing committee to prepare the founding congress of the Party of Labour of Belarus (PT). That took place on November 25, 1993. The PT defined itself as parliamentary and social-democratic, proclaiming wage-labourers its social base and its main function "to pursue the cause of trade unions by political means."[28] It proclaimed its categorical opposition to the government's economic policies, under which living standards had plummeted, industry was collapsing, and "uncontrolled bureaucratic privatization" was occurring.[29] Its own economic programme, on the other hand, was not very clear, except that it wanted to change fiscal and credit policy with a view to promoting a recovery in industry. It also called for a mixed economy, a full-blown welfare state, and for state regulation to be exercised by "economic means," that is, through indirect methods rather than by direct state administration of enterprises, as under the old system.[30] In 1994, Bukhvostov was elected under the banner of the PT to the Supreme Soviet from the town of Gomel. In parliament, he promoted labour interests, including a bill that gave wages priority claim to enterprise funds. (The bill was vetoed by Lukashenko.)

Lukashenko's coup in 1996 raised ASMB's political opposition to a qualitatively new level. Bukhvostov was among the minority of deputies who refused to enter the newly-created pseudo-parliament. From then on, practically every issue of the union's bulletin or newspaper carried no-holds-barred criticism of the government and, in particular, of the President. The government became the union's main target, at least as far as the national office was concerned. Bukhvostov told the Third Congress in September 2000: "The issue of a radical increase in wages is first and foremost a political issue. Political decisions must lead to reforms in the economy and in the enterprises and then and at the same time to an increase in the welfare of workers. That's what we are working for."

Targeting the government made sense, to the degree that its policies, and especially their more arbitrary aspects, were an obstacle to improving the workers' situation. Moreover, as already noted, the state assumed a great deal of direct responsibility for the economic fate of the enterprises, which continued to be state-owned. The sectoral agreement negotiated with the government had more practical meaning in Belarus, than in Ukraine and certainly Russia, inasmuch as the union was able to go to the government to demand help for enterprises where wages fell below the negotiated minimum and often to get action. For this, ASMU and ASMR's leaders were envious of their Byelorussian colleagues.

The problem was not the union's targeting of the government. It was rather that, in the name of the fight against the government, the national office relaxed its pressure on management and on local union leaders who were subservient to management. This, in turn, was closely related to a more fundamental problem: for all its opposition to the government's economic policies, ASMB did not have a coherent alternative programme of its own, certainly not one that its members could embrace. To the extent that it presented an alternative, it was an essentially liberal one, though generous social and wage policies were unrealistically tacked on. Ironically, this strategy undermined ASMB's ability effectively to oppose the Lukashenko regime, and in the end, threatened not only the political independence of the union, but its very existence.

Not that the national leadership completely dropped its insistence on local unions being independent from management. Bukhvostov, for one, continued to voice criticism of local leaders

> ...who stand on two stools: they nod at management and then they nod at the workers, and in the end they do nothing. What sort of negotiations are they when you come to the director on half-bent knees and say: "We understand but we're afraid that the workers will start pressing; so give us at least a one-per-cent raise"? But when you kick open the door, bang your fist on the table, and say: "These are our demands!"—that's a worker's stand. It's organized pressure that brings results.

Nevertheless, his message was increasingly ambiguous. At the Third Congress, after subjecting the government's economic policy to withering criticism, he said:

> In recent years, we have adopted the tactic of supporting the positions of our social partners—the employers' and directors' organizations—on questions of economic policy. We don't agree on everything but we are acting out of pragmatic considerations. This is not "showing understanding for their situation." We are basing our mutual relations on an analysis of the real situation, an understanding of what and upon whom economic and political policy depends. Of course, if we saw that a specific director was not up to muster, we proposed that the ministry take measures to strengthen management [i.e., remove the director]...We did this in a number of plants. Of late, however, directors have come under strong political pressure and they are being dragged into an anti-union campaign...Since we realize that in the present situation many things are beyond the control of management, we have redirected our demands to the government...
>
> I can understand the behaviour of many of the directors at present. Before 1998, when we organized our protests, I used to meet the directors of the Minsk plants and explain our aims. After all, our main goal

> has always been that the plants should function at capacity. Some agreed with us; other did not agree fully. Our logic isn't complicated: "If you can't solve our problems, Mr. Director, then at least don't interfere; and better yet, help us, because any government is afraid of mass worker protest."
>
> In conducting this policy, we often did show understanding for management's situation. We did that even when management was making use of our members' dues and not transferring them to the union, as happened at the Motor Factory, BATE and others. [This was before Lukashenko's decree prohibiting automatic check-off. After the Congress, ASMB successfully sued directors for the dues.] We negotiated, instead of firmly holding these administrations to account. Were we wrong to act in that way, or should we have yielded to the government's efforts to bait us against management? The government's representatives kept telling us that wages in the plants are management's problem.[31]

In private conversation, Bukhvostov pointed out a series of plants, like the Tractor, Ball-Bearing and the Borisov Starter Factory (BATE), that began to have economic problems after their directors publicly criticized government policy: "We have our conflicts with the directors. But we have to protest against this and stand together with them against the government."

This was also why Bukhvostov did not strongly resist pressure to soften the wording of ASMB's constitution on the membership of managers in the union:

> We discussed that article and its application at length in 1991. At that time, I was a hundred-per-cent convinced of the need to get rid of the directors. Yet, when we got down to work, we came up against the ambiguous position of the director in a situation where property relations are not yet clearly defined. It wasn't easy to get the original article passed, but my authority helped push it through. In practice, however, we left it to each plant to decide. This was formalized by an amendment at the Second Congress. Some directors left on their own, but most don't want to leave and some were even upset at the idea that they shouldn't be allowed to be members.
>
> Personally, I made my choice long ago, and all my trade-union activity from 1987 onward shows whose interests I have defended. No one can doubt where I stand in a dispute between workers and management. On the contrary, I often try to make the lines of conflict clearer in

order to strengthen mobilization and in no case do I blur them. But on other hand, I can't really say the director is always the proper target of our efforts. In our situation, the director is himself in many ways a person without rights. His hands are tied by the decisions of the owner, the state. So I always try to evaluate what management really can do itself.

The root problem is state policy; the state is the prime object of our struggle, the struggle for democracy. The government defines many of the parameters of socio-economic relations. But many of our unions don't understand that we have to shift to the political struggle. The government would love for us to restrict our struggle to the enterprise. They tell us to negotiate with the director and then they tell the director that if he signs anything approaching what the union is asking they'll tear off his head. So from a political point of view, this is an entirely different situation than in Ukraine or Russia, where the unions have more political space, more freedom. If they're weak, then that's because they're passive or don't know how to do the everyday, systematic work of mobilizing. But they have employers they can pressure.

In June 2001, with presidential elections approaching, the Republican Council issued a public statement, under Bukhvostov's signature, defending directors who had come under pressure for criticizing the government. It singled out the case of M. Leonov, director of the Tractor Factory, who had been talking to the political opposition and even publicly expressed some political ambitions of his own.[32] (Following the presidential elections, Leonov was arrested and sentenced to prison for purchasing materials for the factory at inflated prices and failing to repatriate earnings from abroad.) The statement called on employers' associations to join efforts with ASMB to defend directors: "Together we can erect a barrier to lawlessness and administrative arbitrariness and clear the way for the effective operation of the enterprises, and that means to higher wages and the well-being of working people!"[33]

Not everyone in the union agreed with that position, which, among other things, implied that "effective operation" of the plants means the same thing for workers as for management. Moreover, if managers' freedom of action was really so circumscribed by the state, was not that all the more reason to treat them as instruments, willing or otherwise, of the state, and not as potential allies? Why defend them and even allow them to be union members? Granted that the government was the ultimate source of the workers' problems, but did it really make sense to call for a political alliance with directors and to be less demanding on them about transferring union dues? N. Boiko, president of the

Motovelo Factory (he had led the strike in April 1999 as the local vice-president) took issue with Bukhvostov: "If the director's hands are tied by the government, then that's his problem. He has a directors' association to defend him. That's not our job." N. Pokhabov, a plumber and shop chairperson at BATE, considered that his union president purposely exaggerated the director's political problems in order to justify his own reluctance to confront the him to defend the members' interests. Staff members of the national office confirmed that BATE's president would have been loyal to management regardless of whether the director had come under pressure for publicly criticizing Lukashenko. Pohabov also pointed out that no one was forcing directors to stay in their posts, which offered them ample material reward. It was well known, for example, that close relatives of BATE's director headed commercial firms that were trading in the starters produced by the plant. Even if delays in paying wages and transferring dues were related to the director's fall from political grace, the union should not let management off the hook. "It's not a personal matter," explained Pokhabov. "The director is part of a system, and that was his choice. If all the local unions put pressure on management by threatening to stop production, the government would have no choice but to let them raise wages and to force them to transfer the unions' dues."

The mixed messages coming from the national office took pressure off subservient local leaders and undermined the efforts of forces in the union that were trying to defend independent positions. (See the next chapter.) No one openly challenged Bukhvostov's position, but even among the national leadership some expressed doubts. Evdokimchik, the Vice President (formerly a highly skilled worker at the Minsk Ball-Bearing Factory, who had headed its strike committee in April 1991 and was subsequently elected plant president), told a workers' seminar in May 2001:

> We have made a lot of progress in promoting independence from the state, both in the union as such and in workers' consciousness. But as far as our relationship with management is concerned, we haven't yet achieved clarity. You can justify that in various ways. But the fact remains that we haven't kicked out management. Some argue that if we do that, management will turn around and destroy the union. Not all members of the Presidium feel that even top management should be excluded. I feel that they should, but I'm not sure workers understand that. They tend to focus on the personal traits of managers. But, you know, being a "good guy" is not a profession.

One could, in fact, discern at least three positions within the union on the issue of union-management relations. People like Evdokimchik, Boiko and Pokhabov were not necessarily opposed to a political alliance with directors and even with liberal forces against Lukashenko, though they expressed some doubts. But they did not feel that was reason to make concessions to management in the enterprises. Bukhvostov, on the other hand, even while calling for union independence from management, gave priority to the political struggle against the Lukashenko regime and was, as a result, prepared—at least up to a point—to show more tolerance toward management. A third position, by far the most widely shared among local union leaders, favoured "social partnership."

That was the position of Mariya, president of the union at the Moghilev Trailer Factory. Very self-assured, she was candid in her support of "partnership." She had been president since the plants' opening in 1985, and apparently not much had changed since then. Her members had sat out April 1991. "We get along fine with director," she said. "There have been no real conflicts. We always find common ground. But our demands have to be reasonable. The main thing is that people have to work. We need discipline and quality." To support her position, she noted that employment had not declined at the factory, as it had almost everywhere else. They were still 4000 employees, and the director guaranteed jobs to the technical school graduates when they returned from their military service, though she admitted that few took up the offer, since wages were so low. On the other hand, the collective agreement provided subsidies for births, weddings, funerals and for single mothers. In addition, sixty per cent of union's dues were spent on "material aid." Bargaining that year, 1999, had been difficult, and the union had had to make concessions. "We have to explain to the workers that neither we nor the director are to blame, but the government, since it ties any increase in wages to increased production." Despite this, Mariya was not exactly rushing into battle with the government. During the course of the Republican Council's discussion of plans for a national protest, she intervened with the suggestion to turn to "real business": how the Council might show its recognition of labour veterans for their long years of service.

In an interview to ASMB's paper, A. Kudelevich, president of the Tractor Factory, argued that union-management partnership was still relevant because of the difficult economic situation: the drop in demand, the scarcity of capital, the prevalence of barter.

> In these conditions, we understand that we are in the same boat and if we don't row in the same direction, we simply won't survive. We have a normal, healthy collective, and if we explain the situation and seek a way out through our joint efforts, then nothing unexpected arises. We have no problem with our partnership. There are only problems on the macroeconomic level, that of the country as a whole. Of course, it's sometimes hard to explain to people why the administration can't find

twenty-two million to transfer to the union its dues, when it can find 2.5 billion rubles to pay wages. But we explain the situation to our members and we meet with understanding and support.[34]

A Self-Defeating Strategy

Both Mariya and Kudelevich justifed their "partnership" with management by pointing to the government's policies as the obstacle to improving the workers' situation. Bukhvostov would certainly not have approved their expressions of solidarity with management, but the fundamental logic of his strategy was not so different form theirs. The irony was that in practice that logic undermined the very goal for which the strategy (at least in Bukhvostov's case) had bene conceived: ending the dictatorship and changing economic policy. In reality, the union leaders that were subservient to management and justified this by blaming government policy did not themselves mobilize their members for the collective actions that were directed against the government. The main reason they did not, whatever their own political views, was that their directors were under strong pressure from the government to keep the workers from participating, and they were not about to defy their directors. The local unions that seriously mobilized their members were those that were independent from management, those that were not afraid to confront it. Boiko of the Motovelo explained:

> In general, relations with management are okay and we usually come to some kind of agreement. But when there are demonstrations, the director begs me not to send people. The KGB also pays me visits me but they don't put pressure; they only ask for information. But the pressure on the director is strong, and so is his pressure on us. But I tell him that we're going anyway, that if the committee doesn't organize it, other people would, in the shops. It would be chaos. So why not do it in an organized way? After the demonstration, the chief engineer says to me: "Great job!"

When ASMB in 1998 decided for tactical reasons to call off a demonstration directed at the government, Bukhvostov had to go to the Ball-Bearing plant to explain personally the decision to calm down the angry workers. But because there were few unions in ASMB like Motovelo and the Ball-Bearing Factory, from the mid 1990s onwards, ASMB was never able to bring more than 5000-6000 of its members into the streets of Minsk. The vast majority of the protesters were from only a few of plants, like Ball-Bearing, Motovelo, Special Instrument, the Gear factories. The giants, like the Tractor, Motor and Truck factories, usually sent token delegations of only 200-300 people each.[35] "We cannot be satisfied by the work of a series of union committees in mobilizing for our mass actions," Bukhvostov told the Third Congress. "Here there are objective and subjective factors...More than 70,000 of our members work in Minsk. If our demands were actively supported by even half of those who are working, the effect would be totally different."[36]

It was as if a tacit agreement had been made between the national office and the local leaders: the latter gave their formal support to Bukhvostov in his fight with the government, and in return Bukhvostov left them in peace to be "partners" with the management. In the estimation of the president of the Gear Factory, at least half of the Presidium in reality opposed Bukhvostov's position toward the government. Only a minority of the plant presidents were even members of the PT, which by the time of the presidential elections in 2000 had a membership of only 1300.

But there was also some open opposition to the politics of the national office. In 1995, when the post of national vice president became vacant, the Republican Council decided to elect two vice-presidents for political balance. One was S. Fedorovich, conservative president of the Tractor Factory. The other was Evdokimchik, who represented the anti-"partnership" current. As vice-president, Fedorovich came out publicly against Bukhvostov's tough stand towards the government. The differences came to a head in the fall of 1998, when Fedorovich opposed a planned demonstration to back the demand for higher wages. The government was desperately trying to prevent the action. Fedorovich lost out and eventually left ASMB. But some local leaders continued to complain that Bukhvostov was getting carried away with politics, that he was rejecting dialogue with the government, that the union's paper was overly politicized, and that he was neglecting the everyday, concrete concerns of the members. Bukhvostov acknowledged this opposition at the Third Congress:

> In 1997, we demanded that wages reach 200-250 U.S.$ by 1999. The Council and myself were accused of playing political games. Unfortunately, there were also some colleagues in this union who did not fully understand the role and task of unions and union politics, the importance of the union's actions in defence of the working person's interests. They want results and aren't satisfied with the mere existence of unions that do not go beyond declarations. It was clear that the enterprises could not radically raise wages unless the state's policy changed...Some activists and elected leaders are frightened by our Council's principled position. We can hear complaints that we don't make enough use of negotations and meetings with government officials, that we should stay

within the limits set by the government, etc. But over the course of 1995-2000, myself and other leaders met personally with all the top government officials. Our union's power and authority helped us in these talks. They take our union into account. But the results are insufficient.[37]

A few days before that congress, the union of the Tractor Factory publicly come out in support of an alternative for ASMB president—an assistant director and former vice president of the union at the tractor plant. The factory's delegation to the congress—which included General-Director Leonov, the same one that Bukhvostov would publicly defend a year later!—denied that they were acting under pressure from the government. The problem, they argued, was over-politicization of the union, in particular its fraternization with the political opposition. Bukhvostov was putting too much emphasis on struggle rather than dialogue and consultation. One delegate complained about that the "whole atmosphere of the [president's] report and the video [portraying the struggles of the previous five years] is saturated with struggle, struggle, struggle. I think that if struggle is going to be the basis of the union's policy, there will surely be no victors in that struggle." Despite this challenge, Bukhvostov was easily re-elected by a vote of 182 against 60.[38]

A few months later, in February 2001, the plant committee of the Minsk Motor Factory, which had also supported the challenge to Bukhvostov, openly defied the Republican Council's decision—for which its own delegates to the Council had voted!—by publicly refusing to participate in a demonstration to demand higher wages. It sent out a fax to the other unions in Minsk, complaining that the demonstration was "overly politicized" and "threatened the stability of the state." Of course, unions like those of the Motor and Tractor Factories were not going to mobilize anyway, and no one had illusions about that. But this was open defiance, and an article in ASMB's paper condemned it as "strikebreaking." Subsequently, things were smoothed over at special Presidium held at the Motor Factory, and the paper was made to apologize.[39]

The vote in favour of Bukhvostov at the Third Congress was much larger than the actual support for his policies among local leaders. Most, in fact, were deeply ambivalent about him. They were not themselves prepared to stand up to their directors or to defy Lukashenko, but they did not mind—at least until it directly threatened their own comfortable lives— having a bold, forceful leader behind whose broad back they could hide. They knew well that if wages in ASM were among the highest in the economy and paid more or less on time, they owed that in large part to Bukhvostov's aggressive policies. But a union can only go so far on the force of its president's personality and the active support he receives from only a handful of factories, and not the largest at that.

A Worker Ideology?

Management's opposition to participation of its employees in actions against the government and the consequent refusal of the plant leaders to mobilize for them do not fully explain the weak participation in these actions in past years. After all, workers took part in wildcats against management, bypassing their passive unions to do it. Another element of the explanation is ASMB's failure to offer its members a realistic, acceptable alternative to Lukashenko's policies. Many of the union's criticisms of government policy—especially its arbitrary, partisan, and repressive features—could make sense to workers. But they did not add up to a coherent alternative. In private conversation, the union's economist admitted this. The same emerged from discussions with PT activists, who were not clear what to tell workers about the party's economic alternative to Lukashenko's policies. To complicate matter, ASMB's economist noted that the government had adopted some of ASMB's proposals.[40]

Bukhvostov often spoke of the need to cultivate an independent "workers' ideology" among members. That was the declared goal of the unions' educational activity. But despite its references to "social guarantees" and "social justice," the economic programme defended by ASMB and the PT had a pronounced liberal accent. The PT's platform for the 2001 presidential elections emphasized the restoration of democracy, and had an only small section on the economy. It called for a "socially-oriented market economy with different forms of property" that would give people a decent living standards, for "defence of the economic sphere from the arbitrariness of state leaders," "protection of the right of citizens to economic independence," "state support for entrepreneurship," "creation of conditions for domestic and foreign investment."[41] In themselves, these goals did not necessarily amount to a liberal programme but they were vague enough to allow ASMB and the PT to enter into an electoral coalition with rightwing parties opposed to Lukashenko and which had the blessing and financial support of the U.S. State Department and other Western governments (via the permanent mission of the Organization for Security and Cooperation in Europe).[42]

Bukhvostov told the PT's Third Congress on the eve of the presidential elections that the union was fighting "for social justice, democracy, and economic freedom."[43] But could "economic freedom" mean the same thing for workers as employers, even in a country under dictatorship? The union's programme could not help but raise doubts in workers' minds. They were, after all, well aware of the consequences of the economic policies promoted by the West in Russia and Ukraine from information gained from television broadcasts and reports from friends and relatives. Lukashenko also made sure they were informed, since his legitimacy was based largely on the rejection of those policies. Workers could respond positively to the union's condemnation of government repression and arbitrariness but they had to worry about whether Lukashenko's removal might open the way for "shock therapy" in Belarus. (Similar things had happened in recent years in countries like South Africa, South Korea, Mexico after the elections of parties running on a platform of democratic reform.) Many saw the choice as one between Lukashenko's "velvet dictatorship," that was nevertheless defending the country, however ineptly, against international capital, and a formally democratic regime that would carry out the programme of international and domestic capital at the people's expense and against their will.

When asked about their economic programme, ASMB's national leaders, staff and PT activists spoke vaguely about "social-democracy" and the "Swedish model," seemingly oblivious to the profound changes that both had undergone over the past two decades. PT activists often argued that privatization was a necessary condition for investment. At a seminar for PT activists, the REP's national president complained that Lukashenko's policies had cut Belarus off from IMF aid. Zlenko invited him to visit Ukraine to see for himself the consequences of that "aid." Asked what he would answer a worker at the Tractor Factory with its 22,000 employees if he asked about the destruction of Russia's machine-building sector under liberal economic policies, Bukhvostov replied: "I couldn't tell him anything." Vetchinkin spent several hours discussing ASMB's economic programme with Bukhvostov and summed up his position this way: "Let the liberals do their dirty work; we'll be in the opposition to defend the workers." That was not far off the mark. Bukhvostov saw the role of unions as one of permanent opposition in society, where exploitation is an inescapable fact of life. The inevitability of exploitation was proved, in his view, by the Soviet experience. It showed that workers can make a revolution but that a new minority will always end up dominating and exploiting the majority.

The point, of course, is not that ASMB or the PT would have had more success with a socialist programme, which would have been completely unrealistic in the circumstances, except as a distant strategic goal. The point is rather their failure to adopt an independent class position. That led them into a strategic, and not just tactical, alliance with forces hostile to workers and to adopt positions that could not rally the mass of workers. It was not enough to condemn Lukashenko's authoritarianism and arbitrariness. The workers needed answers to their socio-economic concerns. Although the united democratic opposition chose V. Goncharik, President of the BFP, as their candidate in the presidential elections, his platform had nothing—and because of the nature of the coalition, could not have had anything—that might have allowed his government, had he won, to resist the tremendous pressure that the West would have immediately brought to bear on it. Indeed, the choice of Goncharik as candidate of the united opposition was largely the result of his promotion by the U.S. embassy and the OSCE's representative. There were more popular candidates, but, Goncharik's candidacy was calculated to deflect accusations that the opposition was pro-Western and unpatriotic. (The U.S. had pumped fifty million dollars into to the political opposition in the two years before the elections.)[44] The chief of staff of Gonacharik's campaign, a leader of the Woman's Party, kept the unions at arms length, and partly as a result, most of ASMB, including the national office, did not work as actively as it might have in the campaign. Many rank-and-file trade unionists were put off by the negative campaigning of right-wing forces that made broad use of wild, personalized accusations against Lukashenko.

Lukashenko claimed a landslide victory, and even ASMB recognized that he had won a majority. According to a monitor from the British Helsinki Human Rights Group, the main source of unfairness was unequal access to the media, especially electronic. Vote tampering was not a major factor. At a polling station in Minsk monitored by an OSCE-sponsored observation group, no fraud was observed: there Lukashenko received sixty-one per cent of the vote to Goncharik's thirty-five. And Lukashenko's popularity was known to be stronger outside the capital.[45] It should, however, be noted that Lukashenko's showing in the capital was helped by wage increases made in the preceding months, and wages in Minsk were almost always paid on time. There were clear signs that his popularity fell significantly afterwards, though his power, at least internally, remains quite secure.[46]

The nature of ASMB's participation in the elections is evidence of the absence of independent, strategic thinking in the union. One has to wonder whether a purely electoralist party (the question of its programme aside) like the PT made any sense in Byelorussian circumstances. The regime was, after all, a dictatorship. As an electoralist party, the PT had not tried to develop firm roots among the union rank and file. And it would not have been able to even had it tried, given the nature of its programme. In general, the electoral challenge to Lukashenko had a marked adventurist character. At least for the U.S. embassy and the right-wing parties and groups, it seems to have been based on hopes of a "Yugoslav scenario," with Lukashenko in the role of Milosevic and Gonacharik playing Kostunica. But neither of the protagonists fit their assigned roles. It is hard to avoid the impression that the right-wing coalition partners were playing more to a Western, than the Byelorussian, audience, counting on blatant electoral fraud to intensify Western pressure to help them bring down Lukashenko.

The "Opposition Syndrome"

The balance of political forces within the country was such that the opposition could not have dislodged Lukashenko, even if he had resorted to massive fraud. When the results were announced, and with the opposition shouting "fraud," a mere 2000 people came out in Minsk to demonstrate.[47] But had a "Yugoslav scenario" come to pass, the unions would have been in no shape to defend their members in the new political situation. Goncharik's victory would have expanded civil liberties and union rights, but repression was not the only, nor probably the main, cause of the unions' weakness. In the months following Lukashenko's banning of automatic dues check-off, only a few of ASMB's local affiliates were able—or really even tried!—to organize hand-collection of dues. That is a measure of their weakness as an independent force. And after the elections, it was enough for the government merely to refuse to talk to the FPB for its affiliates to force Goncharik to resign and to replace him with an official from Lukashenko's administration. Gonacharik, among other things, was blamed for sabotaging dialogue with the government by refusing to congratulate Lukashenko on his electoral victory and for trying to contest the results in Constitutional Court (which refused to receive the complaint). But what really panicked the FPU's affiliates and set them scurrying to sacrifice Gonacharik was the government ban of automatic dues check-off that came three months after the election. It is hard to see how this labour movement could have defended a Goncharik government against internal, but especially international, pressure to adopt a liberal economic strategy, with all the negative consequences that would have for their members.

The local ASMB leaders who criticized Bukhvostov for politicizing the union and for choosing confrontation over dialogue with the government were obviously justifying their own desire for an easy, secure life. But the criticism itself was not without substance, at least in the sense, as argued earlier, that the political struggle led by the national office was conducted at the expense of building strong, independent organizations in the enterprises. The increasing emphasis on the priority of the fight against the dictatorship pushed ASMB's national leadership into a political alliance with right-wing forces that, while hostile to Lukashenko, were no friends of labour. This, in turn, assured that ASMB would not develop its own economic programme based upon workers' interests.

As a result, ASMB was poorly prepared for Lukasheno's next step. In December 2002, the new head of the FPB spoke at ASMB's Republican Council and demanded Bukhvostov's head. He was easily rebuffed by a vote of fifty-three against eleven, with thirteen abstentions.[48] But in March 2003, the directors of three ASMB plants with 28,500 employees, including 22,000 at the Minsk Truck Factory, under pressure from the government, had little trouble persuading the local union leaders to disaffiliate from ASMB. By the fall of 2003, more than a dozen local unions and 68,000 members had left ASMB. Their decisions depended entirely on the directors. Nowhere were the members consulted, although pro-forma delegates' conferences, dominated by management, ratified the decisions after the fact. At BATE, for example, it was enough for the general-director to inform the president that he would not negotiate with a union affiliated to ASMB for the plant committee to vote to disaffiliate. Only one person opposed the decision, Pokhavov. Here, too, no one bothered to ask the members. It was only Bukhvostov's personal intervention with the director—not with the union!—that got the decision reversed. The reversal, by the way, indicates that the director's freedom of action vis-à-vis the government was not so limited as some union leaders claimed.

These defections illustrate ASMB's main failure: despite comparatively favourable starting conditions, it had not created independent, democratic organizations in the majority of its enterprises. And so at BATE as at MAZ, it all depended on the director. It would, of course, be wrong to say that the national office had been inactive on the issue of union independence. Moreover, one has to recognize that its capacity to intervene in the internal affairs of the enterprises was limited. But promoting independence from management had ceased to be a priority, and the national office was itself sending out mixed messages on the matter. Nor did it make full use of the means of influence it had at its disposal. For example, it might have used the PT to organize and support rank-and-file forces that favoured independence in the conservative plants. That would certainly have improved the state of democracy within ASMB, where Bukhvostov more or less decided policy and the plant presidents formally acquiesced and then went about doing what they wanted. The national leadership could also have given higher priority to the goal of limiting the arbitrary power of management in the enterprise that discouraged activism. As a result, the more active elements among the rank and file were crushed under the weight of the inactive majority. Some joined the alternative unions, but they too were eventually crushed by management, often with the active support of the local ASMB leaders. Bukhvostov himself had a positive attitude to the alternative unions but he did not do much to help them in face of the hostility of his local leaders.

Instead of giving more encouragement and support to these independent elements, Bukhvostov admitted at the Third Congress that the Republican Council had not been as demanding as it might have been toward directors who failed to transfer dues because they were under political pressure from a government that was trying to bait the union against them. It is more than ironic that V. Dybal', the MAZ president who took his union out of ASMB, appears in a video made by the FPB for the presidential campaign speaking out in defence of his director against the government that was persecuting him. Not long after the elections, that director made peace with Lukashenko and told Dybal' to take his union out of ASMB. Dybal' readily obeyed and was rewarded by being made deputy director. (He was replaced in the union by another manager.) The national office was bitter over this betrayal. But one would have had to be blind not to see it coming. Bukhvostov said he was not surprised.

But it was not just the local leadership that bent so easily to the director's will: the rank-and-file did not resist either, except for tiny pockets. Only two shop committees at MAZ did not go along with the disaffiliation—in stamping and body assembly—but most of the workers in these shops did. (Disaffiliation by law is an individual decision.) An adjuster, an activist of the Party of Communists of Belarus (a split-off from the Communist Party of Belarus that opposed Lukashenko), who had never before been active in the union, assumed the leadership of a small group of ASMB loyalists at MAZ that numbered 120 in summer 2003. They were supported by ASMB's national office but they were under heavy pressure from management, which illegally barred representatives of the national office from the plant.

This weak rank-and-file resistance was only partly the result of intimidation by management and enticements offered by the "new" union, including at MAZ free dental care, loans for acquiring apartments, subsidized holidays and other goodies. The fact was that these local unions had done little over the years to promote membership participation and commitment. As "partners," they had no interest in it. As a consequence, most workers could not easily see what difference disaffiliation would make: as an ASMB-affiliate, the union had been an adjunct of management, and as an "independent" union it continued to be. The workers knew little of the national leadership's policies, since their plant committees did not distribute its paper. The subservient character of the union at MAZ was one of the reasons the plant once had one of the largest alternative unions with a membership of 1200 members in 1999. But by 2002, it had dwindled to less than 200.

Of course, a different strategy based on class independence would not have guaranteed success either. But the one that was followed made defeat much more likely. What happened at BATE or MAZ need only be compared with events at the Minsk Ball-Bearing Factory, which had the most independent and democratic organization in ASMB and probably in all of Belarus. (See the next chapter.) Its president, having already beaten back management's efforts to dislodge him, thanks to his rank-and-file support, easily withstood management's pressure to disaffiliate from

ASMB. The Ball-Bearing Factory was not quite unique, but there were very few unions like it. When Bukhvostov and Evdokimchik consulted with the plant presidents in the summer of 2003, it was clear that most would probably fold under pressure. The presidents complained that they had no protection. And they really did not, since they had always relied on management rather than build a base of support among the members.

By that time, ASMB's membership was down to 101,000 working members. The government might have continued to press local unions, through the directors, to disaffiliate, but the FPU apparently did not support that scenario, which would have still left Bukhvostov at the head of a rump ASMB and in possession of its official status and offices in the federation's building. Kozik had to get rid of Bukhvostov without destroying ASMB. This did not prove difficult. In October, ASMB plant presidents who made up the majority in the Presidium met behind Bukhvostov's back and decided to convoke a Republican Council to propose that it call a special congress for December 25, 2003. There would be only one question on its agenda: replacing Bukhvostov. When the Presidium met, of the plant presidents, only Lozovskii of the Ball-Bearing Factory defended Bukhvostov's. The Council met on October 16 and voted to convene the special congress. Then on October 23, the BFP's Council voted to remove Bukhvostov from the federation's executive. In preparing the ASMB congress, the directors helped to make sure that the "correct" delegates were chosen. Representatives of the ASMB's national office were illegally kept out of the plant conferences that elected the delegates, but Kozik was allowed to speak to them. Some activists who protested, including Nikolai Pokhabov at BATE, were fired. He had worked there for almost twenty years. Sensing what was coming, Bukhvostov and a few dozen supporters held a protest demonstration in the centre of Minsk, after the authorities had refused them permission, sending him instead to the city's outskirt. As expected, Bukhvostov was arrested and sentenced to ten days. This evoked expressions of outrage from around the world (Bukhvostov is a member of the executive of the International Metalworkers' Federation) but his own union was silent.

At the congress itself, it was only thanks to the presence of representatives of international and foreign labour organizations that Bukhvostov was even allowed to speak. And yet, his opponents accused him of authoritarianism, apart from his neglect of union functions for politics, the main reproach. In their declaration, they stated that "We support the course adopted by the Byelorussian Federation of Trade Unions for the strengthening and development of social partnership."[49] Despite all the effort that went into making sure the correct delegates were chosen, despite the presence at the congress of representatives of the government and top administrators from the enterprises (union members, some were elected delegates), and despite the open ballot (illegally adopted by the congress), in the end only 227 of the 396 delegates voted to remove Bukhvostov. That gives some idea of the potential for independent trade-unionism that still existed in the union and that the deposed leadership had been unable to develop.

Immediately after the vote, Bukhvostov invited his supporters to found a new independent union. Over forty of the delegates took part in the founding congress of the Independent Union of Auto and Farm-Machine Workers of Belarus and elected Bukhvostov as its president. This opens a new chapter in the history of the Byelorussian labour movement. It remains to be seen, however, what lessons the leaders and members of the new union will draw from the defeat. One thing is clear, there will be no managers in the new union. For this, at least, they can thank Lukashenko.

Notes

1. ASMB, Informatsionnyi material uchastniku seminara predsedatelei profkomov predpriyatii ASM stran SNG, 21-23 aprelya 1988, g. Minsk, 1998, p. 3.
2. BFTU, *Informatsionnyi material uchastniku vneocherdnogo IV s'esda Federatsii profsoyuzov Belarusi*, Minsk, 2002, p.2.
3. ASMB, *Informationno-spravochnyi material k III-emu s'ezdu profsoyuza*, Minsk, Sept. 2000, pp. 21-2.
4. Ibid, p. 18.
5. For example, see the aftermath of the April 1991 events at the BelAZ Truck Factory in "Krizis na BelAZe," in A. Bukhvostov, *O profsoyuznom i rabochem dvizhenii 1989-2000 gg.*, Minsk, 2001, pp. 18-19.
6. See the interview with Nikolai Belanovskii in D. Mandel, *Rabotyagi*, pp. 147-70.
7. ASMB, *Sbornik dokumentov soveta profsoyuza*, Minsk, 1991, p. 5.
8. D. Mandel, *Rabotyagi*, p. 154.
9. Op. cit., pp. 155,163-64.
10. ASMB, *Materialy III-go s'ezda*, p. 21.
11. A. Bukhvostov, *O profsoyuznom..."* p. 23.
12. Op. cit., p. 31.
13. ASMB, *Informatsionno-spravochnyi material k III-emu s'ezdu*, p. 18.
14. *Ibid.*
15. ASMB, *Materialy III-ego s'ezda profosyuza ASM*, Minsk 2000, p. 17.
16. , *Byulleten'*, Moscow: Shkola trudovoi demokratii no. 12, 1999, p. 30.
17. See, for example, the campaign for higher wages that began in July 1998 and continued into January 2001, in *Rabochaya solidarnost'*, nos. 20-39, 1998; 1-3, 1999; 8, 2001; ASMB, *Informatsionno-spravochnyi material k III s'ezdu*, pp. 44-48.
18. A. Bukhvostov, *O profsoyuznom..."* p. 149; ASMB, *Khronika deistvii profsoyuza ASM*, Minsk, Sept. 2000, p. 27.
19. *Rabochaya solidarnost'*, no. 36, 8-14 Oct. 2001. For a similar strike at the Minsk Motor Factory in August 1999, see ASMB, *Khronika deistvii profsoyuza*, p. 49

20. See, for example, the strike in 1998 in the stamping shop of the Tractor Factory, *Belarusskii chas*, May 22, 1998.
21. ASMB, *Materialy III-go s'ezda*, p. 29.
22. ASMB, *Metodicheskie materialy po organizatsii profsoyuznogo obucheniya*, Minsk, 1999.
23. ASMB, *Informatsionno-spravochnyi material k III-emu s'ezdu*, p. 19.
24. ASMB, *Materialy III-go s'ezda...*, p. 29.
25. Resolution of III Central Council of ASMB, Dec. 5, 2001 (unpublished).
26. ASMB, *Materyaly III-go s'ezda...*, article 3.6, p. 6.
27. Bukhvostov, *O profsoyuznom...*, p. 27.
28. *Belorusskaya partiya truda: programmnye dokumenty*, Minsk, 1994, pp. 3, 11.
29. *Ibid.*, p. 13.
30. *Ibid.*, p. 12.
31. ASMB, *Materialy III-go s'ezda*, p. 27
32. *Rabochaya solidarnost'*, no. 24, July 20-27, 2001, p. 1.
33. "Zayavlenie Soveta ASMB," June 19, 2001 (unpublished).
34. *Rabochaya politika*, no. 12, Mar. 23-29, 2001.
35. ASMB, *Khronika deistvii ASM*; ASMB, *Informatsionnyi material uchastniku II-go plenuma*, May 29, 2001. A low point was reached in May 2003, when only 2000 came out for a demonstration organized by ASMB and REP against low wages.
36. ASMB, *Materialy III-go s'ezda*, p. 29.
37. ASMB, *Materialy k III-emu s'ezdu*, p. 21.
38. *Rabochaya solidarnost'*, no. 34-5, Sept. 16-30, 2000.
39. *Ibid.*, no. 6, 16-22 Feb., 2001; ASMB, *Informatsionnyi material uchastniku II-go plenuma Soveta profsoyuza*, Minsk, May 29, 2001, p. 10.
40. On this, see for example, ASMB, *Informatsionno-spravochnyi material*, p. 7.
41. *Platforma Beloruskoi partii truda na predstoyashchikh prezidentskikh vyborakh 2001 goda*, Minsk, 2001.
42. D. Chandler, "Democracy Verusus Dictatorship? The 2001 Belarus Presidential Elections," *Labor Focus on Eastern Europe*, no. 69, 2001, pp. 54-70.
43. Belorusskaya partiya truda, *Materiayli pyatogo s'ezda*, Minsk, 2001, p. 6
44. Op. cit., pp. 55 and 59. The promotion of a united candidate was a fatal error in many respects. For one thing, it meant that the opposition had much less television time than if there had been several candidates.
45. Op. cit., 56.
46. EIU, *Country Profile: Belarus*, Apr. 2003, p. 8.
47. Chandler,"Democracy Versus Dictatorship," p. 64.
48. *Rabochaya politika*, no. 48, Dec. 19, 2002.
49. "Declaration of Delegates to the Special Fourth Congress of ASMB" (unpublished).

Chapter Eleven
THREE FACTORIES

This chapter presents three unions at different degrees of independence from management. Together, they illustrate the complexities of the issue in Byelorussian circumstances and the influence of the national leadership's policies on it.

The Borisov Starter Factory (BATE)

Borisov is a small town of 150,000 about seventy kilometres from Minsk. In 2001, BATE employed 4700 people. There are three other ASM plants in the vicinity, the largest being the BELAZ Truck Factory in nearby Zhodino with over 7000 workers. In the Soviet era, BATE was a quasi-monopoly manufacturer of starters for tractors, trucks and cars, making them almost entirely on its own with few outside parts. After the fall of the Soviet Union, most of its goods still went to Russia. Although much of its equipment is in need of replacement, the plant is lighter, cleaner and generally more orderly than what one usually finds in Russia and Ukraine. (That comparison holds for most Byelorussian enterprises.) There is less unused space and idle equipment, and one sees more young faces in the shops. Wages in 2001 were about average for the sector. The enterprise still had most of its "social sphere," including subsidized cafeterias, summer camps, a vacation centre, and it was still constructing housing for its employees, though the latter's contribution to the cost was rising.

BATE's director, N. Busel, was a respected figure in Borisov, a holdover from Soviet times who had been a deputy in the Supreme Soviet dissolved by Lukashenko in 1996. Busel allowed himself public criticism of government policies and even some disparaging remarks about the President himself. The plant became the object of frequent government inspections, and in 1997 its accounts were frozen because of taxes owed to the state, a debt that might have been forgiven had the director been more loyal. It also had trouble obtaining affordable credit. At a delegates' conference in 1998, a state official suggested that the enterprise would be better off without Busel, since he refused to cultivate good relations with the government. He suggested that the employees choose another director. (They held eighty-seven per cent of the shares in the enterprise.) But the conference reaffirmed its support of Busel. Despite this pressure, Busel left the plant in 2002 at the age of 70 a wealthy man by Byelorussian standards and moved to Moscow to avoid prosecution for economic crimes. With the arrival of a new director (a former deputy of Busel), the plant's accounts were unfrozen, and the union received two-years-worth of dues that management owed it. It was the new director who told the union committee that he would not negotiate with an affiliate of ASMB and then relented after Bukhvostov spoke with him. At BATE, the managers, director included, are union members.

BATE's workers struck on the first day of the April 1991 movement, after receiving news of the strike in Minsk. But the union's president, S. Buzo, stood aside. On the second day, at management's suggestion, the workers limited their participation to sending delegations of ten people from each shop to the demonstration. Some workers, reacting to Buzo's inactivity, unsuccessfully tried to organize election of a strike committee. But otherwise, nothing much changed. A few of the shops had independent chairpersons, but there was no attempt to depose the president or to form an alternative union. Buzo was a leader who relied on management's support to keep his job, which is why he agreed so quickly to the director's request to disaffiliate and why Bukhvostov took up the matter up with the director rather than with him. Buzo rarely appeared in the shops and did little to keep his members informed. Over the years, different shops were the scene of wildcats, mostly over late wages. Some were led by the shop committees, but the plant committee was usually invisible.

Buzo also did not take action against management when it failed to transfer dues for two years. He argued that it was not the fault of the director but of the government. He waited three months, hoping the government would rescind its decree, before attempting to organize hand-collection of dues. The more independent unions were collecting most of their dues within a few weeks. When it came to collective actions directed at the government, Buzo voted for Bukhvostov's positions and, with the director's support, usually sent a busload of workers to demonstrate in Minsk. But he always rejected Pokhabov's suggestions to organize protests in Borisov itself. To be fair, he had been warned by the mayor that if that happened, he would not find work anywhere in Borisov. However, however, the government failed to force the removal of leaders in plants where they had the support of their members.

Pokhabov complained that his suggestions at meetings of the plant committee usually met with a wall of silence. When the new director demanded important concessions during the negotiations, Buzo offered no leadership. And when the plant committee voted to disaffiliate, it was Pokhabov who called the national office and made the rounds of the plant to see who was prepared to organize a new ASMB affiliate. He found about forty people. His own experience in the shops convinced him that there was a potential for independent trade-unionism. Workers eagerly grabbed ASMB's paper when it arrived from Minsk. The main factor missing was leadership.

But leadership was not forthcoming from the national office either. It was not as if Pokhabov did not get support and recognition. He was a respected and vocal member of the Republican Council and a delegate from ASMB to the BFP's Council. The national office included him in several delegations that went abroad for education. But it did nothing to encourage him to organize opposition at BATE to counter Buzo's passivity and subservience to management, not even after Buzo quickly acquiesced to taking his union out of ASMB. Buzo later played an active role in the Bukhvostov's removal. Of course, the national office's intervention in local affairs was a sensitive matter. But, it did not do even what it could. For example, it took the intervention of the School for Worker Democracy for the national office to give funds to Pokhabov to organize rank-and-file education in Borisov, even though it had been sitting on unused money earmarked for that kind of activity. Buzo, unlike some of his counterparts in the other plants, did not support that educational work though he did not try block it either.

Pokhabov himself was an active shop leader, who quickly organized the hand-collection of dues after Lukashenko's decree. He even assumed the leadership of wildcats that broke out in other shops, when the chairpersons stood aside. But he invested most of his energy in the PT. He organized a sixty-member section of the party in Borisov, one of the most active in Belarus and one that worked seriously in the presidential elections for Goncharik. Goncharik received the most votes of any circumscription of the Minsk region in Borisov. Pokhabov ran as a PT candidate in the municipal elections of 2003 and with a staff of twenty volunteers (volunteer work is very rare in post-Soviet society) he won, though the government stole the victory from him. Officially he received forty-nine per cent of the vote, whereas he needed fifty per cent plus one to be elected. His political work was done without any material reward and almost any budget, in the face of police surveillance and intimidation.

Pokhabov's attitude to Buzo was marked by a certain ambivalence. Sometimes he denounced him as a "conciliator" and time-server; at other times, he expressed pity for him, since was only a few years from retirement. That, he said, is why he did not try to dislodge him. A similar ambivalence characterized his attitude to management. On the one hand, he argued that Lukashenko's persecution of Busel was no reason for the union to "consider his situation" and refrain from putting pressure on him. He felt it was wrong for the national office not to have gone after the directors at once for their failure to transfer dues. After all, it was theft of union funds. On the other hand, he was proud that his name was in the plant's honour book as a valued worker, and his personal relations with his shop supervisor and with the general director were good, something that made life easier for him in a number of ways. Almost until the end, when he was dismissed, management did not seriously harass him, even though he always defended his members against management and generally won. He did complain, however, that "They sometimes criticize me in public, trying to belittle me, to lower my authority among workers." On the other hand, the new director paid his tuition for an external university programme in economics, until the KGB intervened to put a stop to it.

Management itself was thus by no means an unambiguous actor. The new director confided in Pokhabov that he hated the political pressure that was being exerted on him against the union. At one point, he even suggested Pokhabov oust Buzo from leadership of the union. When the director refused to relent on his decision to fire an otherwise disciplined elderly worker who had been caught with a bottle of vodka under his belt (he had not drunk from it), Pokhabov just told the worker to keep on working, and the director let it go. Worker-management relations were thus complex, as they tend be to everywhere. The problem was that ASMB's national leaders were sending confusing messages, rather than offering clear guidance and support to local activists who wanted their unions to base their action on the workers', rather than management's, interests. The position of the national office allowed Buzo to justify his subservience to management in the name of the struggle against the government, a struggle he did not actively support. It discouraged shop-floor activists like Pokhabov from organizing opposition to leaders like Buzo, who headed most local unions.

In light of this, it is not surprising that Pokhabov did not organize opposition to Buzo but concentrated his efforts on the PT. He himself explained that he had decided to focus on politics, since he could or would not do anything about Buzo. But for all his veneration of Bukhvostov, who was indeed an impressive, courageous leader, he became increasingly disenchanted with the national office's strategy, or, as he saw it, its lack of strategy. He grew especially critical when he saw how easy it was for Lukashenko, acting through the directors, to get the local presidents to disaffiliate. As the pressure mounted in his own plant, he shed his ambivalence toward Buzo and expressed anger with Bukhvostov for continuing to deal with him as if the treachery had never happened. As for his director, he agreed that being "a good guy" is not a profession: "I've said it in the plant committee and I said it in the Council, it makes no sense to have directors and assistant directors in the union. But I get no answer. The Council should publish clear directives on the question of management's presence in the union." By the summer of 2003, he concluded that things might have turned out differently for ASMB had it excluded management. He even took the radical position that the union should bar engineering-technical personnel from membership because they are too vulnerable and easily bent to management's will.

Although a PT activist, he became critical of what he saw as the overpoliticized policy of the national leadership to the detriment of problems within the plants, although he was obviously coming at the issue from a radically different angle than the union's conservative leaders. For example, about ASMB's weekly paper, he said: "How long can you keep devoting a whole paper to criticizing Lukashenko? People already know all that and are sick of reading about it. The paper should write about the workers in the plants, their struggles against the administration, how the union concretely helps them. It should share positive experiences, like the those of the ball-bearing plant, where management knows that it can't run the factory without the union's cooperation." He also felt the national office was not sufficiently active in face of the looming final showdown. "Instead of sitting in their offices, they should been in the factories, consulting with the live elements of the union."

The Minsk Precision Tool-and-Dye Factory (SIITO)

SIITO, which employed about 1200 people in 2001, used to be a department of the Minsk Tractor Factory. Though it is financially autonomous and accepts orders from other enterprises, it still does most of its work for the Tractor Factory, on whose territory it is physically located. Its director is also appointed by the general director of the Tractor Factory. Since SIITO has no "social sphere" of its own, it depends on the Tractor Factory for many of the workers' benefits, including housing, especially dormitory space for young workers, access to vacation resorts, and the like. The average wage at the plant has been relatively high for the sector because of the skilled nature of the work force.

SIITO's workers did not elect a strike committee or participate in the early strikes of April 1991 but they did take part in the second, more organized wave later that month. They subsequently elected a new union president, in the words of one of the workers, a "BNF (Byelorussian National Front)-type who was forever awaiting the revolution and didn't have a clue about day-to-day union work." When he left for a job at the Tractor Factory, SIITO's director expected his hand-picked candidate to be rubber-stamped by the delegates' conference. But some of the delegates posed pointed questions to the director, and the assembly found the answers wanting. A majority rejected the director's candidate in favour of Tamara Svigach, a quality-controller with twenty years of seniority. She had never held a union position. But since the plant was small, people knew each other, and Tamara was known seen as a principled person, someone with dignity who would not be afraid to stand up to the director.

And in fact, she began to clash with him almost at once. "He had been appointed only four months before I was elected," she recalled, "and his main objective was to crush the union committee, to utterly humiliate it. In four short months, he had already so intimidated the committee that they were afraid even to open their mouths. To tell the truth, had I known then what this work would involve, there is no force on earth that could have made me accept it. No one knows how many tears I shed in those first months." There were many contentious issues, including management's concession demands on the length of vacations, arbitrary dismissals, refusal to pay bonuses, unpaid vacation supplements, the failure to transfer dues to the union, insufficient protective gear, the refusal to provide a women's hygiene room, and much else. Svigach carefully went over all the financial documents she could obtain and concluded that there was a lot of waste and that management was negligent in seeking support that was available from the government. An assistant to Bukhvostov recalled the delegates' conference in 1999 on the collective agreement:

> I had already heard from Tamara that there were serious problems relating to health and safety, protective equipment, the woman's room. These were very real, concrete issues [that negotiations had not resolved]. She wasn't blowing them out of proportion, even if the women's room required some capital outlay. These issues were at the core of her report to the conference. And delegates raised additional ones from the floor. What impressed me most was her composure, even though she posed the problems head-on. I was favourably surprised to see a leader who could be so firm and yet never lose her temper or resort to rudeness. The director tried to wriggle out by saying there was no money. But Tamara cited figures that showed he was wrong. Then he said: "I don't understand why Tamara didn't come to see me and resolve these problems amicably." But she cut him off: "I came to see you at least twenty times." Then I spoke in support of the union's position. Our Council still carries weight with directors. They know we have direct access to the Minister, though our influence is fast declining. Over the years, we've had some seven directors dismissed.

When it came to vote, the majority supported Tamara. Most of the workers are skilled instrument-makers. You could tell from the quality of the discussion that these are reflective people. Tamara's problem is that she's the right person at the wrong time. She just can't tolerate the crap that goes on these days. The Tractor Factory has always considered the plant as one of its shops, even though it is independent now. Its union doesn't like her and keeps her at a distance. But in the Council we hold her in high regard and we supported her election to the Presidium.

Bukhvostov similarly spoke of "Tamara's tragedy." The national office really did support her. When she came for advice, it was forthcoming. She was included in a delegation that visited Canadian trade unions to study their education, and she was a member of the Presidium. She, in turn, made sure the union's literature reached her members and she could be counted upon to bring out 200-250 workers to ASMB's collective actions. Yet, although she was very impressed by the large research department of the Canadian Autoworkers' Union and the services it provided its affiliates, she was not ready to cut back her union's spending on "material aid" in order to commit a greater share of the dues to national office. "It would have to prove itself first. If I cut that aid, the workers would have my hide."

Despite the support the national office gave her, its ambiguous position on union-management relations and its indulgence toward subservient plant presidents contributed in important ways to weakening Svigach's position in her plant. For though she could count on a majority at delegate's conferences, if she did the preliminary groundwork—which meant making sure every shop held a meeting before the conference to debate the issues and to elect delegates, and that she was present at each one—she often found herself in a minority in the plant committee, which was made up of representatives from the shops, many of whom were shop-committee chairpersons. The blue-collar members of the committee were the most dependable. They were sober, skilled workers that management did not have "on a hook" for violations. And in any case, they did not fear dismissal, since wages were not great and they could find work elsewhere. But the white-collar members of the committee, and especially the managers, were a different story. And as elsewhere, SIITO's workers had a tendency to elect managers to head their shop committees. Svigach explained:

> I tell the workers: "Can't you see that it takes so long to resolve the problems that I bring to management precisely because they sense that I don't have the whole plant behind me?" Sure, we're a small plant, and I know everybody. That's a big plus. I make the rounds of the shops every day.

But I'm the only full-time union person and I can't be everywhere and do everything. Half of the shop-committee chairpersons are supervisors. Can you grasp that?

At the last meeting of the instrument shop, they elected a new chairman to replace the one who had resigned. By the way, he left because the director finally got to him. He couldn't take it anymore. He didn't want to leave, and I promised that we'd defend him, come what may. But in the end, he came to me and said: "I'm tired. I can't take it anymore." You can imagine the moral pressure he was under. So at the shop meeting, I discussed candidates with the workers. But they kept coming back with the same person: the assistant shop supervisor. So I said: "OK, let's talk this over. I know he's a good person and he'll look after your needs. But suppose that tomorrow the director puts his foot down and says he has to follow orders that are harmful to you? After all, that's his job, and he doesn't want to lose it. He's not a machine-operator or even a line engineer. He's an administrator." But they just replied: "No, we have confidence in him. And, anyway, he's got more free time than we do, and we don't want the extra work," and so forth.

He really is a conscientious, competent manager. But what if it's a matter of mobilizing for a demonstration, or picketing, or distributing leaflets? He might even relay information about the action to the workers. But that's as far as he'll go. To mobilize, you have to talk to each worker, inspire them with your will and enthusiasm. So I'm forced to do that myself. But I'm one person, not the whole union.

One meeting of the plant committee discussed the case of a building engineer who had been deprived of her bonus (in effect, she had been fined) because the roof was leaking. But the roof had been leaking for over a year. It had not been fixed because management did not issue the materials. Svigach explained:

I told them: "We have to put a stop to this arbitrariness. You might be next." But they replied that even if the roof wasn't her fault, her work generally was careless and so she didn't deserve the bonus. In sum, they condoned the director's arbitrariness. In another case, I fought for a whole year to force the director to pay a bonus that was coming to workers and I finally won. But in the committee, I was criticized for needlessly antagonizing the director. I fought against the bonus system. I explained that in the end take-home pay was the same; so why go through a hundred calculations that leave so much room for arbitrariness? But they wouldn't listen. I also told them: "You demand that management distribute milk [it is believed to protect people in harmful conditions] but you won't demand an end to the conditions." They just looked at me in wonder and said: "But that would mean giving up special pensions and wage supplements [for dangerous or harmful work]!"

But even more injurious to the union than the presence of managers was the hostile attitude of the leaders of the union at Tractor Factory. That union, it will be recalled, was very close to management and, together with the director Leonov, they tried to depose Bukhvostov at ASMB's congress in 2000. But SIITO, as noted, was heavily dependent on the Tractor Factory, despite its formally independent status. In the summer of 2000, the workers downed tools over unpaid wages, rejecting Svigach's proposal to begin the lengthy legal procedure for a legal strike. But she assumed the strike's leadership and led the workers, not to her own director, but to the administration building of the Tractor Factory. A three-hour demonstration, duly filmed by the police, resulted in payment of the wages the following day. Both the management and the union leaders of the Tractor Factory tried to undermine Svigach, withholding information and keeping her at arms length, whereas she normally would have been invited to the meetings of its plant committee. But more damaging was the example they gave. Their subservience to management gave comfort and encouragement both to her director and to her opposition in the plant committee. When in 2000 her director came to demand concessions that the union at the Tractor Factory had already granted, Svigach was hard put to convince her committee to resist. By the same token, the slowness of the national office to react to the directors' failure to transfer dues (at SIITO, over a year's worth were owing), its public declaration of support for Leonov, and its call for a political alliance with directors, were, to say the least, unhelpful.

The conflictual relations between Svigach and her director came to a head in the summer of 2001, when he told her to her face that we was going to get rid of her. She proposed to her committee to convene a special delegates' conference to pose the question of the director's removal. Too many problems had accumulated without any hope of a negotiated resolution: the failure to transfer dues, insufficient protective gear, non-payment of vacation supplements, etc. The director was willfully flaunting the law and violating the collective agreement, grounds for asking for his dismissal. And now he wanted to take control of the union. Svigach was confident of support at a conference but she could not get the backing of a majority of her committee. They wanted to give the director another chance and told her to continue talking to him.

At the collective-agreement conference in the fall of 2001, she dropped a bombshell: she was leaving the plant in three months. No one believed her; they thought she was grandstanding. But she did leave and never looked back. People were even more shocked to learn that she had left to devote herself to an evangelical Protestant church which, as it turned out, she had joined even while leading the union. (These churches, usually led by pastors from the U.S., have been proliferating in the former Soviet Union.) Asked about her decision, she gave mostly personal reasons. But she also said that she was hurt by the lack of solidarity within union, the difficulties she had encountered in her own committee, and especially her hostile treatment by the union at the Tractor Factory.

At the election conference a few months later, two candidates vied for plant president: the director's choice, a former Komsomol leader and presently a section supervisor, and Ninel' (Lenin written backwards), a programmer for numerical machines. She had been a member of Svigach's committee and had attended educational courses organized by ASMB's national office. She was an active, committed trade-unionist who had usually supported Svigach, although she felt that she had sometimes been too uncompromising and that had hurt the union's cause. In her view, Svigach proceeded too often on her own rather than investing more effort into persuading others to support her. At the same time, she admitted that the director was a petty tyrant (*samodur*): "they all take Lukashenko as their model." The director, of course, was dead set against her election, all the more so as she was a woman: "After Tamara, no more women (*nikakoi baby*)!" he declared. But Ninel' went through the shops before the conference, explaining how she intended to work as head of the union. Many members already knew her from her picture on the wall of honour as a top employee.

As a result, most of the discussion had already taken place in the shops before the conference. On the day of the conference, the director (illegally) issued orders to the guards not to let in any representatives from ASMB's national office. But as Evdokimchik was being turned away at the gates, a group of women workers on their way out from work witnessed the incident and rushed back into the plant to alert the others. Soon, a large crowd appeared and forced open the way for him. In an open ballot, Ninel' garnered seventy per cent of the vote. Although she had washed her hands of the plant, Svigach had apparently left a legacy. But more than that, this election confirmed the existence of a strong untapped potential at the base of ASMB for independent trade-unionism.

After her election, Ninel' came under constant pressure from management, although the director first tried to buy her with the offer of an administrative job. There was also an unsuccessful attempt to get her to disaffiliate from ASMB on the part of the deputy director for information (in effect, a KGB agent). When she resisted, he told her: "You don't understand who you are dealing with. We have broken people like you." But he abandoned the effort, which may have been his own initiative and not that of the director. In her first eighteen months, Ninel' negotiated the resolution of two wildcat strikes over unpaid wages. Only younger workers participated in the strikes, as the working pensioners and engineering-technical staff were afraid. Eventually, her relations with management took on a degree of normalcy.

Asked if the presence of management in the union complicated her work, Ninel' replied:

> Of course, it would be much easier if management were not in the union. The administration is actually pushing its managers now to get elected to the committees, where they act as its eyes and ears. We have two committee chairmen in large shops who are assistant supervisors, and in others there are foremen. But worst of all, my own vice-president is the deputy director for personnel and workers' services. He is a member of the plant committee as the delegate of the "white house" [the administration building]—they have the right to elect a shop committee and a representative to the plant committee. The director wasn't able to get his candidate elected president of the union, so he pushed for this guy to be my vice-president as a compromise. If there's anything really sensitive, I can't take it to the whole plant committee. For example, we have a conflict over management's attempt to fire three women for absenteeism. In fact, they were at work, but the timekeeper did not have their passes. I'll protect them, of course. We have a lot of single mothers, who are often in bad, unskilled jobs. They're looked down upon by society and they're terribly vulnerable. Their kids get sick, and they turn to the union for protection. But my vice-president insists on firing them! How can we discuss the administration's lawlessness when he is sitting right there?

Ninel' consulted regularly with other independent plant presidents in Minsk and with the national office. She highly valued the education the latter had given her. But she too felt that the national office could have done more about management's influence in the union. It could at least have issued a directive against electing managerial personnel to union positions. An engineering-technical employee herself, she confirmed the widely-held view that blue-collar workers were far more dependable from a union point of view. But sober, disciplined workers were leaving the plant because of the low wages, and it was hard to keep the younger workers, when the ones with more seniority kept the best-paying jobs for themselves. She was organizing leisure activities for young workers in an effort to keep them. Management increasingly had to hire workers who drank, and those, of course, are easily influenced. In a conversation in May 2003, she felt the enterprise really did not have money to raise wages. Orders were down, the quality of the metal was poor, and the equipment was old and losing precision. The workers were cursing the director and Lukashenko.

As for the Tractor Factory, she was being watched closely by its union leaders, who as before, kept sensitive information away from here. There were signs that SIITO might to be reintegrated into the Tractor Factory. Meanwhile, the latter's union leaders were clearly contemplating disaffiliation from ASMB. SIITO's workers, unlike those of the Tractor Factory, understood the need for an independent union. They could see the difference between the day-to-day work of their union and that of the Tractor Factory. The latter, for example, had conceded double pay for weekend work in return for time off during the week. SIITO's union had refused to make the concession. All the same, Ninel' was not sure what she would do if there was renewed pressure for disaffiliation. It would be hard to withstand the combined pressure of management and the union of the tractor plant.

The Minsk Ball-Bearing Factory

6500 people were employed at the Minsk Ball-Bearing Factory in 2000. In the union's estimation, it was about twenty-percent overstaffed, mainly with excess managerial and technical personnel. The average age was relatively young, forty-three, and about a quarter of the work force was under thirty 30. Until 2002, wages at the plant were at the top of the sector, about twenty per cent above average and forty per cent above the average national wage. The plant's equipment is relatively modern, though also increasingly in need of replacement, and production more or less steady, with seventy per cent of the output sold to Russia.

The workers here had been very active in April 1991. Evdokimchik, a well-paid, highly skilled machinist at that time who led the strike committee, recalled:

> I was just an ordinary worker. I never held, nor did I want to hold, a union position. True, I enjoyed some authority among the workers and I chaired our shop's work-collective council. I had a certain level of consciousness but, in general, I solved my problems on my own. Sure, I was dissatisfied with the union, but it seemed impossible to change it, since it was such an integral part of the state-party machinery. Neither it nor the director played any role in the events.

After the strikes, the workers replaced the old plant committee with the strike committee. At first, the new committee worked with both the alternative unions, led by V. Bykov (who was close to the BNF) and with ASMB. "We did that for six months," recalled Evdokimchik. "But we finally had to choose. Our union's constitution gave the committee the right to decide on affiliation. We saw that ASMB was really working, while Bykov's organization wasn't serious." Later, when Evdokimchik became national Vice-President of ASMB, Vladimir Lozovskii, a foundry worker and union vice president, replaced him. This was another rare case where workers headed the union, and that was no small factor in its independence from management. (Both Evdokimchik and Lozovskii subsequently obtained law degrees, studying in the evenings.)

The new leaders of the union immediately established a strike fund. With much patience and effort, they convinced their members to cut back spending on "material aid" to fifteen per cent of the dues (later raised to twenty-five at the demand of the members) and to put thirty per cent into education. They excluded the director and his assistants from the union, but left lower managerial personnel. Thanks to the relatively large group of activists that emerged from the April 1991 events, the union was able to break management's hold on most of the shop committees and to replace the managers and white-collar employees at their head with workers. (In later years, this was partly reversed, as management pressure on union activists intensified.) But not all of the strike leaders became union officers. Some remained "unexposed" (*nezasvechennye*), informal leaders. These were people who knew their shops thoroughly and enjoyed authority among the workers. They conducted agitation on behalf of the union, spoke out at meetings in support of its positions, and mobilized for its actions. But by remaining "unexposed," they avoided the worst of management's harassment. These were the real core of the union's strength on the shopfloor, who served as a counterweight to shop leaders who preferred to avoid confrontation. The union also was able to introduce proportional representation of workers and engineering-technical staff at the delegates' conferences.

The union's educational programme was designed to reinforce and broaden its activist base and, more generally, to create a receptive milieu in the shops for the union's message. Paid time off was negotiated for ten one- or two-day seminars a year for the members of shop committees and for group leaders, though getting them released became an on-going struggle. (There are 266 group leaders, each representing about twenty-five members.) The union also organized special training for health and safety activists. A full-time vice-president, N. Kuz'min, was put in charge of the education. He was a former machinist with twenty-one years seniority who had earned a history degree in evening courses and had gone through the national office's course for union educators. Apart from concrete union issues, the seminars dealt with economics, politics, history and human rights. In Kuzmin's evaluation:

> This work yields results. It is part of our largely unnoticed work aimed at moving workers away from the ideology that tells them that the élite [*verkhy*] will take care of our needs without our participation and towards an ideology that says that only we can solve our problems, that no one else is going to do it for us. Why is our union in a somewhat better position than those of other plants? Because for the past five years we have been conducting this education. It may be only a rudimentary programme, but at least we don't have to explain fundamental truths to our people.

The union also put out a lot of information for its members, including weekly leaflets on union business, especially application of the collective agreement. The worker who maintains the photocopying machine said that it went through ten years of normal use in its first three years. Although the collective agreement gives the union access to the plant's in-house paper, its articles are often censored by the editor, who is appointed by the director. The union always made sure every shop received its quota of ASMB's paper.

Despite the attention to education and information, the union leaders continued to consider that struggle educates best. They do not shy away from conflict. Lozovskii explained:

> Our director is constantly pointing to the tractor and truck plants as examples of harmonious relations between unions and management. The KGB people also ask me: "How come your plant is always on fire, when everywhere else things are so quiet?" We try to reach agreements by negotiating. If we don't succeed the first time, we go back again, and a third time. But when negotiation fails, we go to our people, we explain and we organize them to exert pressure. At other plants, when the union can't reach agreement, it just lets the issue drop. In old days, when unions were part of the state system, they could resolve certain problems without the workers. Now we tell them that we can't do anything by ourselves. So we educate and discuss with the workers, we support and organize them in large and small conflicts. We try to show them that the union can become something that management and the government have to consider. If there were a dozen large plants like ours, the situation in the country would be totally different, and we'd have nothing to fear. But when you are only four or five, you can be repressed. And when the others see the repression, they grow even more cautious.

The union makes a concerted effort at all stages to involve the membership in setting priorities for negotiations and in the negotiations themselves. Although legal strikes are effectively ruled out, the union exerts pressure on management by holding meetings in the shops and delivering the minutes to the director. It has clandestinely organized "wildcats" and demonstrations under the administration's windows. It has proposed votes of non-confidence in managers and obtained their removal. But the main thing in the union's favour was that it built a base in the shops such that the director knew he could not run the plant without its cooperation. Although government pressure on the director was real enough (He often turned up the radio in his office when discussing matters with Lozovskii), what mostly moved him to try to get rid of Lozovskii was the limits that the union placed on his own power.

That happened in the fall of 2000. The director carefully prepared the delegates' conference. At meetings with his shop managers, he instructed them on how to ensure the election of the "correct" delegates. But the union also did its work. The conference was long and stormy. It took three and a half hours just to decide whether to hold an open or secret ballot. Management's delegates favoured, of course, the open ballot. As usual, the director was seated on the stage with the union president. It took three votes, and each time the managers ostentatiously rose from their seats to watch how the other delegates' voted. The open ballot finally won.

The discussion then turned to Lozovskii's record. Emotions ran high. A long list of delegates signed up to speak. Most of the criticism directed at Lozovskii concerned his involvement in politics. (His union had been very active in the Goncharik's presidential campaign earlier that year.) That activity allegedly had a negative impact on the enterprise, since management could not obtain the government support that was available to more loyal plants. "But there was another issue that was left unspoken," explained Kuz'min. "Management wants itself to have more influence on the collective than the union committee. They don't like the fact that we have such strong influence and that we use is to resolve the workers' problems, for example when the collective-agreement conference supported us against the director on the level of indexation." The turning point in the discussion came when a foreman, until recently a worker, pointed out that the conference had already voted to approve the work of the union committee during its last mandate. It made no sense, therefore, to single out Lozovskii for censure. If there were problems at the plant, then perhaps it was the director who was doing a poor job.

Lozovskii won with close to eighty per cent of the vote, and his supporters were elected to the other positions in the plant committee. After the conference, the committee excluded some thirty per cent of the managerial personnel from the union, formally for not paying dues for three consecutive months while the union was collecting them by hand. (It later arranged for automatic transfer through a bank.) That was the only available constitutional grounds for excluding them. The director immediately instructed them to pay up and get back on the union. After the failed attempt to depose Lozovskii, the director tried to persuade him to disaffiliate, offering him a nice salary, a well-furnished office, one-hundred-per-cent dues checkoff, and a lot more. But Lozovskii had already rejected better offers.

Lozovskii shared Bukhvostov's political views and strategy. The difference was that his union's political involvement did not deflect it from the task of building union power on the shop-floor or from holding management responsible for workers' problems in the enterprise, even if their ultimate source was the government. This paid off both for the plant's workers and for ASMB as a whole, since the union at the ball-bearing factory was far and away the strongest affiliate in ASMB and the staunchest supporter of the national office. From around 1995, half of ASMB's participants in national protests were from this one factory. And as noted, participation in protests directed at the government involved defying management and standing up to government intimidation. The media always issued dire warnings, the police came out in force, often dressed in military camouflage, and the whole thing was put on film.

One such demonstration was called for July 15, 1998. The plan was for the workers to gather in their respective factory yards at 4:30 pm, after the shift, and to march out in columns to the site of the demonstration. The government wanted by all means, short of direct repression, to prevent it. And so at two p.m., management shut off power and sent the workers home early. It counted on most not waiting around for two and a half hours for the demonstration. And, indeed, the workers went home. But at 4:30, close to 2000 reappeared, almost a fourth of the total turnout for Minsk. "I was sure the demonstration had failed," recalled Lozovskii. "When I saw them returning, I cried. That's the work of our activists!"

This was one of the few enterprise unions that consistently wanted to strengthen the national office. Half the money in ASMB's (voluntary) strike fund came from the Ball-Bearing Factory. Lozovskii was a strong critic of the weak solidarity and unity in the union. His union's representatives argued for an increase in the national office's share of the dues. They also wanted to amend the constitution to give it the capacity to impose discipline on the affiliates. If Lozovskii was at all critical of Bukhvostov, it was for not using the disciplinary powers that the constitution already granted him. On the other hand, while Lozovskii recognized that it was the more independent unions that supported Bukhvostov and were prepared to delegate more power and resources to the national office, he did not seem to see any link between the latter's strategy and the limited progress that had been made toward establishing the independence of the local unions.

CONCLUSION

Studies of post-Communist labour movements have understandably focussed on their weakness. But the failure of these unions to defend their members should be put in perspective. Organized labour even in the wealthy capitalist democracies has been forced onto the defensive over the past two decades and has ceded positions previously won in hard struggles. Of course, the losses have not been nearly as dramatic as in the post-Communist countries. But then the conditions were much more favourable for resistance.

The factors, in their various combinations, that contributed to the weakness of the unions in the auto and farm-machinery sector of Russia, Ukraine and Belarus should be sufficiently clear from the preceding pages. Rather than review them, this conclusion will briefly discuss three underlying and interrelated issues raised by the unions' failures, as well as by their victories, exceptional and limited though the latter were.

The first issue is whether a different outcome was possible. Were the losses, and especially the extent of the losses, inevitable? What were the respective contributions of "objective" circumstances and "subjective" factors? In one form or another, this is a question with which labour leaders and activists constantly grapple in developing and assessing strategies.

A second issue, which was at the heart of the analysis in this volume, is class independence. What exactly does that mean under capitalism? What is its significance for the labour movement? And why is it so elusive in the countries studied (though, of course, not only there)?

And finally, what can one say about the nature of civil society in these post-Communist countries? Its anaemic character is common to all post-Communist states. In fact, labour, for all its weakness, is probably its strongest component. An underdeveloped civil society and the overwhelming presence of the state were characteristic of Russia for hundreds of years before Communism. What are the perspectives for change?

"Objective" and "Subjective" Factors

Was the outcome a foregone conclusion? The odds were certainly stacked against the labour movement: an unprecedented depression and the resulting insecurity and decomposition of the industrial working class; the social and ideological upheaval wrought by "shock therapy" that caught workers completely unprepared; the absence of experience of self-organization and traditions of struggle. And behind all this was an extremely unfavourable international balance of forces. But that does not mean the outcome was inevitable, however much union leaders who did nothing to avoid it find that conclusion comforting.

It is useful for purposes of analysis to distinguish between "objective" circumstances, like those enumerated above, and "subjective" factors, the action of the unions. But the distinction does not correspond to real life, something Marx pointed out in one of his earliest works, the justly famous Theses on Feuerbach. He criticized mechanistic, deterministic materialism for leaving no room for human agency and he even had some praise for idealism for developing "the active side," although abstractly. That was also the position of E.P. Thompson, historian of the English working class. According to Meiksins Wood:

> It is essential to his historical materialism to recognize the "objective" and "subjective" are not dualistically separate entities (which lend themselves easily to the measurement of "necessity" and "agency"), related to one another only externally and mechanistically, "the one sequential to the other" as objective stimulus and subjective response. It is necessary somehow to incorporate in social analysis the role of consciousness and active historical beings, who are "subject" and "object" at one, both agents and material forces in objective processes.[1]

The relative, conditional nature of the distinction becomes clearer if by "objective" circumstances we understand those factors that lie beyond the influence of the "subject," in this case, the workers and their organizations. These circumstances posed limits to the action of the unions. When the distinction is presented in this way, it is easier to see that what separates the "objective" and "subjective" is "only" the time frame and the scale of the action. For example, in depressed economic conditions, the traditional union weapons of strikes, work-to-rule, and the like, that hit at profits lose their effectiveness. There is much truth to the argument that "if there is no enterprise, there is no union," which was frequently advanced by union leaders to justify concessions to management. They argued that concessions they made to management were inevitable in view of the "objective circumstances," particularly the economic crisis and government policy. The director could do nothing about these. Leaving aside the question of what was or was not within the director's power, one can ask if the government's economic policy, which bore a major share of responsibility for the depression, really lay beyond the influence of the unions.

This certainly seemed the case from the vantage point of isolated, local unions. But why did they not press their national leaders to organize them for serious political struggle? Only the relatively few unions that resisted in the enterprises exerted that kind of pressure or supported national leaders, like Zlenko and Bukhvostov, who actively opposed the government. Those local unions did not resign themselves to their isolation. Nor did they accept the demoralization of their members as an "objective" constraint beyond their influence. The workers' passivity and the local leaders' own vulnerability to persecution by management were among the "objective" circumstances often cited by the local leaders. Yet, most of them did nothing to encourage activism among their members or to build their confidence. On the contrary, they often went out of their way to discourage them, inadvertently showing that they did believe they could influence the disposition of the "masses" to act.

Still, it is legitimate to ask whether those who resisted came out ahead. Maybe "partner-like" relations with management and investment of the workers' limited energies in individual adaptation to the "objective" situation were the more rational choice. After all, those that tried to resist were unable to break out of their isolation and become a political force capable of influencing the government.

One can answer that question on different levels. The first is that even localized resistance often did yield results, though they were necessarily partial and fragile. On the other hand, concessions made by unions without offering any resistance, without demanding a non-monetary quid-pro-quo or guarantees for the union and its members, did not save jobs or lead eventually to higher wages and better conditions. They did, however, undermine the unions' potential to improve their members' situation once the economic situation became more favourable. "Partnership" helped to extinguish any lingering faith workers might have had in their ability to fight collectively for a better life through the union. The rare unions that resisted at least preserved the potential to fight. Even when they could not prevent layoffs, workers who resisted were changed by their experience.² They stand out from the others for their dignity and active outlook towards the social conditions that oppress them. "We showed them that we are human beings," said a participant of the Vinnitsa struggle. They showed they they wanted to and could be subjects of their own destiny, makers of their history. They are the hope of their country.

On another level, because human action is conscious (purposeful), the outcome of a strategy of collective resistance cannot usually be predicted in advance without first engaging in it. In another one of his theses, Marx states that "Man must prove the truth, that is, the reality and power, the this-sidedness of his thinking in practice. The dispute over the reality or non-reality of thinking that is isolated from practice is a purely *scholastic* question." In the same vein, Lenin, who rejected the deterministic interpretation of Marxism predominant among the reformist wing of socialism, was fond of the phrase "On s'engage, puis on voit." Gramsci put it the most clearly:

> In reality, one can foresee only the struggle but not the concrete moments of the struggle, which can but be the result of opposing forces in continuous movement, which are never reduced to fixed qualities since within them quantity is continuously becoming quality. In reality, one can "foresee" to the extent that one acts, to the extent that one applies a voluntary effort and therefore contributes concretely to creating the result "foreseen." Prediction reveals itself thus not as a scientific act of knowledge but as the abstract expression of the effort made, the practical way of creating collective will.³

The argument should obviously not be taken too far. Marx, after all, based the claim to the "scientific" character of his socialism on the presence of real historical, that is, "objective," conditions that finally made possible the age-old dream of a just and free society. Nor was Lenin inviting his party to engage in adventures or "Blanquism," though his opponents accused him of that. Both Marx and Lenin showed on many occasions that they understood the necessity of breaking off, or even of not joining, battle, when the forces arrayed were obviously too unequal. But even retreat for them had to be part of a strategy of resistance and eventual counter-offensive. Again to quote Gramsci:

> The active politician is a creator, an initiator; but he neither creates from nothing nor does he move in the turbid void of his own desires and dreams. He bases himself on effective reality, but what us this effective reality? Is it something static and immobile or is it not rather a relation of forces in continuous motion and shift of equilibrium? If one applies one's will to the creation of a new equilibrium among the forces which

> one really believes to be progressive and strengthening it to help it to victory—one still moves on the terrain of effective reality, but does so in order to dominate and transcend it (or to contribute to this). What "ought to be" is therefore concrete; indeed it is the only realistic and historicist interpretation of reality, it alone is history in the making and philosophy in the making; it alone is politics.[4]

The overwhelming majority of unions in the countries studied here had only one strategy: to subordinate themselves to the will of management and the state and to depend on their kindness. Among the "traditional" unions (those inherited from the Soviet period), there were few exceptions to this, and almost all, at least in the auto and farm-machinery sector, were in Belarus and Ukraine. These exceptions were largely the consequence of exceptional leaders, who in their turn enjoyed the support of exceptional, progressive national and regional leaders. The latter were also absent in Russia.

On the other hand, the rank and file of these unions were not themselves particularly exceptional. They belonged to a very sizeable minority of workers in all three countries that manifested a will to resist. They showed it in widespread, but isolated, wildcat strikes and civil disobedience, in their broad response to several of the FNPR's national protests, in the enthusiastic reaction to the 1998 "rail wars" and miners' picket, in the creation of alternative unions. This active minority was not strong enough on its own to force a change in the predominant strategy of the labour movement. But with leadership willing to unite their will to resist behind a strategy based on class independence, they might have succeeded in awakening the demoralized majority and drawing them into the movement.

To return then to the original question: in retrospect, the most probable outcome happened. But it was not the only one possible, especially the enormous scale of the losses that workers and the society as a whole suffered. Labour leaders who espoused "social partnership" cannot evade a share in the responsibility for the disaster.

Class Independence

This study has argued that the rejection of class independence by most of the union leaders and workers doomed the labour movement to failure. It is true, of course, that "objective" circumstances favoured the predominance of "social partnership": the demise of the Soviet system in the form of a "revolution from above" rather than "from below" that therefore left in tact so much of the totalitarian legacy; the unfavourable international correlation of forces; the economic crisis. But there was still a choice. A small minority opted to rely on their own collective forces, rather than on the benevolence or presumed enlightened self-interest of the managers/owners and the state.

The essence of class independence is reliance by workers on their own forces. That does not, of course, rule out alliances. But it does rule out subordination of workers' interests to those of the ruling class. The analysis presented here illustrated the close relationship between class independence, on the one hand, and solidarity and democracy, on the other, two additional, key elements of the labour movement that were largely absent from the unions studied. It also showed that a strategy based on class independence cannot bear fruit unless it is pursued simultaneously on the economic level, that is, in relation to management, and on the political, in relation to the state. That is a lesson that the alternative unions in Russia, at least those that have survived until now, seem to have learned. However haltingly, they have begun to search for forms of independent political action. From a different angle, it is also the lesson of the defeat of ASMB in Belarus. ASMB adopted an independent policy vis-à-vis the state but failed to pursue one in the enterprises, in relation to management. It also did not establish its independence in relation to Belarus's still embryonic bourgeoisie and to its Western backers: it adopted a softer, "social" version of their programme and went into the 2000 the presidential elections in coalition with them. This also undermined the effectiveness of its political action.

Under capitalism, class independence can obviously only be a strategic orientation, not a goal to be realized. For the very essence of capitalism is labour's subordination to capital. Class independence can be realized only by the abolition of capitalism and its replacement with a self-managed society, one without bosses and (private) owners. Unions that strive for independence but accept the inevitability of capitalism end up trapped in their own contradictions. On the other hand, unions that pursue a coherent strategy based on class independence do not obviously pose socialism as an immediate or even necessarily a mid-term goal. But they do not accept the legitimacy of the capital's power either in the enterprise or in the larger society. They consider that power a usurpation made possible by the correlation of class forces. Their long-term strategy is therefore to change the balance of forces, to build the workers' power, pushing back capital's until the very existence of capital can be confronted. It is this long-term perspective that gives socialist trade-unionists their staying power and has historically made them the pioneers of the labour movement when most viewed the conditions as hopeless.

Of course, even the most militant union leaders rarely adopt that strategy, except in periods of the most intense class struggle. In practice, unions accept the inevitability of capital, though they try to circumscribe its power (unless, of course, they fully buy into "partnership"). That is probably not so surprising. Unions are created by their members to negotiate with capital, not to overthrow it. It is normally left to socialist activists in the union movement to defend a consistent policy of class independence. Their relative absence today is part of the world-wide crisis of the labour movement. But as Marx tried to show 150 years ago and as historical experience has since largely confirmed, the struggle within the framework capitalism is sooner or later—usually sooner—a losing proposition for workers. When the balance of forces shifts in capital's favour—as it inevitably does if the system as such is not challenged—unions are incapable of resisting the offensive. Capital may not be able or want to reclaim all that it previously conceded, but the gap between the real and the possible deepens enormously. The situation is even more unambiguous in the case of the post-Communist countries under study. Workers in the wealthy capitalist countries can at least compare their situation favourably with that of the workers of the periphery. But the capitalism that has been created in the post-Communist countries is itself peripheric and has very little to offer workers.

Civil Society

Russian society has a long history of domination by absolute state power. Historically, not only the labouring classes were deprived of avenues of political influence, but the socially dominant classes, too. In feudal Russia, the nobility were only the "top slaves" of the Tsar. In the Soviet Union, the nomenklatura was completely subordinate to Stalin and after him to the Politburo. Stalin, like Ivan the Terrible whom he admired, destroyed much of the ruling "class," replacing it with new people completely loyal to his person. The two periods when the socially dominant group was able to assert a measure of influence over the state—under Nicolas II after the revolution of 1905 and under Brezhnev in the 1970s and early 1980s—were followed by the overthrow of the entire system, state and dominant social group together.

This pattern appears to be repeating itself. The popular classes today have no formal or informal avenues of influence on state policy. That weakness has enabled Putin to establish the state's predominance over the bourgeoisie too, since it is isolated socially and can really count only on some limited political support from abroad (the "Western" bourgeoisie and its states). The entire system is extremely fragile and depends upon preserving the present weakness of civil society. That is one of the reasons why Putin has moved to strengthen the central state's power and why the bourgeoisie has not really been tempted to assert itself politically.

A comparative study of the "transitions" in Russian and Ukraine concluded: "If Ukraine and Russia had a developed civil society in the form that it exists in Western Europe or North America, those countries would be plunged into anarchy for a long time."[5] If it is recognized that one person's "anarchy" is another person's "class struggle," the conclusion is a just one. The secret of "shock therapy's" success, from the point of view of the West and the Russian bourgeoisie, was precisely its rapid liquidation of the early shoots of "civil society" that had appeared under Perestroika. It was a condition for the formation of a bourgeoisie in Russia.

This helps to explains why Belarus, the only country to refuse "shock therapy," has developed the most dictatorial regime: the refusal of "reform" left of the embryonic "civil society" in tact. Despite all the internal contradictions and divisions of the labour movement, it was only in Belarus that the leadership of the large industrial unions and of the main union federation labour movement directly challenged the government. The greater challenge from society (not only, of course, from the labour movement) called forth the more repressive response from the state. On the other hand, Lukashenko's dictatorship cannot be explained in terms of any "systemic" need. His policies enjoyed a significant measure of popular support and would have enjoyed even more under a less arbitrary and authoritarian regime. Moreover, they cannot hold out for long against international pressures without the kind of conscious, popular support that can only emerge from democracy.

Labour activists and educators who want to activate workers and help them overcome demoralization are confronted with a chicken-and-egg problem. Significant and lasting solutions to the workers' problems require political action. But the basis for organizing workers for political action is the enterprise. Workers first have to appropriate their unions and make progress through them if they are going to be in a position to organize resistance against the state. But how does one organize and mobilize in the enterprise when "objective" conditions are so daunting, when the possibilities of making significant gains seem so limited?

There is no easy answer. But dignity is a good starting point. A worker who respects his or herself may be not be in a position to throw off oppression but he or she will at least not internalize it. The workers' sense of dignity played an important role in the Russian labour movement leading up to the revolution of 1917. Its most striking expression was the demand for "polite address" from foremen and higher management ("you" in the second person plural, rather than the singular, used for servants, children, animals and in close friends). It figured prominently on the list of demands that workers presented management in the vast strike wave that swept Russia in 1912-14, and especially in Russia's industrial heartland, St. Petersburg.[6] Both the strikers and the political authorities considered the demand political.

The awakened sense of dignity was, in turn, linked to social activism. A contemporary observer remarked:

> The spiritual process is an active one. Once the voice of the individual has begun to speak in the worker, he can neither sit under a bush…nor

limit himself to talk…The strength of this process is in its dynamism: the upper strata of the proletariat raise of the backward ones to their own level.[7]

But dignity was also linked to the aspiration to class independence, especially powerful in the younger generation of urbanized workers. In his memoirs, A. Buzinov, a Petersburg metalworker, recalled the shift in outlook that occurred after the failed revolution of 1905-06, during which the liberals turned against the popular democratic movement. At workers's meetings, "from each word spoken…a sharp line separating the workers from the ruling class emerged." The self-made agitators that emerged from among the "conscious workers," were

> always hammering away at the same point—I would say—of class independence [literally, "separateness," [*klassovaya obosoblennost*] from the exploiters. In the persons of these agitators, life had hammered a wedge between workers and owners that no party agitator, who was not as closely tied to the masses as they, could have done.[8]

A police survey of the labour movement in the Petrograd from November 1915 noted that because of the high inflation, the most discussed issue was food co-operatives, for which the factory owners were now offering support. But worker agitators were speaking out against accepting it. According to the report, when the workers at the Ericson Telephone Factory discussed whether to participate in a cooperative opened by the Society of Factory and Mill Owners, "the majority pointed out the Society it totally dependent on the factory owners, and since cooperation is one of the forms of the general workers' movement, it is necessary to think along lines of our own worker societies, independent of the owners." The attitude was the same in relation to insurance and sick funds: "One observes of late in the worker population the tendency toward the separation of their activities from any sort of pressure from the authorities or the entrepreneurs. Here, too, one feels the shift towards pure autonomy…This tendency…can be observed at all workers meetings without exception."[9] And the same was true in politics: workers supported the socialist parties exclusively, boycotting the liberals and further-right parties in elections. During the upsurge of 1912-14, the majority of industrial workers supported the Bolsheviks, whose distinguishing feature, in relation to the other socialist parties, was their opposition to a labour alliance with the liberals.

The issues of dignity and social activism among the popular classes had already become central concerns of the progressive intelligentsia in Russia in the mid-nineteenth century, if not earlier. They were a central theme of Vikor Nekrasov's epic poem, *Who Can be Happy in Russia?*, which he began to write soon after the (very partial) emancipation of the serfs in 1861. In the poem, seven wanderers set off to find the answer to the question "Who can be happy in Russia?" inquiring among all strata of the population. They find only one really happy person, Grisha Dobrosklonov, the one who dreams of another Russia, where "each peasant would live free and happy." He is not blind to the peasants' many shortcomings, their ignorance, servility, egoism. But he also sees that "the Russian people is gathering forces and learning to be citizens," and he follows the call to "be a friend to the oppressed and the exploited." The poet tells us that his fate—common among those in Russia who have dreamed of freedom and acted on the dream, will, alas, be "Siberia and consumption."[10]

Few people when the poem was written shared Grisha's optimism or commitment. But the forces did eventually gather, and the people broke their chains. The present study told of some of the people who today, like Grisha Dobrosklonov 140 years ago, are dreaming of another Russia, Ukraine and Belarus and struggling in conditions that to most people seem just as hopeless. But they too believe the people will gather forces and learn to be citizens. The outlook might really be better than it appears, since the present imposing power of the state in all three countries rests on extremely fragile social foundations. But as in 1917, the fate of their struggle will depend upon similar struggles in the rest of the world, and especially in the most developed countries, whose pressure—military, economic and ideological—has always been a crucial factor in the evolution of Russian (now also Byelorussian and Ukrainian) society.

Notes

1. Meiskins Woods, *Democracy Against Capitalism*, p. 92.
2. This can be readily be observed in worker education.
3. Q. Hoare and G. Smith, *Selections from the Prison Notebooks of Antonio Gramsci*, N.Y.: International Publishers, 1971, p. 438.
4. *Ibid.*, p. 172.
5. G. Simon, "Ukraina i Rossiya: dve strany I–odna trasnformatsiya," p. 6.
6. H. L. Haimson, "The Workers' Movement on the Eve of the First World War," paper presented at the Annual Meeting of the American Historical Association, 1973. See also Mandel, *The Petrograd Workers and the Fall of the Old Regime*, pp. 14-17.
7. L.M. Kleinbort, *Ocherki rabochei intelligentsii*, Petrograd, 1923, p. 16.
8. A. Buzinov, *Za Nevskoi zastavoi*, Moscow-Leningrad, 1930, pp. 126, 101.
9. M .G .Fleer, *Rabochee dvizhenie v gody voiny*, Moscow-Leningrad, 1925, pp. 222-23.
10. N. A. Nekrasov, *Komu na Rusi zhit' khorosho*, Minsk: Staliya, 2002, pp. 258, 275.

BIBLIOGRAPHY

This bibliography lists all books and as well as articles of a more-or-less academic nature that were consulted in the research. Trade-union documents, articles from the trade-union press and from mass-circulation newspapers and magazines are referred to only in the notes.

Anotonova, V.G., ed., Ocherki istorii profosyuzov Kharokovshchiniy, Kharkov: Tornado, 1999.

Ashwin, S., *Russian Workers:The Anatomy of Patience*, Manchester: Manchester University Press, 1999.

Ashwin, S, and Clarke, S., *Russian Trade Unions and Industrial Relations in Transition*, Houndsmills, Basingstoke: Palgrave Macmillan, 2003.

ASMU, *Profosyuzy i rynochnaya ekonomika*, Kyiv, 1999.

Bahro, R., *The Alternative in Eastern Europe*, Manchester: NLB, 1978.

Baron, S.H., *Bloody Saturday in the Soviet Union, Novocherkassk,1962,*. Stanford: Stanford University Press, 2001.

Belousov, A.R., "Uroki postkrizisnogo rosta," in E. Yasin, ed., *Modernisatsiya ekonomiki Rossii*, Moscow: Vysshaya shkola ekonomiki, 2002.

Blasi, J., Kroumova, M., and Kruse, D., *Kremlin Capitalism: Privatizing the Russian Economy*, Ithaca: ILR Press, 1997.

Bol'shakova, O.A., et al., *Samoupravlenie na promyshlennykh predpriyatiyakh v usloviyakh perekhoda k rynku: iz opyta Vol'zhskogo avtomobil'nogo zavoda, 1991-1995 gg.*, Togliatti: Tol'yattinskii politekhnicheskii institut, 1995.

Borisov, V., "The Strike as a Form of Worker Activism in a Period of Economic Reform," in S. Clarke, ed., *Labour Relations in Transition*, Cheltenham: Edward Elgar, 1995.

Bracegirdle, P. and Mandel, D., "The AFL-CIO Comes to the Community of Independent States," *Socialist Alternatives*, vol. 2, no. 2, 1993.

Bukhvostov, A., ed., *Chernobyl'–nezatikhshaya bol'*, Minsk 1999.

Bukhvostov, A., *O profsoyuznom i rabochem dvizhenii 1989-2000 gg.*, Minsk, 2001.

Buzgalin, A. and Kolganov, A., *Krovavyi oktyabr' v Moskve*, Moscow: Ekonomicheskaya demokratiya, 1994.

Buzinov, A., *Za Nevskoi zastavoi*, Moscow-Leningrad, 1930.

Carr, E.H., *Socialism in One Country*, Baltimore: Penguin, vol. 1, 1970.

Carr, E.H., and Davies, R.W., *Foundations of a Planned Economy*, Harmondsworth, U.K., Penguin, 1974.

Chandler, D., "Democracy Verusus Dictatorship? The 2001 Belarus Presidential Elections," *Labor Focus on Eastern Europe*, no. 69, 2001.

Chase, W.J., *Workers, Society and the Soviet State: Labor and Life in Moscow, 1918-29*, Chicago: University of Illinois Press, 1990.

Clover, C., "Le Donbass: une économie de prédation," *Courrier des pays de l'Est*, Feb. 2000.

Daucé, F., "Les mouvements de mères de soldats à la recherche d'une place dans la société russe," *Revue d'études comparatives Est-Ouest*, June 1997.

Deutscher, I., *Soviet Trade Unions*, London: Oxford University Press, 1950.

Derzhavnii komitet statistiki Ukraini, *Statistichnii shchorychnik Ukraini za 1999 ryk*, Kyiv: Tekhnika, 2000.

Economist Intelligence Unit, *Country Report: Belarus*, June 2003.

Economist Intelligence Unit, *Country Profile: Russia*, London, 2003.

Economist Intelligence Unit, *Country Report: Russia*, London, Aug. 2003.

Economist Intelligence Unit, *Country Profile: Ukraine*, London, 2003

Europa World Yearbook, 1998, London: Europa Publications, 1998.

Feshbach, M., "A Comment on Recent Demographic Issues and a Forbidding Forecast," *Johnson's Russia List*, Aug. 11, 1999. (www.cdi.org/Russia/Johnson.).

Filtzer, D., *Soviet Workers and the Collapse of Perestroika*, Cambridge: Cambridge University Press, 1994.

Filtzer, D., *Soviet Workers and de-Stalinization*, Cambridge: Cambridge University Press, 1992.

Filtzer, D., *Soviet Workers and Stalinist Industrialization*, Cambridge: Cambridge University Press, 1986.

Finberg, L., "Leçons de l'élection présidentielle ukrainienne," *Courrier des pays de l'Est*, Feb. 2000, no. 102.

Fleer, M.G., *Rabochee dvizhenie v gody voiny*, Moscow-Leningrad, 1925.

Gaiduk, K., *et al.*, *Belarusskaya eknomika na pereput'e*, Berlin and Minsk, 2003.

Gaponenko, L.S. "Rabochii klass Rossii nakanun'e velikogo Oktyabrya," *Istoricheskie zapiski*, no. 73, Moscow, 1963.

Goskomstat Rossii, *Rossiiskii statisticheskii ezhegodnik, 1999*, Moscow, 2000.

Goskomstat Rossii, *Rossiiskii statisticheskii ezhegodnik, 2001*, Moscow, 2001.

Goskomstat, *Rossiya v tsifrakh 2002*, Moscow, 2002.

Goskomstat, *Rossiya v tsifrakh 2003*, Moscow, 2003.

Goskomstat SSSR, *Narodnoe khozyaistvo SSSR za 70 let*, Moscow, 1987.

Grigoriev, V.M., *et al.*, *Profsoyuznaya rabota na mashinostroitel'nykh predriyatiyakh*, Moscow: Profinzdat, 1972.

Gritsenko, N.N., *et al.*, *Istoriya profsoyuzov Rossii*, Moscow: Akademiya truda i sotsial'nykh otnoshenii and FNPR, 1999.

Haimson, H.L., "The Workers' Movement on the Eve of the First World War," paper presented at the Annual Meeting of the American Historical Association, 1973 (unpublished).

Hoare, Q. and Smith, G., *Selections from the Prison Notebooks of Antonio Gramsci*, N.Y.: International Publishers, 1971.

Husson, M., "Mondialisation, nouvel horizon du capitalisme," in *Mondialisation et impérialisme*, Paris: Les cahiers de Critique communiste, 2003.

IMF, *Ukraine: Selected Issues*, IMF Country Report, no. 3/173, June 2003.

Kagarlitsky, B., "'Political Capitalism' and Corruption in Russia," *Labour Focus on Eastern Europe*, no. 71, 2002.

Kahn, A. and Ruble, B., *Industrial Labor in the USSR*, N.Y.: Pergamon, 1979.

Kantorovich, V., "The Russian Health Crisis and the Economy," *Communist and Post-Communist Studies*, no. 34, 2001.

Kapelyushnikov, R., "Krupneishie i dominiruyushchie sobstvenniki v rossiiskoi prommyshlennosti," *Voprosy ekonomiki*, no. 1, Jan. 2000.

Klebnikov, P., *Godfather of the Kremlin: Boris Berezovsky and the Looting of Russia*, N.Y., Harcourt, 2000.

Kleinbort, L.M., *Ocherki rabochei intelligentsii*, Petrograd, 1923.

Kornievski, O., "Unemployment in Ukraine: Estimates and Forecasts," *National Security and Defence*, no. 2, 2000 (www.uceps.com.us/eng/all/jounral2000).

Kotz, D. and Weir, F., *Revolution from Above*, N.Y.: Routeledge, 1997.

Kozlov, V.A., *Massovye besporyadki v SSSR pri Khrushcheve i Brezhneve*, Novosibirsk: Sibirskii khronograf, 1999.

Krylov, K.D., *Zakonodatel'stvo Rossii o professional'nykh profsoyuzakh*, Moscow: Profizdat, 1996.

Kuzio, T., *Ukraine Under Kuchma*, N.Y.: St. Martin's Press, 1997.

Kuzio, T. and Wilson, A., *Ukraine: Perestroika to Independence*, CIUS: Toronto, 1994.

Kudryavstev, A., *Yaroslavskaya zastava*, Yaroslavl', 1999.

Maksimov, B., "Borot'sya ili gulyat' za svoi schet?", 2002 (unpublished).

Maksimov, B., "Gegemon, gde on?", in D. Mandel and G. Rakitskaya, eds., *Govoryat rabochie Kirovskogo zavoda*, Mosocow: IPPS, 1998.

Maskimov, B., "Kuda vedut lideri," 2000 (unpublished).

Maksimov, B., "Torzhestvo profsoyuznoi demokratii," 2001 (unpublished).

Mandel, D., "Conversion in a Russian Defence Plant: Interview with N. Prostov," *Socialist Alternatives*, vol. 2, no. 2, 1993.

Mandel, D., "Economic Reform and Democracy in the Soviet Union," in Miliband, R., Panitch, L. and Saville, J., *Socialist Register 1988: Problems of Socialist Renewal East and West*, London: Merlin Press, 1988.

Mandel, D., *Factory Committees and Workers' Control in Petrograd in 1917*, Amsterdam: IIRE, 1993.

Mandel, D., ed., *Looking East Leftwards*, Montreal: Black Rose Books, 1998.

Mandel, D., ed., *Novocherkassk 1-3 yunya 1962 g.: zabastovka i rasstrel*, Moscow: Shkola trudovoi demokratii, 1998.

Mandel, D., *Perestroika and the Soviet People: Rebirth of the Labour Movement*, Montreal: Black Rose Books, 1991.

Mandel, D., *The Petrograd Workers and the Fall of the Old Regime*, Houndsmills, Basingstoke: Macmillan, 1983.

Mandel, D., *The Petrograd Workers and the Soviet Seizure of Power*, Houndsmills, Basingstoke: Macmillan, 1984.

Mandel, D, *Rabotyagi: Perestroika and After Viewed from Below*, N.Y.: Monthly Review Press, 1984.

Marx, K., *Capital*, N.Y.: International Publishers, vol. I, 1972.

Mathews, M., *Poverty in the Soviet Union*, Cambridge: Cambridge University Press, 1986.

Minstat Belarusi, Goskomstat Rossii, *Belarus' i Rossiya, 1999*, Moscow, 1999.

Nekrasov, N.A., *Komu na Rusi zhit' khorosho*, Minsk: Staliya, 2002.

Pavlenko, V., ed., *Trudovvoi kodeks Rossiiskoi federatsii*, Moscow: Trud i pravo, 2002.

Pavlevski, J., *Le niveau de vie en USSR*, Paris: Economica, 1975.

"Profspilkovyi rukh v Ukraini," *National'na bezpeka i oborona*, no. 8, 2001.

Profsoyuzy i ekonomia, no. 7, 2001.

Rakitskii, B., *Ugol ataki*, Moscow: Institut perspektiv i problem strany, 2003.

Reddaway, P. and Glinksi, D., *The Tragedy of Russia's Reforms: Market Bolshevism Against Democracy*, Washington: U.S. Institute of Peace, 2001

Roche, M., *Thérapie de choc et autoritarisme en Russie: la démocratie confisquée*, Paris, L'Harmattan, 2000.

Rosefielde, S., "Premature Deaths: Russia's Radical Economic Transition in Soviet Perspective," *Europe-Asia Studies*, vol. 53, no. 8, 2001.

Rutgaizen, V.M. and Shevnyakov, Yu.E., "Raspredelenie po trudu," *EKO*, no. 3, 1987.

Sapir, J., *Le chaos russe*, Paris: la Découverte, 1996.

Sapir, J. *Le krach russe*, Paris: la Découverte, 1998.

Shmakov, M., *Profsoyuzy Rossii na poroge XXI-ogo veka*, Moscow, 1999.

Simon, G., "Ukraina i Rossiya: dve strany –odna trasnformatsiya, *Connections*, no. 2, Apr. 2002.

Statkomitet SNG, *SNG v 2001 g.: statisticheskii ezhegodnik*, Moscow, 2002.

Statkomitet SNG, *SNG v 2001 g.: statisticheskii spravochnik*, Moscow, 2002.

Statkomitet SNG, *SNG v 2002 g.: statisticheskii spravochnik,* Moscow, 2003.

Stiglitz, J., *Globalization and Its Discontents*, N.Y.: W.W. Norton, 2002.

Swain, A., "The First and Last Ukrainian Plan? Dismantling the Coal Mining Industry," *Labour Focus on Eastern Eruope*, no. 60, 1998

Thompson, E.P., *The Making of the English Working Class*, London: Penguin, 1991.

Trokhin, S., "Kogda nachinaetsya ponedel'nik," *Al'ternativy*, no. 3, 1999, p. 43.

U.S. Census Bureau, *Statistical Abstract of the United States: 1999*, Washington, 2000.

Voprosy ekonomiki, no. 3, 1991.

Van Zon, H., *The Political Economy of Independent Ukraine*, N.Y.: St. Martin's Press, 2000.

Van Zon, H., *et al.*, *Social and Economic Change in Eastern Ukraine*, Aldershot: Ashgate,1998.

Wahl, A., "European Labor: The Ideological Legacy of the Social Pact," *Monthly Review*, Jan. 2004.

Wilson, A., *The Ukrainians*, New Haven: Yale University Press, 2000.

Wolczuk, K., "Constituting Statehood: the New Ukrainian Constitution," *The Ukrainian Review*, fall 1998, no. 45.

Wood, E. Meiksins, *Democracy Against Capitalism*, Cambridge: Cambridge University Press, 1995.

Zabastovka v tsekhke 45-3 Volzhskogo avtomobil'nogo zavoda, 27 sentyabrya – 3 oktyabrya 1994 goda: dokumenty i materialy, Moscow: Institut perspektiv i problem strany, 1998.

Zakon Ukraini "O professional'ykh soyuzakh, ikh pravakh i granatiyakh," Donteskii oblsatnoi sovet profsoyuzov: Bibliotechka profosyuznogo lidera, 2002.

Zviaglyanich, V., "State and Nation: Economic Strategies for Ukraine," in S. Wolchik and V. Zviaglyanich, *Ukraine: the Search for a National Identity*, N.Y.: Roan and Littlefield, 2000, p. 253.

INDEX

A
Abramov, M. 24,34,80,99-100
AFL-CIO 24,126,127
alternative unions (see also Edinstvo) 24,41, 60,91-92,108,119-121,125-126,128,130, 142,148-149,181-182,218,223,230,245, 260,269-270
Ashwin, S. 10

B
BATE (Borisov Starter Factory) 101,233, 235,244-246,249-253
BNF (Byelorussian National Front) 217, 253,260
bonus system 8,43,145,256
Borisov Starter Factory (see BATE)
bourgeoisie 1,25,51,74,119,158-159, 175,270-272
Bukhvostov, A. 6,17-18,24,219,222,224, 226-241,243-248,250-252,254-255,257, 264,267
Byelorussian Federation of Trade Unions (see FPB)

Byelorussian National Front (see BNF)
Byrdina, Tatyana 182,187-193

C
civil disobedience 72,107,110, 113, 116, 269
civil society 153, 266, 271-272
class independence 21,245,265,269-271,273
coalminers 4,13,17-19,24,131,181,198 (see also NPG)
collective agreement 5,40,63-64,68-69,72,77, 83,85-88,98,122,133-134,136,138-139, 144-145,160,177,180,189,191,205,209, 226,236,254,257,262
Communist Party of the Soviet Union 1,17
Communist Party of Belarus 245

Communist Party of the Russian Federation (see KPRF)
Communist Party of Ukraine 155-157,165,207

D
Deripaska, O. 34-35,98,125,151
dignity 19,47,50,88,143,187,197,212,254,268, 272-273
Dudnik, V. 181-183,194,211
Duma 28-30,54,74-75,114-115,118,126,135, 149,158

E
Edinstvo 16,18,45,58,75,89,91,101,103,123, 128-152,182
Evdokimchik, A. 230,235-236,238,258,260

F
FPB (Byelorussian Federation of Trade Unions) 218,223-224,226,242-243, 245-246,251
Federation of Independent Trade Union of Russia (see FNPR)
Federation of Trade Unions of Ukraine (see FPU)
Fefelov, A. 64,75,101
FNPR (Federation of Independent Trade Union of Russia) 29,37-38,53,60-61,68,70,73-77,81, 89-91,96-97,99,101-104,109-111,114-115, 117,120,131,150,156,227,269
FPU (Federation of Trade Unions of Ukraine) 161-162,167,174-175,181-182,186,194, 210-211,243,246

G
GAZ (Gorkii Automobile Factory) 35,56,60-61,64-65,94,133,151
Gomel 17,218,224

Goncharik, V. 218,242-243,251,263
Gorbachev, M. 2,9,11-12,14-16,18-20,23, 49,114,188
Gramsci, A. 268,274

H

health and safety 3,5,7,43,50,94,97,124,141, 143,169,196,227,254,261

I

IMF (International Monetary Fund) 25-26, 28,30,33,37,39,53,55,111,117,155-156, 158-159,163-166,215,241
Isaev, A. 70,74-75,103
Ivanov, A. 16,129,131,135-136,140,148-150

K

KamAZ (Kamaz Truck Factory) 91
Karagin, A. 99,138,145
Kharkov Bicycle Factory 7,183,187-193,215
Kharkov Tractor Factory 170,194
Kirov Tractor Factory 83-84
KPRF (see Communist Party of the Russian Federation) 29,111,114-115,117,119, 121,127,149
Krylov, V. 58,106,117,122-125
Kuchma, L. 156-160,166,174,193,208
Kyiv Motorcycle Factory 172

L

labour code 3,5,8,40-42,57,60,62-63,68,89, 91-92,97,107,138,140-142,147,149,160, 183,227
labour competition 65,93,174,176
labour disputes committee 40,62,91,123, 140,189,203
Lenin, V. 11,22,151,258,268,
Likino Bus Factory 84
Lozovskii, V. 246,262-264
Lukashenko, A. 215-218,231-233,235-236,239 -243,245,247,249,251-253,258,260,272
Luzhkov, Yu. 74-75,115

M

Maksimov, B. 58,101,103
Marx, K. 30,74,164,266,268,271
material aid 67,90,95,130,236,255,261
MAZ (Minsk Truck Factory) 9,244-245
Meiksins Wood, E. 24,266
Minsk Ball-Bearing Factory 218,235,245, 260-264
Minsk Bicycle and Motorcycle Factory (see Motovelo)
Minsk Gear Factory 227
Minsk Precision Tool and Dye Factory (see SIITO)
Minsk Tractor Factory 104,151,226,253
Minsk Truck Factory (see MAZ)
Moroz, O. 157,161,175,207
Motovelo (Minsk Bicycle and Motorcycle Factory) 214-215, 235

N

Nekrasov, V. 273-274
Nikolov, N. 197,205-206,208,210-211
nomenklatura 2,9,14,153,155,271
Novikov, Yu. 63-64,66-69,72,79,93-94, 100-101,103-104
Novocherkassk 3
NPG (Independent Union of Miners) 14,18, 110,115,118,127

O

Onoprienko, I. 172-174

P

Perestroika 4,11-12,14,20,22-24,105-106, 126,164,195,272
Pokhabov, N. 235-236,246,250-252
Popov, V. 106,112,116,121,123,125
privatization 15,23,25,29-30,32,34,53-54,61, 112,117,155,159,180,188,205,215,241
PT (Byelorussian Party of Labour) 149,240-242,244,251,253
Putin, V. 28,30-32,34-35,38,54-55,57-58, 75,77,87,102,149-150,159-160,271

INDEX

R
REP (Radio-Electronics Workers' Union) 217-218,224,226,229,241,248
revolution 1-2,18-19,21-22,58,125,151,195, 241,253,269,271-273

S
School for Worker Democracy 90-91,124,147, 178,183,186,203,211,229,251
sectoral agreement 67,71-73,96-98,122,171, 174,179-182,185,187,202-203,206,227,231
Shmakov, M. 126
shock therapy 10,19,24,28,31-32,47,55,59, 106,111-112,132,155,175,217,219-220, 223,241,266,271-272
SIITO (Minsk Precision Tool and Dye Factory) 253,255,257,260
skilled workers 26,49-50,197,255
Smirnov, A. 56,62,99,109,111,121,126
socialism 2,8,14,20,59,81-82,149,151,268,270
socialist competition 65
Socialist Party 157,175,182
Sotsprof 136,148-149
Soviet system 1,5,10,15,19,21,39,42,48,59,65, 129,145,151,156,231,269
STK (work-collective council) 12,15-16,21,129,131-132,260
Stoyan, A. 174-175,193
Svigach, T. 254-258

T
Thompson, E.P. 19,24,266
TIE (Transnationals Information Exchange) 90-91,147,178,182,229
Tutaev Motor Factory 43,47-48,102,105-127, 150,195
Tyutyunov, P. 196-206,208-212

U
Union of Labour 74-75,111
United Russia 75

V
VAZ (Volga Automobile Factory) 14-15,20, 33-34,39,42,55,60,62-63,70,80,83-85,91, 94,102,128-152
Vetchinkin, V. 161,168-170,175,183-187, 190,192,241
Vinnitsa Ball-Bearing Factory 195-212,268
Volga Automobile Factory (see VAZ)
Volosyuk, N. 98,106,109,121,126

W
wage arrears 37,46,98,106-107,109,120, 133-134,136,158,171,173,189,207
wage system 8,12,40-41,44-46,62-63,69, 84,93,122,144-145
Washington consensus 25,213,217
women 36,44,48-49,89,124,138,161,258-259
work-collective council (see STK)

Y
Yaroslavl 105-127 passim
Yaroslavl Diesel Apparatus Factory (see YZDA)
Yaroslavl Fuel-Pump Factory (see YZTA)
Yaroslavl Motor Factory (See YMZ)
Yeltsin, B. 9,15,17-18,20,28-30,35-36,49, 52-53,55,73-76,108,110-112,114-117, 120,130,149,156-157,217
YMZ (Yaroslavl Motor Factory) 12-13,35-86- 88,105-106,109,111,113,118-119,122,127
YZDA 94,105-106
YZTA 49,98,106,109,119,121

Z
ZAZ (Zaporizh'e Automobile Factory) 155,174
ZIL 64,78,101
Zlenko, V. 7,22,163-164,167-186,192-193, 199-200,205,211,224-225,241,267
Zolotarev, P. 18,58,131,136,141-142, 146-147,152

also by DAVID MANDEL

PERESTROIKA AND THE SOVIET PEOPLE

The economic and political situation of a society attempting to be re-born is the subject of this work. With a chronological perspective in mind, this book describes the nature of the crisis that led to a regime-initiated perestroika.

> This book is an excellent starting point for discussion about the meaning of present economic reform strategy, a debate which is more necessary now than it was in 1991. —*Canadian Journal of Political Science*

> ...refreshing for anyone trying to make sense of what is going on in Russia...an iconoclastic, controversial, and welcome work. —*Canadian Book Review Annual*

> ...gives a glimpse of Soviet life and social movements, of which we have seen too little in the mainstream media. —*Peace Magazine*

> 207 pages
> Paperback ISBN: 1-895431-14-X $16.99
> Hardcover ISBN: 1-895431-15-8 $45.99

FORMER "STATE SOCIALIST" WORLD
Views From the Left, Volume 1

This collection of essays, and interviews, by some of the foremost democratic socialist thinkers of today, brings together social scientists in the West with their Russian counterparts.

> Contents include: "The Russian Working Class and the Labour Movement in Year Four of 'Shock Therapy'," David Mandel; "A Letter from the Kirov Factory," Boris Maksimov; "Gender and Post-Communist Restructuring: How Women Pay the Price," Valentine M. Moghadam; "The Greens and the Labour Movement: An Experience in Co-operation," Kirill Privezentsev; "The G-7 and 'Market Reform' in Russia: 'Shock Therapy' Against Democracy," Michel Roche; "The Transitional Period in Russia: The Present Stage and Possible Futures," Galina Rakitskaya; "Interview with Grigorii Artemenko: The Left in the Ukraine," David Mandel; "Interview with Tomas Kraus: Change of Régimes in Eastern Europe," Alexsandr Buzgalin; "The Shattering of Yugoslavia: An Exceptional Case?," Catherine Samary; and "The End of the Deng Era," Roland Lew.

> 190 pages, index
> Paperback ISBN: 1-55164-036-8 $19.99
> Hardcover ISBN: 1-55164-037-6 $48.99

LOOKING EAST LEFTWARDS
Former "State Socialist" World, Volume 2

This collection, covering Russia, the Ukraine, Belarus, Hungary, Poland, China, and Cuba combines a unique variety of genres, interviews, diaries, and essays, that provide both analytical insight and a concrete sense of the complex socio-political and cultural processes at work in these societies. Key, in this account of the "post-Communist" regime, is an essay by the editor, entitled "Travels Through Russia, Belarus and the Ukraine: Diaries, Summer—Fall 1996," observations and analysis based on extensive travels and participation in rank-and-file union education.

Other essays include: Boris Maksimov, "Letter from the Kirov Factory, April 1996"; Vladimir Shimanovich, "The 18th Brumaire of Aleksandr Lukashenko," an interview with the Vice President of the Belarussian Party of Labour; Vladimir Zlenko, "The Union Movement in the Ukraine: The Hard Road to Renewal," an interview with one of Ukraine's most dynamic labour leaders, President of the Union of Auto and Agricultural Machine-Construction Workers; Vladislav Kelle, "Nationalism and the Future of Russia"; Ruslan Kostenko, "The Left in Russia"; Denis Paillard, "Zyuganov's Russia," a critical look at the ideology and politics of Russia's main opposition party; Jan Malewski, "Solidarnosc After Fifteen Years: The Reactionary Despair of the Betrayed"; Laszlo Andor, "The Hungarian Trade Union Movement: 1989-1996"; Catherine Samary, "Capitalist Restoration in Eastern Europe: A Process without Historical Precedent."

Jacqueline Heinen looks at the social and economic situation of women in the Poland in "When Unemployment Means Marginalization: The Case of Poland"; Roland Lew, "Chinese 'Socialisme' and Social Emancipation"; Janette Habel, "Cuba: Social Tensions and Political Uncertainties"; and Liudmila Bulavka, a specialist of popular culture, analyzes the crisis of Russian cinema through the work of the director of the prize-winning film on Stalin's purges *Burnt by the Sun*, in "N. Mikhalkov the Monarchist Artist on Socialism with Tenderness."

250 pages, index
Paperback ISBN: 1-55164-098-8 $24.99
Hardcover ISBN: 1-55164-099-6 $53.99

# of related interest

EUROPE: CENTRAL AND EAST
Marguerite Mendell, Klaus Nielsen, editors

These essays help to put the mass of changes in the former USSR and the eastern bloc into a larger historical and sociological perspective. The writers consider the social complexity which surrounds any political and economic system—an "embeddedness," which establishes itself very slowly and over many years. Inspired by the "great transformation" model Karl Polanyi substantiated, they analyse the changes as long evolutionary processes. Apart from the editors, contributors include: John Campbell, Mihailo Crnobrnja, Agnes Czako, Endre Sik, Jerzy Hausner, Bob Jessop, Tadeusz Kowalik, Domenico Mario Nuti, Birgit Muller, Yakov M. Rabkin, Hilary Wainwright, and Claire Wallace.

Marguerite Mendell is professor of economics at Concordia University, Quebec. Klaus Nielsen is associate professor of economics at Roskilde University, Denmark.

298 pages
Paperback ISBN: 1-895431-90-5 $19.99
Hardcover ISBN: 1-895431-91-3 $48.99

send for a free catalogue of all our titles

C.P. 1258, Succ. Place du Parc
Montréal, Québec
H2X 4A7 Canada

Or visit our website at http://www.web.net/blackrosebooks

to order books
In Canada: (phone) 1-800-565-9523 (fax) 1-800-221-9985
email: utpbooks@utpress.utoronto.ca

In United States: (phone) 1-800-283-3572 (fax) 1-651-917-6406

In UK & Europe: (phone) London 44 (0)20 8986-4854 (fax) 44 (0)20 8533-5821
email: order@centralbooks.com

Printed by the workers of
MARC VEILLEUX IMPRIMEUR INC.
Boucherville, Québec
for Black Rose Books Ltd.